Evolution of Destination Planning and Strategy

Larry Dwyer • Renata Tomljenović • Sanda Čorak
Editors

Evolution of Destination Planning and Strategy

The Rise of Tourism in Croatia

palgrave
macmillan

Editors
Larry Dwyer
University of Ljubljana
Woolloomooloo, Australia

Sanda Čorak
Institute for Tourism
Zagreb, Croatia

Renata Tomljenović
Institute for Tourism
Zagreb, Croatia

ISBN 978-3-319-42245-9   ISBN 978-3-319-42246-6   (eBook)
DOI 10.1007/978-3-319-42246-6

Library of Congress Control Number: 2016957567

Cover illustration: © Jan Wlodarczyk / Alamy Stock Photo

Printed on acid-free paper

This Palgrave Macmillan imprint is published by Springer Nature
The registered company is Springer International Publishing AG
The registered company address is: Gewerbestrasse 11, 6330 Cham, Switzerland

ACKNOWLEDGEMENTS

The chapters of this book have been developed in conjunction with the research and consultancy activities of the Institute for Tourism and its associates. The central message of this book is that tourism planning and development needs to be located not only within the context of tourism but within its broader economic, social, cultural, political and environmental concerts. While Croatian tourism development is a success story, the problems it deals with are common to destinations worldwide. To understand these problems, situate them in the broader economical and socio-political contexts and reflect upon them realistically, researchers need to have a thorough understanding of real-life practices and challenges.

This book has been made possible by many individuals and organisations that have worked with the research team of the Institute for Tourism. We are grateful to the managers and staff of tourism boards and professional associations who have spent with us a lot of time discussing the issues that they face and proposing solutions and organised many workshops and site inspections to get us in touch and facilitate our understanding of many facets of tourism from operators' perspectives.

Much of the research that the chapters are based on has been supported by national tourism institutions – the Ministry of Tourism, Croatian National Tourism Board and the Croatian Chamber of Commerce – and we are grateful for their support and cooperation.

Our thanks also go to the colleagues in international and Croatian tourism scholarly communities who have cooperated with us on many research projects and endeavours.

We would like to thank all the authors for their contribution as well as the Institute's administrative staff for their assistance and support.

The Editors

CONTENTS

1   Introduction   1
    Larry Dwyer, Sanda Čorak, and Renata Tomljenović

2   Crafting a National Value-Driven Tourism Vision   15
    Renata Tomljenović and Irena Ateljević

3   Managing Tourism Development Process
    in Croatia: Can European Union Accession Help?   37
    Ivo Kunst

4   Shaping Destination Identity: Challenges
    of Branding Croatia   67
    Neda Telišman-Košuta

5   The Influence of Political Factors in Fashioning
    Destination Image   79
    Božo Skoko, Katarina Miličević, and Damir Krešić

6   Tourism Destination and DMO Transformation   99
    Sanda Čorak and Snježana Boranić Živoder

7   Tourism Attraction System   119
    Eduard Kušen

8   Implementation of Tourism Satellite Account: Assessing
    the Contribution of Tourism to the Croatian Economy   149
    Neven Ivandić and Zrinka Marušić

9   Abandoned Tourism Resorts in Croatia: The
    Consequences of Discordant Spatial Planning
    and Tourism Development Policies   173
    Jasenka Kranjčević

10 Sustainability Issues in Management of Tourism
    in Protected Areas: Case Study of Plitvice Lakes
    National Park   201
    Izidora Marković Vukadin

11 Identifying Trends in Tourism Demand Using
    Longitudinal Survey   221
    Zrinka Marušić, Ivan Sever, and Sanda Čorak

12 Longitudinal Assessment of the Carrying Capacity
    of a Typical Tourist Island: Twenty Years On   245
    Jakša Kivela and Zoran Klarić

13 Gastronomy Tourism: Croatia, a Land of Wine
    and Plenty, or Beyond Pizza and Grill!   265
    Jakša Kivela

14 Tourism Future: Towards Transformational Tourism   279
    Larry Dwyer, Irena Ateljević, and Renata Tomljenović

Index   295

CONTRIBUTORS

Irena Ateljević, PhD received her doctoral degree in human geography in 1998 at the University of Auckland, New Zealand. She is currently positioned as a Senior Research Fellow at the Institute for Tourism, Zagreb, and within the Cultural Geography Group at Wageningen University (Netherlands), as a Visiting Professor. Her primary research interests lie in the transformative role of tourism in the broader context of a transmodern paradigm shift.

Sanda Čorak, PhD is a Scientific Advisor and the Managing Director of the Institute for Tourism, Zagreb. She obtained her PhD degree in economics (marketing) at the University of Zagreb. Her research interests are tourism market research and segmentation, destination marketing, governance and sport tourism. She is the Editor of the international academic journal *Tourism* and a Senior Lecturer at the University of Applied Sciences (VERN Zagreb).

Larry Dwyer, PhD is a Professor, Faculty of Economics, University of Ljubljana; Adjunct Professor Griffith Institute for Tourism (GIFT), Griffith University; and Honorary Professor of Travel and Tourism Economics in the School of Marketing, Australian School of Business, University of New South Wales. He publishes widely in the areas of tourism economics, management, policy and planning, with over 200 publications in international journals, books, book chapters, government reports and monographs.

Neven Ivandić, PhD is a Research Fellow at the Institute for Tourism, Zagreb, Croatia. His research interests include tourism economics, strategic planning and management both on destination and firm level. He is one of Croatia's foremost experts in compilation of tourism satellite account and assessing tourism contribution on national and regional economies. His extensive experience spans research and consulting both in Croatia and abroad, also having served on supervisory boards of several renowned Croatian hospitality companies.

Jakša Kivela, PhD a Visiting Fellow at the Institute for Tourism, received his doctoral degree from the Royal Melbourne Institute of Technology (RMIT) on the topic of customer loyalty and consumer behaviour in restaurants. For the past 20 years, he has taught at the School of Hotel and Tourism Management at the Hong Kong Polytechnic University specialising in Hospitality and Tourism Management, Culinary Arts Practice, Wine Studies and China Business. Specifically, he has published in leading tourism and hospitality journals.

Zoran Klarić, PhD is a Senior Research Fellow at the Institute for Tourism, Croatia. His research interests include spatial aspects of tourism such as tourism planning, carrying capacity and environmental interpretation. He was engaged on numerous projects in Croatia and abroad as tourism expert for UNEP, UNWTO, Plan Bleu and GIZ, especially in Montenegro, Bosnia and Herzegovina, Egypt and Cyprus. He published over 70 scientific and professional papers in national and international scientific and professional journals.

Jasenka Kranjčević, PhD is a Senior Research Fellow at the Institute for Tourism, Croatia. Her research interests include tourism role in spatial distribution of tourism, architecture as touristic product, architectural touristic heritage and tourism history. She is the member of scientific project Heritage Urbanism (HERU) – Urban and Spatial Models for Revival and Enhancement of Cultural Heritage at Faculty for Architecture, University of Zagreb. She published over 30 research papers.

Damir Krešić, PhD is a Research Fellow at the Institute for Tourism, Croatia. He graduated from the Faculty of Economics and Business, University of Zagreb, with a degree in Finance, completed his master's degree in Foreign Trade and got his PhD in Tourism. His main areas of expertise are destination management and marketing, destination master planning and ICT application in tourism. During his career, Damir has successfully collaborated with public and private sector as well as with variety of tourism stakeholders and acquired an in-depth understanding of Croatian tourism.

Ivo Kunst, PhD is a Senior Research Fellow at the Institute for Tourism, Zagreb, Croatia. He obtained a bachelor degree, a master's degree and PhD in economics, all at the University of Zagreb, Department of Economics. His main research interests include tourism economics, tourism development and strategic management. Apart from publishing over 25 research articles, during his professional career, he served on supervisory boards of several Croatian hotel companies and held managerial positions in several leading Croatian companies in the non-tourism sector.

Eduard Kušen, PhD a Visiting Fellow at the Institute for Tourism, is an architect graduate, and he has received his PhD in architecture. Prior to joining the Institute for Tourism, he worked in building design, product design and spatial planning. In his multidisciplinary approach, he links tourism planning with urban planning, physical planning, architecture and protection (conservation) of natural and cultural heritage. He has published several books on tourism attractions and resources, more than hundred scholarly and professional articles.

Izidora Marković Vukadin, PhD is a Research Assistant at the Institute for Tourism, Croatia. Her areas of research interest include spatial planning in tourism, analysis of tourist resources, sustainable development, environmental protection and nature-based tourism. She has also finished her PhD in management of protected areas and has working experience with the institutions in nature protection sector and DMOs. In addition, she participated on a dozen of scientific conferences with submissions and published more than ten research papers.

Zrinka Marušić, Mag. Math is a Senior Adviser at the Institute for Tourism, Croatia. She obtained a master's degree in mathematics and statistics from the Faculty of Science, University of Zagreb, and university specialist's degree in business economics from the Faculty of Economics. Her main research interests include quantitative research methods in tourism, measurement of tourism consumption and tourism economic contribution, and valuation of public goods in tourism.

Katarina Miličević, PhD is an expert associate at the Institute for Tourism, Croatia. She is also a Managing Board Member of the Croatian Youth Hostel Association and a part-time Senior Lecturer at Zagreb School of Economics and Management, the only AACSB-accredited college in Croatia. She has finished her undergraduate and graduate study at the Zagreb School of Economics and Management and got her PhD from the Faculty of Economics, University of Ljubljana, Slovenia. The main areas of her scientific interest and professional expertise are related to destination competitiveness, tourism management and marketing, and destination branding.

Ivan Sever, PhD is a Research Assistant and Institute for Tourism and a PhD student at the University of Ljubljana, Slovenia. His research interest is focused on research methodology and data analysis techniques in tourism studies. He has authored or co-authored several research papers and is a member of Croatian Statistical Association.

Božo Skoko, PhD is a Professor at the Faculty of Political Science of the University of Zagreb, where he is a Head of the Public Relations and Journalism Department. The areas of his scientific research include communication, international relations, national identity and image and destination branding. He is a long-time strategic communications consultant and co-founder of Millenium promocija, the leading Croatian public relations agency. He has published five books and over forty scientific papers on public relations, media, country branding and managing identity and image of Croatia.

Neda Telišman-Košuta, MSc is a Senior Adviser at the Institute for Tourism, Zagreb, Croatia. Her research interests include the study of destination image and branding, brand delivery in the tourism context and destination development. During the course of her career, she has tried to bring her research based and academic knowledge into an extensive professional portfolio of projects focusing on destination marketing and development strategies both in Croatia and in other countries of South-Eastern Europe.

Renata Tomljenović, PhD a Senior Research Fellow at the Institute for Tourism, Croatia, received her doctoral degree at the Griffith University, Australia. Her research interests include tourism role in fostering social transformation, socio-cultural impacts of tourism and tourism planning. She is the Managing Editor of the international academic journal *Tourism* and serves on a number of editorial boards.

Snježana Boranić Živoder, PhD a Research Fellow at the Institute for Tourism, Croatia, received her doctoral degree at the University of Zagreb. Her research interests are destination marketing and management, destination branding and tourism planning. She is also a Senior Lecturer at the University of Applied Sciences (VERN, Zagreb).

LIST OF FIGURES

Fig. 2.1   Keywords of basic value propositions generated by workshop
            participants   29
Fig. 2.2   The basic value propositions for the three pillars of
            national tourism vision   30
Fig. 2.3   The vision statement   31
Fig. 3.1   Croatian regions according to the level of tourism
            development   44
Fig. 7.1   Basic functional classification of tourism attractions   129
Fig. 7.2   An illustration of a basic tourism destination consisting
            of a cluster of tourism places—Riviera of Opatija
            (Northern Adriatic, ca. 1900)   137
Fig. 7.3   A schematic of the relationship between tourism attractions
            and basic tourism destinations and tourism places   138
Fig. 7.4   Photo of the model (Kušen's System of Tourism
            Attractions, 2009)   141
Fig. 7.5   Two-dimensional model projection   142
Fig. 7.6   Process of conversion of a tourism resource into a
            tourism product   145
Fig. 9.1   Location of the two abandoned tourism zones in Croatia   190
Fig. 9.2   Policy networks between tourism and physical planning   195
Fig. 10.1   Location and main characteristics of Plitvice Lakes
            National Park   207
Fig. 10.2   Distribution of visitors in NP Plitvice Lakes in 2013   211
Fig. 10.3   Changes of land cover in area of NP Plitvice Lakes from
            1991 to 2012 with illustrations   214

Fig. 11.1   Secondary motives for visiting Croatian coastal destinations   231
Fig. 11.2   Length of stay in Croatian coastal destinations   233
Fig. 11.3   Use of information sources by tourists in Croatia   234
Fig. 11.4   Average daily tourist expenditures in Croatia in Euro
             (at current prices)   236
Fig. 12.1   Island of Vis, Croatia   246
Fig. 12.2   Komiža's open garbage dump   259

LIST OF TABLES

Table 3.1   Response rate by stakeholders and regions   45
Table 3.2   Tourism development at the local level (%)   47
Table 3.3   Availability of local development plans (%)   48
Table 3.4   Plan implementation (%)   49
Table 3.5   Stakeholder cooperation in the process of tourism
             development (%)   51
Table 3.6   Potential constraints to tourism development (%)   52
Table 5.1   First associations with Croatia among respondents from
             former Yugoslav countries (%)   91
Table 5.2   First associations with Croatia in six European countries (%) 93
Table 5.3   First associations with Croatia among respondents from
             the GCC countries (%)   94
Table 6.1   Objectives of tourist development policy in the
             city/municipality (%)   108
Table 6.2   City/municipality development plans (%)   109
Table 6.3   Implementation of programs and projects defined
             by planning documents (%)   109
Table 6.4   Possible constraints of tourism development (%)   110
Table 6.5   Skills and competences of employees in tourism boards (%)   112
Table 6.6   Cooperation in the field of tourism development (%)   113
Table 7.1   Contribution to the functional classification system
             of tourism resources   125
Table 7.2   Basic functional classification of tourist motives/activities 127
Table 7.3   Lew's Composite Ideograph of Tourist Attraction Typology   128
Table 7.4   An example of a subdivision of types of attractions
             belongs to the geological features of a destination   131

Table 7.5	Evaluation of tourism attractions	132
Table 7.6	Draft of a Tourism Attraction Registry data sheet	133
Table 7.7	A contribution to the classification of key data (characteristics) for each tourism attraction	134
Table 8.1	Methodological approach for assessment of internal tourism expenditures in Croatia in 2011	156
Table 8.2	Methodological approach for assessment of output, intermediate inputs and gross value added of tourism industries in Croatia in 2011	159
Table 8.3	Methodological approach for assessment of TSA Table 6 in Croatia in 2011	160
Table 8.4	Total domestic supply and internal tourism consumption (elements of TSA Table 6) for Croatia in 2011	161
Table 8.5	Tourism gross value added and internal tourism consumption for EU countries (million Euro)	164
Table 9.1	Number of beds in the hospitality industry in the period 1955–1984	180
Table 9.2	Planned accommodation facilities in Yugoslavia for 2000 according to a study from 1984	181
Table 9.3	Accommodation facilities in Croatia (permanent beds) by type of accommodation and hotel category, structure in per cent and rate of change	187
Table 9.4	Occupancy rates (permanent beds) according to main types of accommodation and hotel categories in per cent	188
Table 9.5	Population of Malinska municipality 1961–2011	191
Table 9.6	Number of tourist arrivals and overnights in Malinska municipality 1960–2008	191
Table 9.7	Population of Kupari in 1948–2001	193
Table 9.8	Number of tourist arrivals and overnights in Kupari, 1936–1938	193
Table 9.9	Number of tourist arrivals and overnights in Kupari, 1962–1965 and 1980	193
Table 10.1	Number of visitors and overnight stays in Plitvice Lakes National Park, 1970–2011	210
Table 11.1	Tourist satisfaction	235
Table 12.1	Tourism indicators for Vis, 1981, 1988, 2014	248
Table 12.2	Vis' tourism-related issues and vulnerabilities	256
Table 12.3	Indicators of nautical tourism growth	257
Table 13.1	The demographic characteristics of the sample	269
Table 13.2	Croatia's gastronomy tourism—Alliance/relationship matrix	273

CHAPTER 1

Introduction

Larry Dwyer, Sanda Čorak, and Renata Tomljenović

Tourism in Croatia

There are several reasons for the increasing interest shown towards Croatian tourism in recent years. The recent accession of Croatia to the EU is creating general and scholarly interest in the country's primary, secondary, and tertiary industries. In terms of tourism, Croatia is a rising star. Although occupying only 1.3 % of the EU territory (European Union, 2016), and accounting for less than 1 % of the total EU population (Eurostat, 2015), it realizes 61 million of tourist nights or 5.1 % of EU total. When the number of tourist nights is put in proportion to the population size, Croatia is the most popular destination of the European Union, alongside Malta and Cyprus. Most of its tourism activity is realized in the Croatian Adriatic (officially the EU NUTS2 region). The Croatian Adriatic is a popular destination for foreign tourists and comprises one of ten EU regions that collectively account for over 90 % of foreign visitors to Europe (Eurostat, 2016). Tourism is important to Croatian economy,

L. Dwyer (✉)
University of Ljubljana, Ljubljana, Slovenia

S. Čorak • R. Tomljenović
Institute for Tourism, Zagreb, Croatia

© The Author(s) 2017
L. Dwyer et al. (eds.), *Evolution of Destination Planning and Strategy*, DOI 10.1007/978-3-319-42246-6_1

1

contributing 10.4 % to the national GDP and 13.3 % to the national employment (Ivandić, Marušić, Šutalo & Vuglar, 2014). A long history together with the impressive recent performance of Croatian tourism industry combined with a scholarly approach to key issues of destination strategic planning and development makes this book timely, both in terms of its Croatian and, broader, Adriatic/Mediterranean context and themes covered.

Croatia, is an independent state since 1990 when it seceded from the former Yugoslavia. Geographically, it is an Adriatic and Central European country, easy to reach by road from main European outbound markets. Its 56,000 km^2 in a shape of a boomerang is divided into three geographical zones—lowland Pannonian to the north and north-east, mountain Dinaric, and the coastal Adriatic. Although there is a strife to disperse tourism demand geographically throughout the country, tourism is primarily developed along the Adriatic. It is a narrow strip of karst coastline and islands bordered inland by steep mountain ranges. The total coastline length stretches to 1,777 km due to many inlets and bays making it, after Greece and Italy, the longest shoreline in Europe. Of that, three quarters is made of elongated islands that stretch parallel the shore. With 718 islands and islets, 289 rocks, and 78 reefs along the coastline, Croatia is sometimes described as the 'land of a thousand islands', and these islands are important for the geographical identity of the country. With a population of 4.4 million, it is one of the more sparsely populated countries of Europe with a population density of 76 per km^2 (Croatia, 2016).

The popularity of Croatia as tourism destination is still on the rise. After independence, it has been promoted as the 'Mediterranean as it once was' to achieve clear geographical positioning as an independent state and to appeal to memories of its loyal old guests and to the nostalgia-driven market segments of new ones. As it has gradually widened the product portfolio with an array of products appealing to special interest, it has since moved to lifestyle positioning. It has clearly captured the market attention as its destinations are increasingly voted among the best on various travel portals, by travel association and travel magazines.

Coinciding with similar developments all over Europe, tourism started to develop in the mid-nineteenth century along the coast, as citizens of polluted industrial towns of Central Europe flocked to the coastal health retreats, made accessible by newly developed railway and steamship lines. In the post-WW2 era, tourism started to flourish in the

1960s, when fiscal policy measures stimulated significant investments in tourism facilities and transport infrastructure. At the same time, the increase of living standard of the local population and border crossing liberalization enabled an increase in traffic of domestic and foreign tourists. Under the state-run economy, there was a sharp increase in tourism accommodation, from about 40,000 beds in 1955 to 800,000 in 1984 (Large Geographic Atlas of Yugoslavia in Kranjčević, Chap. 9) seeking to increase it to over 2.5 million in 2000 (Kobašić in Kranjčević, Chap. 9). With some decentralization in planning and sovereignties given to private ownership and entrepreneurship, private accommodation started to flourish from the 1970s. By 1990, just before the outbreak of the Homeland war, there were 862,000 beds, of which 32 % in private accommodation. However, owning to the decaying state-run resorts, low quality of private accommodation, shifts in demand, and emergence of competitors, the tourism already started to show signs of an early decline. The steady increase in tourism arrivals and overnights peaked in 1987/1988 of about 10.5 million arrivals and 60 million overnights and then started do decrease to 8.5 million and 55.5 million, respectively, by 1990 (Croatian Bureau of Statistics, 2012). With the outbreak of war, the tourism activity abruptly came to almost a halt. However, tourism has recovered relatively quickly, certainly much quicker that the early post-Homeland war plans have envisaged. By 2010 the numbers of tourist arrivals and overnight matched those of 1988.

In 2015, Croatia recorded 71.6 million overnights, 92 % of which by foreign tourists in about 943,000 of permanent beds, of which 17 % in hotels and resorts, 48 % of private accommodation, and 25 % in camps (96 % of them in coastal area). The major Croatian generating markets are Germany, Slovenia, Austria, the Czech Republic, Italy, Poland, Slovakia, the Netherlands, the United Kingdom, and Hungary. The tourist activity is geographically concentrated on the narrow coastal strip, accounting for 95 % of total overnights, and shows a high degree of seasonality with 63 % of tourist overnights spent in the two summer months (July and August) and 35 % in shoulder seasons (April to June, September, and October) (Croatian Bureau of Statistics, 2016). Tourists express high level of satisfaction with the scenic and natural beauties of the country, friendliness of hosts, and personal safety, perceiving it as an excellent family destination, testified furthermore by a very high level of repeat tourists (83 % to Croatia, 61 % to the same destination) (Institute for Tourism, 2015).

In spite of these positive trends, Croatian tourism is still facing significant challenges. In essence, it is a mature tourism destination dependent on the sun&sea product, with a pronounced seasonality, typical for all warm-sea destinations. However, while its Mediterranean competitors started to restructure its tourism sector in the 1980s, Croatia—due to the breakup of Yugoslavia and war—has started to upgrade its tourism infrastructure after 2010. The steady growth of tourism since then is a result of expansion and upgrading of bed capacity, rather than in an increased occupancy rate, although there is a trend of increase in the product breadth and depth. The *Strategy for Croatian Tourism Development to 2020* (Ministry of Tourism, 2013), adopted by the government, aims to address the main challenges faced by its tourism sector—seasonality and geographical concentration of tourism activity; overreliance on natural beauty and cultural heritage as key tourism attractions with a subsequent lack of new purpose-built attractions; slow introduction of products for special interest markets, coupled with traditional approach to marketing; growth based on expansion of private accommodation; and insufficient investment in tourism infrastructure, especially hotel capacity.

The main goals of the Strategy are to increase its attractiveness and competitiveness to ensure a top-20 ranking on the Travel and Tourism Competitiveness Index, achieve 7 billion Euro investment in tourism, increase foreign tourism expenditure by 6 billion Euro, generate 30,000 new jobs (20,000 direct and 10,000 indirect jobs), increase capacity by 100,000 beds, and spread tourism more equally temporarily and geographically. Achieving these goals requires creative and practical solutions based on a sound theoretical approach to the issues of effective strategy implementation with support of a broad range of stakeholders, efficient destination management, improved marketing and branding, effective spatial planning, improved and expanded tourism attractions, timely statistics on the scope and impacts of tourism, and sound management of natural and cultural resources to ensure sustainable tourism development. The chapters of this book are addressing a number of issues related to the struggles to improve performance of Croatian tourism industry while ensuring its long-term sustainability.

THE INSTITUTE FOR TOURISM, ZAGREB

This book is prepared by the researchers of the Institute for Tourism, Zagreb. It is one of the 25 public research institutes in Croatia and among the oldest tourism research institutes in Europe. Its history dates back to

1959, when it was set up by the Croatian Chamber of Economy for the purpose of providing consultancy and microeconomic studies for the tourism industry. In 1986, it was turned into a public scientific institute and given its current name. It now employs 28 staff, of which 20 are scientists.

The mission of the Institute is to foster sustainable tourism development through its scientific, professional, and educational activities. In the focus of its research interest are four broad themes: economic impacts of tourism, visitor behavior and experiences, sustainable destination development and governance and transport, and environment and tourism. The Institute mostly conducts applied research focused on solving practical problem faced by the theory and practice of tourism development, both globally and in the context of Croatian tourism. In this way the research conducted directly contributes to the economy and, in general, to the sustainable local and regional development of Croatia. The research that the Institute conducts is mainly based on the positivist paradigm that generally dominates in tourism research and is, accordingly, quantitative. However, reflecting the increasing importance of the interpretive and critical studies with qualitative research method, with a team of social geographers focused on tourism, local community, sustainability, and the management of development, research by the Institute gradually includes those based on an interpretative paradigm.

From its beginning, the Institute has gained a wealth of experience in tourism planning and development. Applying the theoretical knowledge and scientific rigor, the Institute is engaged in development and management plans for tourism destinations, development of specific tourism products, restructuring and development of hospitality enterprises, as well as planning an implementation of operational solutions. The knowledge and experience gained from the scientific and applied work are disseminated widely to the Croatian professional community through specialized tailor-made educational programs, participation in the educational programs of Croatian universities and professional associations, and development of on-line educational courses for on-line staff in tourism and hospitality.

Through research, consultancy, and education, the Institute affects tourism development of many local communities and, by recommendation and the development of performance indicators, facilitates the formation of a national tourism policy and the adoption of different measures. More recently, the Institute was in charge of development of the abovementioned *Strategy for Croatian Tourism Development to 2020*, largely founded on the results of its primary research, adopted by the government, and followed by a series of action plans to operationalize national strategic goals, such as product development (nautical tourism, bike tourism, rural tourism, congress tourism, cultural tourism, social tourism), accommodation sector (small/family-run hotels, private accommodation), fostering business climate (competitiveness, small- and medium-sized tourism enterprises, education for tourism), and sustainability (green tourism). It was involved in strategic and marketing plans from major tourism regions and destinations of Croatia, and it is facilitating tourism development in continental Croatia through planning and education. It is also the forerunner in product developments, in particular heavily involved in research and planning of nautical tourism, cultural and river cruise tourism. Its longitudinal market survey of summer tourists along Adriatic and occasional product demand surveys such as cultural tourism, national and nature park, transit tourism, and nautical tourism (known as TOMAS surveys of tourist motivation, activities, satisfaction, and expenditures) are used widely for the purpose of planning, product development, and promotion.

Internationally, apart from the international-interdisciplinary journal *Tourism*—one of the oldest tourism journals in the world for which the Institute is best known—it nurtures partnerships with colleagues from similar institutions, particularly from English-speaking countries (Australia, Canada, New Zealand, UK, USA) whose works prevail in the international academic journals and from Western European countries as well as countries in the region. It is an excellent and productive cooperation, as colleagues abroad have profound theoretical knowledge, but are somewhat distanced from tourism practice. With this partnership with academics worldwide, the Institute reaches a global scientific community, while the cooperation with the UN World Tourism Organization (UNWTO) serves to make the Institute relevant to the global professional audience. The core of the cooperation with the UNWTO is on determining new segments of the tourist demand and the harmonization of research instruments in order to achieve greater data comparability on an international level. The work that is conducted at the Institute, as this book clearly demonstrates, is of relevance to the international scholarly and professional community.

OVERVIEW OF BOOK CONTENT

The book combines two aspects. The first is a theoretically oriented approach to destination planning and development. The second aspect comprises a problem solving focus on Croatian tourism. The contents will be of interest to all scholars, students, and practitioners engaged in various aspects of destination development planning and management as well as those interested in how Croatia is approaching its tourism development.

Against this background, the book is structured in 14 chapters, roughly organized according to the planning process.

In Chap. 2, *Crafting a National Value-Driven Tourism Vision*, Renata Tomljenović and Irena Ateljević start from the premise that the crafting of destination image and identity is the most critical aspect of a strategic approach to tourism development. This chapter outlines a novel and innovative approach to crafting a value-driven vision for tourism development. The proposed value-driven approach is based on the need to depart from the classical market-driven competitive positioning that is argued to foster long-term unsustainability for the tourism industry with serious disturbance to the fabric of social, cultural, and environmental life. The value-driven approach calls up an awakening of more human values of reciprocity and stewardship that go beyond currently dominant economic and competitive concerns. The chapter starts with a theoretical discussion of market versus value-driven visions framed within the current discourse of conscious travel and responsible business practices. It then provides a historical insight into the visions that have, supposedly, guided Croatian tourism development since the 1990s, before presenting results of a series of workshops and consultations with the Croatian tourism stakeholders for the purpose of defining Croatian tourism vision to 2020.

In Chap. 3, *Managing Tourism Development Process in Croatia: Can EU Accession Help?*, Ivo Kunst presents a provocative analysis of the relationship between planning and implementation, highlighting the opportunities offered by EU accession to improve the quality of destination management. Although international tourism receipts, particularly in times of declining economic activity, have traditionally been used to stabilize the Croatian economy, successive Croatian governments have treated tourism predominantly as a 'gift from heaven' and have not shown much interest to oversee its development. In 2015, the Travel and Tourism Competitiveness Report ranked the competitiveness of Croatian tourism 33rd in the world. A survey of local authorities and DMO directors revealed that Croatia's rather poor tourism competitiveness stems predominantly from the inefficient implementation of tourism development strategies at the destination level. The survey results also indicate that most of the constraints impeding Croatia's tourism competitiveness could be effectively neutralized using the EU structural and cohesion funds. This chapter also suggests that the access to these funds will be largely conditional upon the overall quality of Croatia's integration into the economic, fiscal, and regulatory system of the European Union.

Chapter 4, *Shaping Destination Identity: Challenges of Branding Croatia* by Neda Telišman-Košuta, focuses on destination image and identity delivered through consistent branding, analyzed through Croatia's attempt to move away from a 'sea, sun, and summer' only destination against the lack of capacity to deliver consistent branding strategies. Striving to extend its image beyond that of the three S markets and to improve its competitive position, much of recent destination development and marketing planning in Croatia has dealt with branding to some extent. However, destination branding has largely remained strategy on paper. Interviews with regional and local tourist boards across Croatia reveal their perceived incapacity to act as branding managers due to insufficient finances, human resources, knowledge, and authority. The power of destination branding is seen to be curtailed by lack of 'destination thinking' and 'destination leadership'. In view of these limitations, it is suggested that future research should explore possibilities of destination brand management stemming from collaboration and leadership theories.

Political issues of tourism development are addressed in Chap. 5, *The Influence of Political Factors in Fashioning Destination Image* by Božo Skoko, Katarina Miličević, and Damir Krešić. The chapter examines the role of tourism in creation of national identity against the historical background of relatively recent formation of a nation state. The authors argue that political factors as well as tourism promotion can play an important role in the formation of national brands and that strong national brands can substantially increase a nation's competitive advantage in the global market. This is particularly true for countries in transition such as Croatia that have gained independence and face the imperative of creating a completely new national image. During the last two decades, Croatia has successfully repositioned its image from an unknown Yugoslav republic, victim of war and newly formed Balkan state, to an attractive tourism destination. Tourism promotion has played an important role in this process with the Croatian National Tourist Board relying heavily on tourism attractions to disassociate the image of Croatia from its neighbors, especially from other former Yugoslav countries. The chapter presents research of Croatia's image in the most important Western tourism generating markets, countries in the Middle

East as well as in neighboring countries. The research also identifies additional attributes and strategies that could be used to create a stronger, global brand for Croatia.

Management issues are addressed in Chap. 6, *Tourism Destination and DMO Transformation* by Sanda Čorak and Snježana Boranić-Živoder. Due to the strong competition that characterizes the European tourism market, many countries face the challenge of improving the efficiency and efficacy of destination management. Croatia, from its inception as an independent state, has been developing its destination management approach based on a system of tourism associations (DMO), from local through regional to the national level. In recent years it has been found to be difficult to follow the rapid changes taking place in the tourism market. Based on research carried out in the public sector, poor destination management has been identified as one of the limiting factors of tourism development of Croatia. A central question arises as to how to ensure the efficient yet consistent destination management organization and its structure in a face of rapidly and continually changing organization and business environment and against the rapid growth of tourism arrivals and overnights. This chapter identifies the weaknesses and advantages of the existing destination management system. It also analyzes possible ways to transform the system in order to preserve the existing foundation and strengthen the system to be able to meet all tasks of destination management in a competitive tourism market.

Whereas the first five chapters deal with the key aspects of tourism planning and management—defining a guiding vision, identifying the challenges of delivering it in practice through sound management, building destination identity/brand and national (tourism) image, and setting up and continuously innovate destination management structure—the focus of the book thence shifts to identify some important tools necessary for sound decision making in both planning and implementation stage.

In Chap. 7, *Tourism Attraction System*, Eduard Kušen argues that although tourism attractions are a basic resource for long-term tourism developments, they are not given the proper attention, both theoretically and practically. For tourism planning, an important yet theoretically underdeveloped area is its relationship and interdependence with spatial planning. The chapter presents an innovative approach to tourism attractions from the lens of spatial planning from the identification, classification to evaluation of tourism attractions. While advancing the theory of tourism resources and attractions, it also presents a highly practical planning and management tool. This new system of tourism attractions is tested through the series of case studies. It is argued that one cannot understand the importance of tourism attractions for the development of tourism without full knowledge of the integrated process of converting a tourism resource into a market-ready tourism product.

For sound decision making, but especially for advocating tourism interests to the broad range of stakeholders, the economic contribution of tourism is an important issue. Chapter 8, *Implementation of Tourism Satellite Account: Assessing the Contribution of Tourism to the Croatian Economy* by Neven Ivandić and Zrinka Marušić, addresses tourism's contribution in Croatia based on the Tourism Satellite Account (TSA) approach. While Tourism Satellite Account is the recommended method by the UN World Tourism Organization, its application is less straightforward in the case of developing countries and countries in transition. The chapter demonstrates technical aspects of compiling core TSA tables within the available tourism statistic data in Croatia. The adopted approach is compared to solutions implemented in other European countries. The resulting TSA macro-aggregates show that the contribution of tourism to the Croatian economy is higher than in many other tourism developed countries. Taking into account TSA scope as confined to the direct effects of tourism demand on production, employment, investment, and government revenues and expenditures, the chapter then discusses the role of TSA in the wider context of the tourism planning process. Although the TSA cannot be directly used as planning tool due to its descriptive character, it helps in the fine tuning of tourism statistics and creating the basis for construction of different stochastic and deterministic economic models. As an example of such TSA extension, the chapter presents an application of input-output model based on TSA in order to measure the indirect effects of tourism demand in Croatia.

In Chap. 9, *Abandoned Tourism Resorts in Croatia: The Consequences of Discordant Spatial Planning and Tourism Development Policies,* Jasenka Kranjčević explores the challenges brought about by the abandoned tourism zones or resorts in Croatia. It is argued that resorts' demise is primarily a result of poor planning, incompatible policy networks between different government bureaus and sectors, complex ownership structures, a web of incompatible laws and regulations, and unrealistic expectations together with lack of institutional/bureaucratic cooperation. It is further argued that the resorts' closures may have resulted from incompetent management and 'creative' accounting, as well as the Homeland war. With all indicators showing a continued demand for tourism land, it simply defies logic to still have abandoned resorts idle away on valuable land and in prime locations. Current legislative incompatibility and a lack of inter-departmental and inter-sectoral will are some of the consequences of socio-political changes of the 1990s. Other factors include the transition to the market economy, bureaucratic inertia, and insecurity. Not surprisingly, the rights and obligations of tourism industry stakeholders have not been clearly defined nor articulated, including, among others, the use of tourism land. Since the government continues to plan for and allocate new areas for tourism development, the abandoned tourism resorts are an indication of an irresponsible and irrational use of valuable land, allowing further degradation and pollution of local and regional land resources, and a gross mismanagement of the existing natural, economic, and cultural capital.

While sustainable development is generally honored in principle in tourism planning, there is a question of its practical implementation. Tourism in general, including tourism in protected areas, inevitably changes and disturbs the socio-cultural and natural environment. In Chap. 10 *Sustainability Issues in Management of Tourism in Protected Areas: Case study of Plitvice Lakes National Park*, Izidora Marković espouses the principles of the development and management of protected natural areas in the world as the basis for finding the most appropriate model of management for the Plitvice Lakes National Park, a UNESCO-protected national heritage. The analysis shows that the main factors that have negative impact (global, regional, and local) on the area of Plitvice Lakes are the impact of tourism, residential function, agriculture, transport, and unresolved communal infrastructure. Plitvice Lakes National Park is a representative example of developmentally loaded protected natural areas, which requires the application of the new development paradigm with the aim of permanent protection of its natural phenomena. The future development of Plitvice Lakes National Park requires continuous research on economic, social, and environmental processes, to better align future development with the principles of sustainable development, particularly through spatial planning and management.

Of essential importance to sustainable tourism development is a consistent data collection exercise and research agenda able to track and analyze changes in tourist demand. In Chap. 11, *Identifying Trends in Tourism*

Demand Using Longitudinal Survey, Zrinka Marušić, Ivan Sever, and Sanda Čorak propose an approach to tracking the changes in behavior and characteristics of tourists that enables Croatian tourism marketing experts to gain rich data at the regional and national level. The authors identify tourism as a complex and dynamic phenomenon, affected by various economic, social, cultural, political, technological, and environmental trends. These trends affect the characteristics and expectations of tourists as well as tourism flows and therefore have implications for destination management and the types of products and services that tourism businesses need to develop. The key challenge for successful tourism industry is the ability to recognize and adapt to these trends. Tourism destinations that fail to adapt have difficulty maintaining their competitiveness and delivering tourism products and services that stimulate satisfaction and create loyalty. Furthermore, the movements on tourist market are strong, and people tend to search for new destinations and new experiences. To deal with these challenges, tourism researchers should look beyond the present manifestations of tourism and use research designs that are able to examine and monitor the underlying mechanisms of change. Longitudinal research is particularly appropriate for such purposes (to study the patterns of change over time) and as such is a key process for understanding tourism development. Although the number of longitudinal surveys in tourism is increasing, only a few assess the changes in behavior and characteristics of tourists in the destination itself. This chapter presents a methodological guide and empirical trend study to stimulate much needed research in this area. Presented empirical case study is based on longitudinal survey of attitudes, activities, and expenditures of Croatian tourists in the period from 1987 to 2014.

Chapter 12, *Longitudinal Assessment of the Carrying Capacity of a Typical Tourist Island: Twenty Years On* by Jakša Kivela and Zoran Klarić, highlights the tourism growth of Vis Island over a twenty-five-year period, from when the first carrying capacity was conducted in 1991 to today. An examination and understanding of changes, both negative and positive, highlight what models of tourism development are appropriate for this ecologically fragile small, remote island. The chapter focuses on the limits of what acceptable change planning process must be without putting at risk the island's natural and cultural heritage. Importantly, guidelines for regulating future tourism development that does not adversely alter the cultural-social-biophysical endowments of Vis Island are recommended.

The issues addressed are relevant to the tourism development of Adriatic islands generally.

Gastronomic tourism, while important to Croatia, has been under-researched in the wider scholarly literature. In Chap. 13, *Gastronomy Tourism: Croatia a Land of Wine and Plenty, Or Beyond Pizza and Grill!*, Jakša Kivela argues that although the literature supports the view that there is a connection between tourism and gastronomy, there is little empirical evidence to show, for example, whether or not there is a culinary-tourism market segment. Does a destination's gastronomy contribute to the tourists' quality of experiences while visiting the destination? And, do tourists return to the destination to re-sample its cuisine? The most recent literature suggests that gastronomy is becoming an important attribute in the development of niche travel and niche destinations. A question whether motivation to travel for gastronomy is a reasonably valid construct to use for tourism market segmentation purposes is answered based on research conducted on two islands in the South Adriatic, popular by foreign tourists. This study was undertaken during the summer season on the islands of Vis, Hvar, and Korčula in Croatia between 2010 and 2013. These middle-Adriatic islands are well-known tourist destinations that offer authentic Dalmatian gastronomy. The results of this study suggest that motivation to travel for gastronomy is a reasonably valid construct to use for tourism market segmentation purposes. The results of the data analysis reveal that gastronomy plays a considerable role in the way tourists experience a destination and indicate that quite a few travelers would return to the same destination to savour its unique gastronomy. Implications for research and suggestions for destination planners are also discussed.

Chapter 14, *Tourism future: Towards Transformational Tourism* by Larry Dwyer, Irena Ateljević, and Renata Tomljenović, ties together the main propositions of the book grounded in the standard tourism planning framework to dwell on the future of tourism and tourism research. Linked to the first chapter on value-driven national vision, this chapter discusses how travelers shape tourism development and addresses the power of tourism to transform societies towards more healthy state of being. The chapter identifies current and emerging tourism practices with a transformational potential, identifying the benefits that Croatia could potentially derive by embracing new tourism practices, identifying the implications for the future of tourism in Croatia, and for emerging destinations globally.

REFERENCES

Croatia. (2016). *Croatia.eu: Geography and population.* http://croatia.eu/article. php?lang=2&id=11. Date accessed 15 Feb 2016.

Croatian Bureau of Statistics. (2012). *Statistical report no. 1463 – Tourism, 2011.* Zagreb: Croatian Bureau of Statistics.

Croatian Bureau of Statistics. (2016). *First release, tourist arrivals and overnight stays in rented accommodation, 2015.* http://www.dzs.hr/default_e.htm. Date accessed 13 Apr 2016.

European Union. (2016). *Living in EU.* http://europa.eu/about-eu/facts-figures/living/index_en.htm#goto_1. Date accessed 15 Feb 2016.

Eurostat. (2015). *Key figures on Europe – 2015 Edition.* Luxembourg: Publications Office of the European Union.

Eurostat. (2016). *Eurostat yearbook – Tourism statistics.* http://ec.europa.eu/eurostat/statistics-explained/index.php/Tourism_statistics. Date accessed 15 Feb 2016.

Institute for Tourism. (2015). *TOMAS Summer 2014 – Attitudes and expenditures of tourists in Croatia.* Zagreb: Institute for Tourism.

Ivandić, N., Marušić, Z., Šutalo, I., & Vuglar, J. (2014). *Satelitski račun turizma RH za 2011. godinu i izračun neizravnih i ukupnih učinaka turizma u RH [Tourism Satellite Account of the Republic of Croatia for 2011 and Estimation of Indirect and Total Impacts of Tourism].* Zagreb: Institute for Tourism.

Ministry of Tourism. (2013). *Croatian Tourism Development Strategy to 2020.* Official Gazette of the Republic of Croatia 55/2013. http://narodne-novine. nn.hr/clanci/sluzbeni/2013_05_55_1119.html. Date accessed 20 Nov 2014.

Crafting a National Value-Driven Tourism Vision

Renata Tomljenović and Irena Ateljević

INTRODUCTION

To speak about crafting a national tourism vision for any country today inevitably demands to ask first what the vision for the planet as a whole is, in the current context of the overwhelming crises at every level, from the environmental and economic to the social and cultural. When one looks at the scientific warnings, the vision for the future looks rather bleak as the facts speak for themselves. The structure of the world's ecosystems changed more rapidly in the second half of the twentieth century than at any time in recorded human history (Millennium Ecosystem Assessment, 2005). The world population is growing rapidly which is putting more pressure on the earth's recourses; there are many oil spill disasters; we produce huge amounts of waste and also plastic, causing, for example, 'plastic soup' in the oceans; there is loss of habitat; and thanks to our economic 'development' (a word suggesting it is developing in the right direction), CO_2 levels are increasing (Millennium Ecosystem Assessment, 2005), causing global warming. When all other life-threatening practices

R. Tomljenović (✉) • I. Ateljević
Institute for Tourism, Zagreb, Croatia

© The Author(s) 2017
L. Dwyer et al. (eds.), *Evolution of Destination Planning and Strategy*, DOI 10.1007/978-3-319-42246-6_2

are added in terms of pesticides, pops and other poisons in our waters and food chains, acidification and so on., it is not surprising that some prestigious scientists are warning us that the face of humanity and Gaia (Greek name for the Earth) is disappearing (Lovelock, 2010). Economically, the world is not doing any better either. The Wall Street led 2008 economic crisis that exposed the corruptive nature of the global political economy, has seriously put into the question our worship of the unconscious neo-liberal market economy model. In the words of Robert Skidelsky, a renowned British economist:

> ...[this] crisis also represents a moral failure: that of a system built on debt. At the heart of the moral failure is the worship of growth for its own sake, rather than as a way to achieve the 'good life'. As a result, economic efficiency – the means to growth – has been given absolute priority in our thinking and policy. The only moral compass we now have is the thin and degraded notion of economic welfare. This moral lacuna explains uncritical acceptance of globalization and financial innovation...taking us back to the primary question: what is wealth for? The good life was one to be lived in harmony with nature and our fellows. Yet we destroy the beauty of the countryside because the unappropriated splendors of nature have no economic value. We are capable of shutting off the sun and the stars because they do not pay a dividend. (Skidelsky, 2009, p. 1)

The moral failure has also led us to the continuously widening socio-economic gap in which the poorest 40 % of the world's population account for 5 % of global income only while the richest 20 % account for its three-quarters (Ateljevic, 2011). Yet, longitudinal studies in rich countries of the West show that increasing income (beyond basic needs) does not increase happiness either (Layard, 2005). This growing dissatisfaction with our dominant lifestyle model is clearly illustrated in increasing suicidal rates, cancer disease and the consumption of antidepressants worldwide (World Health Organization, 2002, 2012) but also in the growing need for transformative holidays and travel. Namely, there have been emerging strong arguments (by scholars and practitioners) on value-driven (tourism) consumption and travel, which some frame as 'transmodern' tourism of the future (Ateljevic, 2009), while others speak of transformative tourism (Lean, 2009; Reisinger, 2013) or conscious travel (Pollock, 2015). According to these claims, it appears that the current unsustainable, suicidal, material paradigm increasingly pressures people (worldwide, albeit predominantly in the West) to search for some 'higher values' in which

CRAFTING A NATIONAL VALUE-DRIVEN TOURISM VISION 17

travel often appears to provide means to change both—one's own life and the impact one makes on places one visits. In other words, transmodern/transformative/conscious travellers are recognized to be re-inventing themselves and their world; they value the slow, small and simple and aim for self-reliance; they are connected and communicative; they care about the places they visit; they seek meaningful experiences that help them develop; they require their host/producers of tourism experience to think globally but to act locally. More broadly, marketers have already captured them as the market of LOHAS—conscious consumers with lifestyle of health and sustainability (Lohas, 2015; Worldwatch Institute, 2004; Cohen, 2007).

In this context, the value-driven approach to the formulation of the tourism vision that is proposed here is based on the obvious need to depart from the market-driven competitive positioning that has been underpinning the global tourism industry for too long, as it is proving to be seriously disturbing the fabric of social, cultural and environmental life. The value-driven approach calls upon awakening more human values of reciprocity and stewardship that go beyond currently dominant economic and competitive concerns, the values that will ensure the quality of local and global life and greater responsibility for planetary assets. The chapter starts with a theoretical discussion of market versus value-driven visions framed within the current discourse of conscious travel and responsible business practices. The fairly limited literature on the concept of vision informed the methodology and was applied to a recent tourism envisioning conducted in a series of workshops and consultations with the Croatian tourism stakeholders for the purpose of defining Croatian tourism vision to 2020. In order to further justify this fairly radical and new approach to tourism envisioned for the national level, a brief historical background into the visions that have, supposedly, guided Croatian tourism development since the 1990s is provided. Then the methodology is presented with which the first key scientific contribution of this chapter is laid out as this methodological approach may prove to be useful in other envisioning attempts around the world that aspire to motivate more responsible and conscious tourism practices.

Methodology section is followed by discussion of findings that highlight two further widely applied aspects that may be of interest to the international audience of both academics and practitioners. Firstly, Croatia has been very much an illustrative example of the unconscious socio-economic global practices outlined above along with a pervading sense of failure of the Croatian economy and governance. Secondly and consequently, the fairly successful tourism industry is proving to be almost the only hope for the livelihoods of many as it involves not only significant direct employment but a whole range of associated industries around it (from building industries to agriculture, transport, retailing, etc.). Thus, with tourism at the forefront of the economy but also affecting the environment and social values, it was a unique setting for exploring, with tourism stakeholders, as to how value-driven tourism vision could spearhead wider societal transformation. It is also assumed that this proposition would be alluring to the tourism industry itself, which has always fought for national respect and affirmation in the context of being dominantly perceived as a 'carefree/sun/sea-consumption based' industry. Yet the experience will display the complexity of the political process involved in the course of envisioning tourism strategy and how, despite the local aspirations for a 'different tourism', the new vision could not and has not been pursued and adopted in the final strategic planning process.

LITERATURE REVIEW ON (TOURISM) ENVISIONING

The visioning has become a well-established practice in tourism planning. In the broadest sense, the visioning has emerged from corporate policy planning, as a part of strategic planning. This corporate style planning is a rational and cost-benefit-driven process based on assessing a company's strengths and weaknesses and recognizing opportunities and threats from the external environment, leading to a set of strategies to achieve goals (Ruhanen, 2007). Within the corporate domain, it is seen as a tool to increase productivity and competitiveness (Shipley & Newkirk, 1998) and act as an effective mechanism that can mobilize people into action (Nanus, 1992). The concept of visioning in strategic tourism planning is not new. It is almost a mandatory that every tourism strategy features a vision. Yet, surprisingly, the topic of visioning is more frequently discussed by professionals. Thus, while various manuals and practical advice on vision abound, this subject has received scant attention by tourism scholars.

The scholarly articles on tourism/destination vision are rare and far apart. Ritchie (1999) has reported a vision building exercise for the Canadian national park based on values and a consensus building approach. Smith (2003) has outlined the approach of visioning Canadian tourism to be focused more on 'strategic visioning' as an extension of strategic planning based on the classical approach to situational analysis, with vision having strong marketing orientation. Ruhanen (2007), discussing the urgency and challenges of integrating sustainability objectives into destination planning for competiveness, advocates the strategic visioning process. She argues convincingly of the need to build the vision on stakeholder consultation and outlines the role and properties of vision without dealing with theoretical or methodological issues. Yeoman and Ledderman (2005) presented vision of Scottish tourism, but the thrust of their work is scenario development. From what little is available on tourism-related scholarly articles, two propositions are common. Firstly, the vision should be based on stakeholder values (Ritchie, 1999) and an outcome of a broad participation of stakeholders (Ruhanen, 2007). Therefore, the statement made by Ritchie (1999; p 274) fifteen years ago that 'the concept of visioning has not as yet received extensive attention in the tourism, or tourism-related, literature' holds true even today.

The subject of vision is also bypassed by scholars in general. In the broader context, visioning has received some attention in transformational studies where the notion of 'guiding vision' appears and it is considered the central element of governance strategies for transition management in the multi-level multi-actor network. Späth and Rohracher (2010) assessed the transformational potential of the guiding vision in the context of technology development, concluding that visioning has the potential to initiate and guide transformation needs and become a strong social norm. To do so the vision has to (A) resonate with sentiments shared by the wider public, (B) be concretized to a degree that make it deployable as a moral standard, (C) be sufficiently convincing and backed by credible knowledge and authority, (D) be launched into various societal spheres in order to align various actors in command of useful resources and (E) be inscribed into plans and policy guidance at various levels.

Visioning has also received some attention in visionary/spiritual/ transformation leadership literature bound mostly to the corporate world. While it is outside the scope of the theme of this chapter, that literature is relevant in as much as it puts the concept of values and, more specifically, spirituality, in the focus. Cacioppe (2000a, 2000b) amply illustrates how companies are now commonly writing visions and value statements that not only provide directions for business operations but also aim to motivate and inspire their employees to be committed to a worthwhile purpose. However, as he points out, often the two dominant paradigms—materialistic versus spiritual—collide. While at the individual level people are revaluating their most important values and life purposes, the organizations often remain locked in a materialistic, profit-driven corporate philosophy. Thus, he questions if the transformation can be done entirely through intellectual process, such as rational and analytical strategic planning.

However, vision is a theoretically marginalized construct in general. Van der Helm (2009) argues that it is precisely the lack of theory explaining appropriateness of vision and absence of clear methodology for vision formulation, which has resulted in vision seen as trivial, albeit necessary exercise, not worthy of scholarly attention. In an attempt to develop the theoretical underpinning of vision, van der Helm (2009) has outlined a typology of visions based on the context in which it appears (religious, political and social) and the field of use (business, community or policy vision). If applying this typology, a national tourism vision is a combination of community and policy vision. Community vision is developed within a network or group of actors through interactive process for the purpose of building a common ground or shared platform on which to build the strategy and hold actors together. It is also a policy vision where a network of policy-relevant actors develops foresight to influence network decision-making process and assumes the existence of policy network in which the vision has to become active.

Apart from the vision context, the equally relevant and theoretically still unresolved issue relates to the qualities of vision, where the central question is how visionary a vision has to be or, in other words, whether a vision can be too visionary. Van der Helm (2009) claims that the good vision is always future oriented and needs to provide sufficient contrast between past and present. Its purpose is to foster change by influencing human thinking that will then lead to change in behavior. This is contrary to Ritchie's (1999) earlier proposition made within the context of tourism that the vision should reflect the values of stakeholders for whom it is developed and, in the context of tourism planning, the values of stakeholders should be a fundamental component of a vision that seeks to capture the public will regarding the national treasure (Ritchie, 1999). If the vision has to reflect the current values of stakeholders as Ritchie claims, this would perpetuate the current practice, rather than induce change. However, if the vision is too future oriented than it would appear too ambitious and unattainable and thus failing to motivate stakeholders. Yet, there is a consensus that a good vision needs to be inspirational/motivational and perceived as relevant and authoritative (van der Helm 2009; Späth & Rohracherm, 2010) to be implemented and it is likely that an implementable vision needs to strike a balance and opt for incremental change.

To be effective, the issue of vision ownership, ambassadors and leaders is as important as the vision itself. Joy (2011, p. 40) is convinced that, to induce change, the vision needs a leader who has to be 'one step ahead of the values expressed in the norms of an institution and, finally, those of followers'. To the contrary, Späth and Rohracherm's (2010) case study of the transformational role of vision illustrates that vision, even when embraced by powerful actors, can be opposed by others with different views and, furthermore, points out that this aspect of vision is often underplayed in the literature on vision. Similarly, van der Helm asks the question of how vision is to be evaluated if an effective one should induce change. Yet, the actual change induced by vision is often incremental 'moving reality slowly into direction indicated by vision' (van der Helm, 2009).

Once these views of 'desired visions' for change are applied to the case of Croatian tourism future, it inevitably invites us to go back to our opening claims of the need to move from the market and competition model of unsustainable industrial practices to a value-driven approach of conscious tourism. From the position of academics interested in transmodern/transformational/conscious potentialities of tourism who also had the recent opportunity to inform the political process of envisioning the future of Croatian tourism at all levels (local, regional and national), the section on methodology will provide further details on how this process was approached. Yet, before that, the next section will set further context by laying out the historical evolution of tourism visions in Croatia.

HISTORY OF NATIONAL TOURISM PLANNING IN CROATIA

In Croatia, national integrated strategic plans rarely address tourism specifically, but, rather, tourism is treated horizontally, as part of other policies. Thus, for example, the first document developed in preparation for the EU accession—the *National Strategic Reference Framework 2012–2013* (Republic of Croatia, 2010)—suggests that 'green' becomes national brand due to the low level of environmental pollution, and, along this line, it is suggested that the investment made in 'green' brand will bring a high return rate, especially through tourism. Yet, while side-tracked in national strategic documents, the practice of national tourism planning is longstanding in Croatia.

The first strategy was developed in 1993 by the Institute for Tourism (Ministry of Tourism & Institute for Tourism, 1993), when the country was still involved in war and goals proposed dealt with the tourism recovery, market (re)positioning and brand identity. Even under these circumstances, the full evaluation and protection of the tourism resources was one of the strategic objectives. The same year a detailed *Tourism Master Plan* was developed by Austrian consultants and sponsored by the Austrian government (Horwath Consulting and Institute for Tourism, 1993). The master plan singled out the nature, people and tourism development as the three most important factors of Croatian economic growth/success in which the interest of the local population was strongly promoted. Then in 1998, the *Long-Term Development Concept of Croatian Tourism* was articulated for the next ten years by the Institute for Tourism (1998). The two pillars of the concept were the (A) growth in tourist numbers and income and (B) transition from the mass to sustainable tourism by improving product quality and market positioning based on product differentiation. Five years later the comprehensive *Strategy of Croatian Tourism Development to 2010* was launched, based for the first time on visioning tourism future (Ministry for Tourism, 2003). The vision addressed tourism's contribution to overall development, commitment to sustainability and investment-based growth as expressed in the document: 'tourism contributes significantly to the economic development of the Republic of Croatia and wellbeing of its citizens, based on the sustainable use of natural, cultural and heritage potentials, actively participating it their preservation and improvement, creating environment attractive to investors' (Ministry for Tourism, 2003, p. 18).

While these documents were developed, the level of commitment to their implementation remained questionable due to the lack of strategic leadership to drive the strategies forward. In that vacuum, the Croatian National Tourist Board has developed the marketing plans of Croatian tourism often including a formulation of the broader strategic framework. The first of such plans was developed in 2001 and another one ten years later. The one for the 2010–2014 defines vision for the Croatian tourism combining international market position while addressing tourism's role in the national economic and social context: 'Croatia will be globally recognized as a highly valued life-style destination, while, at the same time, succeeding in preservation of national natural and cultural values and tourism will become a highly competitive and sustainable sector that significantly contributes to the national economy' (THR and Horwath Consulting 2007, p. 7).

An in-depth analysis of the Croatian tourism development conducted for the purpose of national tourism planning has demonstrated that the aims of these policy documents were only partially met. Tourism has recovered to its pre-1990s level in 2010, ten years sooner than anticipated by early tourism plans, to reach about 14.3 million arrivals and close to 72 million overnights in 2015 (Croatian Bureau of Statistics, 2016). The national tourism competitiveness improved over time, as has product quality, especially in the accommodation sector. Today, Croatia has about 40 % of its accommodation in four to five star hotels compared to 22 % in 1989. The quality of private accommodation, camps and marinas has also improved. Tourism has become an important contributor to the national GDP, which stands at around 10.4 % (see Chap. 8), with ninety thousand jobs being created directly (Croatian Bureau of Statistics, 2014) and many more indirectly. Croatia's traffic access has been greatly improved with the expansion of the network of highways connecting the inland to the coastline (Šolman 2010; Institute for Tourism, 2005).

However, Croatia's tourism product is still lagging in scope, quality and creative imagination. In spite of the ambitious aims, it has not managed to extend the season beyond a few summer months and to diversify the product portfolio. The country fails to devise effective and coordinated destination management structures, which would truly work on an integrated framework to protect socio-cultural and environmental heritage while providing local economic livelihoods. Slow administration processes by local and regional authorities, lack of any joint visions by key stakeholders, low levels of creative entrepreneurship and poor control of destination tourism development (in particular uncontrolled building expansion) are just a few of many inherited problems associated not only with tourism industry but society in general.

Furthermore, the paradigm of economic growth with an accompanied mechanistic approach to problem-solving and the more recently unleashed forces of neo-liberalism continue to shape the public and private sector policy approach. As a result, tensions are mounting. Higging-Desboiles (2006) critiques the neo-liberal paradigm that has swept across the contemporary tourism sector, where tourism is an industry focused on profit, while people and places are turned into profit-generating products. She reminds us that in the most important international documents, charters and memorandums up to the 1980s, tourism was considered a force that had the potential to transform and enrich people and communities and encourage openness to new ideas, creativity and integration.

This rhetoric is currently mirrored in Croatia too. The obsession with economic growth and an investor-led push for resort development has now overshadowed a human face with which the Croatian tourism begun in the early stages of its development. Namely, in the early days, tourism was not considered to be one of the Yugoslavian/Croatian strategic priorities. It was somehow left to an organic growth of erratic, 'mushroom' developments driven by small-scale entrepreneurship of family-based businesses (Ateljevic & Doorne, 2003). These businesses were often unregistered and grew up out of a simple demand by independent tourists who were often driving around and virtually knocking on people's doors asking for some accommodation. Once the contact between the locals and tourists was established, they would often become repeated visitors and almost a part of the family (Corak, Mikacic, & Ateljevic, 2013). In developing this way, it was the source of national pride as guests from developed Western countries were respected and valued, from whom locals were learning and to which they passed on their love of life and local hospitality (Ateljevic & Corak, 2006). Paradoxically enough, it was an approach to tourism practice that in many ways now corresponds to the new demands of conscious tourism described earlier.

Furthermore, the political and legal pressures for greater sustainability of all our practices keep on rising, due to Croatia's recent membership to the European Union in July 2013, whereby the 'Innovation European Union 2020' strategy pushes its vision for smart, green and inclusive growth. In the words of José Manuel Barroso, President of the European Commission (2015):

> Europe 2020 is the EU's growth strategy for the coming decade. In a changing world, we want the EU to become a smart, sustainable and inclusive economy. These three mutually reinforcing priorities should help the EU and the Member States deliver high levels of employment, productivity and social cohesion. Concretely, the Union has set five ambitious objectives - on employment, innovation, education, social inclusion and climate/energy - to be reached by 2020. Each Member State has adopted its own national targets in each of these areas. Concrete actions at EU and national levels underpin the strategy.

This sustainability vision has been put to Croatia during the EU pre-accession times when its Strategic Reference Framework 2006–2013 for the national economic development vision was established. It was not only the fundamental programming document for coordinating Croatian policy with the EU policy but also the only document envisioning a vision for Croatia's future. The vision has been that of sustainable and balanced regional development, people with knowledge and skills, social inclusion, macro-economic stability and efficient financial market, with state administration transformed into an efficient service for citizens and entrepreneurs. The relevance of this document for the purpose of this chapter is that it explicitly calls/pledges for radical personal and societal transformation by adopting a new value system and behavior patterns based on the openness to the world, foreign investment, new knowledge, technologies and innovation, readiness to learn and accept challenges, dedication to persistent and hard work and willingness to succeed and to take responsibility for both successes and failures. In the later planning period, the Croatian government has, for the most part, followed strategic directions closely aligned with the Europa 2020.

It is in this conflicting space of inherited problems from Croatia's (tourism) economic and social past, the political pressures from the European Union, the global neo-liberal pressures of uncontrolled economic growth, the increasing demand for responsible values based on products by conscious consumers and the huge gap between strategic documents and the material reality, that the vision for Croatian tourism was created and proposed.

METHODOLOGY

Conceptually, the approach to the visioning exercise consisted of creating the vision internally and externally. The internal or 'sectorial' vision answered the question of what the tourism industry is and what role it aims to play. The need for creating an internal vision, similar to the company vision, has grown out of two key aspects: (a) many of the factors influencing tourism are not under influence of the tourism industry, and (b) the industry in itself is highly fragmented and in need of the culture of cooperation, partnership and inter-based self-organization that is yet to be mastered. The external tourism vision is configured in relation to society/communities and visitors/tourists. This is a clear statement that the social and environmental benefits are not an accidental yet are welcomed by-products of tourism (as it was the case in previous strategic documents) and an aspect at the *core* of the future tourism development. The second conceptual underpinning was the value system adopted as the basic foundation of vision building. The starting premise was that for the implementation of the strategy, *behavioral change* is needed and that behavior patterns rest on *values*.

In the creation of the national tourism vision, the participatory approach was adopted through two steps. In the first step, consultations with a broad range of tourism stakeholders were carried out via three regional workshops with an aim to identify the main issues and their solutions that generally encapsulate their aspirations and view of the future. Then a survey of public sector leaders and DMO general managers was conducted to ascertain their attitudes to tourism and views on a range of tourism development issues. Finally, a population survey on attitudes and response to tourism development was carried out. The results of this research are reported in Chaps. 3 and 6, but in the context of the visioning exercise, the most relevant conclusions that came out were the following:

• Stakeholders acknowledged the importance of income creation but are acutely aware that economic growth needs to be balanced with the social and environmental values.
• They want future development to be based on our cultural and natural heritage and our way of life, believing that Croatia's economic stagnation has preserved the environment and the wide pristine nature is a rarity in Europe as is the social, hospitable nature of Croatians.
• The unique market positioning is built on the fact that Croatia is a clean, healthy, beautiful and scarcely populated country, which are attributes that will be increasingly hard to find in a future overpopulated and industrialized Europe.
• To always keep in mind that tourism development should be for the betterment of residents and its growth within the limit of environmental capacity and socially just practices.
• There was an awareness that tourism has a great potential for nationwide economic and social revitalization, through the integration with other economic sectors, cultural production and social life.

While the first step entailed the research agenda in order to gain insights into the opinion and attitudes of a wide range of stakeholders with research methods allowing generalization, the second step entailed an articulation of vision. It was conducted through the visioning workshop with the tourism leaders from public and private sectors under an assumption that they will, based on their role in tourism development, become ambassadors of the vision and, with their political, economic and social influences, work toward its implementation. The workshop was conducted in March 2012. A list of potential participants was developed in consultation with the tourism experts and the Ministry of Tourism. In total, 28 leaders were identified representing the public sector (Ministry of Tourism, Parliamentary Committee for Tourism, National Tourism Board), trade associations (Chamber of Commerce, hotels, travel agencies), DMO managing directors of leading tourism regions, managing directors of leading hotels and academics and journalists specialized for tourism. It was originally intended to be a two-day event under the auspices of the Minister of Tourism to give legitimacy to the process and attract all participants. However, the visioning exercise unfortunately took place in the immediate post-election period, and the Minister of Tourism, who was just taking over the office, declined his support. Thus, a half-day workshop was conducted instead, attracting 18 participants with the lowest participation from the hotel sector.

To prepare participants for the visioning session, a discussion paper was prepared and delivered to each participant beforehand. The discussion paper was deliberately polemical, designed to challenge existing patterns of thought. It briefly outlined past attempts to plan tourism development, highlighted the achievements and discussed the weaknesses. In particular, it was highlighted that these weaknesses were dealt with in every strategic document, yet little was done to remedy them. Consequently, the question was raised if it was for the lack of a clear, motivating vision able to unite stakeholders and steer actions and/or leaders driving strategy implementation. The future challenges were briefly addressed, positioned between the neo-liberal paradigm of tourism as an industry and a re-emerging paradigm of tourism as a social and transformational force, drawing on the conclusion from the stakeholder-wide consultations conducted earlier as well as our scientific insight into global trends. Finally, the concept of vision built on values was then introduced and three basic questions were set out: What do we want to be as an industry? How do we want to contribute to society? What kind of tourism do we want?

The visioning workshop was divided into several parts. Firstly, a short presentation was made to set the scene and introduce the concept of value-based vision. After the presentation, participants were invited to evaluate or discuss this approach, and, in general, they found it to be meaningful and timely. The consensus, though, might be due to the participant pre-selection as the discussion paper had announced the line of reasoning and the methodological approach, and those not receptive to such an approach could have simply decided not to attend the workshop. The vision building exercise was structured in two phases. Firstly, participants were asked to identify key propositions of the vision grouped around the three main questions. Every participant shared his/her view of the tourism future by explaining his/her reasoning. During the short break, the researchers have summarized the responses, and, based on that, the four key ingredients for each of the three pillars of vision were derived.

OUTCOMES (RESULTS AND DISCUSSION)

The approach adopted for crafting the national tourism vision based on values and structured around the clearly identified three questions, however logical and theoretically justified, was a novel approach. At the outset, the first question was whether participants would be willing to cooperate or whether they would revert quickly to problems and have a 'blame-oriented' discussion. Yet, on the contrary they seemed to get fully engaged and enthusiastic to talk about new visions and values that should be(come) key drivers of 'their industry'. Hence, at the end of the workshop, a set of core values was identified. The following is not simply a compilation of what was said but the values that were reached through group consensus.

Figure 2.1 provides the visual overview of key words and basic value propositions.

In other words (Fig. 2.2), the participants had visioned that, by the end of 2020, the tourism industry will be:

- *Responsible* to tourists, people working in the industry and communities hosting them;
- Truly *valued* and affirmed as a nationally important economic sector;
- *Liberated* from the red tape—huge numbers of uncoordinated laws and regulations;
- *Successful* in business operations, overall management and balanced/*sustainable* growth;
- Competitive and *progressive* through innovative product development, excellent service quality and optimized seasonality.

They had boldly envisioned that tourism should be a priority in the overall national development. They see tourism as increasing the general standard of living (material aspect) and, in particular, an activity that can

Fig. 2.1 Key words of basic value propositions generated by workshop participants

transform domestic production and foster spiritual growth. They firmly believed that tourism can become a platform or an initiator of broader social transformation of the value system built on trust and partnership, healthy attitudes to people and the environment and an openness to new worlds, new knowledge and new ideas to overcome the ego and an ethnocentric value system dominant today. Dwelling upon these ideas, the participants wanted to believe that, if tourism is affirmed and its development well managed and coordinated, it will induce (catalyze) the transformation of personal and social values at the core of the national development goals and the key force introducing a new paradigm based on lifestyle of health and sustainability.

Finally, they envisioned the picture that they would like Croatia to portray to its visitors (external vision). The main starting point is authenticity based on the premise that we already possess and value the key tenants of the new paradigm—preserved nature (green and blue) and pride in our culture—while as a people, we are pleasant, open, spontaneous, hospitable and warmhearted. Most of all we, as hosts, are the source of positive energy with which we inspire our visitors as well as ourselves.

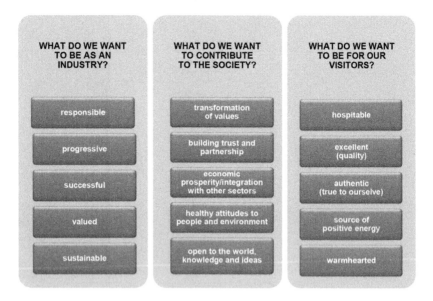

Fig. 2.2 The basic value propositions for the three pillars of national tourism vision

In the consensus building second phase, it became clear that the participants have, in projecting a tourism future, had envisioned overall national prosperity and wellbeing. Their starting point is that tourism is a Croatian success story (regardless whether by accident or design), but that it is only a fragment of what tourism can become and contribute to society if it manages to mobilize political and economic leaders, free up entrepreneurial spirit and unleash creative potentials of individuals and communities. In the end all those key consensual findings were translated into the vision statement for 2020.

Turning it into the vision statement, by 2020, tourism is recognized and valued as the economic priority of Croatian national and local sustainable development (Fig. 2.3). The culture of cooperation and partnership, mutual trust and respect are the values at the core of tourism success. Tourism is taken seriously by the central government, and this model of value-driven tourism vision is applied at the regional and local level. The public sector fully supports entrepreneurship, employment and

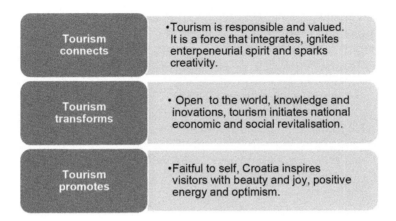

Tourism connects
•Tourism is responsible and valued. It is a force that integrates, ignites enterpeneurial spirit and sparks creativity.

Tourism transforms
• Open to the world, knowledge and inovations, tourism initiates national economic and social revitalisation.

Tourism promotes
•Faitful to self, Croatia inspires visitors with beauty and joy, positive energy and optimism.

Fig. 2.3   The vision statement

investment in tourism while clearly articulating its interests and aims. It is an active and constructive partner to the public sector. Liberated from governmental red tape, the private sector encourages creativity. Tourism not only proclaims sustainability principles but applies it in all its facets, in particular though:

- Responsibility to people that work in tourism or whose livelihoods are dependent on tourism, so that work in tourism becomes a source of pride and self-worth.
- Responsibility to communities by always bearing in mind that successful tourism is consistent with the aspirations of those that live off and with tourism, and tourism products are those equally valuable/ usable to locals as they are to visitors.
- Responsibility for environmental management so that sound environmental practices are applied daily in production and use. Through genuine care about the visual appearances of our towns and villages as well as their infrastructural and energetic needs, tourism shows that it cares for the wellbeing of communities and the environment.

By adopting a value system based on responsibility, unity, cooperation and partnership, economic prosperity and social and ecological sustainability, tourism can be a force that initiates national transformation.

What we do in tourism impacts on everything else, as tourism is integrated with economic, cultural and social politics. Through income and jobs, tourism leads the economy. This is carried out through optimism, positive energy, enthusiasm and self-respect and social transformation of the Croatian people. A space is created where entrepreneurial spirit, creativity, innovation and education merge into one.

We have created innovative and unique tourism products based on our way of life and natural and cultural heritage, and, by nurturing the authentic, we have remained true to ourselves. Therefore, we are an ideal destination for all those that find joy and fulfilment in developing new skills. All those who search for a healthy environment and an oasis of peace are able to recuperate intellectually, emotionally and physically in Croatia.

THE EPILOGUE OR 'WHEN TWO WORLDS COLLIDE'

While the process of envisioning and the resulting vision statement was clearly inspiring, ambitious and pleasantly surprising (especially for researchers), in reality, the vision is (as yet) ignored. Once the key vision statements were attempted to be integrated into the final document on tourism strategy of Croatia 2020, many have been lost or diluted in the process of filtering by primarily the Ministry of Tourism to which the document was presented. Thus, the originally proposed vision has been modified and turned into the more official, bureaucratic language. When presenting the strategy at various public and media events, the aim of Croatia coming into the top-20 most competitive tourism countries (on the Travel and Tourism Competitiveness Index) has, in effect, turned out to be the key vision of Croatian tourism.

It is possible to identify two key reasons that lie behind such an outcome. Firstly, due to the political inconsistency of central government change over, when elections have brought up a new party in power, resulting in the lack of strong governmental leadership. So, while the former Ministry of Tourism signed the contract with the Institute for Tourism to develop the strategy, the newly elected government needed to approve the finalized document. In the current political culture of Croatia where one government likes to oppose everything that the previous government does, this change has seriously halted the whole process. The second reason struck even deeper. Individual leaders obviously remain torn between the human values that they intimately harbor (outcome of the workshop) and the broader context so much infused with the neo-liberal 'mantra' of economic growth, jobs, bottom line and competitiveness. Also it might be attributed to certain level of embarrassment attached when people start to express and share their feelings in the public arena, despite the fact they form the social and individual fabric of our lives. In a fairly safe space of enclosed workshops, it was easier to express it, than when it was needed to be taken out in the open.

Obviously, the shift in values leading to behavioral change needs to be accompanied by a shift in processes and organization structures that supports it—not only in the context of tourism but in the current government prevalent world view of valorizing economic rationalism ahead of social, cultural or any other alternative perspectives. Yet to dare and be a pioneer of social change is not always easy as Alain de Botton (2000, p. 13) in his study of human history and philosophy neatly captures this critical tension between the personal and the collective/political:

> ... [It] is not only the hostility of others that may prevent us from questioning the status quo. Our will to doubt can be just as powerfully sapped by an internal sense that societal conventions must have a sound basis, even if we are not sure exactly what this may be, because they have been adhered to by a great many people for a long time ... . We stifle our doubts and follow the flock because we cannot conceive of ourselves as pioneers of hitherto unknown, difficult truths.

Yet, even one of the most prolific tourism writers and researchers Michael Hall invites us all to work on change in these critical times of ours:

> ... I also realize that for me it is time for a change. I feel that growing sense of disenchantment and unease in my research and in the structures I am embedded in that, if it cannot be given an outlet, it will lead to further disenchantment. Perhaps others feel this as well in terms of their own situation. Perhaps others, like me, read Sartre at 17 and never came back. I then return to Harvey's (2000:255) 'spaces of hope': The lesson is clear: until we insurgent architects know the courage of our minds and are prepared to take an equally speculative plunge into some unknown, we too will continue to be the object of historical geography (like worker bees) rather than active subjects, consciously pushing human possibilities to the limits. What Marx called 'the real movement; that will abolish the existing state of things' is always there for the making and for the taking. This is what gaining the courage of our minds is all about. (Hall, 2004, p. 152)

REFERENCES

Ateljević, I. (2009). Transmodernity – remaking our (tourism) world? In J. Tribe (Ed.), *Philosophical issues of tourism* (pp. 278–300). Bristol: Channel View Publications.

Ateljevic, I. (2011). Transmodern critical tourism studies: A call for hope and transformation. *Revista Turismo em Análise, special issue: Critical Issues in Tourism, 22*(3), 497–515.

Ateljevic, I., & Corak, S. (2006). Croatia in the new Europe: Culture versus conformity. In D. Hall, M. Smith, & B. Marciszewska (Eds.), *Tourism in the new Europe: The challenges and opportunities of EU enlargement* (pp. 288–304). Oxfordshire: CAB International.

Ateljevic, I., & Doorne, S. (2003). Unpacking the local: A cultural analysis of tourism entrepreneurship in Murter, Croatia. *Tourism Geographies, 5*, 123–150.

Cacioppe, R. (2000a). Creating spirit at work: re-visioning organizational development and leadership – Part I. *The Leadership & Organization Development Journal, 21*(1/2), 48–54.

Cacioppe, R. (2000b). Creating spirit at work: Re-visioning organizational development and leadership – Part II. *The Leadership & Organization Development Journal, 21*(1/2), 110–119.

Cohen, M. J. (2007). Consumer credit, household financial management, and sustainable consumption. *International Journal of Consumer Studies, 31*, 57–65.

Corak, S., Mikacic, V., & Ateljevic, I. (2013). An ironic paradox: The longitudinal view on impacts of the 1990's homeland war on tourism in Croatia. In R. Butler & W. Suntikul (Eds.), *War and tourism* (pp. 161–175). New York: Routledge.

Croatian Bureau of Statistics. (2014). *Employment and wages, 2014 – statistical report no. 1549.* Zagreb: Croatian Bureau of Statistics.

Croatian Bureau of Statistics. (2016). *Tourist arrivals and nights in 2015 – first release no. 4.3.2.* Zagreb: Croatian Bureau of Statistics.

De Botton, A. (2000). *The consolations of philosophy.* London: Hamish Hamilton.

European Commission. (2015). Europe 2020. http://ec.europa.eu/europe2020/index_en.htm. Date accessed 10 Feb 2015.

Hall, C. M. (2004). Reflexivity and tourism research: situating myself and/with others. In J. Phillimore & L. Goodson (Eds.), *Qualitative research in tourism: ontologies, epistemologies and methodologies* (pp. 137–155). London: Routledge.

Higging-Desboiles, F. (2006). More than an "industry": The forgotten power of tourism as a social force. *Tourism Management, 27*, 1192–1208.

Horwath Consulting and Institute for Tourism. (1993). *Glavni turistički plan Hrvatske [Master plan for Croatian tourism development].* Zagreb: Horwath Consulting.

Institute for Tourism. (1993). *Strategija razvoja turizma Hrvatske [Strategy for Croatian tourism development]*. Zagreb: Institute for Tourism.

Institute for Tourism. (1998). *Koncept dugoročnog razvoja hrvatskog turizma [Long-term Development Concept of Croatian Tourism]*. Zagreb: Institute for Tourism.

Institute for Tourism. (2005). *TOMAS transit survey 2005*. Zagreb: Institute for Tourism.

Joy, L. (2011). *How does societal transformation happen? Values development, collective wisdom, and decision making for the common good*. Quaker Institute for the Future – Pamphlet 4. Belize: Caye Caulker.

Layard, R. (2005). *Happiness: Lessons from a new science*. New York/London: Penguin.

Lean, G. L. (2009). Transformative travel: Inspiring sustainability. In R. Bushel & P. Sheldon (Eds.), *Wellness and tourism: Mind, body, spirit, place* (pp. 191–205). New York: Cognizant.

Lohas. (2015). Lifestyle of health and sustainability – LOHAS online, http://www.lohas.com. Date accessed 16 June 2015.

Lovelock, J. (2010). *The vanishing face of gaia: A final warning*. London: Penguin Books.

Millennium Ecosystem Assessment. (2005). *Eco-system and human well-being: Biodiversity synthesis*. Washington DC: World Resources Institute.

Ministry of Tourism. (2003). *Strategija razvoja hrvatskog turizma do 2010 [Strategy of Croatian Tourism Development to 2010]*. Zagreb: Ministry of Tourism of Republic of Croatia.

Nanus, B. (1992). *Visionary leadership*. San Francisco: Jossey-Bass.

Pollock, A. (2015). *Social entrepreneurship in tourism: The conscious travel approach. Tourism innovation partnership for social entrepreneurship*. UK: TIPSE.

Reisinger, Y. (2013). Preface. In Y. Reisinger (Ed.), *Transformative tourism: tourist perspectives* (pp. XII–XIV). Wallingford: CABI.

Republic of Croatia. (2010). *National strategic reference framework 2012—2013*. Zagreb: Republic of Croatia/Central Office for Development Strategy and Coordination of EU Funds.

Ritchie, B. J. R. (1999). Crafting a value-driven vision for a National Tourism Treasure. *Tourism Management, 20*, 273–282.

Ruhanen, L. M. (2007). Destination competitiveness: Meeting sustainability objectives through strategic planning and visioning. In A. Matias, P. Nijkamp, and P. Neto (ed), *Advances in modern tourism research: Economic perspectives* (1st ed.) (pp. 133–152). New York: Physica-Verlag Heidelberg.

Shipley, R., & Newkirk, R. (1998). Visioning: Did anyone see where it came from? *Journal of Planning Literature, 12*(4), 407–416.

Skidelsky, R. (2009). *Keynes: The return of the master*. London: Allen Lane.

Smith, S. L. J. (2003). A vision for the Canadian tourism industry. *Tourism Management, 24*(2), 123–133.

Šolman, S. (2010). The role of road transport in Croatian tourism. *Acta Touristica Nova, 4*(2), 231–250.

Späth, P., & Rohracher, H. (2010). 'Energy regions': The transformative power of regional discourses on socio-technical futures. *Research Policy, 39,* 449–458.

THR & Horwath Consulting. (2007). *Strategic marketing plan for Croatian tourism 2010 – 2014.* Zagreb: Croatian National Tourism Board.

Van der Helm, R. (2009). The vision phenomenon: Towards a theoretical underpinning of visions of the future and the process of envisioning. *Futures, 41*(2), 96–104.

World Health Organisation. (2002). *World health statistics.* Geneva: WHO Press.

World Health Organisation. (2012). *World health statistics.* Geneva: WHO Press.

Worldwatch Institute. (2004). *State of the world 2004: A Worldwatch Institute report on progress toward a sustainable society.* New York: W. W. Norton & Company.

Yeoman, I., & Ledderman, P. (2005). Scottish tourism: Scenarios and vision. *Journal of Vacation Marketing, 11*(1), 67–83.

CHAPTER 3

Managing Tourism Development Process in Croatia: Can European Union Accession Help?

Ivo Kunst

INTRODUCTION

Mostly due to its geographical position on the eastern shore of the Adriatic Sea, its numerous islands and favorable climate, the tourist industry in Croatia has developed over a rather long period of time. Although for many years the prevailing rationale for tourism development was the generation of the foreign currency receipts needed to remedy the growing trade deficit, Croatia's recent governments have become increasingly aware that tourism has grown into one of the most important contributors to the country's economic development. This change in attitude can be attributed mostly to a high direct share of tourism in Croatia's gross domestic product (10.4 percent) (Ivandić, Marušić, Šutalo & Vuglar, 2014), as well as to the tendency of the receipts generated by the tourism industry to grow moderately even in years of considerable economic downturn (Croatian National Bank, 2012). Irrespective of the fact that a large (and

I. Kunst (✉)
Institute for Tourism, Zagreb, Croatia

© The Author(s) 2017
L. Dwyer et al. (eds.), *Evolution of Destination Planning and Strategy*, DOI 10.1007/978-3-319-42246-6_3

37

growing) share of tourism receipts in Croatia's gross value added might be influenced by the prevailing recessionary trends in other economic sectors, the nominal value of tourist spending in Croatia could be significantly higher, especially in view of the expected improvement of the country's image in the years following Croatian accession to the European Union. Such a conclusion is strongly supported by the rather recent evidence from Malta, Cyprus and Slovenia, small Mediterranean countries that have all joined the European Union (EU) in year 2004 (Kunst, 2007). As a result of adopting new tourism development strategies during the EU accession process, and their effective execution following the accession, all three countries have been able to achieve increased tourist receipts and to attract substantial foreign direct investment (Theuma, 2006; Scot & Topcan, 2006; Konečnik, 2006; Alipour & Hall, 2006; Attard & Hall, 2004; Bramwell, 2003). Further, adopting more stringent environmental legislature and protection of most valuable spatial resources from potential degradation, these countries have been able to markedly improve their image on the international market and significantly increase the level of their tourism competitiveness. In order to rise to the occasion and capitalize on the unique opportunity that the imminent EU accession represents, Croatia's government needs to efficiently manage the tourism development process at all levels. This implies coordination of tourism policies, instruments and activities at the national, regional and local levels.

Unlike most economically developed countries, where the idea of strategic management and long-term guidance of the tourism development process has been applied for years (Getz 1986; Hall 2000; De Carlo, Cugini & Zerbini, 2008; Dodds, 2007; Villa, Costa & Rovira, 2010), tourism development in Croatia has been characterized not so much by the lack of strategic planning, but by an ineffective operationalization of the strategies adopted. The unavailability and/or inadequate capacity of communal infrastructure; the substandard quality of the transport infrastructure, especially at destination level; the lack of appropriate tourism signage; and a rather poor interpretation of attractions are ample evidence, additionally borne out by the shortness of the tourism season and the uncompetitive operational results of the hotel industry. Not surprisingly, Croatian tourism in the year 2015, according to the *Travel and Tourism Competitiveness Report* (World Economic Forum, 2015), was placed only 33rd in the world, not only a long distance behind Spain (1st), France (2nd) and Italy (8th), the most developed Mediterranean tourism countries, but also behind Portugal (15th) and Greece (31st).

This relatively unfavorable assessment of Croatia's tourism international competitiveness has been largely influenced by the fact that the country is still globally perceived mainly as a destination for summer 'sun and sea' family holidays (Rutin, 2010). The existing dominant image and the marketing that highlights it further significantly impede penetration into new consumer niches. It also represents one of the main causes for the pronounced seasonality in tourism demand, as well as for the marked concentration of tourist activities along the narrow coastal strip. In terms of the increasing competition on the tourism destinations market, as well as in view of the rapid growth in the diversification of tourist interests (Robinson & Novelli, 2005), reliance on 'sun and sea' market positioning represents a significant development constraint. Further, such a market positioning cannot contribute to a long-term improvement in the competitive position of Croatia as a tourist destination.

In addition to the excessive reliance on the 'sun and sea' product, the current competitive position of Croatia's tourism largely reflects a significant number of organizational shortcomings and/or regulatory restrictions, which have not been addressed. Apart from an insufficient understanding of the various complexities of tourism development, the primary reason for the existence of these constraints should be sought primarily in the lack of cooperation between the several ministries responsible for the creation of a stimulating and enabling environment for the development of the tourism sector. Most ministries, pressed for time to be able fully to harmonize the country's legislation (regulatory system) with the requirements of the acquis, prepared sector-specific legislation independently and without sufficient cooperation with other relevant stakeholders. Such lack of cooperation and/or coordination more often than not led to legislative solutions that brought about considerable negative impacts regarding the overall competitiveness of Croatian tourism and also on the dynamics and the volume of entrepreneurial activity in the tourism sector (Kunst, 2011). Further, and aside from the lack of cooperation and coordination at the central government level, the insufficient competitiveness of Croatian tourism can also, in part, be attributed to the lack of vertical communication between the government and the authorities at regional and local level and to a rather low level of cooperation among various tourism development stakeholders at the destination level (local authorities, destination management organizations, public sector institutions, private businesses, local residents) (Kunst, 2011).

Given the long-term harmful effects of various development constraints on Croatia's tourism competiveness, and having in mind the growing opportunity cost associated with delays in their removal, this chapter has three main aims. First, to investigate to what extent local authorities and executives in charge of destination management organizations (DMOs) at the local level are at present able to steer the tourism development process in their respective communities. Second, to identify a number of development constraints that constitute major obstacles to growth in tourism competitiveness at destination level. Third, to determine under what conditions and to what extent it will be possible to make use of the available EU funds in order to neutralize the existing shortcomings of Croatian tourism competitiveness. Accordingly, the remainder of the chapter is divided into five sections: the first part refers to the relevant theoretical concepts and contains a review of the literature, the second part addresses the research method, the third part is devoted to the presentation of the most relevant findings, the fourth part discusses the activities to be undertaken in order to improve the country's tourism competitiveness in view of the availability and effective utilization of EU funds, whereas the fifth part summarizes the previous discussion.

UNDERLYING THEORY

The process of globalization is reflected in the tourism industry in various ways (Knowles, Diamantis & El-Mourhabi, 2001; Fayed & Fletcher, 2002; Hjalager, 2006; Dwyer 2015). Noteworthy are issues such as the general availability and easy access to all relevant information; the new and innovative ways of market communication, new sales channels and more affordable air transport; and the increased interest in exploring different countries and learning more about their cultures and ways of life. In view of increasingly dynamic global changes the impacts of which are difficult to predict, it is reasonable to expect that whatever it was that guaranteed success today certainly will not be enough to guarantee success tomorrow. In such a dynamic macroenvironment, tourism destinations are forced to continuously innovate their existing development strategies in order to distinguish themselves from the ever-growing number of potential competitors (Omerzel Gomezelj & Mihalič, 2008) and to create a favorable market environment for long-term sustainable socioeconomic growth (Pearce, Barbier & Marakandya, 1990). Devising new and/or innovating existing competitive strategies as well as viable market communication strategies implies differentiation at the destination level. Successful differentiation includes both differentiation in the set of available destination experiences and differentiation in each of the tourism products offered to the market (Calantone, di Benetto, Hakam & Bojanič, 1989; Echtner & Ritchie, 2003). It is assumed, moreover, that successful and sustainable market differentiation, in order to ensure long-term sustainability of the tourism development process on a national, regional and/or local level (Inskeep, 1991; Dredge, 1999), calls for strategic management. Consequently, tourism policy at destination level must focus on the improvement of competitiveness by means of creating an institutional framework capable of monitoring, controlling and increasing the quality and efficiency of the tourism sector, while protecting the destination's resource base (Goeldner, Ritchie & McIntosh, 2000).

Regardless of the fact that the development strategy of each and every tourism destination should be the result of the active involvement and creative participation of all stakeholders from the public, private and civil sector (Jamal & Getz, 1995), the responsibility for the effective implementation of the agreed-upon strategy typically lies in the hands of the local authorities and institutions in charge of tourism destination management. Further, effective implementation of the goals and objectives set forth by the strategy implies the establishment of appropriate control mechanisms and also the undertaking of appropriate remedial action if the need arises. Given the different and often conflicting interests of various stakeholder groups, where local politicians are most often motivated by the need to increase tax revenues and the urge to be re-elected, private sector operators by the need to generate profits and civil organizations and local residents by the need to preserve the environment and cultural heritage within the destination (Altinay, Var, Hines & Hussain, 2007), long-term destination sustainability implies continuous adjustment of interests, during the process of strategic planning, as well as during the day-to-day implementation of the agreed-upon development strategy.

However, only when all relevant development stakeholders agree on the key issues of the desired future of the destination will it be possible to guide the development process in the desired direction by means of coordinated action (Wehrmeyer, Clayton & Lum, 2002). In this regard, the market position and competiveness of any tourism destination in the future will depend greatly on the speed of the vision-implementation process. Further, this process will be more successful, the higher the congruence in views among the key development stakeholders, and the higher the number of jointly agreed and undertaken activities to 'provoke' the achievement of a desired future. Therefore, regardless of its position in the destination life cycle (Butler, 1980; Getz, 1992; Digance, 1997; Butler, 2009), each destination's success in the future is inextricably linked with the efficiency of its strategic management.

Strategic management of tourism destinations should be understood as an iterative and multi-criterial collaborative process that presupposes the active involvement and direct participation of all key development stakeholders' representatives (Getz, 1986; Jamal & Getz, 1995; Hall, 2000; McClamrock, Byrd & Sowel, 2001; Vanhove, 2005; Enz, 2010). It consists of two interrelated stages: (i) the strategic planning phase, during which the stakeholders need to come up with a shared vision for the destination, accompanied by a set of strategic objectives, and (ii) the strategy implementation phase, during which the agreed-upon vision and the development goals and objectives need to be materialized.

Strategic planning, in its broadest sense, can be defined as a formal process during which one envisions a desired future, assesses objectives and provides instruments/mechanisms for its achievement (Krallinger & Hellebust, 1993; McClamrock et al., 2001; Kaufman, Oakley-Browne, Watkins & Leigh, 2003). It includes a more or less detailed analysis/critical examination of the former development path, as compared with the competition and with destination potential, as a crucial point of reference for setting up the new development vision. The development vision, further, represents a starting point for the determination of key strategic objectives, for example, how can one get from 'here' to 'there', for defining the role of both the public and the private sector entities, as well as for the setting up of priority actions. The strategy implementation phase implies the establishment of appropriate control mechanisms (Choi & Sirakaya, 2006; Yilmaz & Bititci, 2006; WTO, 2004; Miller, 2001; Manning, 1999) on the basis of which one can fairly accurately determine whether there is the need to introduce corrective actions.

It is particularly important to underline that successful strategic management of tourism development at the national level implies both efficient implementation of a national tourism development strategy and defined development objectives at the regional and local levels. Regional and local development objectives should not only be consistent with the strategic directions set forth at the national level but should also take into consideration the specific needs and development goals of the local stakeholders. This can best be achieved through a community-based approach to strategic planning (Jamal & Getz, 1995; Tosun & Dallen, 2001).

In such an institutional and regulatory planning environment, it is reasonable to expect that the implementation of the development objectives set forth at the national level will depend heavily on their fulfilment at the regional and local level.

RESEARCH METHOD

In order to obtain reliable information on whether the tourism development process in Croatia is being managed in an efficient manner, especially at destination level, a survey of local public sector stakeholders in charge of the tourism development—local government officials (city/municipal mayors) and local tourism board representatives (DMO directors)—was implemented. The main purpose of the survey was to provide reliable information for the purpose of the development of the *Croatian Tourism Development Strategy to 2020*.

The survey addressed various issues of relevance to tourism development at the local level in order to provide insights into the current state of affairs in the area of tourism destination management and to detect potential problems in the sphere of local tourism development and/or destination competitiveness.

Through a battery of statements and questions, the survey was structured in such a way as to address (i) the level of support to regional/local tourism development; (ii) the state of tourism planning related to both the existence of local tourism (master)plans and tourism marketing plans and the efficiency of their implementation; (iii) the current level of cooperation between different stakeholders; and (iv) the major barriers to tourism development perceived at a destination level. For data collection a questionnaire, combining closed and open-ended questions, was used. In regard to the type of question, dichotomous or multiple response and the five-point Likert scale have been used.

The survey was conducted via e-mail in September and October of 2011. Survey participants were mayors of all 556 cities/municipalities and managers of all of 267 local tourism boards. Results are presented in total and comparatively for three Croatian regions (Fig. 3.1) characterized by different levels of economic and tourism development: (i) North Adriatic, consisting of three northern coastal counties with the most developed tourism product and the most tourist activity; (ii) the South Adriatic, consisting of four southern coastal counties with a well-developed tourism

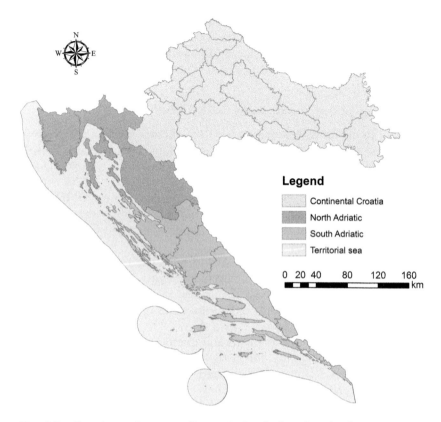

Fig. 3.1   Croatian regions according to the level of tourism development

product; and (iii) the inland part of Croatia, consisting of 14 counties where tourism development is mostly in the initial development phase. Planned and obtained sample and response rate are presented in Table 3.1.

RESULTS AND DISCUSSION

The results of the research are presented in two subsections. The first subsection discusses the survey results regarding the effectiveness of Croatia's tourism development management, whereas the second subsection addresses the main constraints to the improvement of Croatia's tourism competitiveness.

Table 3.1 Response rate by stakeholders and regions

	Local government				Local tourism boards			
	Croatia total	North Adriatic	South Adriatic	Inland	Croatia total	North Adriatic	South Adriatic	Inland
Planned sample size	556	89	131	336	267	69	85	113
Obtained sample size (number of respondents)	337	57	72	208	146	44	46	56
Response rate (%)	60.6	64.0	55.0	61.9	54.7	63.8	54.1	49.6

Is Croatian Tourism Development Managed Effectively?

The results obtained from the survey clearly indicate that the tourism development process in Croatia is not being managed in the most efficient way. Despite the fact that the city and/or municipal mayors generally agree in the assessment that tourism is important for the economic development of their cities/municipalities (47.4 per cent), a large number (64.2 per cent) are of the opinion that tourism in their respective jurisdictions is not developing fast enough (Table 3.2). This is especially true in the inland parts of Croatia (71.2 per cent). Further, almost 60 per cent of the mayors, with notable regional differences, believe that tourism development in their area does not have enough support from the national level. The opinions and/or attitudes of the tourism board managers are closely aligned to those of the mayors. In fact, 63 per cent believe that tourism is important for the economic development of their areas, more than half (55.2 per cent) are of the opinion that the tourism development is not sufficiently supported from the national level. As for the dynamics of tourism development, more than half of the managers (55.9 per cent) believe that tourism is not developing fast enough in their cities and/or municipalities.

Although the insufficient government support for tourism development perceived at the local level is mostly due to the lack of funds in the state budget, insufficient funding is reflected in the quality of existing tourism infra- and superstructure and in the highly uneven spread of tourism-related facilities throughout the country. Despite the fact that tourism attractions in the inland regions of Croatia, especially within the larger cities, are quite diverse and worth visiting, tourism activity in the coastal regions of the North Adriatic and South Adriatic at present accounts for 96 per cent of all overnight stays in the country. Further, these two regions account for 96 per cent of Croatia's commercial accommodation. In contrast, the region Inland Croatia accounts for only 4 per cent of the country's commercial accommodation and generates only 4 per cent of the total, statistically registered, overnights (Croatian Bureau of Statistics, 2015). In addition, due partly to insufficient government support to tourism development at the local level, even in the North and South Adriatic, tourism activity takes place only along the narrow coastal strip. At the same time, most of the coastal hinterland, as well as the inner parts of the islands, are almost entirely unprepared for tourism.

Table 3.2 Tourism development at the local level (%)

Statements on tourism development in a town/ municipality[a]	Local government				Local tourism boards			
	Croatia total	North Adriatic	South Adriatic	Inland	Croatia total	North Adriatic	South Adriatic	Inland
Tourism is at present important for the economy of your city/ municipality[a]	47.4	68.4	68.6	34.3	63.2	67.4	82.6	43.6
Pace of tourism development in your city/ municipality is not fast enough	64.2	49.1	55.7	71.2	55.9	40.9	57.8	66.1
We have problems in managing the tourism development in our city/ municipality	38.3	28.1	26.1	45.5	43.1	39.5	55.6	35.7
We do not have sufficient support for tourism development from the central government	59.5	62.5	49.3	62.1	55.2	53.5	53.3	58.2

[a]Those that agree or strongly agree with a statement on the five-point Likert scale

Regarding the importance of strategic planning at the local level (Table 3.3), the results highlight the fact that only about 59 per cent of Croatian cities/municipalities have long-term economic development plans, and tourism development is incorporated in only two thirds of them.

Table 3.3   Availability of local development plans (%)

Availability of long-term development plans	Local government				Local tourism boards			
	Croatia total	North Adriatic	South Adriatic	Inland	Croatia total	North Adriatic	South Adriatic	Inland
Economic development plan of the city/municipality	58.6	42.9	54.2	64.4	n/a	n/a	n/a	n/a
Tourism development is incorporated in this plan[a]	75.2	93.2	74.1	70.7	n/a	n/a	n/a	n/a
Tourism masterplan as a separate document	20.5	46.4	16.4	14.6	36.1	72.7	15.6	23.6
Tourism marketing plan	n/a	n/a	n/a	n/a	18.2	46.5	8.9	3.6

[a]For those who have economic development plans

However, for a country where tourism represents one of the vital economic activities, it is surprising that only 20.5 per cent of the cities/municipalities have separate long-term tourism development plans. Moreover, the practice of tourism planning is unrelated to the stage of tourism development as evident in South Dalmatia. Although the tourism industry in South Dalmatia represents one of the primary sources of income for the local community, only 16.4 per cent of the mayors and 15.6 per cent of tourism board managers steer the tourism development process with a help of a tourism masterplan.

Concerning the issue of the implementation, a vast majority of mayors (81.2 per cent) and tourism board managers (72.3 per cent), whose cities and/or municipalities have tourism masterplans, believe that the objectives set forth by the masterplans are being implemented slower than recommended or not implemented at all (Table 3.4). In such circumstances it is, therefore, not surprising that a relative large proportion of both city and/or municipal mayors (38.3 per cent) and tourism board directors

Table 3.4 Plan implementation (%)

Implementation of plans and projects	Local government				Local tourism boards			
	Croatia total	North Adriatic	South Adriatic	Inland	Croatia total	North Adriatic	South Adriatic	Inland
Mostly according to the recommendations of the plan	13.6	8.0	0.0	24.1	23.4	25.0	42.9	8.3
We follow the plan recommendations, but at a somewhat slower pace	51.5	68.0	58.3	34.5	48.9	50.0	42.9	50.0
Plan recommendations are mostly not being implemented due to lack of finance	21.2	8.0	16.7	34.5	17.0	14.3	14.3	25.0
Plan recommendations are mostly not being implemented since it is not operable	3.0	8.0	0.0	0.0	6.4	10.7	0.0	0.0
Plan recommendations are mostly not being implemented due to a lack of human resources	4.5	4.0	0.0	6.9	0.0	0.0	0.0	0.0
Something else	6.1	4.0	25.0	0.0	4.3	0.0	0.0	16.7
Total	100.0	100.0	100.0	100.0	100.0	100.0	100.0	100.0

(43.1 per cent) find it extremely difficult to manage the tourism development process in their distinctive destinations.

Apart from many harmful effects, such as excessive number of newly built holiday homes and/or apartments for rent, unauthorized use of publicly owned maritime property for private purposes and gradual destruction of the spirit of the place of the destination or overloaded communal infrastructure systems, the lack of effective implementation of local tourism masterplans is adversely affecting dynamics and the quality of tourism strategy implementation at the national level. As the existing constraints at the destination level cannot be effectively removed, they could only intensify, leading to a further deterioration of Croatia's global tourism competitiveness.

As for the vertical and horizontal cooperation with other tourism development stakeholders (Table 3.5), the majority of city/municipal mayors believe the best cooperation is being achieved with the tourism board managers (59.2 per cent), private sector operators (46.2 per cent) and the county administration (42.9 per cent). At the same time, a much smaller proportion of mayors is satisfied with the present level of the cooperation with the Ministry of Tourism (29.0 per cent), other relevant ministries (21.3 per cent) and other national governmental institutions (23.7 per cent). The attitudes of the city/municipal mayors are strongly confirmed by the opinions of the tourism board managers. According to them, local tourism boards cooperate best with the local private sector operators (69.9 per) and local government (85.4 per cent). At the same time, only one third of the managers express their satisfaction with the quality of cooperation with the Ministry of Tourism (34.3 per cent), whereas less than one fifth found the cooperation with other relevant ministries satisfactory (18.9 per cent).

What Are the Major Obstacles to Croatian Tourism Competitiveness?

When it comes to the factors that either decelerate the pace of tourism growth in Croatia or reduce its competitiveness on the global scale, the viewpoints of the city/municipal mayors and tourism board managers clearly indicate several crucial development constraints. These constraints should, therefore, represent priority problem areas on which the authorities should focus attention in the years to come (Table 3.6).

Table 3.5 Stakeholder cooperation in the process of tourism development (%)

Good cooperation with:[a]	Local government				Local tourism boards			
	Croatia total	North Adriatic	South Adriatic	Inland	Croatia total	North Adriatic	South Adriatic	Inland
Ministry of Tourism	29.0	31.6	22.5	30.6	34.3	38.6	27.3	36.4
Other relevant ministries	21.3	29.1	21.7	19.0	18.9	15.9	15.9	23.6
Other governmental institutions	23.7	34.5	27.1	19.3	n/a	n/a	n/a	n/a
County administration	42.9	50.9	47.9	38.9	45.1	52.3	46.7	38.2
City/municipal administration	n/a	n/a	n/a	n/a	85.4	90.9	75.6	89.1
State and other public sector companies/institutions	n/a	n/a	n/a	n/a	41.7	47.7	42.2	36.4
Inspection authorities	27.3	34.5	23.5	26.6	52.4	72.7	43.2	43.6
Local tourism board	59.2	75.4	61.4	53.4	n/a	n/a	n/a	n/a
National tourism board	n/a	n/a	n/a	n/a	66.2	79.5	66.7	54.7
Other tourism boards within the county	n/a	n/a	n/a	n/a	77.8	86.4	77.8	70.9
Other tourism boards outside your county	n/a	n/a	n/a	n/a	49.3	38.6	46.7	60.4
Private sector	46.2	62.5	45.7	41.5	69.9	86.4	62.2	63.0
Relevant civil and professional associations	43.9	47.3	40.3	44.2	58.0	70.5	45.5	58.2

[a]Those that agree or strongly agree with a statement on the five-point Likert scale

Table 3.6 Potential constraints to tourism development (%)

Potential constraints[a]	Local government				Local tourism boards			
	Croatia total	North Adriatic	South Adriatic	Inland	Croatia total	North Adriatic	South Adriatic	Inland
Investment climate and/or level of bureaucracy	65.6	68.4	70.8	63.0	68.5	61.4	65.2	76.8
Tourism offer (accommodation, F&B, other)	64.7	40.4	63.9	71.6	52.1	34.1	43.5	73.2
Unclear ownership titles	40.1	56.1	59.7	28.8	32.9	31.8	47.8	21.4
Communal infrastructure	31.2	33.3	37.5	28.4	28.1	38.6	37.0	12.5
Transport infrastructure	25.5	33.3	34.7	20.2	30.1	34.1	39.1	19.6
Marketing/promotion	35.0	29.8	29.2	38.5	18.5	9.1	15.2	28.6
Human resources	20.2	22.8	26.4	17.3	29.5	31.8	26.1	30.4
Legal framework	16.6	21.1	18.1	14.9	25.3	34.1	17.4	25.0
Spatial planning/spatial management	13.7	17.5	13.9	12.5	24.7	27.3	37.0	12.5
Excessive real-estate construction	6.5	14.0	13.9	1.9	19.9	27.3	37.0	0.0
Illegal construction	6.2	10.5	11.1	3.4	10.3	9.1	21.7	1.8
Other	0.3	1.8	0.0	0.0	0.7	0.0	0.0	1.8

[a]Possibility to give more answers

It is perceptions of the city/municipal mayors and tourism board managers that the biggest constraint to competitiveness of Croatian tourism is the unfavorable investment climate (65.6 and 68.5 per cent, respectively). This corresponds to the prevailing international perception of Croatia as an excessively bureaucratic and highly corrupt country with inefficient judiciary (Transparency International, 2014; US Department of State, 2015). Apart from this negative overall perception, the investment climate in the tourism sector is additionally burdened by the oligopoly nature of the Croatian hotel sector at a national level and monopoly nature at destination level (Kunst, 2011). Mostly due to a poorly chosen privatization model and its uncritical implementation during the first half of the 1990s, Croatian tourism is nowadays, especially in comparison to other economic sectors, controlled by very large, regionally dominating, corporations that control the whole tourism development process along the most of the Adriatic coast. This, in turn, to a large extent prevents equal opportunity market entry to potential (international) competitors. In such circumstances, it is difficult to shake off the impression that the local monopolists represent one more unnatural and unnecessary barrier to new tourism development projects. This, in turn, negatively affects the current investment demand and the medium-term interest of international investors.

Alongside the unfavorable investment climate, the existing tourism 'hardware' in terms of abundance, quality, diversity and/or availability of a variety of tourism-related facilities represents the second major constraint that, over the medium term, might further diminish the competiveness of Croatian tourism. Apart from the insufficient quality of existing accommodation facilities perceived by 40.1 per cent of city/municipal mayors and 47.3 per cent of tourism board managers as obstacles, most respondents found the supply of other non-accommodation, leisure and tourism-related services also rather undeveloped and/or unavailable. The lack of quality in existing accommodation stems predominantly from its unfavorable structure. Out of approximately 914,000 beds available in all statistically registered commercial accommodation facilities as of August 2015 (Croatian Bureau of Statistics, 2015), only 13 per cent relate to hotel accommodation. The remaining 87 per cent represent the accommodation available in campsites (26 per cent), other collective accommodation (14 per cent) and rooms/suites for rent within the households (47 per cent). The accommodation structure dominated by households and campsites, mostly due to the highly seasonal nature of their business, seriously limits the market positioning of Croatian tourism, as well as the country's tourism receipts.

It also causes a number of problems in the planning and/or optimization of various communal systems (infrastructure) whose size needs to be determined according to the demand at peak season and not according to the average annual needs. This greatly increases not only the construction costs of these systems but also their annual operating and maintenance costs. As for the underdeveloped non-accommodation product, this applies mainly to the lack of breadth and depth in the supply of food and beverage outlets (51.3 per cent of the city/municipal mayors and 52.7 per cent of tourism board managers), entertainment facilities (36.2 per cent of the city/ municipal mayors and 39.7 per cent of tourism board managers) as well as to the insufficient supply of additional activities (39.2 per cent of the city/municipal mayors and 37.0 per cent of tourism board managers). In addition, the relatively poor tourism value chain at destination level during the summer is reduced still further during the other months of the year (Marušić, Čorak, Ivandić & Sever, 2011).

Furthermore, the unresolved property issues and unclear ownership titles (40.1 per cent of city/municipal mayors and 32.9 per cent of tourism board managers) represent the third most important obstacle to the Croatian tourism competitiveness. Notwithstanding the still unfinished privatization process, due to which the state still holds a strong equity interest in 14 Croatian hotel companies, the biggest problem concerning the unresolved property issues relates to the undefined legal treatment of the un-privatized land used by the privatized hotel companies. Although the hotel companies used such land prior to their privatization in the 1990s, the government's idea was to exclude the land not covered by tourism facilities from the privatization process and to offer it to the privatized hotel companies on a long-term lease basis. Unfortunately, despite several attempts to find a reasonable formula to assess the market value of such land and charge the hotel companies for using it, the state and the hotel companies have not found a mutually acceptable solution so far. As a result, the privatized hotel companies still use publicly owned land without any service charge and in a legally unregulated manner. Nevertheless, all legal entities using state-owned land plots for private entrepreneurial activities are prohibited from carrying out any investments on these plots. Further, since such land plots cannot be used for business-related arrangements with other legal entities (concessions, leases, etc.), the present stalemate situation blocks the investment and severely undermines the market survival of all tourism facilities situated on such properties.

The results also indicate that underdeveloped and/or deficient communal systems (31.2 per cent of city/municipal mayors and 28.1 per cent

of tourism board managers) as well as inadequate transport infrastructure (25.5 per cent of city/municipal mayors and 30.1 per cent of tourism board managers) pose a significant limitation to the competiveness of
Croatian tourism. With the exception of telecommunications, the current
state of other communal systems, especially in smaller urban settlements,
cannot follow the growth of tourism demand. In this respect, most urgent
issues perceived by mayors and tourism board managers are fecal discharge
(70.3 per cent and 50.7 per cent, respectively) and solid waste management
(19.3 per cent and 36.3 per cent, respectively), while the least investment
is needed for enhancement of the existing electricity and water supply systems, which are, regardless of occasional problems during peak season, able
to meet most of the consumers' needs. In terms of transport infrastructure,
most city/municipal mayors and tourism board managers support further
investment in quality and capacity of national, regional and local roads
(36.5 per cent and 34.2 per cent, respectively) as well as the improvement
in the overall transport infrastructure at the destination level. This particularly applies to the quality of local public transport (42.4 per cent of city/
municipal mayors and 50.7 per cent of tourism board managers), availability of bike trails (35.9 per cent of city/municipal mayors and 31.5 per cent
of tourism board managers), tidying up of pedestrian areas (33.8 per cent
of city/municipal mayors and 23.3 per cent tourism board managers) and
offering more parking space (21.7 per cent of city/municipal mayors and
36.3 per cent of tourism board managers). These attitudes strongly cor-
respond to the views expressed by visitors to various tourism destinations
situated within the Croatian coastal counties (Marušić et al., 2011).

Largely as a result of a rather traditional market communications, and
regardless of its quite diverse product portfolio, Croatia has, so far, not
been able to successfully move away from its dominating 'sun and sea'
image. Hence, one should not be surprised that the surveyed city/munici-
pal mayors and tourism board managers are of the opinion that the existing marketing/promotion mix represents another serious limitation to
increasing Croatia's tourism competitiveness on the global market (35.0
per cent and 18.5 per cent, respectively). In this regard, the survey results
indicate the need for a thorough restructuring of the country's existing
tourism brand architecture.

The quality of human resources, as measured by the knowledge and
skills level of the employees in the tourism industry, has also been recognized as one of the major obstacles to improving the competitive level
of Croatian tourism (20.2 per cent of city/municipal mayors and 29.5
per cent of tourism board managers). In view of the ever-increasing

importance of the experiential component in the positioning of tourism destinations (Pine & Gilmore, 1998), the market sustainability of each tourism destination increasingly depends on the versatility, adaptability, communication skills and creativity of the human capital. However, the system of formal education and lifelong learning in Croatia is not sufficiently adapted either to the requirements of the tourists or to the needs of the tourist industry. Effective and goal-oriented improvement in the human capital department requires day-to-day cooperation among educational institutions and employers in order to create curricula capable of producing professional profiles able to adapt continuously to the requirements of the tourism industry.

Finally, the attitudes of the city/municipal mayors and tourism board managers suggest that the existing legal framework is also reflected negatively in the present competitive ranking of Croatia's tourism (16.6 per cent of city/municipal mayors and 25.3 per cent of DMO directors). Such a viewpoint stems predominantly from the fact that tourism is directly and/or indirectly associated with a number of other economic activities, all of which are regulated by autonomous laws and bylaws that, more often than not, do not take into account the various negative side effects reflected in the operational results of the tourism industry. The sheer number of corresponding non-tourism legislation, as well as the fact that the majority of laws and bylaws are created by different governmental bodies, allows for the potential existence of various legislative inconsistencies. In other words, the laws and bylaws affecting tourism are often not fully aligned with each other. Further, since it is often difficult to comprehend them unequivocally, one can conclude that the existing legal framework in Croatia not only hampers the daily operations of a number of legal entities in tourism but also diminishes the efficiency of the judiciary, thus creating an atmosphere of legal uncertainty (Kunst, 2011).

AVAILABILITY OF EU STRUCTURAL FUNDS: VITAL BUT NOT SUFFICIENT PREREQUISITE FOR THE INCREASE IN CROATIA'S TOURISM COMPETIVENESS

The results clearly indicated the main factors due to which Croatia's tourism competitiveness still lags behind most European Mediterranean destinations. Although the study was not designed to offer specific answers on how to improve Croatian tourism competitiveness, respondents' attitudes provide sufficient insight to formulate concrete actions.

A detailed insight into the National Strategic Reference Framework (Republic of Croatia, 2010) brings about an encouraging conclusion: Croatian development priorities in the use of EU funds relate primarily to (i) the improvement of transport and energy infrastructure, as well as environmental protection infrastructure, (ii) the enhancement of competitiveness in various spheres of the economy, (iii) the provision of a more balanced regional development, (iv) the promotion of employment and education of the workforce and (v) enhancement of the efficiency of the state administration and judiciary. In other words, it would be possible to use the available EU structural and/or cohesion funds so as to systematically eliminate most of the present limitations that impede the country's tourism competitiveness, provided that these are recognized as strategic priorities in the national tourism development strategy.

However, it should be noted that the mere availability of EU funding for improving the country's tourism competitiveness does not necessarily imply that Croatia will be either competent enough to take advantage of them or that they will be used appropriately. To what extent will Croatia be able to make use of this opportunity will largely depend on the quality of the nominated projects in terms of their relatedness to the most relevant issues of Croatian tourism. In other words, Croatia should nominate primarily those projects that are expected to ensure maximum net benefit. To make this possible, it is necessary to evaluate the contribution of each potentially interesting project on the basis of cost-benefit analysis and rank them accordingly. Furthermore, since the preparation of each project calls for the preparation of the complex and extensive documentation, following the proscribed best practice procedures, one could argue that the likelihood of EU funds provision greatly corresponds to the skills of human resources in the public sector. In this regard, one should stress the need for continuous capacity building in the area of EU project documentation preparation.

With all that in mind, and taking into account the limitations to Croatia's tourism competitiveness, it seems that the Croatian government should immediately embark upon a series of structural reforms related predominantly to the education quality of future (and present) tourism professionals and to the improvement of the investment climate in the country. The improvement in the quality of education for future (and present) tourism professionals should result in more efficient implementation of international best practices not only at the level of individual legal entities but in the context of responsible management of tourism development at the destination level as well. The improvement of the investment climate, on the other hand, resulting in a gradual increase in private investment demand, should substantially enrich and diversify the existing tourism offer at the (micro)destination level. To achieve these goals, priority action areas of the government in the short term, apart from the urgent completion of hotel and tourism companies privatization, include (i) deregulation and liberalization of the tourism regulatory framework, (ii) taxes reduction, (iii) improvement in the existing education system for tourism professionals, (iv) reform in the system of spatial planning and (v) reorganization of the existing system of tourism development management.

Deregulation and liberalization of the tourism regulatory framework is needed mostly because of its lack of functionality and, to some extent, of its inappropriateness. Although the existing regulatory framework for tourism development and/or management, in a formal sense, constitutes of a relatively small number of laws and/or bylaws, legal entities involved in the tourism business in Croatia must also be aware and adhere to the provisions of 65 other non-tourism, laws and/or bylaws. The mere number of these laws and/or bylaws indicates a legal overregulation. In such circumstances, 'creative chaos' prevails since, more often than not, relevant legal provisions are interpreted differently and on a case by case basis. On the other hand, the inappropriateness of the tourism regulatory framework has a lot to do with the accelerated harmonization of Croatian legislation with the EU acquis, in which the government officials were made to (non-selectively) adopt certain legal provisions from countries that are economically, socially and/or politically significantly more advanced. Therefore, certain provisions in many laws and/or bylaws are set too rigidly or in a manner inappropriate to the level of Croatia's overall development. In such regulatory conditions, it is very unlikely to expect increased investment activity neither from domestic, tourism-related, legal entities nor from international potential investors.

Despite the preferential status of most tourism and/or hospitality services with regard to the value added tax, the overall fiscal and para-fiscal burden of the tourism business in Croatia is significantly higher than in most of the countries in the relevant competitive framework. In this regard, in order to increase the level of Croatia's tourism competitiveness, a desirable reform of the existing tax system should, inter alia, include the adjustment of the present rate of the value added tax (in line with the competitive environment), but also relieve the existing tax burden on wages. In addition to these tax cuts, one should also abolish a range of various para-fiscal levies and adjust the remainder of them in a way that would reflect the seasonal nature of the tourism business and the actual occupancy of installed capacity. Tax relief, furthermore, should not necessarily be the same for all tourism-related businesses but would have to take into account their specificities.

Although it started more than twenty years ago, the process of privatization in the Croatia's tourism and hospitality industry is not yet finished. Unlike some other economic sectors and/or industries in which state ownership can justify the protection of vital national interests, this cannot possibly be the case in the domain of tourism. Namely, tourism is an economic sector which is worldwide most directly linked to private entrepreneurship. Regardless of that fact, fourteen relatively large tourism and hospitality legal entities in Croatia are still being owned by the state. Despite the fact that most of these companies operate along the Adriatic coast and are, therefore, privileged to tourism companies not exposed to such favorable geographic location, their economic performance is rather poor. Namely, most of them record below-average profitability and often losses. Also, due to the hard budget constraint, as well as to the prevailing bureaucratic management, such companies are, as a rule, under-capitalized and overstaffed, with obsolete products and with no development vision. Therefore, the rapid and efficient privatization of such companies would significantly improve not only their operational business results but also the quality of the integrated tourist product of the destinations in which they operate.

Reform of the present tourism education system with the aim to improve the skills level of Croatian tourism professionals is mostly needed since the formal education system in Croatia, especially in terms of rapid and revolutionary changes in communication technologies, is not properly adjusted neither to the private sector needs nor to the needs of effective destination management. In other words, due to the impossibility of finding and securing a sufficient number of well-trained employees, both on to micro and macro level, Croatia's tourism competitiveness might be progressively endangered in the years to come. Although in the past fifteen to twenty years, often under the supervision of internationally recognized experts, most of the prominent hotel companies in Croatia made a significant step forward in the introduction of internationally accepted standard operating procedures in all important areas of day-to-day business, this is still not enough since Croatia continues to lag behind its competition in the number of top quality managers and skilled professionals in the private sector. The situation is even worse in the public sector, especially in the area of destination management at the local level. In this sense, the reform of the education system in line with the needs of the tourism sector should ensure not only the establishment of several specialized institutions of higher education and/or business schools but also the provision of contemporary equipment and practicums at the vocational school level. Furthermore, when it comes to the 'software', the reform of the tourism educational system should also: (i) harmonize the curricula to the specific needs of the tourism and hospitality enterprises, (ii) introduce lifelong learning and (iii) establish contacts/cooperation with selected international centers of excellence in order to ensure dissemination of best business practices in the shortest possible time.

As for the reform of the existing spatial planning system, the changes are necessary especially in order to ensure enhanced protection of the still undeveloped natural space from the partial interests of local politicians and/or politically protected/sponsored influential entrepreneurs. Despite the relatively sound spatial planning methodology which requires harmonization of plans of lower rank with those of higher order (town/city—county—state), a decentralized spatial planning system brings about a bad practice of production of 'pre-ordered' spatial plans that closely reflect the interests of influential investment lobbies and/or politically 'protected' individuals at local, regional and/or national level. In other words, despite the long tradition of spatial planning and the abundance of excellent spatial planners, the spatial plans in Croatia are more and more being produced in a manner that often neglects the professional standards of the discipline itself. In such circumstances, in order to avoid/minimize corruptive behavior, it seems that the whole spatial planning system should be (partially) centralized.

In addition to initiating and implementing much-needed structural reforms so as to improve the investment climate and foster entrepreneurial activity in the country, the increase of Croatia's tourism competitiveness asks for the improvement of the whole system of managing the country's tourism development process, both locally (level of a tourist destination) and 'vertically' (top to bottom). Regarding the needed improvement at the level of the individual tourist destinations, and due to the increasing number of participants in the integrated tourism product, there is a rising need for mutual coordination and/or systematic guidance of their entrepreneurial activities. That is the task of both local tourist boards who should provide solutions to possible problems/deficiencies in the destination's offer and local government who should safeguard the implementation of the suggested solutions. However, since the local government officials at the destination level often do not comprehend the role of local tourist boards too seriously, and since they themselves do not have the sufficient level of knowhow required for the effective management of the tourism development process, it would be vital to introduce obligatory 'tailor-made' educational courses for all (newly elected) city/municipal leaders (and their closest associates) in all parts of the country with potential for tourism development. Accordingly, this would require the design and implementation of various educational and/or training programs, involving not only the experts of the Ministry of Tourism, and the National Tourism Board (NTB), but the selected education institutions and consultants as well. On the other hand, in order to increase its internal efficiency and functionality, the vertical improvement of Croatia's tourism management system asks for: (i) a clear division of authority among the NTB, regional tourism boards and local tourism boards as well as for (ii) a more efficient communication and the establishment of a clear line of command between the Ministry of Tourism, the counties and the cities/municipalities.

CONCLUSION

Although international tourism receipts, particularly in times of low and/or declining economic activity, have traditionally been used to stabilize the economy, reduce the current account deficit and decrease the unemployment rate during the tourist season, most Croatian governments have, so far, treated tourism predominantly as a 'gift from heaven'. Regardless of evident improvements in volume and receipts over the years, tourism development in Croatia is still being managed ineffectively and without an agreed-upon strategic direction. As a result, overall tourism activity in most parts of the country is still being characterized not only by the lack of vertical coordination in goal setting at the national, as compared to the local level, but also by the inability to effectively implement most of the policy recommendations entailed in tourism masterplans at the local/destination level. The conducted primary research, which gave a sound insight in the attitudes of Croatia's public sector key tourism development stakeholders, strongly supports this conclusion. In such circumstances, tourism in Croatia is still developing haphazardly and very much extensively, mainly along the most attractive area along the Adriatic coast, whereas the inland part of the national territory and its attractions are so far being largely neglected.

Similar to the situation in some other countries of the Mediterranean (Altinay, Var, Hines, & Hussain, 2007; Shamsul Haque, 2007; Altinay & Bowen, 2006; Tosun, 2000), tourism development at destination level is often under the influence of 'muscle flexing' and political sponsorship of the eligible local elite who, by means of a variety of bureaucratic procedural tricks, easily safeguard their privileged position/status, which allows them successfully to pursue personal gains at the expense of public interest. Such behavior is inevitably reflected negatively not only in the quality of the overall tourism experience but also on investment demand, including the development of small family businesses.

Although Croatian tourism has taken a big step forward in enhancing its international competitiveness during the last fifteen years, especially by modernizing the existing hotel industry and improving the quality of its destination management at the local level through the introduction of a new tourist board system, it has so far not been able to diversify its tourism product in order to extend its existing customer base and attract a broader array of new market segments. In this context, Croatia has so far not been able neither to shift away from the image of a summer 'sun and sea' and yachting destination nor to activate the resources of the inland parts of the country in order to attract various types of rapidly growing 'special interest' and 'adventure' market niches (Lew, 2008; Robinson & Novelli, 2005; Trunfio, Petruzzellis & Nigro 2006).

Notwithstanding the fact that Croatian tourism still lags behind most of the countries of the European Mediterranean in terms of competiveness, Croatian accession to the European Union represents a unique opportunity significantly to improve the present situation in several ways: (i) as a result of becoming a member of the 'elite club', Croatia and its tourism will be exposed to larger presence in the media; (ii) due to constant pressure by the Commission, Croatia will be forced to embark upon much-needed structural reforms in order to improve the presently unfavorable investment climate and the country's overall economic performance; and (iii) easier access to available EU funds, providing these are used for the effective removal of various constraints affecting the country's competiveness. However, since 'real life' usually unfolds somewhat worse than hoped for, mostly due to various types of stakeholder resistance or 'system error', it cannot be expected that all the constraints impeding Croatia's tourism competitiveness will be neutralized effectively in medium term.

Nevertheless, it seems logical to assume that the more attention the government devotes to the problem of tourism sector competitiveness, the more effective remedial action can be expected. A key prerequisite for the materialization of such a scenario is the government's awareness that tourism activity can and should play a significant role in the economic development of the country. Only then will it be possible effectively to deregulate the complex inter-sectorial legislation currently blocking tourism development, improve the tourism-related infrastructure, diversify the product and successfully implement the rules and logic of strategic management at the national, regional and local levels.

REFERENCES

Alipour, H., & Hall, D. (2006). The mediterranean enlargement: An overview. In D. Hall, M. Smith, & B. Marciszweska (Eds.), *Tourism in the new Europe – The challenges and opportunities of EU enlargement* (pp. 199–212). Wallingford: CAB International.

Altinay, L., & Bowen, D. (2006). Politics and tourism interface: the case of Cyprus. *Annals of Tourism Research, 33*(4), 939–956.

Altinay, L., Var, T., Hines, S., & Hussain, K. (2007). Barriers to sustainable tourism development in Jamaica. *Tourism Analysis, 12*(3), 1–13.

Attard, M., & Hall, D. (2004). Transition for EU accession: the case of Malta's restructuring tourism and transport sectors. In D. Hall (Ed.), *Tourism and transition: Governance, transformation and development* (pp. 119–132). Wallingford: CAB International.

Bramwell, B. (2003). Maltese responses to tourism. *Annals of Tourism Research, 30*(3), 581–605.

Butler, R. W. (1980). The concept of the tourist area life-cycle of evolution: implications for management of resources. *Canadian Geographer, 24*(1), 5–12.

Butler, R. W. (2009). Tourism destination development: Cycles and forces, myths and realities. *Tourism Recreation Research, 34*(3), 247–254.

Calantone, R. J., di Benetto, C. A., Hakam, A., & Bojanic, D. C. (1989). Multiple multinational tourism positioning using correspondence analysis. *Journal of Travel Research, 28*(2), 25–32.

Choi, H. C., & Sirakaya, E. (2006). Sustainability indicators for managing community tourism. *Tourism Management, 27*(6), 1274–1289.

Croatian Bureau of Statistics. (2015). *Tourism 2015, first release – number 4.3.1/8.* Zagreb: Croatian Bureau of Statistics.

Croatian National Bank. (2012). *Bulletin 187.* Zagreb: Croatian National Bank.

De Carlo, M., Cugini, A., & Zerbini, F. (2008). Assessment of destination performance: a strategy map approach. *Tourism Review, 63*(2), 25–37.

Digance, J. (1997). Life cycle model. *Annals of Tourism Research, 1997, 24*(2), 452–455.

Dodds, R. (2007). Malta's tourism policy: Standing still or advancing towards sustainability? *Island Studies Journal, 2*(1), 47–66.

Dredge, D. (1999). Destination place planning and design. *Annals of Tourism Research, 26*(4), 772–791.

Dwyer, L. (2015). Globalisation of tourism: Drivers and outcomes. *Tourism Recreation Research, 40*(3), 326–339.

Echtner, C. M., & Ritchie, J. R. B. (2003). The meaning and measurement of destination image. *Journal of Tourism Studies, 14*(1), 37–48.

Enz, C. A. (2010). *Hospitality strategic management – concepts and cases.* New Jersey: John Wiley & Sons.

Fayed, H., & Fletcher, J. (2002). Globalization of economic activity: Issues for tourism. *Tourism Economics, 8*(2), 207–230.

Getz, D. (1986). Models in tourism planning. Towards integration of theory and practice. *Tourism Management, 7,* 21–32.

Getz, D. (1992). Tourism planning and destination lifecycle. *Annals of Tourism Research, 19*(4), 752–770.

Goeldner, R., Ritchie, J., & McIntosh, R. (2000). *Tourism. Principles, practices, philosophies* (8th ed.). New York: John Wiley & Sons.

Hall, C. (2000). *Tourism planning: Policies, processes and relationships.* Essex: Prentice Hall.

Hjalager, A. (2006). Stages in the economic globalization of tourism. *Annals of Tourism Research, 34*(2), 437–457.

Inskeep, B. (1991). *Tourism planning: An integrated and sustainable development approach.* New York: van Nostrand Reinhold.

Ivandić, N., Marušić, Z., Šutalo, I., & Vuglar, J. (2014). *Tourism satellite account of Croatia for 2011 and calculation of indirect and total contribution of tourism to Croatian economy.* Zagreb: Ministry of Tourism of Republic of Croatia and Institute for Tourism.

Jamal, T. B., & Getz, D. (1995). Collaboration theory and community tourism planning. *Annals of Tourism Research, 22*(1), 186–204.

Kaufman, R., Oakley-Browne, H., Watkins, R., & Leigh, D. (2003). *Strategic planning for success: Aligning people.* New York, John Wiley & Sons: *Performance and Payoffs.*

Knowles, T., Diamantis, D., & El-Mourhabi, J. (2001). *The globalization of tourism and hospitality – a strategic perspective.* London: Continuum.

Krallinger, J. C., & Hellebust, G. K. (1993). *Strategic planning workbook.* New York: John Wiley & Sons.

Konečnik, M. (2006). Slovenia: New challenges is enhancing the value of the tourism destination brand. In D. Hall, M. Smith, & B. Marciszweska (Eds.), *Tourism in the new Europe – the challenges and opportunities of EU enlargement* (pp. 81–91). Wallingford: CAB International.

Kunst, I. (2007). Croatian tourism and EU accession. *Tourism and Hospitality Management, 13*(2), 437–458.

Kunst, I. (2011). Direktna strana ulaganja u hrvatski turizam – stanje i ograničenja [Direct foreign investment in Croatian tourism – current state and constraints]. *Turizam, 59*(2), 225–241.

Lew, A. A. (2008). Long tail tourism: New geographies for marketing niche tourism products. *Journal of Travel & Tourism Marketing, 25*(3/4), 409–419.

Manning, T. (1999). Indicators of tourism sustainability. *Tourism Management, 20*(1), 179–181.

Marušić, Z., Čorak, S., Ivandić, N., & Sever, I. (2011). *TOMAS ljeto: stavovi i potrošnja turista u Hrvatskoj [TOMAS Summer: attitudes and expenditure of tourists in Croatia]*. Zagreb: Institute for Tourism.

McClamrock, J., Byrd, J. J., & Sowel, S. L. (2001). Strategic planning: Policies, leadership and learning. *The Journal of Academic Librarianship, 27*(5), 372–378.

Miller, G. (2001). The development of indicators for sustainable tourism: results of a Delphi survey of tourism researchers. *Tourism Management, 22*, 351–362.

Republic of Croatia. (2010). *National strategic reference framework 2012—2013*. Zagreb: Republic of Croatia, Central Office for Development Strategy and Coordination of EU Funds.

Robinsion, M., & Novelli, M. (2005). *Niche tourism: An introduction*. In M. Novelli (Ed.), *Niche tourism: Contemporary issues, trends and cases* (pp. 1–11). Oxford: Elsevier Butterworth-Heinemann.

Omezrel Gomezelj, D., & Mihalič, T. (2008). Destination competiveness – applying different models, the case of Slovenia. *Tourism Management, 29*(2), 294–307.

Pearce, D., Barbier, E., & Marakandya, A. (1990). *Sustainable development, economics and environment in the Third World*. Aldershot: Edward Elgar.

Pine, J.B. & Gilmore, J. H.. 1998. Welcome to the experience economy. Harvard Business Review, July-August.

Rutin, J. (2010). Coastal tourism: A comparative study between Croatia and Tunisia. *Tourism Geographies: An International Journal of Tourism Space, Place and Environment, 12*(2), 264–277.

Scott, J., & Topcan, L. (2006). Building bridges in borderlands of the new Europe. In D. Hall, M. Smith, & B. Marciszweska (Eds.), *Tourism in the new Europe – the challenges and opportunities of EU enlargement* (pp. 224–236). Wallingford: CAB International.

Shamsul-Haque, M. (2007). Theory and practice of public administration in Southeast Asia: Traditions, directions and impacts. *International Journal of Public Administration, 30*, 1297–1326.

Theuma, N. (2006). Malta: Re-imaging the mediterranean destination. In D. Hall, M. Smith and B. Marciszweska (ed), *Tourism in the new Europe – The challenges and opportunities of EU enlargement* (pp. 213-223). Wallingford: CAB International.

Tosun, C. (2000). Limits to community participation in the tourism development process in developing countries. *Tourism Management, 21*(6), 613–633.

Tosun, C. M., & Dallen, J. (2001). Shortcomings in planning approaches to tourism development in development countries: the case of Turkey. *International Journal of Contemporary Hospitality Management, 13*(1), 352–359.

Transparency International. (2014). *Global corruption barometer – Croatia.* www. transparency.org/country. Date accessed 22 May 2016.

Trunfio, M., Petruzzellis, L., & Nigro, C. (2006). Tour operators and alternative tourism in Italy: Exploiting niche markets to increase international competitiveness. *International Journal of Contemporary Hospitality Management, 18*(5), 426–438.

US Department of State. (2015). *Investment climate statement – Croatia.* http:// www.state.gov/e/eb/rls/othr/ics/2015/241530.htm. Date accessed 22 May 2016.

Vanhove, N. (2005). *The economics of tourism destinations.* Oxford: Elsevier Butterworth – Heinemann.

Vila, M., Costa, G., & Rovira, X. (2010). The creation and use of scorecards in tourism planning: A Spanish example. *Tourism Management, 31*, 232–239.

Wehrmeyer, W., Clayton, A., & Lum, K. (2002). Foresight for development. *Greener Management International, 37*, 24–36.

World Economic Forum. (2015). *Travel and tourism competitiveness report.* Geneva: World Economic Forum.

WTO. (2004). *Indicators of sustainable development for tourism destinations.* Madrid: OMT.

Yilmaz, Y., & Bititci, U. S. (2006). Performance measurement in tourism: a value chain model. *International Journal of Contemporary Hospitality Management, 18*(4), 341–349.

CHAPTER 4

Shaping Destination Identity: Challenges of Branding Croatia

Neda Telišman-Košuta

NEED FOR (RE)SHAPING DESTINATION IDENTITY

Tourism is one of Croatia's most important economic sectors having generated 8.6 billion Euro in tourism expenditure in 2013 (Croatian National Bank, 2014; Institute for Tourism, 2014) and directly contributing 10.4 per cent of the GDP in 2011 (Ivandić, Marušić, Šutalo, & Vuglar, 2014). It is also a sector performing today below its full potential largely due to Croatia's persisting one-dimensional image as a 'sea, sun and summer only' destination.

Although tourism in Croatia originated in the 1880s as a seaside, health-oriented winter pastime for the Austro-Hungarian nobility and wealthy entrepreneurs, the country readily responded to the 1960s trends of democratized travel when the summer vacation became a middle class 'right' across Western Europe. The large West German, Austrian, Italian and even Dutch markets naturally flowed to the warm, close and affordable Adriatic coast in the summer where hotels, campsites and, in a then socialist country, privately owned accommodation were being rapidly developed to welcome them. In the 1990s, a new wave of sunseekers

N. Telišman-Košuta (✉)
Institute for Tourism, Zagreb, Croatia

© The Author(s) 2017
L. Dwyer et al. (eds.), *Evolution of Destination Planning and Strategy*, DOI 10.1007/978-3-319-42246-6_4

resulted from the release of pent-up Eastern European demand following the breakup of the Soviet bloc. Despite its extraordinary diversity of natural and cultural heritage as a country located on the crossroads of Alpine, Pannonian, Balkan and Mediterranean Europe, this interplay of both demand and supply side forces has resulted over the past 50 years in Croatia's tourism destination identity to become equated with 'budget seaside summer holidays'.

Recent research conducted by the Croatian Tourist Board (2013) confirms that Croatia is perceived in its most important tourist generating markets as first and foremost a 'sun and sea' destination with an overwhelming 81 per cent of respondents opting for this portrayal of the country. Furthermore, 52 per cent associate Croatia 'very strongly' with the 'sun and sea' product versus a significantly lower number of 'very strong' associations of Croatia with 'nautical tourism' (24 per cent), 'health and wellness' (12 per cent), 'wine and gastronomy' (12 per cent) or 'business tourism' (6 per cent). Research of Croatia's image among those who have never visited the country, conducted by the Institute for Tourism (Telišman-Košuta & Marušić, 2011) in representative European source markets, revealed that dominant top-of-mind associations of Croatia are 'beautiful coastline, sea and islands' with 'beaches', 'warm' and 'sun' following close behind, these also being the prevailing image attributes across markets, age groups and income levels. Viewed from this perspective, it is not surprising that tourism activity in Croatia is concentrated along a narrow coastal sliver from mid-June to mid-September. In fact, the Adriatic coast has been consistently attracting upward of 95 per cent of total overnights registered in Croatia with slightly over 90 per cent occurring in the summer months (Croatian Bureau of Statistics, 2015).

Besides stretching the limits of coastal capacity during the summer, the existing concentration of tourism activity leaves huge potential of shoulder seasons and inland destinations of Croatia untapped. Extending the tourism season and extending the spatial distribution of tourism activity have been a 'mantra' of strategic tourism development and marketing planning for decades. Most recently, on the national level, both the *Croatian Tourism Development Strategy to 2020* (Ministry of Tourism, 2013) and the new *Strategic Marketing Plan of Croatian Tourism* (Croatian National Tourist Board, 2015) emphasize seasonal and spatial distribution of tourism as their principal goals. Numerous similar regional and local level documents, including those from the coastal counties seeking to attract tourist away from the saturated beaches and further inland, set the same priorities.

This is the context within which there has been a steadily growing interest in destination branding throughout Croatia over the past decade. Destination branding has come to be seen, from the national to local levels, as a means of changing images and, thus, of changing visitation patterns. Consequently, most recent destination development and marketing planning in Croatia have dealt with destination branding to at least some extent. Regardless of the depth to which branding may have been tackled, the destination brand concepts and delivery action plans contained in these planning documents have, however, largely remained strategy on paper.

THE POWER OF DESTINATION BRANDING: A CRITICAL REVIEW

The surge of interest in destination branding being seen in Croatia reflects broader international enthusiasm the concept has generated in the course of the past 20 years both among tourism academics and practitioners. First academic papers and books on destination branding appeared in the late 1990s (Pike, 2005), the arguments therein built on a significant existing body of literature exploring the country of origin effect, positive correlations between destination image and likelihood to visit and the power of brands to increase the value of goods and services. The main line of thinking was that in a globalized world with ever-increasing competition among destinations, visitors often make their travel choices based on simplified perceptions of places making the brand and no longer just the price or the product, the key factor of destination success (Morgan, Pritchard, & Pride, 2004). A number of influential authors in the field, including Kotler and Gertner (2002), Olins (2004) and Anholt (2009), argued that, similar to branding goods and services, tourism destinations can be branded to differentiate themselves by projecting powerful and convincing brand images. Anholt (2009, p. 8) went further stating that '... a destination's brand equity ... becomes an asset of enormous value – probably more valuable than all its tangible assets, because it represents the ability of the place ... to continue to trade at a healthy margin for as long as its brand image stays intact'.

Destination branding has very quickly developed into one of the hottest subjects in tourism marketing. It also continues to be a controversial one. Reacting to the ensuing view, all too often held by the political establishment, of branding as a 'quick fix' for destination ambiguity or even anonymity, pioneering authors on the subject were quick to point out that branding is not something that can be 'done to' or 'invented about' a destination and that images, being constructs created from numerous diverse information sources, cannot be influenced through marketing communication such as advertising or public relations alone (Anholt, 2009). Thus, Olins (2007) writes of the need for destinations to discover 'the truth' about themselves and communicate it through everything they do, while Anholt (2007) introduces the notion of 'competitive identity' meaning a joint, coordinated effort by diverse stakeholders to transmit a destination's fundamental and permanent values. Buncle (2009) describes a destination brand as DNA that defines the destination, and, while a destination can present itself in different ways, adapting the message to different market segments, this underlying core characteristic is always the same. In their view, branding must be based on the reality of a place which is relevant for potential visitors and concisely communicated to them in, what can be expected to be, a long-term process of image building.

Discerning a destination's true identity, relevant to both hosts and guests, is undoubtedly a difficult task. The delivery of that core brand concept by all the different destination stakeholders in a coordinated manner over a longer-term period is, however, the real challenge. As Buncle (2009) notes, 'living the brand' through the products and services being delivered, through contacts with the local population, through marketing communication, including delivery in the Web 2.0 environment, so that a visitor's experience matches the brand's promise, is the most critical element of destination branding. Acknowledging these difficulties, and without disputing the importance of image to destination competitiveness, there is currently growing questioning of the feasibility of branding in a destination context.

Several problem areas have been identified in the literature. There is the issue of limitations of reduction or, in other words, the question of whether something as complex as a destination can be reduced to a clear, simple core. While traditional product or service brands have clear cores, the essence of a destination is seldom so clear since places possess layers of history and multiple meanings and are constantly changing (Morgan et al.). Concern is being expressed regarding the possibility of destinations to generate effective brand positioning strategies in heterogeneous markets as those typically encompassed by tourism (Pike, 2008). Some authors go further, questioning whether destination branding is, in fact, an impossible mission (Nicholaisen & Blichfeldt, 2012). The main points being raised revolve around issues of power in creating, controlling and in, generally, managing destination brands. Contrasting product and place brands, it is argued that destinations, unlike firms and corporations, do not have the mechanisms to ensure coordinated functioning of all diverse stakeholders contributing to the delivery of the destination brand. Destination management organizations (DMOs), although in theory cohesive entities, in reality lack the power to coordinate the destination marketing mix which is the basic prerequisite of destination branding. They also have little influence over the sources and the processing of information upon which visitors shape destination brand images. With DMO responsibility generally limited to promoting the destination, they themselves are actually likely to equate branding with promotion. There is, thus, no single entity that owns the destination brand and no single entity that can manage it, ultimately raising the question whether branding is a manageable task in the tourism destination context at all (Blichfeldt, 2005).

PERCEIVED CHALLENGES TO DESTINATION BRANDING IN CROATIA

Destination branding has generated substantial interest in Croatia seen both as a tool in repositioning the country's image to 'more than a sea, sun and summer' destination and a means in increasing the appeal of some of the country's lesser known regions. Similar to a number of other tourism-oriented countries, destination branding in Croatia is considered mainly to be the tourist boards' realm of responsibility. With only a few exceptions of destination and/or place branding projects in the country having been financed or co-financed by local or regional governments, most of this type of work completed so far has been commissioned by tourist boards.

The Croatian tourist board system is a pyramid-like structure organized hierarchically along national, regional (county) and local (town or municipality) levels of responsibility. The system has thus far functioned in the capacity of destination marketing organizations, while the intention of pending new regulation is to increase its involvement in destination management, transforming it, in fact, into more efficient destination marketing and management entities. Although the extent of the system's legally foreseen, not to mention realistically expectable, managerial leeway remains to be seen, the tourist boards are one of the few 'points of unity' representing 'the destination perspective'. In this sense, the tourist boards' understanding of branding in the destination context, as well as their organizational and leadership capacity, can be expected to bear significantly on the state of destination branding and, particularly, on brand implementation throughout Croatia.

Addressing what seems an important research gap, especially in light of the leverage image has on destination competitiveness, a limited initial probe into Croatian tourism board system's readiness for destination branding sought to explore their understanding of the concept, its significance, manner of implementation, responsibilities it entails and perceived barriers.[1] Some of the issues raised in Croatia and presented below echo the strengths and limitations of destination branding being discussed in the broader international context.

Understanding the Concept

Destination branding is understood within Croatia's tourism board system as a process of identifying some distinguishing feature(s) of a destination which will ensure its visibility and recognition. It involves two distinct phases. The first stage focuses on research of destination characteristics and guests perceptions, while the second is devoted to execution of brand strategy.

The distinguishing feature upon which a destination brand can be built is predominantly seen to be some unique physical asset in the destination, such as a beach, a monument or a man-made attraction allowing the destination to be branded as a place 'with THE beach', 'THE church', 'THE water park' and so on. Destination brands can also be created around quality of products and services, in which case all the sub-brands must be of the same quality, making up, for example, a 'five star destination'. To a lesser degree, branding is seen as exploiting something intangible, such as 'a story'.

Understanding the Significance

There is a certain amount of skepticism as to the added value of destination branding. Questions are raised regarding the recognizability or the reputation of destinations being, in fact, the result of 'natural' processes which have nothing to do with destination branding strategy. Some consider it just a 'fancy' new term or a 'fashion', invented by consulting and advertising agencies, for basically finding and asserting a destination's most valuable asset which is something that has been done all along.

Implementation Practice

Current destination branding practice in Croatia is associated with promotion. Branding is, for all practical purposes, equated with destination logos, slogans and promotional materials even though it is clear that these elements alone cannot create awareness of a destination. At the same time, tourism promotion is the only aspect of destination branding which is dealt with consistently.

Perception of Responsibility

The tourist boards are somewhat defensive as to their own responsibility for destination branding. Namely, they do not see themselves as being the ones in position to play the leading role in the destination branding process since they do not have the finances, the manpower nor the knowledge to do so. Moreover, brand delivery is considered to be outside the boards' realm due to the fact they do not own or manage the facilities and services offered to visitors and thus they do not have any real influence over the visitor experiences that make up the brand. In their view, the responsibility for destination branding resides with the government at every level.

Doubt is also expressed as to the reality of every little town being branded, making it imperative a strong national and regional brands are created which the smaller destinations could become a part of. The viability of the local perspective is also questioned in the sense that locally worn 'rose colored glasses' can sometimes hinder a community's ability to realistically discern their own significantly differentiating features.

Perception of Barriers

The multiple barriers to destination branding perceived by the tourist boards fall into two main groups of related issues. Uppermost is the lack of 'destination thinking'. Despite the publicly often proclaimed 'importance of the destination', in reality diverse destination stakeholders are impatiently pushing their own interests. The lack of a longer-term perspective is regarded as a particularly critical issue. Thus, the political elite are seen as having only an election-to-election, 4-year horizon during which they are interested mainly in advancing their party's political agenda and in keeping the opposition at bay or discredited. Elections resulting in change of political option usually also result in a new political program which often disregards previously done work. The private sector is short tempered and does not understand long processes in general. The resulting lack of unity, continuity and perseverance is counterproductive to any attempts at destination branding. All are perceived as symptomatic of Croatia, very difficult and slow to change.

In addition to, or even ensuing from, this lack of 'destination thinking', there is presently no clear leader of the destination branding process. Because destinations are complex, multi-layered systems, it is unlikely a 'natural' brand leader would emerge from within such a structure. The tourist boards realistically have the mandate and the capacity only to promote destinations while individual companies are focused on their business. The only logical option is for the government to take on this task since only a governmental body could have the legitimacy for a process as all-encompassing as destination branding. Yet, local governments are seen to be all too often basically incapacitated for sustaining a broad-based and lengthy effort such as destination branding due to their short-termed and partisan political agendas.

FUTURE RESEARCH

Croatia's readiness for destination branding has been examined based on a small-scale exploratory research focusing on the perspective of local and regional tourist boards. Consistent with issues raised in the literature, the insights gained show limitations to destination branding stemming from lack of 'destination thinking' among diverse stakeholders, as well as from lack of brand-directed leadership within destinations. Despite the tourist boards' coordinating function within a destination, they do not see themselves capable of assuming the role of destination brand managers and being responsible for brand delivery due to insufficient finances, manpower, knowledge and authority. Expressing some skepticism regarding its added value, destination branding is presently seen as having mainly a promotional function.

An obvious next step in future research would be to test the above discussed results on a larger, representative sample of tourist boards and to do so using more sophisticated research instruments. Moreover, the study should be extended to include perceptions and challenges of destination branding among other relevant stakeholders, namely, residents, hospitality companies, other non-tourism businesses in destinations and local or regional governments. Not trying to pre-empt these research results, but anticipating the difficulty of destination-wide brand delivery to be the uppermost issue, another research track should also explore other possible models of destination brand management in Croatia going beyond the established tourist board or DMO structure.

Since destination brand management and delivery is apparently an unrealistic expectation to have of DMOs, or for that matter of probably any single organizational entity, it would be sensible to seek alternatives which would be better suited to the complex destination environment. This may entail a shift from present modelling of destination management on corporate business practice towards other systems based on knowledge of group and network dynamics. In this sense, it would be important to gain further understanding of academic work on collaborative potential of destinations and particularly of the more recent destination leadership studies. Acknowledging that tourism more than most other economic sectors involves the development of some kind of cooperative function encompassing both formal and informal collaboration, partnerships and networks (Scott, Cooper, & Baggio, 2008), it is argued that organizations functioning in tourism destinations should adjust their strategies '... toward achievement of collaborative advantage rather than competitive advantage' (Fyall, Garrod, & Wang, 2012). In other words, organizations within destinations must learn to cooperate internally so that destinations they make up can compete externally. This presupposes destination leadership which, like network leadership, implies '... leading, organizing and communicating with the individual stakeholders and the destination network as a whole ... through motivating, encouraging and inspiring human actors by setting long-term values and directions' (Pechlaner, Kozak, & Volgger, 2014). The need for a new paradigm in destination leadership must, however, allow for different social and historical characteristic of nations.

NOTE

1. The research study was part of the Institute for Tourism exploratory work intended to guide future research on challenges of destination branding. It encompassed individual in-depth interviews with 20 regional (county) and local (town or municipality) tourist board directors from diverse parts of Croatia selected on the basis of their extensive experience in the tourist board system. The interviews were taped and the information was analyzed using content analysis tools. The study was conducted in May 2014.

References

Anholt, S. (2007). *Competitive identity: The new brand management for nations, cities and regions.* New York: Palgrave Macmillan.

Anholt, S. (2009). Why national image matters. In ETC & UNWTO (Ed.), *Handbook on tourism destination branding* (pp. 8–17). Madrid: UNWTO.

Blichfeldt, B. S. (2005). Unmanageable place brands. *Place Branding, 1*(4), 388–401.

Buncle, T. (2009). Introduction. In ETC & UNWTO (Ed.), *Handbook on tourism destination branding* (pp. 24–30). Madrid: UNWTO.

Croatian Bureau of Statistics. (2015). *Statistical databases – Tourism 2014.* http://www.dzs.hr/default_e.htm. Date accessed 19 March 2015.

Croatian National Bank. (2014). *Annual report 2013.* http://www.hnb.hr/publikac/godisnje/2013/e-god-2013.pdf. Date accessed 19 March 2015.

Croatian National Tourist Board. (2013). *Market research program 2013.* http://business.croatia.hr/Documents/3012/Program-trzisnih-istrazivanja-2013.pdf. Date accessed 20 October 2014.

Croatian National Tourist Board (2015). *Strategic marketing plan of Croatian tourism 2015-2020.* http://www.mint.hr/UserDocsImages/SMPHT-2014-2020-Sazetak.pdf. Date accessed 6 April 2015.

Fyall, A., Garrod, B., & Wang, Y. (2012). Destination collaboration: A critical review of theoretical approaches to a multi-dimensional phenomenon. *Journal of Destination Marketing & Management, 1*(1), 10–26.

Institute for Tourism. (2014). *Research study on tourism activity of domestic population.* http://www.iztzg.hr/hr/institut/projekti/istrazivanja/. Date accessed 6 April 2015.

Ivandić, N., Marušić, Z., Šutalo, I., & Vuglar, J. (2014). *Tourism satellite account of Croatia for 2011 and calculation of indirect and total contribution of tourism to Croatian economy.* Zagreb: Ministry of Tourism of Republic of Croatia and Institute for Tourism.

Kotler, P., & Gertner, D. (2002). Country as brand, product and beyond: A place marketing and brand management perspective. *Brand Management, 9*(4–5), 249–261.

Ministry of Tourism. (2013). *Croatian tourism development strategy to 2020.* Official Gazette of the Republic of Croatia 55/2013. http://narodne-novine.nn.hr/clanci/sluzbeni/2013_05_55_1119.html. Date accessed 6 April 2015.

Morgan, N., Pritchard, A., & Pride, R. (2004). *Destination branding: Creating the unique destination proposition.* Oxford: Elsevier Butterworth-Heinemann.

Nicholaisen, J. & Blichfeldt, B.S. (2012). *Destination branding: Mission impossible?* TRU Progress Working paper no. 9. Aalborg University Denmark. http://vbn.aau.dk/files/68473670/TRUprogress_9.pdf. Date accessed 10 April 2015.

Olins, W. (2004). Branding the nation: The historical context. In N. Morgan, A. Pritchard, & R. Pride (Eds.), *Destination branding: Creating the unique destination proposition* (pp. 18–25). Oxford: Elsevier Butterworth-Heinemann.

Olins, W. (2007). *On Br@nd*. London: Thames and Hudson.

Pechlaner, H., Kozak, M., & Volgger, M. (2014). Destination leadership: A new paradigm for tourist destinations? *Tourism Review, 68*(1), 1–9.

Pike, S. (2005). Tourism destination branding complexity. *Journal of Branding and Brand Management, 14*(4), 258–259.

Pike, S. (2008). *Destination Marketing: An Integrated Marketing Communication Approach*. Oxford: Elsevier Butterworth-Heinemann.

Scott, N., Cooper, C., & Baggio, R. (2008). Destination networks: Four Australian cases. *Annals of Tourism Research, 35*(1), 169–188.

Telišman-Košuta, N., & Marušić, Z. (2011). *Image of Croatia as a tourism destination on foreign markets*. Zagreb: Institute for Tourism.

CHAPTER 5

The Influence of Political Factors in Fashioning Destination Image

Božo Skoko, Katarina Miličević, and Damir Krešić

INTRODUCTION

During the last two decades, Croatia has successfully repositioned its image from an unknown Yugoslav republic, victim of war and newly formed Balkan state, to an attractive tourism destination which has become a member of the European Union in 2013. Although in the public domain of some countries, especially countries in northern Europe or Arab countries, Croatia is still somewhat associated with the war and the legacy of former Yugoslavia, the perception of Croatia has substantially changed over the past two decades. The main argument of this chapter is that tourism promotion has been the major force helping Croatia to improve its image distorted by the unfavorable political condition and, at the same time, to dissociate its image from the image of

B. Skoko
Faculty of Political Science, University of Zagreb, Zagreb, Croatia

K. Miličević (✉) • D. Krešić
Institute for Tourism, Zagreb, Croatia

© The Author(s) 2017   79
L. Dwyer et al. (eds.), *Evolution of Destination Planning and Strategy*, DOI 10.1007/978-3-319-42246-6_5

other Yugoslav countries and to become recognizable as a unique, small, Central European and Mediterranean country. Recent promotional efforts of Croatian tourism, characterized by the slogans 'Croatia – The Mediterranean as it once was' and 'Croatia – Full of life', fueled by the increasing global demand for original, different and well-preserved places, have additionally strengthened the positioning of Croatia as an attractive Mediterranean and Central European tourism destination. However, apart from positioning itself as an attractive 'sun and sea' destination, other comparative advantages of Croatian tourism, such as its tourism offer in the continental parts of the country, rich cultural heritage and political stability in a politically unstable region of the Europe, remain insufficiently and poorly perceived by the international community. Tourism has undoubtedly had a significant influence on building the contemporary brand of Croatia as a country. However, Croatia still has to undertake additional efforts to position itself as a new member of the European Union as well as an important political and economic entity in this part of Europe. Therefore, this chapter will try to demonstrate how promotional activities, implemented by the Croatian Tourist Board, have improved unfavorable image of Croatia in the international community, caused by war and war-related sufferings and directed the attention to the natural beauties of Croatia, positioning Croatia as an attractive tourism destination, providing authentic and quality tourism experiences. Through the example of Croatia as a tourism destination, this chapter also examines the role that tourism promotion has played in the evolution of the Croatian national brand which influenced Croatia's current image in the minds of different target markets. The focus of the chapter is not on every singular promotional activity, but on the sum of all effects resulting from multiple activities and the way these effects impact the brand awareness of Croatia. This chapter is structured as follows. In the introductory section, the chapter provides an overview of the specific situation faced by Croatia due to the unfortunate war events. This is followed by the discussion on how Croatia used natural beauties and tourism promotion in order to disassociate its image from the war events and from the image of the rest of ex-Yugoslav countries. Finally, the chapter presents research results about Croatia's image in the region, European Union (EU) countries and GCC countries, providing evidence that the current image of Croatia in the international community is largely determined by the tourism promotion activities.

CHALLENGES OF CROATIA'S INTERNATIONAL POSITIONING AFTER THE BREAKUP OF YUGOSLAVIA AND CROATIA'S INDEPENDENCE

Croatia was a former Austro-Hungarian, and thus Roman Catholic, constituent member of Socialist Federal Republic of Yugoslavia, which was founded in 1943, during the Second World War. The Republic of Croatia (then called Socialist Republic of Croatia) was one of the six Yugoslav republics for nearly 50 years, until the 25th of June 1991, when Croatian Parliament adopted a Constitutional Decision on Independence and Sovereignty of the Republic of Croatia. The independent Republic of Croatia was established in rather unfavorable historical circumstances. The late 1980s and early 1990s period of the last century was marked by the collapse of communism in Eastern European countries, the disintegration of multinational Yugoslavia and the Serbian military aggression against Croatia and Bosnia and Herzegovina. However, unlike other European socialist countries which, during the democratic changes of 1989, relatively easily shifted from socialist to capitalist economic and social system, Croatia has, through its struggle for independence, produced a number of specific characteristics which are even today important determinants of Croatia's image. It should also be emphasized that Croatia, alongside Slovenia, was one of the economically most developed countries among socialist countries of Eastern Europe (Vukadinović, 2000). Due to the fact that it relatively easily avoided direct war conflicts, Slovenia has succeeded admirably in shaking off the negative perceptions of being 'Balkan', mainly through successful promotion of branded export goods (Elan skis, Gorenje appliances, Laško Pivo beer and others), through well-funded tourism campaigns and through NATO and subsequent EU membership (Anholt, 2007). Contrary to Slovenia, instead of taking advantage of a good starting positions, Croatia was thrown in the vortex of war, which resulted in a large number of human casualties, material damage and huge military expenditures, and in the end, after the liberation of the territory, the process of rebuilding the homes and return of war refugees. Because of the problems caused by the war in the former Yugoslavia, Croatia was also faced with a poor international image. Although Croatians have a relatively long tradition as a nation, due to 70 years of living in two Yugoslav states (1918–41, 1945–90), and to strong Yugoslav propaganda dominated by Serbs, Croatia has been largely either unknown or associated with negative stereotypes. One of the most common was the one that propagated the image of Croatia as a pro-fascist and undemocratic state in the international community. This was due to the fact that in period 1941–45, some parts of Croatia were governed by the quisling regime of the Independent State of Croatia, which was an active ally of Hitler's Germany and which often pursued discriminatory policy against ethnic minorities, such as Jews, Serbs, Roma and others. However, even though the Independent State of Croatia did not have the support among the majority of Croatian people, and even though most Croatians subsequently joined the anti-fascist movement, this fact remained a basis for deliberate and malicious propagation of negative stereotypes about Croatia in the international community during the communist regime (Sanader, 2000). The negative stereotypes tied to the Croatia and consequent negative image of Croatia in the international community is still partially present, and Croatia has not completely recovered from this negative propaganda to this day. Besides, the communist regimes were actively involved in the altering or removing the national identities in many other post-communist and transition countries because strong and internationally recognizable identities were considered to be major threats to the unitary political systems. This was also true for Croatia. According to Anholt (2007, p. 118), 'one of the most damaging effects of Communism was the way in which it destroyed the national identity and the nation brands of the countries. By stopping the export of their national products and by preventing people from travelling abroad, and in many other ways, the Communist regime effectively deleted the old, distinctive European nation brands'. For example, regardless of the fact that the city of Dubrovnik was most notable brand image (Hall, 2002), even tourists who vacationed for years in Dubrovnik associated this city not with Croatia but only with Yugoslavia. The importance of such an iconic landmarks for development of national brand is additionally stressed by Clancy (2011, p. 294), who argued that 'outsiders frequently know nations largely through constructs experienced by tourism, thus we may not know much about Croatia but we might likely construct the image of Croatia through the knowledge of the beauty of the Dalmatian coast and the Old City of Dubrovnik'. This is additionally confirmed by the fact that the former Yugoslavia had a relatively positive image in the international community and was already developing a recognizable country brand, which was largely based on tourism and the natural beauties of Croatia. Therefore, it could be ironically argued that, during Yugoslav era, the most important attributes of Croatian national identity were largely used with the purpose of deconstructing that very identity.

On the other hand, the positive image that Yugoslavia enjoyed in the international community played an important role in covering the undemocratic nature of the political regime in the former Yugoslavia and consequently blurred the insights of the international community into the causes of disintegration of Yugoslavia and eventual causes of inevitable war (Miličević, Skoko & Krešić, 2012). Because the ex-Yugoslavia was the founder and an important member of the Non-Aligned Movement, and because it developed a special Yugoslav model of socialist system, western countries perceived it, not only as the bridge between East and West but also as a bridge between North and South. In this context, it is also important to recall the role that the lifetime president of Yugoslavia, Josip Broz Tito, played in the international community. In his decades in power, as one of the founders of the Non-Aligned Movement, he played an active role in international politics and with his specific socialist system—the so-called socialism with a human face—gained many supporters and had a very positive image in the western countries which was, however, substantially different from reality (Sanader, 2000). In addition to the quite positive image that Yugoslavia enjoyed among western intellectuals, the political and media establishment, the long-term Serbian propaganda aimed against Croatia and Croats must also not be ignored. This propaganda left a substantial mark on international public opinion and prepared the ground for the negative attitude of the international community regarding Croatia's secession from Yugoslavia (Miličević et al., 2012).

So in the early 1990s, as a new sovereign state on the map of Europe, Croatia faced two major challenges. Similar to many other transitional countries, Croatia suffered from an image forged during an earlier and very different political era, which constantly obstructed its political, economic, cultural and social aspirations (Anholt, 2007). Therefore, in a relatively short period of time, it had to position itself on the international political stage and win the favor of the international community while at the same time defending its territory in an imposed war. In such circumstances, it is extremely difficult to create recognizability with the European public and take care about its image. The outbreak of the war drew global attention, and Croatia was largely perceived as a victim of aggression. However, at the same time, Croatia was faced with a multitude of misinformation, prejudices, stereotypes and disorientation, which further complicated understanding of the situation in the former Yugoslavia, as well as the relationships between individual nations and the former republics. Thanks to the decision by citizens in a referendum on Croatia's independence (an overwhelming 94.2 per cent of Croatian citizens supported leaving the Socialist Federal Republic of Yugoslavia), the presenting of the truth about the events in the former Yugoslavia and strong lobbying activities, Croatia managed to secure international recognition from the majority of European countries in January 1992. Subsequently, international communication was somewhat facilitated for Croatian government institutions. Due to a better visibility in the international community, Croatia was able to begin the process of disassociation of its image from the rest of its surroundings, especially from the former Yugoslav countries.

In this period, the war associations were still creating a very negative context of Croatian image. It took a lot of political and diplomatic efforts to convince the international community that Croatia's right to self-determination and independence as well as the necessity for international recognition of Croatia was grounded from the historical and ethical standpoint but also from the standpoint of international law (Sanader, 2000). Since the interrelationship between national identity and tourism branding has been commonly discussed in the tourism research literature (Hall, 2002; Huang & Santos, 2011), it is not surprising that international recognition and definition of Croatia in regard to other nations was the first and foremost prerequisite of international branding of Croatia. Furthermore, additional efforts were needed in order to win the media war and to eliminate prejudices against Croatia and to place objective information which would position the newly founded country on the political map of Europe. The Croatian government realized that, in order to make a perceptual separation of Croatia from other Balkan countries, it was very important to provide the international community with new and up-to-date information about Croatia, information not connected with war and the suffering of the Croatian people. Tourism provided huge potential for this, since Croatia has a very indented coastline and, unlike other Yugoslav republics, had a long tourism history, first as a part of the Austro-Hungarian monarchy and later as a part of Yugoslavia.

Under these circumstances, it was vital, following the cessation of conflict, that Croatia should establish a national tourism marketing policy which, closely allied to national image rebuilding, would, as a brand, convey a distinct image to (Hall, 2004):

- Differentiate clearly the country from its neighbors;
- Reassure former markets that quality and value had been restored;
- Secure long-term competitive advantage through the country's major tourism attributes.

In order to emphasize its differentiation compared to other former Yugoslav republics, Croatia began its strong international tourism promotion even while the Homeland War was going on in 1994. The emphasis was on its natural beauty, the Adriatic Sea with its thousand islands and its rich cultural and historical heritage, as well as long tourist tradition, by which its uniqueness and advantages in relation to its neighbors were articulated. In this manner the attention was diverted from the war which, for the most part, awakens negative associations, regardless of compassion. Upon the end of the Homeland War, with its natural advantages and cultural wealth, Croatia invested additional efforts in tourism promotion and development of tourism, which positioned it as one of the leading tourism destinations in the Mediterranean.

Today, Croatia has successfully repositioned its image from Yugoslav country to an attractive Mediterranean tourism destination. Although Croatia is still associated with the war, former Yugoslavia and the Balkan region, this perception has substantially changed over the past two decades (Miličević et al., 2012). The Republic of Croatia became a member of the European Union on 1 July 2013, after years of negotiations, during which it had to meet criteria that were not required by any previous member. On this road, it had to shatter many stereotypes that had existed in certain European centers of power toward countries from the Balkans. However, despite numerous reforms, raising democratic standards and political and economic development, these efforts were practically unnoticed among citizens of the old EU member states. In countries of the EU, Croatia is primarily perceived as an attractive tourism destination. In addition to being familiar with Croatia's unique natural features, one segment of the European public still associates Croatia with the war and the legacy of the former Yugoslavia. The reason for such a 'unilateral' image of Croatia can be sought in the fact that, for two decades, Croatia strategically and continuously carried out tourism promotion and was intensively working on strengthening its tourism image. At the same time, it has ignored promotion of other attributes except for sporadic projects such as promotion of the culture, the economy and sporting achievements. Instead of Croatia presenting itself to its European neighbors in a strategic, creative and pragmatic manner, highlighting the strengths and potentials by which it could enrich the EU, the communication of Croatian political institutions with the world (with the exception of a few successful projects in the area of culture, as was the Croatian festival in France—'Croatie, la voici') was largely reactive and bureaucratic. In fact, due to the lack of pro-activity in relation to the media and international publics, on the eve of Croatia's accession there appeared a number of critical media reports on Croatia's unpreparedness for the EU.

NATURAL BEAUTIES AS A COMPARATIVE ADVANTAGE OF CROATIAN TOURISM

Croatia represents a meeting point of the Mediterranean and Central Europe, the Alps and the Pannonian Plain. Its relatively small area is distinguished by a marked diversity of nature, landscape, traditions and cultures. Therefore, two biggest comparative advantages of Croatia in the international positioning are its preserved natural diversity and natural beauty and a rich and preserved cultural and historical heritage. However, Croatian cultural and artistic heritage was quite unknown to Europe and the world in the 1990s. Even though Croatia is a relatively small country, it has an abundance of monuments, which are integral parts of European artistic achievements, presenting the most prominent extension of Western European culture toward the south-east. Within this context, Croatia is unique in Europe because no less than four cultural circles meet in its territory: the West and the East and the northern, Central European and the southern Mediterranean circle. It has a large number of preserved cities of ancient or medieval origin, and every fairly large city has its individual quality reflecting a specific cultural and architectural period. Croatian cultural abundance permanently testifies to Croatia's connection to key European cultural epochs. Six monuments on the UNESCO World Heritage List (UNESCO, 2016) are particularly distinguished: the intact land division of the ancient Greek plain in Stari Grad on the island of Hvar, the urban core of ancient Split with the palace built by the Roman emperor Diocletian, the early Christian Euphrasian Basilica in Poreč, the Romanesque core of the city of Trogir, the early Renaissance Cathedral of Saint James in Šibenik and Renaissance Dubrovnik surrounded by the striking preserved walls. Croatia is also a European record-holder in nonmaterial heritage under the protection by UNESCO[1].

Extending across 1.3 per cent of the EU territory, Croatia is not a large country (56.6 thousands km²), but it is one of the most environmentally preserved areas in Europe (Miroslav Krleža Institute of Lexicography, 2016). Its 1,777 km of the Adriatic coast (6,278 km with island coastline) represent one of the most distinctive and indented coasts in the world (Miroslav Krleža Institute of Lexicography, 2016) with 1,244 islands and islets (Croatian Tourist Board, 2016). It has an exceptionally clean and clear sea, with clarity for 56 m in some places (Miroslav Krleža Institute of Lexicography, 2016). According to the Environmental Performance Index (2016), it is considered to be among the cleanest countries in the Mediterranean and the 15th cleanest in the world. Croatia is among top EU countries with the largest supply of fresh water resources per inhabitant (Eurostat, 2016). In terms of biodiversity, it belongs to the top countries in Europe, and in environmental terms, it is one of the most preserved European countries. The most valuable parts of the natural heritage of Croatia are protected through 409 different protected areas with the total area of 7,547 km² (8.5 per cent of the area of Croatia). Among the protected areas, the most important ones are two strict nature reserves, eight national parks and eleven nature parks. Four national parks are located in mountain areas (Risnjak, Paklenica, Sjeverni Velebit and Plitvice Lakes) and four in coastal or maritime areas (Kornati, Mljet, Brijuni and Krka) (State Institute for Nature Protection, 2016).

It is indeed difficult to find such natural and cultural diversity in such a small area, as is the case in Croatia. It is simultaneously a Mediterranean and Central European country, mountain and flat country and littoral and continental country. Croatia boasts an indented afforested coast with a multitude of islands just like in southern seas, green coastal grazing lands with drystone walls reminding one of Ireland. Mountain parts are covered with spacious woodlands just like in Scandinavia, romantic lakes, fast rivers and picturesque mountain spaces just like in the Alps, but also brutal karst bare rocky areas with deep passes and canyons such as those in western parts of North America. In wide plains of lowland Croatia, there are spacious preserved swamps which otherwise can only be found in the extreme east of Europe in Russia or Ukraine, while gentle hills are adorned with vineyards and medieval castles and fortifications such as those found in Germany or Austria.

Dalmatia spreads along the Adriatic coast, from the southern slopes of the Velebit massif and Zadar in the north to Dubrovnik and to the Prevlaka in the most southern part of Croatia. The second largest Croatian city, Split, is its regional center. The western part of the country, Istria, as the largest peninsula in the Adriatic Sea, is also a separate historical region which lies against the Croatian Littoral and Rijeka, the biggest Croatian harbor. As a result of its numerous islands and islets, Croatian coast is the third longest in the Mediterranean, behind Greek and Italian coasts. In north-east, Slavonia spreads over the lowland part of Croatia, between the rivers of Drava, Sava and the Danube, and its largest cities are Osijek, Slavonski Brod and Vukovar. In the wider region around Zagreb, the largest cities are Varaždin, Karlovac, Sisak and Bjelovar. The Littoral (Adriatic) and lowland (Pannonian) Croatia are separated by the mountain and karst area of Gorski Kotar and Lika, whose relief only in some places exceeds 1,900 m above sea level.

In brief, thanks to its abundance, diversity and the preserved condition of nature, Croatia has huge potentials for the future. Skoko and Kovačić (2009) convincingly argue that it is extremely important that it expands its protected areas as soon as possible, or in other words, to put as larger part of its territory as possible under protection. By doing this, it will be possible to preserve them for the future from devastation, because only such natural preconditions enable Croatia to develop and present itself as an oasis of tranquility and rest. In this sense, they advocate clean industries, the production of healthy food, innovative program of rest and leisure and strengthening of cultural and health tourism.

Tourism Promotion as a Croatia's Tool for Achieving International Image

The need for destinations to promote a differentiated tourism product is more critical than ever, since today's leading destinations offer superb accommodation and attractions, high quality services and facilities and almost every country as a destination claims unique culture and heritage (Morgan & Pritchard, 2005). Consequently, the marketing of places has become an important managerial activity and, in some cases, the generator of local wealth (Kotler, Haider & Rein, 1993). Although many tourism companies or destinations recognize the importance of integration of marketing communications aimed at strengthening the strategic position of the destination image and its market value, effective implementation of marketing activities remains a great organizational challenge (Magzan & Miličević, 2012). According to Morgan and Pritchard (2005), the battle for customers in tomorrow's destination marketplace will be fought over experiences promised, and this is where place promotion moves into the territory of destination brand management whose outcome is destination image.

Bearing in mind all of the aforementioned Croatia's comparative advantages, it seems only logical for Croatia to use them in its international tourism promotion, which was launched in 1992 under the slogan

'Croatia – a small country for a great vacation'. In that time, the public was presented with the Croatian tourism promotional strategy, and, in collaboration with the PR agency McCann Erickson, a series of promotional posters were printed along with the Croatian image booklet in 12 different languages in the press run of 700,000 copies. It was an edition which presented Croatia as an attractive 'old' tourism destination, which 'reveals itself' to the world again. During 1993 and 1994, Croatia was portrayed in two series of tourism posters, and 1994 saw the publication of the promotional booklet *The Thousand Islands of the Croatian Adriatic* and *Zagreb, the heart of Croatia – the new European Metropolis*. The motifs widely included Croatian tourism sites, an inventory of Croatian tourism places was created, and they were linked to Croatia in a red and black graphism (Skoko, 2004). According to Anholt (2007), tourism is, in most cases, the most important and most powerful of the nation's six 'booster rockets' (brands, policy, investment, culture, people, tourism). The rationale behind this line of thought is that tourism offers the opportunity to brand the country directly.

In addition to this, the Croatian Tourist Board (the umbrella organization in charge of the tourism promotion of the country) organized the advertising of Croatia as a tourism brand in leading world mass media. Within public relations, study trips of foreign journalists to Croatia were organized, along with participation in leading tourist fairs worldwide. Over these years, the Croatian tourism promotion was the only organized and systematic Croatian international communication. It was also the most efficient mode of image management, as other modes (public diplomacy, cultural promotion, etc.) were quite insufficient. Therefore, more often than not, the Croatian leaders in international relations relied on the achievements of the tourism promotion, in order to present Croatia as a likable and nice country, hit by an unwanted war and which has done its best in order to return to a normal life.

With a continued tourism promotion, Croatia succeeded to provide the world with a sufficient amount of information on its advantages and particularities, keeping its distance from the rest of the region and creating a long-term recognizability. In this way, it started to be perceived as an exceptionally attractive country with a great tourism potential, which is evident from the constant growth of tourism demand. This helped in suppressing negative associations with the war and accompanying developments, associated with Croatia in the early 1990s.

In 2002 the Croatian Tourist Board appointed the consulting agency THR from Spain, to develop a strategic marketing plan for the promotion of Croatian tourism around the world, based on which a new wave of tourism promotion was launched under the slogan 'The Mediterranean as it once was'. In this way, Croatia sought to position itself geographically as a Mediterranean tourism destination and to present itself as a culturally authentic destination. Croatia promoted itself simultaneously as a country brand, and then its tourism regions were separately presented as brands Istria, Kvarner and the Zadar, Split, Šibenik and Dubrovnik areas. Regrettably, the continental part of the country was neglected. These areas have substantial tourism potential, but awareness of them has increased only recently. Although the slogan 'Croatia – the world of diversity' was also launched with the objective to present Croatia in its entire diversity, it was used only sporadically. However, the focus of the promotion over the last 20 years or so was on the Adriatic Sea, coast and islands.

Strategic Marketing Plan of Croatian Tourism 2010–14 emphasized a new image of a destination based on the experience and emotions. The Plan suggested the communication of simple elements of the identity which can be offered to the market—preserved coast, unique system of islands, intact hinterland and rich cultural heritage. The Plan defined the basic positioning of the brand of Croatia as a Mediterranean country which has preserved the heritage of its ancestors. Thus, in spite of the efforts to bring the continental Croatian landscapes closer to the world, the Mediterranean heritage was still a foundation of the perception of the brand. The latest communication concept defined by the Croatian Tourist Board resulted with the new slogan for Croatian tourism promotion 'Croatia – Full of life'. The new slogan is a product of marketing company BBDO and its subsidiaries from Croatia, Great Britain and Spain. It was developed in accordance with the *Croatian Tourism Development Strategy to 2020* (Ministry of Tourism, 2013). Tourism development strategy suggested implementation of rebranding activities in order to attract new target markets that are looking for excitement and product diversification.

Croatia's Image in the Region, EU Countries and GCC Countries

In order to critically examine the previously presented arguments regarding the effects of political factors and tourism promotion on fashioning the image of Croatia in the international community, the results of three separate public opinion studies, conducted in the countries of the former Yugoslavia, in the EU countries and the GCC countries, are presented. The public opinion study from 2008, conducted in the countries of the former Yugoslavia, was carried out approximately 10 years after the end of war-related events. The research was conducted by one of the authors of this paper (Skoko, 2010) as a part of his PhD thesis. Although it was expected that the image of Croatia would still be quite burdened with the war, it was surprising to see that major associations connected with Croatia, in all former Yugoslav countries, were related to the sea and tourism, even in Serbia which was in open war with Croatia. The research was conducted on a sample of 5,087 respondents, whereby 1,000 respondents came from Bosnia and Herzegovina, 1,025 from Montenegro, 1,019 from Macedonia, 1,011 from Slovenia and 1,032 from Serbia.

The results showed that, in the regional context, Croatia is most recognizable by the key association of coastal landscape and tourism (Table 5.1). Sea and tourism were the most important features associated with Croatia for 74 per cent of respondents from Macedonia, 71 per cent from Bosnia and Herzegovina, 67 per cent from Slovenia, 38 per cent from Serbia and 37 per cent from Montenegro. However, among respondents

Table 5.1 First associations with Croatia among respondents from former Yugoslav countries (%)[a]

	Total	Bosnia and Herzegovina	Montenegro	Macedonia	Slovenia	Serbia
Sea and tourism	57	71	37	74	67	38
War	16	9	24	5	6	35
Sport achievements	6	4	9	9	6	3
Ustaše[a]	5	5	8	3	2	9
None of the above	4	3	6	0	8	4
Culture	3	3	7	3	3	1
Croatian products	3	2	4	3	1	3
Don't know	3	1	5	2	3	5
European Union	1	2	1	1	2	0
Partisans	1	1	1	0	1	1

Source: Adopted from Skoko (2010)
[a]Fascist collaborators in Croatia during WWII

from Serbia, the associations connected to the war were right next to the positive association to sea and tourism (35 per cent of respondents).

Additional analyses showed that there was no statistically significant difference between respondents from Bosnia and Herzegovina, Montenegro, Macedonia, Slovenia and Serbia with regard to what were their most frequent associations to Croatia. Therefore, it could be concluded that in a relatively short period of time, Croatia was able to build its own distinctive and desirable image in the region and with positive associations of sea and tourism to completely overshadow associations on the effects and consequences of the war.

Similar results were obtained from the survey conducted with the goal of gaining deeper insights into the image of Croatia as a tourism destination in six European countries among population who has never travelled to Croatia but made at least one international trip over the last 5 years[2]. The research was conducted in 2011 by the Institute for Tourism, Zagreb, on the sample of 2,574 respondents, whereby 502 respondents were from Germany, 508 from the UK, 250 from Sweden, 297 from Denmark, 503 from Poland and 514 from Spain.

The following are the internal data of the Institute for Tourism which show that, in those six countries, the dominant image of Croatia was mostly formed through the activities related to the promotion of Croatian tourism (Table 5.2). Respondents perceive Croatia as a coastal country, a country with green and unspoiled nature and a tourism country. At the same time, there are also organic attributes of the image arising from the war and social and political relations from the past, particularly common among older respondents, which lead to the conclusion that this is a case of a previously formed image.

As in the case of the survey in former Yugoslav countries (Skoko, 2010), the findings of this research suggest that Croatia was able to build a positive image thanks to the continuous tourism promotion and positive association with the sea, natural beauty and cultural sites, which are the result of investment in tourism promotion and strengthening of Croatian tourism.

Almost similar results were obtained during the last public opinion study about image of Croatia in the GCC countries. Study was conducted in 2013 in Qatar and the United Arab Emirates where the GCC citizens were questioned about their trip characteristics and the image of Croatia (Michael, Miličević & Krešić, 2014). The study was conducted on a sample of 279 respondents. The majority of respondents were Emirati (63 per

Table 5.2 First associations with Croatia in six European countries (%)[a]

Elements	Total	Germany	UK	Sweden	Denmark	Poland	Spain
Beautiful coastline, sea, islands	28	39	20	34	7	47	13
Beaches	19	23	10	17	10	27	22
Beautiful nature/ landscape, green landscape, mountains and forests, preserved environment	17	15	18	14	15	23	14
Tourist country, new tourist country, country for visiting	16	18	11	11	18	20	16
Warm, sun	15	15	7	24	16	29	3
War	14	12	21	10	30	5	13
History and culture, historic city centers	10	5	12	8	9	9	16

Source: Adopted from Institute for Tourism (2011)
Note: The sample of respondents who reported spontaneous reactions at the mention of Croatia
[a]Possibility of multiple responses

cent) and Qatari (10 per cent). The others (27 per cent) were other GCC citizens and citizens from different countries residing in Qatar and the United Arab Emirates at that time.

Even though Croatia was not much promoted in the Arab countries, few associations connected with Croatia were mostly related to its beautiful nature, landscapes, sea, beaches and islands (Table 5.3). Since Croatia has not developed a recognizable national brand, high on the list were associations with other countries like Russia, Yugoslavia, Bosnia and Herzegovina and Albania or even with entire continents like Africa or Europe.

From the findings of this research, it is evident that Croatia has built its image as a beautiful tourism destination, but it is also recognized by some other elements such as its national football team, history and culture and, unfortunately, by poverty and the war. The lack of branding activities on national level results in many unknown facts about Croatia, such as that Croatia is home country and birth place of Nikola Tesla, the country where the tie, as the most popular male accessory, was invented, the country where ballpoint pen was invented and so on. It is also less known fact

Table 5.3 First associations with Croatia among respondents from the GCC countries (%)

Elements	Total GCC
Beautiful nature/landscape	9
Sea, beaches, islands	8
Association on countries other than Croatia	8
Europe	8
Football team	5
History, culture and architecture	3
Poor, not safe	3
War	1
Note: multiple responses	

Source: Adopted from Michael et al. (2014)

in the international community that Croatia is a country rich in cultural and historical heritage with UNESCO-protected areas and non-material heritage. Croatia is a country rich in water and the country with 1244 islands. Besides the football players, Croatia has world top handball players, skiers, tennis players and water polo players. Finally, it can be concluded that Croatia is much more than attractive tourism destination, but unfortunately, as shown by the aforementioned studies, this has not been fully recognized by the international community mostly because of the absence of a clearly defined national umbrella brand.

CONCLUSION

Croatia is politically and, to a certain extent, economically stable country, currently claimed to be a potential leader of regional political stability[3], and it is the second country from the former Yugoslavia, after Slovenia, who joined the EU. Still, Croatia is underutilizing the power of its image which is something that developed western countries have been using for decades as a powerful tool for achieving political, economic and other interests.

It can be argued that Croatia has done a lot in the last two decades on its international positioning, because it has transformed its image from a completely unknown country to one of the most attractive tourist destinations in Europe. In doing so Croatia has heavily used its natural attributes in order to dissociate itself from the rest of its surrounding, especially from the countries of the former Yugoslavia. However, since Croatia did not simultaneously work on or manage other attributes of its identity, its current image in the world is predominantly determined by natural beauties, sea or, in other words, by tourism promotion. This is the reason why Croatia is, besides for its tourism offer, still a relatively unknown country in the world and some of its competitive advantages are fairly unknown and underutilized even in regional context. This is the main conclusion derived from the results of three surveys concerning the national image of Croatia in the international community presented in this paper. The research results suggest that Croatian national brand is still not sufficiently recognizable in the international community. Elements that are sufficiently recognizable are mostly elements promoted by tourism promotion activities.

In order to become more recognizable in the international community, Croatia must define its own brand and reach consensus about its own identity and vision of the future. In order to place its products on the foreign markets, to attract foreign investments and to gain respect in international relations, Croatia will have to build a strong and distinctive umbrella brand. In this umbrella brand, Croatian natural beauties, Adriatic Sea and tourism offer will certainly play an important role, but Croatia must make efforts to show to the rest of the world its other attributes or to show that it is not just a destination for pleasure but also a country of hard working people, creativity, science and technology and so on. In doing so, Croatia will have to use a more systematic and coordinated approach for building its identity and image, and it will have to combine individual efforts carried out by different government institutions, among which the Croatian Tourist Board will remain one of the most influential, but hopefully not the only one, architects of Croatian identity in the international community.

NOTES

1. UNESCO—the United Nations Educational, Scientific and Cultural Organization is a specialized agency of the United Nations.
2. Countries covered with the survey of the image of Croatia as a tourist destination were Germany, Great Britain, Sweden, Denmark, Poland and Spain.
3. US Secretary of State Hillary Clinton, during her visit to Zagreb on 31 October 2012, referred to Croatia as the 'anchor' of the region, a prosperous country which can be an example to others, and as having a terrific geographic location and an educated workforce.

REFERENCES

Anholt, S. (2007). *Competitive identity*. London: Palgrave Macmillan.
Clancy, M. (2011). Re-presenting Ireland: tourism, branding and national identity in Ireland. *Journal of International Relations and Development, 14*(3), 281–308.
Croatian Tourist Board. (2016). Islands. http://croatia.hr. Date Accessed 23 May 2016.
EUROSTAT. (2016). Water statistics, http://ec.europa.eu. Date accessed 23 May 2016.
Hall, D. (2002). Brand development, tourism and national identity: The re-imaging of former Yugoslavia. *Brand Management, 9*(4-5), 323–334.
Hall, D. (2004). Branding and national identity: the case of Central and Eastern Europe. In N. Morgan, A. Pritchard, & R. Pride (Eds.), *Destination branding* (pp. 87–105). Oxford: Elsevier.
Huang, W. J., & Santos, C. A. (2001). Tourism and national Identity in the United States. In E. Frew & L. White (Eds.), *Tourism and national identities: An international perspective* (pp. 13–25). New York: Routledge.
Institute for Tourism. (2011). *A survey on Croatian tourism image in six European Countries. (Unpublished report)*. Zagreb: Institute for Tourism.
Kotler, P., Haider, D. H., & Rein, I. (1993). *Marketing places: Attracting investment, industry, and tourism to cities, states, and nations*. New York: The Free Press.
Magzan, M., & Miličević, K. (2012). Integrirane marketinške komunikacije kao strategija za održavanje tržišne dominacije i rast profitabilnog poslovanja [Integrated marketing communications as a basis for the market dominance and growth]. In M. Martinović (Ed.), *Marketing u Hrvatskoj—55 poslovnih slučajeva [Marketing in Croatia—55 case studies]* (pp. 209–222). Zagreb: MATE d.o.o.
Michael, I., Miličević, K. & Krešić, D. (2014). *Preparing for tomorrow: Analyzing tourism demand from GCC countries to Croatia*. International conference on tourism milestones, unpublished paper, Sharjah, UAE.
Miličević, K., Skoko, B. & Krešić, D. (2012.). *The Power of Tourism in creating a national brand: The case of croatia*. Proceedings of the Destination Branding & Marketing IV, (pp. 236-247), Cardiff.
Ministry of Tourism. (2013). Croatian tourism development strategy to 2020. Official Gazette of the Republic of Croatia 55/2013. http://narodne-novine.nn.hr/clanci/sluzbeni/2013_05_55_1119.html. Date accessed 20 Nov 2014.
Miroslav Krleža Institute of Lexicography. (2016). Adriatic Sea and islands, http://croatia.eu. Date accessed 23 May 2016.
Morgan, N. J., & Pritchard, A. (2005). Promoting Niche Tourism Destination Brands. *Journal of Promotion Management, 12*(1), 17–33.

Sanader, I. (2000). *Hrvatska u međunarodnim odnosima [Croatia in international relations]*. Zagreb: Golden marketing.

Skoko, B. (2004). *Hrvatska—identitet, image, promocija [Croatia—identity, image and promotion]*. Zagreb: Školska knjiga.

Skoko, B. (2010). *Hrvatska i susjedi—kako Hrvatsku doživljavaju u Bosni i Hercegovini, Crnoj Gori, Makedoniji, Sloveniji i Srbiji [Croatia and Its Neighbors—How is Croatia Perceived in Bosnia and Herzegovina, Montenegro, Macedonia, Slovenia and Serbia]*. Zagreb: AMG.

Skoko, B., & Kovačić, V. (2009). Koncept meke moći država i njegova primjena na Republiku Hrvatsku [The Concept of Soft Power, the State and its Application in the Republic of Croatia]. *Polemos, 23*(12-1), 29–49.

UNESCO. (2016). About World Heritage—Croatia, http://whc.unesco.org. Date accessed 23 May 2016.

Vukadinović, R. (2000). Hrvatska vanjska politika—novo vrijeme i nove zadaće [Croatian Foreign Policy—New Time and New Tasks]. *International studies, 1*, 1–2.

State Institute for Nature Protection. (2016). Protected areas in Croatia—national categories, http://www.dzzp.hr. Date accessed 23 May 2016.

CHAPTER 6

Tourism Destination and DMO Transformation

Sanda Čorak and Snježana Boranić Živoder

Introduction

Tourism destinations are, today, operating in a very complex environment. To stay competitive they have to continuously adapt to rapidly changing market trends, by continuously improving their general and tourism infrastructure, introducing new products and attractions and communicating this effectively with their target markets. At the same time, the internal environment is also changing. The number of stakeholders in the process of tourism development is increasing, and stakeholder management is becoming more complex and time-consuming. The pressure for new products and attractions brings to the market those stakeholders, such as in culture and nature protection, with little experience in tourism. Tourism entrepreneurs pressure for continuous growth, while local communities need to devise the strategies to adjust and respond to these pressures. All this is happening in the period of economic uncertainties, dwindling of public funding and public sector downsizing. In spite of these challenges, many destinations have found it hard to adapt their destination management organizations, traditionally focused on destination

S. Čorak (✉) • S.B. Živoder
Institute for Tourism, Zagreb, Croatia

© The Author(s) 2017   99
L. Dwyer et al. (eds.), *Evolution of Destination Planning and Strategy*, DOI 10.1007/978-3-319-42246-6_6

marketing and promotion, to these new circumstances and Croatia is not an exception. The question of organizing destination management is gaining prominence, and there are various propositions of how to reorganize the system, traditionally set up to market and promote destination.

Croatia has a system of destination management organizations set up almost three decades ago consisting of national, regional and local tourism organizations. They are formally associations of enterprises in tourism and services directly benefiting from tourism, but their membership is mandatory and defined by a national regulation. Their funding is secured by membership fees and tourist bed tax, but in most cases it is insufficient for meeting a long list of tasks related to infrastructure and product development, fostering local resident support for tourism development and marketing. In recent years the system has been criticized for inefficiency and there are calls for reform. However, although those critical of the system are prominent in public discourse and professional circles, their arguments are more ideological than evidence-based. Taking the stance that reforming the system through a top-down approach is too risky without any real evidence, this paper presents the results of research on main issues and challenges faced by the Croatian destination management organizations from the standpoint of their managers and the local and municipal governments. It starts with brief overview of the key themes discussed in the destination management in order to provide a sound contextual framework. It then outlines the trajectory of tourism development and system of tourism organizations in Croatia and evaluation of their effectiveness. It concludes by identifying the main advantages and disadvantages of the current system in a fast-changing social environment and illustrates the constraints and challenges common to many destinations as they strive to improve their destination performance while ensuring sustainable development.

THE ROLE OF DESTINATION MANAGEMENT AND DESTINATION MANAGEMENT ORGANIZATIONS (DMOs) IN TOURISM DEVELOPMENT

The term 'destination management' has established itself in academic and professional circles in recent decades. Many authors have dealt with this topic by studying different aspects, such as the issues of cooperation between stakeholders and the complexity of the destination marketing

(Buhalis, 2000), the role of destination management companies (Schaumann, 2004), challenges of destination management in modern society (Gretzel, Fesenmaier, Formica, & Oleary, 2006), destination management and competitiveness (Sainaghi, 2006) and the like. As a consequence, the term 'destination management' is differently defined (Jafari, 2000; Lengyel, 2007; Magaš, 2008; Čorak, 2008; Bartoluci, 2008). One of the most commonly used is a definition proposed by the UNWTO (2007) according to which the destination management is coordinated management of all aspects that make a destination.

Unlike a decade or two ago, when the destination management was reduced to destination marketing or, even more narrowly, destination promotion, destination management today is far more complex. This complexity is driven by an acute need to ensure sustainable destination development through optimal use of resources and welfare of the local community and achieve competitiveness in a fast-changing social and economic climate. The challenges posed by the contemporary social changes and need for sustainability are reflected in the need to track changes and react to these changes accordingly. Thus, instead of being solely responsible for attracting tourists—what was the focus of the destination tourism activities in the past—they now have to 'deliver' destination experience to tourists promised by marketing activities and to reach a level of satisfaction that will result in their loyalty and a positive 'word-of-mouth' (Laesser & Baritelli, 2013).

Conscious of the role and needs of an efficient destination management that would lead to sustainable development and the achievement of a desired vision, destinations worldwide have established organizations that are commonly referred to as destination management organizations (DMOs) and/or destination management and marketing organizations (DMMOs). In general, DMOs evolved from tourism organizations that have a long history, dating back to more than a hundred years ago. The first such organizations of a local/regional character were founded in the nineteenth century, whereas the first national organizations were set up in the early twentieth century (Pike, 2004). Since then, their roles and activities have changed, depending on the numerous social and economic trends, but mostly due to the development of tourism as a major economic activity in many countries over the past several decades. Thus, those early tourism organizations evolved into DMOs or DMMOs, depending on the level of tourism development and the role of the whole system of tourism organizations in a country.

This transition of tourism organizations to DMOs and their subsequent functions, reflecting broadly a shift from marketing to destination management role, is also noticeable in the academic literature. Two decades ago Gartell (1994), for example, argued that DMOs are marketing organizations that initiate activities in a destination. Subsequently, authors such as Crouch and Ritchie (1999) and Ritchie and Crouch (2003) viewed these organizations as management organizations (including marketing) in charge of ensuring leadership and coordination for a destinations as well as successfully managing the complexity of the tourism system. Still more recently Lally, O'Donovan and Quinlan (2015) added a new perspective by stating that DMOs are facilitators of collaboration among stakeholders in a tourism destination.

Currently, DMOs are responsible for many functions. The UNWTO sees tourism destination as a factory and defines the role of DMOs from an economic perspective, albeit recognizing the key differences between a factory and destination: 'DMO is in charge of tourism destination 'factory' and is responsible for achieving an excellent return on investment, market growth, quality product, a brand of distinction and benefits to all 'stakeholders. Yet, the DMO does not own the factory, neither does it employ the people working in it, nor does it have control over its processes' (UNWTO, 2007, p. 12). Scholars have different views as to what should be the role(s) of DMO. For example, Gartell (1994), although arguing that the DMO is a marketing organization that run 'business' and destination, identified a number of basic areas of activity still in the foci of DMO activities today—coordination, leadership, promotion of development, provision of services for visitors and cooperation with destination actors. Crouch and Ritchie (1999) and Ritchie and Crouch (2003) take a broader view of DMOs as organizations established with an aim to provide leadership and coordination and to manage complex tourism system, including marketing. Furthermore, Presenza, Sheehan and Ritchie (2005) pointed out that DMOs have become more prominent as 'destination developers' acting as catalysts and facilitators for the realization of tourism development. DMOs' trajectory from marketing to management organizations is also well documented by Pike and Page (2014) through a narrative analysis of the first 40 years of destination marketing literature with the focus on the core marketing role of DMOs. They also highlight the need to monitor the way DMOs are increasingly expected to be engaged in and undertake several destination management functions and take on a leadership role.

DMOs continue to be an important topic within the destination management literature (Pechlaner, Volgger, & Herntrei, 2012; Volgger & Pechlaner, 2014; Pike & Page, 2014), in particular in relation to their impact and performance measurement in the context of dynamic social and economic challenges. Pechlaner et al. (2012), in addressing the issue of corporate governance of DMOs, found that DMOs may have a positive effect on destination governance. Volgger and Pechlaner (2014) see the main role of DMOs as initiators and mediators by introducing a flexible interface management system and promoting self-responsibility, self-organization and self-regulations of destination networks. In their study of the relationship between destination success and success of DMO in several Alpine regions, they find that management of DMOs is related to effective destination governance and to success of tourism destinations. Specifically, DMOs are evaluated according to professionalism, networking capability, acceptance within the destination, power and influence within destination, resource endowment and transparency in dealing with its members.

What makes a successful DMO model today is still undefined. Many agree that the most effective DMO should deliver a productive marketing plan for the tourism industry, as well as welfare to community residents by enhancing the profit potential of tourism and importance of sustainability (Pike & Page, 2014; Volgger & Pechlaner, 2014; Borzyszkowski, 2014; Pechlaner et al., 2012; Bornhost, Ritchie, & Sheehan, 2010; Gretzel et al., 2006; Presenza et al., 2005). Murdaugh (2012) identifies three groups of DMO success criteria: performance success, best practices for marketing and management and community leadership. The first relates to the key mission, i.e., the creation of economic impact, the second relates to ensuring the best 'platform' for effective management (planning, research, partnerships and the like), while the third involves activities related to the recognition of these organizations as the key to effective management and tourism development.

EVOLUTION OF DMOs IN CROATIA

Croatia, as a Mediterranean country, is a destination with a long tourism tradition. It started to develop its tourism at the end of the nineteenth century, although the most intensive tourism development took place after the World War II, reflecting the rise of mass tourism. A steady growth of tourism demand from 6.7 million tourist overnights in 1960 (Federal

Bureau of Statistics, 1964) to 45.8 million in 1990 (Croatian Bureau of Statistics, 1992) is a reflection of the attractiveness of Croatia as a summer holiday destination. This popularity was due to the exploitation of beautiful indented coastline and pristine natural environment as the core components of its tourism product that was in high demand by the mass tourism market of the second half of the twentieth century.

However, the growth in tourist arrivals and overnights started to slow down during the 1980s, as Croatia failed to keep up with the huge influx of tourists and qualitative shifts in tourist preferences. Growing competition internationally and decaying resorts and poor infrastructure were some of the factors responsible for a weakening of demand. Finally, with the Homeland War tourism come to a halt from 1990 to 1994/1995. Croatia, now as an independent, sovereign state, has been trying to gain back the tourism flows that it had achieved at the end of the 1980s (Ateljević & Čorak, 2006).

In the process of rebuilding tourism, Croatia has tried to reposition itself by improving its core sun and sea summer tourism and introducing competitive new special interest products such as nautical tourism, cultural tourism, sport and adventure tourism, city tourism, MICE, health tourism, rural tourism and similar (Ministry of Tourism, 2013). This strategy was partly successful, as nowadays a tracking of tourist motivation, activities, satisfaction and expenditure through a continuous national visitor survey shows steady increase in tourist satisfaction with summer tourism, while dissatisfied with shopping opportunities, variety of entertainment and cultural opportunities, quality of local transport (Marušić, Čorak, & Sever, 2015). There are other issues burdening Croatia's tourism product quality. The sense of place of picturesque stone towns and villages is partially lost due to the overbuilding of standardized apartment blocks. Despite the progress made over the last decade, the perception of Croatia as a cheap mass market destination still exists in some of European tourism generating markets (Ateljević & Čorak, 2006).

Many of these problems can be attributed to destination planning and management. In terms of planning, the reintroduction of Croatia as a tourism destination internationally, as an independent state, required a strong marketing effort. The first strategic document *Tourism Master Plan for Croatia* drawn in 1993 (Official Gazette of the Republic of Croatia, 1993) identified the three basic attributes of positioning—rest and relaxation close to home in an ecologically preserved environment at favorable prices. However, with a country still in turmoil and faced with a total lack of any tourism planning at a destination level, the Ministry of Tourism made a decision to initiate development of a strategic marketing plans for each of the 20 counties of Croatia. These plans were primarily drafted for local authorities, and the system of tourism organizations was required to implement them in cooperation with the private sector.

Croatia has a hierarchically organized system of tourism organizations set up immediately after its independence. Historically, these organizations go back to the very beginning of tourism in the mid of the nineteenth century, while the current system is a continuation of tourism associations established in the former Yugoslavia (Vukonić, 2005). At the beginnings of tourism development in Croatia (second half of the nineteenth century), tourism organizations undoubtedly contributed to tourism development by endeavoring to preserve and promote cultural heritage, revitalize settlements and public spaces and organize social life. They took care of the overall revitalization and enhancement of public and private spaces, which was even then recognized as one of the factors of attractiveness of an area (Boranić, Čorak, & Kranjčević, 2014). Today, the tourism organization network in Croatia, as in many other countries, consists of the national tourism board, as well as county and local tourism boards. In total there are around 330 registered tourism boards. Set up as non-profit organizations, they have a wide range of duties and responsibilities related to destination marketing, developing products and infrastructure improvement as well as improvement of quality of life in a destination. They are regulated by the *Act on Tourism Boards and the Promotion of Croatian Tourism* (Official Gazette of the Republic of Croatia, 2008). That Act defines as many as 26 specific tasks, which can be grouped as: (1) promotional activities and provision of information; (2) tourism product development and improvement of conditions for tourism; (3) planning and promotion of tourism development; (4) coordination with tourism development stakeholders, market research, internal marketing and education and raising the local residents' awareness of the possibilities of tourism development; (5) management of the public tourism infrastructure assigned by the community or county government. The umbrella organization—the Croatian Tourist Board—has 16 regulatory tasks, mostly related to promoting tourism at home and abroad, with a number of activities forming the platform for achieving this basic task.

The main source of funding of Croatia's tourism boards is the tourist tax and membership fee, which amount is defined by a national regulation. In general, both the amount of tourist tax paid per person/night and the annual membership fees vary, the former by the intensity of destination development and the latter by the proportion of the company's income derived from tourist expenditure. This income is distributed between local, county and national tourism boards in the proportion 65:10:25. While such funding arrangements ensure steady income for tourism boards and facilitate financial planning in advance, there is inherited tension in the system. First, they are formally an association of private tourism stakeholders, but poorly accountable to them as their membership is compulsory and tourism boards' management is not under pressure to work cooperatively and/or work in their mutual best interest. Second, they are set up by local government, but every aspect of their business operation, from the president, structure of the advisory and management boards, formal qualification of their CEOs, right through allocation of funds, is defined by the Act. Third, the funding arrangements favor well-developed destinations with a larger proportion of accommodation in hotels in resorts that, usually, collect and transfer all the tourist tax collected in contrast to those where private accommodation prevails or with a lower density of tourism activity. As regions with the lower tourism activity are also often economically depressed, the possibility for subsidizing the tourism boards from local municipalities is also small.

These problems reflect on the actual functioning of the tourism boards. Increasingly, tourism professionals, community leaders and academics articulate many issues that such system of tourism managements is creating, such as that the system is too big and therefore not efficient enough, there is no clear division of responsibilities between different levels and not enough coordination among levels, there are too many tasks and finally the system is under the influence of local politics. Expected reform, driven by the Ministry of Tourism in charge of the *Act on Tourism Boards and the Promotion of Croatian Tourism*, is supposed to ensure that the system benefits from pooling human and financial resources through formation of regional and reduction of municipal and county tourism boards. Those tourism boards that are unable to generate sufficient income from membership fees and tourist tax are to be transformed into tourist information centers. In terms of task, it is planned that the Croatian Tourist Board (CTB) will primarily be a tourism marketing organization in charge of promotional activities. Research and development is to be transferred to regional destination management organizations that can financially support such activities and in that way improve the quality of regional tourism products (Horwath HTL Zagreb, 2013).

EFFICIENCY OF THE DMO SYSTEM IN CROATIA

While there is a drive to restructure the system of destination management, the proposed changes discussed above are mostly of organizational nature, and the Ministry's proposition has sparked a heated debate on the most optimal structure of DMOs. Some argue that the system, as is, does not need radical reform but rather some fine-tuning. The proponents of the existing system argue that the system is well organized and smoothly functioning, as evidenced by the increase in tourist arrivals and overnights, increase in tourism expenditures, spread of demand to shoulder season, coupled with continuous improvement of tourist satisfaction and ever-increasing mention of Croatian destinations in the international media. Moreover, it is argued that the proposed changes only relate to the formal organization of tourism boards, rather than tackling the key issues and challenges faced by practitioners on the ground. The critics, supporting radical reorganization of the system, argue that systemic inefficiency is evidenced in the uneven geographical development of tourism making many tourism boards in low-tourism intensity areas redundant, contributing to inefficient use of resources for tourism marketing as each micro-destination is 'pedaling its own boat', insufficient influence in decisions relating to tourism development (i.e., building permits, zoning) and inability to coordinate destination stakeholders. While both sides of the arguments have some merits, a decision to reorganize the system of tourism organizations is largely based on assumptions, impressions or particular interests instead of a sound judgment based on research evidence.

Thus, when drafting the *Croatian Tourism Development Strategy to 2020* (Ministry of Tourism, 2013), the Institute for Tourism conducted a public sector opinion survey on tourism development and management and how it should be improved, with the main aim to flesh out the key issues and challenges faced in the process of managing tourism development. In particular, the survey goals were (1) to determine the attitudes of the public sector toward tourism development, (2) to determine the level of knowledge and skills of the public sector for the development of tourism and (3) to identify possible 'bottlenecks' that the public sector faces in the development of tourism. The survey participants included local government units (municipalities and cities) and tourism boards (system of national, counties, cities and local tourism organizations). The question-

Table 6.1   Objectives of tourist development policy in the city/municipality (%)

Objectives[a]	Tourism boards	Local government
Sustainable tourism development	41.1	31.2
Improvement of tourist image	39.7	35.3
The development/improvement of products	39.0	19.3
The increase in revenues from tourism	30.1	27.0
Extending the season	27.4	12.5
Increasing the number of tourist arrivals	26.0	21.1
Investment attraction	23.3	35.3
Job creation	18.5	43.6
Improving the quality of life of residents	17.8	28.8
Improving the quality of services	15.1	6.5
Year-round performance	9.6	10.1
Stopping of negative demographic trends	6.8	22.0
Something else	.	1.8

[a]Multiple response

naires were sent by mail to 568 local government units and 330 tourism boards with 63 per cent and 50 per cent response rate, respectively.

According to the survey results (Table 6.1), tourism boards and local governments agree that one of the main tasks of tourism development is 'improvement of tourist image' (40 and 35 per cent, respectively). However, tourism boards give greater importance to 'sustainable development' (41 per cent) and 'improvement of products' (39 per cent), while for local government 'job creation' (44 per cent) and 'investment attraction' (35 per cent) are important objectives. For tourism boards 'the increase in revenues from tourism' and 'extending the season' were also very important goals, while 'improving the quality of life of residents' is an important goal for the local government, confirming the expected differences in attitudes of tourism boards directors and local government according to their business missions. As expected, tourism boards are more focused on the specific tourism industry goals, while local governments are more concerned with the development goals such as attracting investments and creating jobs.

Tourism management and development is, in most cases, an ad hoc process, as many municipalities do not have a development plan, let alone a tourism development plan. Furthermore, those that have a plan struggle with its implementation (Table 6.2 and 6.3).

Therefore, a less than optimal level of tourism development in Croatia could be attributed partly to planning and partly to implementation of

Table 6.2 City/municipality development plans (%)

	Tourism boards	Local government
Economic development plan for city/municipality	n/a	58.6
Tourism development is an integral part of your plan (for those who have a plan for economic development)	n/a	75.2
Tourism development plan (master plan/strategic plan)	36.1	20.5
Tourism marketing plan	18.2	n/a

Table 6.3 Implementation of programs and projects defined by planning documents (%)

Implementation of programs and projects	Tourism boards	Local government
Basically the way it is recommended	23.4	13.6
We follow the recommendations of the plan, but at a slower pace than the recommended	48.9	51.5
The plan is generally not carried out because we do not have the necessary financial resources	17.0	21.2
The plan is generally not carried out because it is not operational	6.4	3.0
The plan is generally not carried out because we do not have the necessary human resources	0.0	4.5
Something else	4.3	6.1
TOTAL	100.0	100.0

plans. Although each of 20 Croatian counties and around 250 municipalities and cities have a tourism board, only about 36 per cent of municipalities or cities have tourism development plan. Given that marketing is, traditionally, at the core of their operations, surprisingly only about 18 per cent of municipalities have a marketing plan. Furthermore, only about 50 per cent of the programs and projects envisaged in the planning documents at the county level, and 23 per cent at the level of municipalities was carried out mainly as recommended by the plan. About half of the projects followed the recommendations but at a slower pace. A small number of tourism boards fails to implement the plan due to the lack of allocated funds (17 per cent). Since a majority of the municipality/city tourism boards had not adopted a development plan which would 'facilitate' their function in terms of priorities and implementation of various projects that would lead to the attainment of defined development goals and vision of the tourist destination, the lack of a tourism development and/or marketing plan was the most obvious constraint for tourism development.

According to the opinions of the tourism boards' directors (Table 6.4), these constraints were mostly related to lack of funding (72 per cent). Many countries face similar problems. As Laesser and Baritelli (2013) pointed out, 'financial resources for destination marketing are scarce, so it is advisable to lower the high dependence on public funding by identifying business rationales and revenue mechanism that are financially sustainable by themselves'. The results of the second Biennial Forum on Advances in Destination Management held in St. Gallen (Reinhold, Laesser, & Beritelli, 2015) highlighted the problem of budget cutting in the public sector and hence the need to restructure the tourism organization network with regard to financing and the scope of activities. It was concluded that the existing forms of DMOs and their function have lost legitimacy and that it is therefore necessary to 'educate real destination managers

Table 6.4 Possible constraints of tourism development (%)

Possible constraints[a]	Tourism boards	Local government
Funding	71.9	49.3
The tourist offer (accommodation, catering, etc.)	52.1	64.7
Bureaucracy	43.2	27.3
The investment environment	37.7	48.1
Property relations	32.9	40.1
Transport infrastructure	30.1	25.5
Development vision	30.1	24.3
Business/entrepreneurial optimism	30.1	37.1
The workforce/human resource	29.5	20.2
Utility infrastructure	28.1	31.2
Destination management/strategic partnerships	26.0	19.6
The legal framework	25.3	16.6
Spatial planning/management area	24.7	13.7
Education of staff	21.2	28.8
'Apartmanization'	19.9	6.5
Marketing/promotion	18.5	35.0
Tourist attractions	15.1	22.3
Construction without permits ('wild' construction)	10.3	6.2
Innovations	6.8	11.0
Environmental preservation/sustainability	6.2	4.2
Another restriction	3.8	2.1

according to the new needs or substitute DMOs with consultants and local project managers'.

Additionally, human resources, quality of tourism offer and transport infrastructure were also among the most distinct limitations. Tourism boards noted bureaucracy and local government investment environment, entrepreneurial optimism and surprisingly marketing/promotion as among the many constraints of tourism development. It seems that local government notes the failures of tourism boards' tasks and *vice versa*.

Given the large number of different tasks defined by the aforementioned *Act on Tourism boards and the Promotion of Croatian Tourism*, work in tourism boards requires different specialized knowledge and skills. Continuing and long-life learning is extremely important in order to be able to monitor trends in the environment and carry out promotional, research and other activities that would lead to raising the quality of all aspects of destination product and achieving the desired level of tourism development. As the activities of the tourism boards in the last 20 years have mainly focused on providing information, tourism promotion and keeping records on tourist arrivals, the survey has shown (Table 6.5) that tourism board employees were educated mostly for listed tasks. On the other hand, for some of the set tasks, the degree of competency in a large number of tourist organizations is inadequate. This is most obvious with skills and knowledge needed to conduct research, to monitor destination competitiveness and for tourist infrastructure management.

However, the competence of human resources in tourism today is extremely important. The first three aspects—marketing, management and governance—'contribute to a better understanding of structures and processes that allow more effective coordination, planning and marketing of the tourism destination' (Pechlaner, Kozak, & Volgger, 2013). Due to the particularly turbulent economic and political changes in recent times, that is also the case in Croatia, where an increasing emphasis has been put on the human factor. Topics such as power and influence, motivation and communication, as well as ethical consideration, lie at the heart of the agenda (Pechlaner et al., 2013). As stressed by Pechlaner et al. (2013, p. 2), 'network leadership among destination actors implies the particular challenges of leading, organizing and communicating with the individual stakeholders and the destination network as a whole'. Blichfeldt, Hird and Kvistgaard (2014, p. 80) stated that 'DMOs depend heavily on relationships and interactions with key internal stakeholders and also need to facilitate strong relationships between such stakeholder and thus,

Table 6.5   Skills and competences of employees in tourism boards (%)

Skills and competences for specific activities/tasks[a]	Tourism boards			
	Croatia—total	Northern Adriatic	Southern Adriatic	Continental Croatia
Destination promotion (including PR, e-marketing, advertising, press)	54.2	60.5	46.7	55.6
Provision of information	89.6	90.9	89.1	88.9
Preparation of tourism development/management plans	36.6	46.5	24.4	38.9
Gathering data on the tourism offer	86.1	93.2	82.6	83.3
Organizing manifestations	84.7	84.1	78.3	90.7
Campaigns for the preservation of the tourism destinations and environment	54.9	59.1	47.8	57.4
Conducting research	18.1	25.0	10.9	18.5
Monitoring destination competitiveness	19.6	31.8	13.0	15.1
Record-keeping of tourist stays (check-ins, check-outs, inspection service, etc.)	90.3	95.5	91.3	85.2
Educating residents (significance and effects of tourism, etc.)	39.2	45.5	34.8	37.7
Coordinating tourism development stakeholders of the destination	42.6	56.8	28.9	42.3
Development of destination products	40.6	50.0	28.3	43.4
Management of public tourism infrastructure	21.3	18.6	17.8	26.4

[a]The share of respondents whose answer was 1 (yes) on the scale from 1 (yes), 2 (to some extent) to 3 (no)

the key responsibilities of such DMOs do not relate to management, but to leadership'.

Managing tourism development in the majority of tourism destinations in Croatia has become especially that there is no major tourism leader to direct and coordinate all of the stakeholders and their activities and interests within destinations. Due to the previously mentioned many different tasks in the field of destination marketing and management, and given the current state of skills of human resources, the complete and successful performance of their tasks is very hard to achieve. This is consistent with some previous studies. Socher (2000) stated that due to a fast-changing environment, a lack of managerial authority and the challenges presented

Table 6.6   Cooperation in the field of tourism development (%)

Good cooperation with[a]	Tourism boards	Local government
City/municipal administration/departments	85.4	n/a
Other tourist communities in our county	77.8	n/a
Private sector	69.9	46.2
Croatian Tourist Board (main office)	66.2	n/a
Relevant associations and professional associations	58.0	43.9
Inspection services	52.4	27.3
Other tourist offices outside county	49.3	n/a
County administration	45.1	42.9
Government/public companies and institutions (electricity, water, roads, museums, etc.)	41.7	n/a
Ministry of tourism	34.3	29.0
Other relevant ministries	18.9	21.3
Government bodies	n/a	23.7
Tourism board	n/a	59.2

The share of respondents that evaluated cooperation aspects by marks '4' or '5' on a scale from 1 (very poor) to 5 (very good)

by complex power structures in many destinations, DMOs have found it increasingly difficult to fulfill their assigned tasks.

Under such circumstances of inadequate collaboration and often mutual exclusion of interests of key destination stakeholders, no significant level or intensity of association or partnership has occurred, either in public-private, public-public or public-private collaboration. According to the survey results (Table 6.6), evaluation of collaboration is perceived differently; the tourist board network rated their collaboration with the city administration as very good (85 per cent), while 60 per cent of the surveyed mayors (whose function also includes chairing the Tourism Council) rated this collaboration as very good. Both groups of respondents rated their collaboration with the private sector somewhat lower, especially in the case of the city administration (46 per cent stated that their collaboration is very good compared to some 70 per cent of respondents from the tourist board network). This lack of cooperation obstructs the creation of a comprehensive destination value chain, and thus the creation of the key prerequisites for the development of an entire spectrum of tourist experiences. This ultimately has an adverse impact on the market competitiveness of the integrated tourist products in numerous destinations in Croatia.

IMPLICATIONS AND CONCLUSIONS

The main goal of this chapter was to illustrate the development of destination management and destination management organizations in Croatia identifying their advantages and disadvantages and the need of their transformation according to fast changes in tourism industry, as well as in the environment.

According to survey results and the Institute for Tourism's vast experience, the system of tourism boards in Croatia is well organized and smoothly functioning, as evidenced by increases of tourist arrivals, overnights, tourists' expenditures and satisfaction. Still, systemic inefficiency is reflected in the uneven geographical development of tourism, insufficient use of resources in tourism marketing, political influence at local levels in decisions relating to tourism development and inability to coordinate destination stakeholders' activities.

The challenges mentioned by Gretzel et al. (2006), that DMOs face many problems, adaption to technological changes, management expectations, changing of focus from marketing to destination management, managing new level of competition, recognition of creative partnership as a new lifestyle and finding a new way to achieve success, could apply still today. The need for constant innovation in order to survive in an increasingly competitive market is present but requiring both human and financial resources, which are missing in the case of Croatia, as research has clearly shown. Yuan, Gretzel and Fesenmaier (2003) also argue that financial and human resources are essential to continued innovation by DMO and innovative activities are worthless if they cannot be realized due to lack of money or human resources.

Croatia's network of tourist organizations now faces the need for reorganization, which aims to replace the 'old' concept with a new one that would be more effective and flexible in carrying out their tasks. The basic idea is to create a system that would be 'imposed' as the front-runner of tourism development in the destination, and with closer cooperation among all stakeholders, so that the destinations' development would adapt more quickly to market demands. From the experiences of the Institute for Tourism that conducts the majority of research on Croatian tourism, problems of the system today include: (1) system is too big, (2) there is no clear division of tasks among levels and (3) there are too many tasks not adequately distributed among the levels of tourism boards. Instead of the twenty county tourism boards, it would be more appropriate to create a smaller number of regional DMOs, which would be more focused on promotional activities, while the tourism boards of smaller destinations would be more focused on creating and developing tourism products.

Ideally, addressing these problems would be divided between the local and regional level with a view to a more clear definition of the tasks, to combine human and financial resources more effectively. It is important to note that in some European countries (e.g., Italy, UK), the system has been significantly reduced (Reinhold et al., 2015). However, it is expected that these changes would be difficult to achieve in Croatia, since the organizational setup of the entire system is yet unclear. Having this in mind, it is important to stress that, as stated by Reinhold et al. (2015), DMOs need to become less monolithic and accommodate more flexibility in their (hierarchical) structures, functions, tasks and associated process. The same authors pointed out that DMOs should reorient toward tasks that can be managed and benefit collaboration such as building know-how in specific domains (e.g., events and MICE) and certain back-office processes (human resources, finance, etc.) or supporting regional collaboration in general, each of which is very important also in Croatia.

Economic and social changes necessitate constant adaptation of tourism organizations to new business environments. In the past, the basic issue was how to attract tourists to the destination, while today the main issue is how to provide a quality experience for tourists. Therefore, many destinations face the problem of effectively coordinating the stakeholders. It is easier to answer the question of organizations and systems but much more complex to determine how to motivate, inspire and encourage stakeholders in destinations to work together and to take responsibility. Having in mind the long history and tradition of system of tourism organizations in Croatia, the expected transformation of the system should bear in mind all positive as well as negative sides of the existing system and today's fast-changing environment. Research has shown that issues of human resources and of funding would be the main key success factors regardless of the type of organization implemented in the future.

REFERENCES

Ateljević, I., & Čorak, S. (2006). Croatia in the new Europe: Culture versus conformity. In D. Hall, M. Smith, & M. B. (Eds.), *Tourism in the new Europe: The challenges and opportunities of EU enlargement* (pp. 288–301). Wallingford: CAB International.

Bartoluci, M. (2008). The role of tourism policy in sustainable development of croatian tourism. In L. Galetić & N. Čavlek (Eds.), *Proceedings of the 4th international conference, an enterprise Odyssey: Tourism – Governance and Entrepreneurship* (pp. 248–249). Zagreb: University of Zagreb, Faculty of Economics and Business.

Blichfeldt, B. S., Hird, J., & Kvistgaard, P. (2014). Destination leadership and the issue of power. *Tourism Review, 69*(1), 74–86.

Boranić, S., Čorak, S., & Kranjčević, J. (2014). The transformation of the system of tourism organizations in the context of social changes. In M. Kozak & N. Kozak (eds), *Proceedings book of the 3rd interdisciplinary tourism research conference, 3–7 June 2014* Istanbul, Turkey (pp.485–489). Ankara: Anatolia: An International Journal of Tourism and Hospitality Research.

Bornhost, T., Ritchie, J. B. R., & Sheehan, L. (2010). Determination of tourism success for DMOs & destinations: An empirical examination of stakeholder's perspectives. *Tourism Management, 31,* 572–589.

Borzyszkowski, J. (2014). Cooperation with the environment as one of the basic elements concerning the activity of the present-day DMO. *European Journal of Tourism, Hospitality and Research, 5*(2), 47–59.

Buhalis, D. (2000). Marketing the competitive destination in the future. *Tourism Management, 21*(1), 97–116.

Čorak, S. (2008). Izazovi destinacijskog menadžmenta [Destination management challenges]. In M. Stanić (ed), *Destinacijske menadžment kompanije – Priručnik za razumijevanje poslovanja i uspješni marketing* [Destination management companies – Handbook for understanding of business operations and successful marketing] (pp. 23–32). Zagreb: Association of Croatian Travel Agencies.

Croatian Bureau of Statistics. (1992). *Tourism 1991, Report No. 850.* Zagreb: Croatian Bureau of Statistics.

Crouch, G. I., & Ritchie, J. B. R. (1999). Tourism, competitiveness and societal prosperity. *Journal of Business Research, 44*(3), 137–152.

Federal Bureau of Statistics. (1964). *Statistical Bulletin No. 299: Catering and tourism in 1962.* Belgrade: Federal Bureau of Statistics.

Gartell, R. B. (1994). *Destination marketing for convention and visitor bureaus* (2nd ed.). Dubuque: Kendall/Hunt Publishing Company.

Gretzel, U., Fesenmaier, D. R., Formica, S., & Oleary, J. T. (2006). Searching for the future: Challenges faced by destination marketing organizations. *Journal of Travel Research, 45,* 116–126.

Horwath HTL Zagreb. (2013). *Operativni priručnik za primjenu modela destinacijske menadžment organizacije (DMO)* [Operational manual for application of DMO model]. http://business.croatia.hr/Documents/3217/Operativni-prirucnik-za-primjenu-modela-destinacijske-menadzment-organizacije.pdf. Date accessed 5 April 2016.

Jafari, J. (Ed.). (2000). *Encyclopedia of tourism.* London: Routledge.

Laesser, C., & Baritelli, P. (2013). St. Gallen consensus on destination management. *Journal of Destination Marketing and Management, 2*, 46–49.
Lally, A. M., O'Donovan, I., & Quinlan, T. (2015). *Stakeholder engagement in destination management: Exploring key success factors.* Paper presented at the 11th Annual Tourism and Hospitality Research in Ireland Conference (THRIC 2015), 11–12 June.
Lengyel, M. (2007). *Destination management – Conceptual framework and the case of Hungary.*http://itthon.hu/documents/28123/4381804/UNWTO_DM_conf_Budapest2007_Lengyel_angol.pdf/bfc69281-2435-4ce2-8cdd-cc418beee301. Date accessed 3 March 2016
Magaš, D. (2008). *Destinacijski menadžment – modeli i tehnike* [Destination management – models and techniques]. Opatija: Faculty of Tourism and Hotel Management.
Marušić, Z., Čorak, S., & Sever, I. (2015). *TOMAS 2014 summer– Attitudes and expenditures of tourists in Croatia.* Zagreb: Institute for Tourism.
Ministry of Tourism. (2013). Croatian tourism development strategy to 2020. Official Gazette of the Republic of Croatia 55/2013. http://narodne-novine.nn.hr/clanci/sluzbeni/2013_05_55_1119.html. Date accessed 20 November 2014.
Murdaugh, M. E. (2012). *Destination marketing insights: How to boost performance, increase customers, and maximize market share.* Minneapolis: Mill City Press.
Official Gazette of the Republic of Croatia. (1993). http://narodne-novine.nn.hr/clanci/sluzbeni/1993_12_113_2184.html. Date accessed 07 April 2016.
Official Gazette of the Republic of Croatia. 2008). http://narodne-novine.nn.hr/clanci/sluzbeni/2008_12_152_4142.html. Date accessed 07 April 2016.
Pechlaner, H., Volgger, M., & Herntrei, M. (2012). Destination management organizations as interface between destination governance and corporate governance. *Anatolia – An International Journal of Tourism and Hospitality Research, 23*(2), 151–168.
Pechlaner, H., Kozak, M., & Volgger, M. (2013). Destination leadership: A new paradigm for tourist destination? *Tourism Review, 69*(1), 1–9.
Pike, S. (2004). *Destination marketing organizations.* Oxford: Elsevier.
Pike, S., & Page, S. J. (2014). Destination Marketing Organizations and destination marketing: A narrative analysis of literature. *Tourism Management, 41*, 202–227.
Presenza, A., Sheehan, L., & Ritchie, J.B.R. (2005). Towards a model of the roles and activities of destination management organizations. https://www.academia.edu/1009194/Towards_a_model_of_the_roles_and_activities_of_destination_management_organizations. Data accessed 10 March 2016.
Reinhold, S., Laesser, C., & Beritelli, P. (2015). 2014 St. Gallen Consensus of destination management. *Journal of Destination Marketing & Management, 4*, 137–142.

Ritchie, J. B. R., & Crouch, G. I. (2003). *The competitive destination: A sustainable tourism perspective.* Wallingford: CAB International.

Sainaghi, R. (2006). From contents to processes: Versus a dynamic destination management model (DDMM). *Tourism Management, 27,* 1053–1063.

Schaumann, P. (2004). *The guide to successful destination management.* New York: Johnny Wiley & Sons.

Socher, K. (2000). Reforming destination management organizations and financing. *Tourist Review, 2,* 39–44.

UNWTO. (2007). *A practical guide to tourism destination management.* Madrid: UNWTO.

Volgger, M., & Pechlaner, H. (2014). Requirements for destination management organizations in destination governance: Understand DMO success. *Tourism Management, 41,* 64–75.

Vukonić, B. (2005). *Povijest hrvatskog turizma* [History of Croatian tourism]. Zagreb: Prometej.

Yuan, Y. L., Gretzel, U., & Fesenmaier, D. R. (2003). Internet technology use by American convention and visitors bureaus. *Journal of Travel Research, 41*(3), 240–255.

CHAPTER 7

Tourism Attraction System

Eduard Kušen

INTRODUCTION

Over the last couple of decades, the interest for the overall system of tourism attractions of both tourism scholars and practitioners is dwindling. The phenomenon of tourism attractions is narrowed semantically and in terms of its content to the real tourism attractions, that is, those already accessible to tourists and featuring prominently in tourism marketing, such as the Niagara Falls, the Great Pyramid of Giza, the Louvre Museum and so forth. It is no surprising, therefore, that research interest in tourism attractions is reduced almost exclusively to marketing, while their development aspect is mostly ignored. The un- or underdeveloped tourism attractions are treated mostly as other tourism resources.

Given the theoretical underdevelopment of the tourism attraction phenomenon, the purpose of this chapter is to present the System of Tourism Attractions developed at the Institute for Tourism over the last two decades. It captures numerous and complex relationships that exist in the attraction microcosm between the elements of tourism attractions (potential and real) and the tourism system as a whole. It is unique, integrated, functional, multidimensional system that represents their phenomenology and, at the same time, provides a practical interactive

E. Kušen (✉)
Institute for Tourism, Zagreb, Croatia

© The Author(s) 2017
L. Dwyer et al. (eds.), *Evolution of Destination Planning and Strategy*, DOI 10.1007/978-3-319-42246-6_7

tool for record-keeping purposes in form of the Registry and Atlas of Tourism Attractions. In this way the system fills the current gap in tourism attractions research where the integrity of the process by which tourism resources are converted into tourism attraction products has not yet been sufficiently explored and researched.

A development of the Tourism Attraction System can be, broadly, divided in two stages. In the first stage, the focus of attention were the tourism attractions and the key causal links between them, resulting in the functional classification of tourism attractions as a theoretical framework and a specification of data to be recorded for each attraction—a draft register entry page (Kušen, 1999; Kušen, 2002a, 2002b; Kušen & Tadej, 2003). The System itself and the practical model for the functional document management of the System through the Registry and Atlas of Tourism Attractions (Kušen, 2010) were created in the second stage. In outlining theoretical underpinnings and development and testing of the System, this chapter is divided in the two main parts. The first part deals with the phenomenology of tourism attractions and defines both their form and their relationship with other elements of a tourism system. The second part is focused on the relationship between attractions and destinations to create the System of Tourism Attractions. At the end, the synthesis provides an overview of the newly acquired knowledge on tourism attractions as a synergy of both research stages.

First Stage: The Focus on Tourism Attractions

The main objective was to collect, integrate and systematize the available knowledge and information dealing with the phenomenon of tourism attractions in the broadest possible sense. Methodologically, the deductive-inductive approach was used. Theoretical framework derived from the literature was tested simultaneously through a series of case studies. Interactions between the results of the deductive theory building and the test results of case studies assumed a creative course and yielded a series of original results: the functional classification of tourism resources, a functional classification of tourism motives/activities, a basic functional classification of tourism attractions and a marketing and development assessment of tourism attractions. For practical purposes, specification of data to be recorded for each attraction—a draft register entry page—provided a foundation for the System of Tourism Attractions.

Tourism Attractions Theoretical Framework

When the research into tourism attractions was undertaken during the 1990s, it became evident that scientific and professional literature neglected research into tourism resources that attract visitors especially when it came to their developmental component and function and, especially, within the framework of the long-term planning of tourism development. Only a couple of papers were explicitly dealing with the integrated understanding of the tourism attraction phenomenon.

Mill and Morrison (1985) functionally positioned tourism attraction well in the broad structure of a unique tourism system. This system is presented graphically in the form of a wheel that consists the four key segments, market, travel, tourism destination and marketing, and the four activities that link them together: the travel purchase, the shape of travel demand, the selling of travel and reaching the marketplace. Tourism attractions are located in the third quadrant (tourism destinations) and are highlighted as the especially attractive factors of tourism supply. However, a comprehensive and all-inclusive system of tourism attractions was missing. Few years later Lew (1987) made an ideographic typology of tourism attractions by summarizing data from some 40 papers published by some 30 authors. Most of that research was pragmatically focused only on very few individual and mutually poorly connected parts of attraction phenomenology. As such, it failed to provide a complete explanation or comprehensive picture of the complex mechanism that interlinks not only tourism attractions but also many other elements of tourism. It was Leiper that, in 1990, published a paper under the pretentious title *Tourism Attraction Systems*, an article that failed short in capturing comprehensiveness of such a system. Then, there is ample literature dealing with this issue, yet all of it only partially, in outlines or in passing. In the more practical terms, the paradigm of prevalent attitudes toward tourism attractions is illustrated by a rather less known book—*The ICM Guide to World Tourism Attractions* (2000). The book provides an overview of 222 most significant real tourism attractions worldwide, for example, those attractions that are already well established on the global market. The attractions are classified as Amusement, Cultural, Historical Tourism Market, Human-made, Natural and Religious, with some assigned to two categories. In the context of this discussion, it is important as it best illustrates an ad hoc approach to development of typology of tourism attractions prevailing even today.

Definition of Tourism Attractions

Given the state of Tourism Attraction Research, it is important to discuss the meaning of tourism attraction. The most common perception of tourism attractions is that they are dominantly visual sensations that arouse strong emotions in visitors. There is impression that a large segment of the profession shares this romantic view of tourism attractions. Professional and scientific publications and dictionaries offer a host of tourism attraction definitions. Differences in definitions reflect mostly context in which they are created. Tourists (consumers) experience tourism attractions in one way, whereas geographers, marketing experts or long-term tourism planners have different perceptions.

In line with the objectives of this research, a more complex definition was required, deriving from the basic principles that a system of tourism attractions is a subsystem of a larger tourism system. Within this system, tourism attractions are considered to be a source of energy that moves the entire wheel of a tourism system. They are a magnet that attracts visitors to visit a tourism destination and act as the primary generator of destination tourism development. From this perspective, two aspects are overlooked in the prevalent approach to tourism attractions—the importance of a long-term development vs. short-term marketing approach and the considerations of motives that drive travel decisions with the strong focus on leisure travel, while non-leisure travel motives are mostly ignored.

Probably the most comprehensive definition of tourism attractions is given by Lew (2000, p. 35) that provides a good starting point for dwelling into key issues in tourism attraction definition:

Attractions are more than just a site or an event in a destination. They are an integral part of a larger tourism system that also consists of tourists and markers. Attraction typologies vary considerably depending on whether they are being used for marketing or planning purposes. No site, sight or event is an attraction in itself. It only becomes one when a tourism system is created to designate and elevate it to the status of an attraction. Almost any object—real or intangible—may be designated as having some special quality that allows it to be elevated through advertising to the status of an attraction. The only intrinsic requirement of the object is that it is associated with a location. This differentiates attractions from other consumable goods. Rather than bringing the goods to the consumer, the tourist must go to the attraction to experience it. Thus, the system that creates and supports an attraction must have three major components to exist: an object or event located at a site, a tourist or consumer, and a marker, an image that tells the tourist why the object or event is of interest ...

Lew (2000, p. 35) then continues to specify characteristics of a tourism attraction and their relationship with other tourism resources as well as principles of their evaluation:

...The objects from which attractions are created are typically environmental and cultural resources....From the perspective of the tourist, they consist of objects to see, activities to do and experiences to remember ... The assessment of attractions is a common part of planning and marketing and is undertaken to understand the competitive advantage of one place over others. Attractions are inventoried, and their potential for development (or need for protection) are studied. No single agreed-upon typology of attractions exists to conduct an inventory, in part because most places have their own distinctive qualities. Attraction inventories have been approached in one or more of three ways. The most common approach is to group attractions into nominal categories (also referred to as formal and ideographic). Such categories include cultural artefacts and nature. Examples of the former include special structures (buildings, bridges, and monuments), communities, theme parks, cuisine and works of art. Nature includes mountains and other scenery, vegetation, climate and nature preserves and parks. Depending on the place and the purpose of the attraction inventory, other types of categories are often combined with the nominal ones ... attractions may also be classified into cognitive or perceptual categories (see cognition), such as authenticity, educational, adventurous and recreational. They can be inventoried based on their organizational or structural characteristics, including isolated or clustered, urban or rural, low or high capacity, and seasonal or year-round attraction (see seasonality). The cognitive approach to attraction inventories is used when the destination image is of primary interest for marketing purposes. The organizational approach is used when undertaking community planning and controlling the development process are the main concern.

Although comprehensive, this definition contradicts the adopted principles of attraction being part of the larger tourism system and where both real and potential tourism attractions as well as leisure and non-leisure motives are treated as equally important. The main propositions of this definition are not particularly effective in building an integrated and well-rounded system of tourism attractions.

From the perspective adopted in this research, the potential tourism attractions—those tourism resources that can be turned into real tourism attractions, resources with the immanent 'seed' of tourism attractive-ness—should not be excluded from the overall body of tourism attrac-tions. Based on a critical analysis of available literature and results of case studies, the following definition of tourism attractions was developed and adopted in subsequent development of the Tourism Attraction System: potential and real tourism attractions represent the basic tourism resources of every tourism destination. They determine destination's tourism prod-uct and its overall development. The essence of tourism attractions lies in the fact that they attract tourists and satisfy their needs, travel motives and activities. All potential and real tourism attractions are strongly spatially related, either as spatial elements or their existence is spatially limited to a certain area, which forces tourists to travel in order to experience them.

Tourism Attractions as a Part of Tourism Resource System

As the literature of that time has not successfully dealt with the dis-tinction between potential and real tourism attractions nor proposed a coherent Tourism Attraction System/framework, there was a need to functionally position both real and potential tourism attractions within an integrated system of tourism resources. Lew (1987), in the already mentioned analysis of 30 or so studies dealing with tourism attractions, concluded that in most studies potential and real tourism attractions were considered the basic resources upon which tourism had developed. However, Lew also concluded that researchers had not completely com-prehended the multi-layered meaning of terms related to the nature of tourism attractions as phenomena that appears in a physical environment, as well as inside the heads (thoughts) of tourists. Despite the analysis of a large number of works by a large number of authors, his Framework of Tourism Attraction Research remained literally just a framework replete with interesting views on the phenomenon of tourism attractions, but lacking a real synthesis.

In contrast to Lew, Leiper (1990) built his system of tourism attrac-tions on real tourism attractions and shaped it exclusively on the basis of the relationship between the tourist and the real tourism attraction. This kind of approach is very important for the marketing purpose. However, by overlooking potential tourism attractions and neglecting evaluation of the entire tourism destination attraction base for planning purposes, such an approach fails to ensure a system of tourism attractions satisfying equally marketing and planning purposes.

All tourism attractions (potential and real) are tourism resources, but all tourism resources do not necessarily have to be tourism attractions. A non-selective use of the term tourism resource instead of potential tourism attraction is not wrong in principle, but this benign terminological practice becomes an obstacle in construction of a functional system of tourism attractions with respect to the goals and tasks that are posed before such a system. Therefore, the results obtained through research on tourism resources are presented in a form of a Contribution to the Functional Classification System of Tourism Resources (Table 7.1).

Table 7.1 Contribution to the functional classification system of tourism resources

A. Basic tourism resources (tourism resource base)
   1. Potential tourism attractions
   2. Real tourism attractions
B. Other direct tourism resources
   1. Tourism accommodation and catering facilities
   2. Supporting tourism facilities
   3. Human resources for tourism
   4. Income from tourism
   5. Tourism development zones
   6. Tourism places
   7. Tourism destinations
   8. Travel agencies
   9. Tourism organizations (tourist boards, associations, etc.)
   10. Tourist information and promotional materials
   11. Tourist information system
   12. Tourism education of the local population
   13. Tourism attractiveness of surrounding destinations
C. Indirect tourism resources
   1. Preserved environment
   2. Geographical and transit position
   3. Transport connections
   4. General education level of the local population
   5. Financial potential
   6. Communal and social infrastructure
   7. Quality of spatial organization
   8. Facility design, exterior design, green surfaces
   9. Safety, security and political stability
   10. Other resources

Source: Kušen (2002a), p. 17

In this table, tourism resources are divided into three groups: (1) basic tourism resources (tourism attraction base) comprising of all potential and real tourism attractions; (2) other direct tourism resources, grouping all tourism resources that are managed or significantly influenced by the tourism industry; and (3) indirect tourism resources, featuring all resources on which tourism industry depends but over which it does not have much of an influence.

Tourist Motives and Activities

The preceding discussion has focused on the need to consider both real and potential tourism attractions when building a Tourism Attraction System that can serve the short-term marketing needs as well as the long-term planning goals. The second aspects lacking in the theoretical discourse on tourism attraction were that of the motives driving travel decisions, in particular reference to the non-leisure travel. Lew (1987, p.554) begins his discussion on the essence of tourism attraction with a witty remark: 'Without tourism attractions there would be no tourism (Gunn 1972:24), but without tourists there would be no tourist attractions'. This is just a succinct way to describe the nature of tourism and the preordained bond that exists between tourists, tourist needs and motives for travels and the completely defined types of tourism attractions. Thus, the types of tourism attractions of a destination influence the types of tourism that can be developed. To overcome this gap, the basic functional classification of tourist motifs/activities (Table 7.2) was developed. It was based on the OECD's international classification of international visitors (*OECD*, 1992, p. 194). It installs equality between leisure- and non-leisure-motivated travels, which is very important for the subsequent definition, classification and evaluation of tourism attractions.

Basic Functional Classification of Tourism Attractions

Now, with a working definition of tourism attractions satisfying both marketing and planning purpose and clear positioning of tourism attractions within Tourism Resource System, the foundations were set for development of the basic functional classification of tourism attractions. To date, in both scholarly and professional writings, there is a stubbornly held division of tourism attractions into natural and cultural (human-made), and, sometimes, events are added to them. The current classifications of

Table 7.2 Basic functional classification of tourist motives/activities

1. Leisure motives/activities
1.1. Rest/recuperation
1.2. Sport recreation
1.3. Leisure education
1.4. Pleasure and entertainment
2. Non-leisure motives/activities
2.1. Business travel
2.2. Medical treatment
2.3. Professional education
2.4. Travel conditioned by traffic infrastructure—transit
2.5. Other obligations

Source: Adapted from Kušen (2002a), p. 37; Kušen (2010), p. 414

tourism attractions are one sided (they comprise only real tourism attractions); they are formal (providing a basic division into natural and anthropogenic); they are narrowly described (without significant evaluation); they are non-systematic (without a clear articulation of their vertical and horizontal hierarchy); they are pronouncedly non-functional (they cannot be included either directly or in any general terms into the modern documentation systems or analytical procedures inherent to the tourism resource management processes or the process of planning long-term tourism development). Most of all, they do not reflect the level of theoretical development of tourism in general.

While some authors have expanded the range of tourism attractions, their categories and typology, they have failed to achieve an integrated and closed functional system that would comprise the key multidimensional relationships between the types of tourism attractions, their characteristics/properties and the sites where they are located. Of the existing classification, the most comprehensive is Lew's (1987) Composite Ideograph of Tourist Attraction Typology, where nine categories of attractions are defined, based on a matrix of nature, human and nature-human interface across the top and general environments, specific features and inclusive environments along the side (Table 7.3).

The WTO (1993) also attempted to classify the tourism attraction resources into natural resources, cultural and historical heritage for tourism, climate conditions and infrastructure and tourism services. Classification of tourism attractions was also attempted by Mill and Morrison (1985) in their book *The Tourism System*. Their classification starts with the two basic cat-

Table 7.3 Lew's Composite Ideograph of Tourist Attraction Typology

Nature	Nature-human interface	Human
General environment:		
1. Panoramas	4. Observational	7. Settlement infrastructure
Mountain	Rural/agriculture	Utility types
Sea coast	Scientific gardens	Settlement morphology
Plain	Animals (zoos)	Settlement functions
Arid	Plants	Commerce
Island	Rocks and archeology	Retail
		Finance
		Institutions
		Government
		Education and science
		Religion
		People
		Way of life
		Ethnicity
Specific features:		
2. Landmarks	5. Leisure nature	8. Tourism infrastructure
Geological	Trails	Forms of access
Biological	Parks	To and from a destination
Flora	Beach	Destination tour routes
Fauna	Urban	Information and receptivity
Hydrological	Other	Basic needs
	Resorts	Accommodations
		Meals
Inclusive environment:		
3. Ecological	6. Participatory	9. Leisure superstructure
Climate	Mountain activities	Recreation entertainment
Sanctuaries	Summer	Performances
National parks	Winter	Sporting events
Nature reserves	Water activities	Amusements
	Other outdoor activities	Culture, history and art
		Museums and monuments
		Performances
		Festivals
		Cuisine

Source: Lew (1987) p. 558

egories of tourism attractions—natural and man-made—and then divided further according to purely marketing needs. With the intention of creating a functional classification of tourism attractions, other sources also did not venture off the beaten tracks and therefore could not achieve the set goal.

In filling the existing gap in the theory and practice relating to tourism attractions as argued so far, it was clear that the functional classification of tourism attractions that was proposed must already contain the embryo of a system of tourism attractions in which the DNA of that system is stored. To this end, the first stage was completed with the basic functional classification of tourism attractions. The classification, built on the existing literature and, furthermore, developed, tested and refined through many case studies, was completed at that stage and has not required much change since then.

The basic functional classification (Fig. 7.1) divides real and potential tourism attractions into 16 basic types. Each type of attraction has its number. Types of attractions are ordered according to the approximate time of their creation. Moreover, the order in which types of attractions are

LINKS	CODE	BASIC TYPES OF ATTRACTIONS	GRUP OF ATTRACTIONS		
	1.	GEOLOGICAL FEATURE	NATURAL	ORIGINAL	TANGIBLE
	2.	CLIMATE			
	3.	WATER			
	4.	FLORA			
	5.	FAUNA			
	6.	PROTECTED NATURAL HERITAGE			
	7.	PROTECTED CULTURAL HERITAGE		LEISURE RELATED	INTANGIBLE
	8.	THE CULTURE OF LIFE AND WORK			
	9.	FAMOUS PERSONS AND HISTORICAL EVENTS			
	10.	EVENTS /HAPPENINGS	CREATED		
	11.	CULTURAL AND RELIGIOUS INSTITUTIONS		UPGRADED	TANGIBLE
	12.	NATURAL SPAS SANATORIUMS			
	13.	SPORT AND REKREATION FACILITIES			
	14.	TOURISM PATHS, TRAILS, ROADS AND ROUTS			
	15.	ATTRACTIONS FOR ATTRACTIONS			
	16.	TOURISM PARAATTRACTIONS		NL*	

* NON LEISURE

Fig. 7.1 Basic functional classification of tourism attractions (*Source:* Kušen (2002a, b), p. 61)

listed reflects several types of grouping. First six types belong to natural and the next ten to human-made attractions. In a similar manner, first nine are authentic, while the remainder are modified. Then, all but the last group can be considered leisure driven, with the last 16th belonging to non-leisure attractions. The classification also makes distinction between tangible attractions (Types 1 to 8 and 11 to 16) and non-tangible (Types 8, 9 and 10).

Importantly, the basic classification has also captured complexity of tourism attractions, as there are three basic types of tourism attractions that include parts of other types of attractions. These links are presented in the first column of the table. For example, Protected Natural Heritage (Type 6) includes parts of Types 1, 2, 3, 4 and 5. The Protected Cultural and Historical Heritage (Type 7) includes parts of Types 8, 9, 10 and 11. Likewise, Type 14—Tourist Trails, Roads and Routes—includes parts of Types 1, 2, 3, 4, 5, 6, 7, 8, 9, 10, 11, 12 and 13.

At the very outset, it has become clear that the complexity and diversity of attractions belong to the types of attractions as defined by the basic functional classification which was calling for creation of a detailed classification system dividing the basic type of attraction into sub-types. The method of drafting a detailed classification system was the same as in creating the basic classification system, which means that every basic type of tourism attraction was divided further into a required number of functional sub-types. The sub-types, which are organized and presented as a table, are given codes that link each sub-type with the higher-order attraction type.

Such an approach to the classification system ensures conditions for the creation of a Registry and Atlas of Tourism Attractions. An example of the approach to creation of a detailed classification is presented in Table 7.4, where geological features of a destination (Type 1) are divided into several sub-types at two levels.

Evaluation of Tourism Attractions

While the basic functional classification of tourism attractions together with the detailed classifications offers a comprehensive attraction typology, to fulfill the ambition that such a mechanism serves both planning and marketing purposes, there was a need to evaluate each tourism attraction. Such an approach was already called for by Lew (2000). He has advocated creation of a Registry of Tourism Attraction and stressed out the need to evaluate each resource and plan their develop-

Table 7.4 An example of a subdivision of types of attractions belongs to the geological features of a destination

1. Geological characteristics of a destination
1.1. Relief
1.1.1. Hills and mountains
1.1.2. Lowlands
1.2. Islands
1.3. Karst
1.4. Individual structures
1.4.1. Natural beaches
1.4.2. Grottos and caves
1.4.3. Karrens and rocks
1.4.4. Karst sinkholes and fields
1.4.5. Pits
1.4.6. Canyons, cliffs and waterfalls
1.4.7. Bays and fjords
1.4.8. Mountain tops and viewing points
1.4.9. Eruptive formation
1.4.10. Sediments and similar structure
1.4.11. Fossils
1.4.12. Ichnofossils
1.4.13. River sediments
1.4.14. Exploration fields and mines
1.4.15. Meteorites

Source: Kušen (2002a) p. 69

ment for/integration into tourism system. He has also defined several aims of tourism evaluation as well as some criteria to be used in the evaluation process. However, the system of tourism attractions has not been properly structured and enclosed into a functional whole with real tourism attractions.

Thus, the process of evaluation of tourism attractions was added to the basic functional classification of tourism attractions (Table 7.5). Similar to the development of basic classification, the evaluation system was developed and tested on several case studies. The evaluation consists of seven types of tourism attraction assessment belonging to two basic aspects of evaluation—development and marketing. Development potential of each attraction is assessed based on (1) category (international, national, regional, local), (2) seasonality, (3) length of stay (visitation, overnight), (4) carrying capacities and (5) place in a broader system of tourism attrac-

Table 7.5   Evaluation of tourism attractions

1. Development assessment
 1.1. Category (international, national, regional, local)
 1.2. Seasonality
 1.3. Length of stay
 1.4. Carrying capacities
 1.5. A broader system of tourism attractions
2. Marketing assessment
 2.1. Tourist accessibility
 2.2. The extent of tourist use

Source: Kušen, E. (2002a), p. 176

tions. The marketing assessment consists of evaluation of visitor accessibility and the extent of tourist use. The development assessment of tourism attractions is primarily intended for the long-term planning and protection of the tourism attractions. In contrast, the marketing assessment serves mostly the marketing planning and management.

Finally, such an approach to tourism attraction evaluation facilitates organization and management of tourism attractions documentation. For example, to establish a Tourism Attraction Registry, a data-sheet for each attraction has to be created containing results of the proposed evaluation. The evaluation should be done by tourism experts trained in the attraction assessment. The most demanding and sensitive is the evaluation of the importance/category of tourism attractions (international, national, regional and local), which replaces the existing non-functional division into primary and secondary tourism attractions and the assessment of the *carrying capacity*.

From Theory to Practice: Creation of Registry and Atlas of Tourism Attractions

The cumulative result of the research conducted during this stage was the *Tourism Attraction Registry Data-Sheet*. The Registry of Tourism Attractions was defined as two-dimensional file, at the level of one data-sheet per tourism attraction (Table 7.6). However, with the coding system used to mark each attraction's data-sheet, the Registry as a whole gets a third dimension based on the functional classification of tourism attractions that determines the order of Registry entry. Thus, all the partial research results were directly incorporated into the Registry data-entry

Table 7.6 Draft of a Tourism Attraction Registry data sheet

1. Data-entry fields in the tourism attraction data-sheet
2. ID (ordinal) number
3. Code of attraction type/sub-type
4. Code name
5. Name of attraction
6. Short functional description
7. Location—geographic coordinates
8. Category
9. Seasonality
10. Length of stay
11. Carrying capacity
12. Broader Tourism Attraction System
13. Visitor accessibility
14. Extent of tourism use
15. Entry date and addition

Source: Kušen, E. (2002a), p. 177

sheet, and, as such, they have indirectly determined the framework of the System of Tourism Attractions.

In addition to Registry, the Atlas of Tourism Attraction can also be easily created. A variety of maps can be created by entering the site (geographic coordinates) of a particular tourism attraction on a cartographic (topographic) background. The Registry and maps complement each other and represented an efficient tool for result verification. The Atlas of Tourism Attractions also contains a collection of thematic maps that facilitate visualization of the attraction base, their spatial distribution and a more comprehensive interpretation of data contained in the Registry.

The first stage ended with a draft of the Registry page of tourism attractions in an analogue form. Thus, nearly all conditions were established for the final testing of the proposed classification and evaluation of tourism attractions at the level of a tourism destination, as well as for the creation of a system of tourism attractions.

SECOND STAGE: TOWARD A SYSTEM OF TOURISM ATTRACTIONS

Although tourism attractions are independent entities, they are also *inseparable from the tourism destination* in which they are located. Therefore, in contrast to the research during the first stage that focused on the individual tourism attraction, the goal at this second stage was to explore the relationship between tourism attractions within tourism destination or, in other words, to develop a method of evaluation of a tourism destination attractiveness. Therefore, the definition of the basic tourism destination, especially its spatial positioning and boundaries, becomes a prerequisite for its attraction evaluation and, thus, is the first task at this research stage. As a focus of research shifted from the individual tourism attraction evaluation to the evaluation of destination attraction base, a need has also emerged to expand and upgrade the content of the Registry data-entry sheet (Table 7.7). However, the main goal was to create a System of Tourism Attractions whose multidimensional structure would reflect almost all of the relationships existing within the microcosm of tourism attractions. Thus, a third dimension was added to the Registry of Tourism Attractions—that of the tourism destinations. The addition of that third dimension facilitated an attraction synthesis and a concept of the tourism spatial organization, thus providing an invaluable tool in the process of tourism planning from the destination point of view.

Table 7.7 A contribution to the classification of key data (characteristics) for each tourism attraction

Key data	Original	Interpreted	Evaluated
1. Name of attraction	X		
2. Code/type		X	
3. Location	X		
4. Short functional description		X	
5. Natural/human-made		X	
6. Tangible/non-tangible		X	
7. Potential/real		X	
8. Category			X
9. Seasonality			X
10. Length of stay			X
11. Carrying capacity			X
12. Broader system of tourism attractions			X
13. Tourist accessibility			X
14. The extend of tourism use			X
15. Relevant tourist activities			X
16. Specificities 1, 2, 3			X
17. Data-entry date	X		

Source: Kušen (2010), p. 419

Similar to the first stage, the research in the second stage combined inductive and deductive approach. Concepts were developed based on the available literature and then models developed, tested and refined through the series of case studies. These were mostly various planning documents conducted by the team of the Institute for Tourism, mostly for Croatian tourism destination and regions and in Croatian language. The results of the case study research were published in the article *A System of Tourism Attractions* (Kušen, 2010). In the following year, this System was registered with the State Intellectual Property Office of the Republic of Croatia, under the title Tabulation of Tourism Attractions, as industrial design (Kušen, 2011). Finally, in late 2013 the digital Registry of Tourism Attractions, as a derivate of the previous, analogue Registry, was developed and tested on the case study of the land-locked County of Koprivnica-Križevci in Northern Croatia.

Attraction Evaluation of the (Basic) Tourism Destination

As already discussed, one of the cornerstones of the System of Tourism Attractions is tourism destination. Many published texts deal with the topic of tourism destinations, specifically, tourism destination management from a marketing standpoint. They are, generally, very similar and often repetitive. For the task at hand, a good starting point in understanding the interactive link between tourism attractions and a tourism destination is Dawkin's (2003, p. 134) definition of a region:

> A region will be defined as a spatially contiguous population (of human beings) that is bound either by historical necessity or choice to a particular geographic location. The dependence on location may arise from a shared attraction to local culture, local employment centers, local natural resources, or other location-specific amenities.

To derive definition of a destination that would fit the purpose of development of the System of Tourism Attractions, the spatial aspects of a destination were especially important. Without them it would be impossible to achieve the optimum result in shaping a comprehensive System of tourism attractions. A discussion on tourism destination definition below is a summary of the earlier work—an early discussion on spatial boundaries of tourism destination (Kušen, 2002b) and definitions presented in the later article on the System of Tourism Attractions (Kušen, 2010).

In geographic terms, a tourism destination is a clearly defined area; it is always part of the area strongly marked by prominent physical characteristics, potential and real tourism attractions as well as spatial relations between them and other elements of the tourism offer. There are two types of destinations: a *basic* tourism destination where fundamental tourism metabolism enfolds and which cannot be divided any further and a complex (higher-order) *tourism destination* which is represented by the aggregated characteristics of the basic tourism destinations belonging to it. A basic tourism destination consists of an area featuring one or more tourism places (towns/villages) located close to each other and their functional surroundings. An often referenced example of this is the Opatija Riviera of the Northern Adriatic in Croatia, a stretch of 25 kilometer of seaside walkway connecting three tourism places (Opatija, Lovran and Volosko) and two villages in the hinterland (Veprinac and Kastav), established in the eighteenth century initially as the key infrastructure for the prevalent medical tourism. This example vividly illustrates how certain tourism and recreational facilities could not be provided within the boundaries of any individual town or village but only within their functional surroundings—in a tourism destination (Fig. 7.2).

Theoretically, the boundaries of a basic tourism destination are changeable, and the rate and type of change depends on the development of the tourist places (towns/villages) and the surrounding functional area. Despite that, for the practical reasons of tourism attraction base management and research of tourism development potential, the boundaries of a basic tourism destination need to be fixed for a foreseeable period and, more often than not, adapted to an existing administrative-territorial division (municipality or city). Real tourism attractions, with a tourism infrastructure and supra-structure in the basic tourism destination, define the destination tourism products; however, potential tourism attractions, with other direct and indirect tourism resources, determine the type and structure of a possible long-term tourism development. An area without potential and real tourism attractions simply cannot develop into a tourism destination. On the other hand, an area that is underdeveloped in tourism terms but has significant attraction potential can be considered as a potential tourism destination whose attraction base must be evaluated, protected and developed.

The basic tourism destinations can be categorized in terms of the value and quality of their destination tourism product. Such cases of destination categorization are already emerging in practice, for instance, star ratings ranging between 1 and 5. All of the basic tourism destinations should also preferably be categorized in terms of their tourism potential (especially in

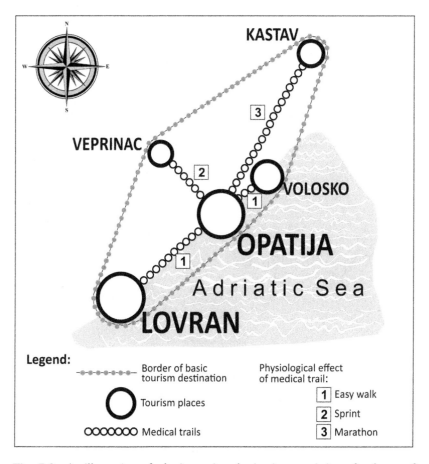

Fig. 7.2   An illustration of a basic tourism destination consisting of a cluster of tourism places—Riviera of Opatija (Northern Adriatic, ca. 1900)

view of their potential tourism attractions). Of course, this is only possible if all potential and real tourism attractions within a specific tourism destination have previously been identified and evaluated (Fig. 7.3).

Basic destinations, as well as complex (higher-order) destinations, represent a framework for the establishment of a Registry of Tourism Attractions. Furthermore, they also serve as a framework for the tourism evaluation of a broader area, which is not only a sum of evaluations of the relevant tourism attractions as it also includes the quality of their spatial distribution within the boundaries of a given tourism destination.

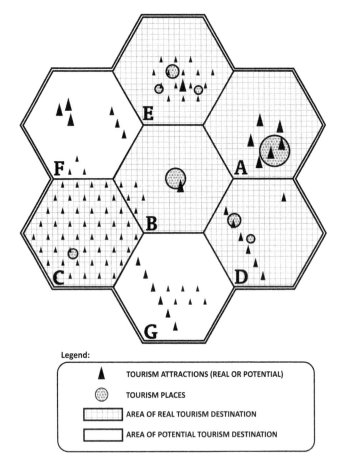

Fig. 7.3   A schematic of the relationship between tourism attractions and basic tourism destinations and tourism places (*Source:* Kušen (2002a) p. 44)

Functional Classification of Tourism Attraction and Registry from a Destination Perspective

The results of the case studies showed that the functional classification of tourism attractions worked well, while only the detailed classification (sub-types) experienced some minor adjustment or expansion. However, with the introduction of the destination dimension, it is the ensuing documentation—the Registry data-entry sheet—that needed more significant change (Table 7.7). Data was divided into three groups: original (taken over from other documents), interpreted by experts and evaluated by trained tourism professionals. Moreover, new data on individual tourism attraction and its relationship to a destination was added, such as divisions into natural vs. human-made, tangible vs. intangible, potential attractions vs. real attractions and so on. Likewise, data on tourist activities that can take place at the attraction as well as the possibility to add some unexpected special features was also introduced. Simultaneously with the ongoing work on the analogue version of the Registry, an integrated and detailed Tourism Attraction System was completed. The two are not the same, although they are very similar; a Registry is an operative practical instrument, while a system is a theoretical model.

Tourism Attraction System

A proposed Tourism Attraction System is, firstly, an innovative and partial elaboration of parts of the Tourism Resource System relating to tourism attractions and tourism destination, and it is elaborated within the framework of their functional phenomenology. It is built on the principle that it has to be relevant to both tourism theory and practice in order to ensure creative and rational management of tourism resources in general and tourism attractions in particular and that it should facilitate long-term sustainable tourism planning and provide a foundation for establishing and maintaining a modern tourism attraction documentation system.

A proposed functional System of Tourism Attractions (both potential and real) comprises a series of precisely defined relationships: between tourism attractions, between attractions and other tourism resources and between all of them and the non-tourism components of a basic tourism destination. It is presented as a three-dimensional table in the shape of a cuboid with five mutually interconnected tables printed on each of its five visible sides.

The essence of the system is merging of the two classifications—the Classification of Tourism Attractions (Fig. 7.1; Table 7.4) and Classification of key data for attraction and tourism destination as a whole (Table 7.7). In this way a three-dimensional system of tourism attractions was created, which ensures that every tourism attraction has a precisely determined position, in terms of the type of attractions to which it belongs and the characteristics that make it recognizable. A series of relations (relationships) that arise from the previously systematized and redefined autonomous segments of the tourism base have been incorporated into both classifications and in the *System* as a whole

The System is wholly 'open', which means that it can be built upon as needed in all directions. However, without full apprehension of its internal structure, every arbitrary change will destroy its basic meaning. Moreover, familiarity with its internal structure is necessary to overcome all problems that may arise in its use, primarily due to the specific nature of a certain type of tourism attractions.

Finally, the System can be applied and used in practice. It provides all necessary inputs for establishing maintaining tourism attraction documentation (i.e. Registry and Atlas of Tourism attractions). It is equally useful in planning a long-term tourism development as it provides a complete insight into the basic tourism resources (potential and real tourism attractions). It facilitates creation of an optimum destination tourism product based on the full familiarity with a destination's tourism attraction base. For tourism policy and decision makers, it can assist in formulating optimum strategic decisions for the development of tourism within their jurisdiction. Finally, when it comes to the long-term development planning and creative land-use management, it ensures that tourism is treated equally to other sectors. As for local communities, the System allows them to participate efficiently in the creation of plans for the economic, social, cultural and spatial development of their communities.

Moreover, the System offers entrepreneurs an insight into the structure of tourism potentials in a particular tourism destination. It also helps tourism associations to efficiently fulfill a range of their tasks and obligations. It also helps in rational use of funds as it replaces a prevalent practice according to which numerous very important tourism strategies and action plans were based on superficial or incomplete insights into tourism attraction base as attractions were only partially identified, randomly systematized, inadequately or erroneously evaluated and, typically, not properly recorded.

The concept of the System is physically represented by the shape of a three-dimensional ceramic model (a cuboid of 6.0 cm by 8.8 cm by 22.5 cm) with tables in Croatian. Accordingly, every tourism attraction and its key characteristics are determined precisely with the help of coordinates in the model (System). The model is presented in Fig. 7.4 with a

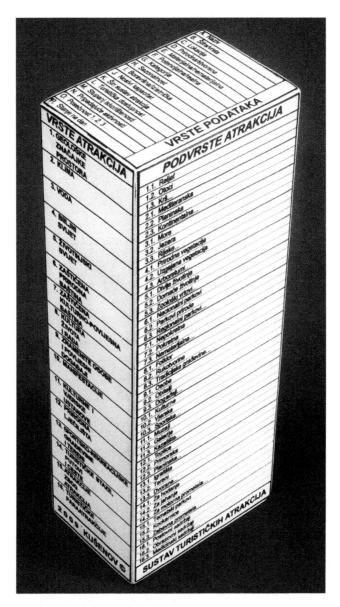

Fig. 7.4 Photo of the model (Kušen's System of Tourism Attractions, 2010)
(*Photo:* Kušen, E)

TYPE OF DATA

Columns:
A. Name
B. Typecode
C. Location
D. Natural/related
E. Tangible/intangible
F. Potential/real
G. Category of importance
H. Seasonality
I. Excursionist/residential attraction
J. Carrying capacity
K. Wider system of tourism attraction
L. Tourism accessibility
M. Degree of usage
N. Activities
O. Special features
P. Condition on a given day

TYPE OF ATTRACTION	SUB. TYPES	GROUP OF ATTRACTIONS
1. GEOLOGICAL FEATURES	1.1. Relief 1.2. Islands 1.3. Karst...	NATURAL / ORIGINAL / TANGIBLE
2. CLIMATE	2.1. Mediterranean climate 2.2. Mountain climate 2.3. Continental climate...	
3. WATER	3.1. Sea 3.2. Lakes 3.3. Rivers...	
4. FLORA	4.1. Natural vegetation 4.2. Cultivated vegetation 4.3. Arboretums...	
5. FAUNA	5.1. Wild animals 5.2. Domestic animals 5.3. Zoos...	
6. PROTECTED NATURAL HERITAGE	6.1. National parks 6.2. Nature parks 6.3. Regional parks...	
7. PROTECTED CULTURAL HERITAGE	7.1. Imovable heritage 7.2. Movable heritage 7.3. Intangible heritage...	LEISURE RELATED / INTANGIBLE
8. THE CULTURE OF LIFE AND WORK	8.1. Folklore 8.2. Handcraft 8.3. Traditional constructions...	
9. FAMOUS PERSONS AND HISTORICAL EVENTS	9.1. Persons 9.2. Families 9.3. Historical events	
10. EVENTS/HEPPENINGS	10.1. Cultural events 10.2. Religious events 10.3. Sport events	
11. CULTURAL AND RELIGIOUS INSTITUTIONS	11.1. Museums 11.2. Galleries 11.3. Theatres...	CREATED / UPGRADED / TANGIBLE
12. NATURAL SPAS SANITARIUMS	12.1. Spas 12.2. Seaside sanitariums 12.3. Mountain sanitariums	
13. SPORT AND RECREATION FACILITIES	13.1. Sport and recreation grounds 13.2. Ballparks 13.3. Gyms...	
14. TOURISM PATHS, TRAILS AND ROADS	14.1. For walking 14.2. For riding 14.3. For motor vehicles...	
15. ATTRACTIONS FOR ATTRACTIONS	15.1. Theme parks 15.2. Casinos 15.3. Fun and leisure vehicles...	
16. TOURISM PARA-ATTRACTIONS	16.1. Business facilities 16.2. Educational facilities 16.3. Medical facilities...	NON-LESURE

SYSTEM OF TOURISM ATTRACTIONS   2009   KUŠEN'S ©   SYSTEM OF TOURISM ATTRACTIONS   2009   KUŠEN'S ©

Fig. 7.5 Two-dimensional model projection (*Source:* Kušen, E. (2010), p. 422)

two-dimensional projection of the Model in English (Fig. 7.5), facilitating reading the model in the photo.

The table on the front side of the Model represents the basic division of tourism attractions (Fig. 7.1), and the table on the right lateral side represents their detailed division (part of Table 7.4). The back side features a table that depicts the different groups into which the various types of tourism attractions are classified. The table on the top side of the Model contains a basic division of mandatory data for each tourism attraction. The left lateral page contains just a table net where the data on the front and top sides of the Model can be cross-referenced.

A Registry of Tourism Attractions

Testing the basic components of the System of Tourism Attractions during the first and second stage has confirmed its practical value in creation of the tourism attraction documentation system—the Registry and Atlas that have, after the entire System was created and successfully tested, got its final form initially in analogue format and, subsequently, in a digital format that offers limitless possibilities for expansion.

A Registry of Tourism Attractions of any tourist destination, basic or of a higher order, is a method for keeping written data about all potential and real tourism attractions. Its functionality lies in the multidimensional connectivity between data entered in its analogue version and the added interactive possibilities in the digital version. This Registry is open to the expansion of data in all directions, including keeping data on other direct and indirect tourism resources. However, it also offers connectivity with a cartographic tourism attraction data management system, especially the Atlas of Tourism Attractions. If applied correctly, it can change the current practice of managing tourism attractions in Croatia and elsewhere, whereby great financial resources were wasted. Over the past 20 years, a large amount of money was invested into collecting tourism attraction data when various tourism plans and other documents were drafted. However, the data has not been managed, if it was kept at all.

As part of the aforementioned Croatian-Hungarian project based on Kušen's System of Tourism Attractions and the analogue Registry of Tourism Attractions, it was possible to create a digital version in late 2013, toward the very end of the Second Research Phase. This digital version offers numerous new solutions that only digital technology can provide and which can return the tourism attractions to marketing in their full extend. Due to the unlimited amount of information available through the digital Registry, and because of the ability to promptly update and organize data, some parts of the Registry data can be made available to the final user, an individual tourist, in marketing purposes.

SYNTHESIS: CONVERSION OF A TOURISM RESOURCE INTO A TOURISM PRODUCT

A System of Tourism Attractions as a theoretical model with the accompanying Registry and Atlas of Tourism Attractions with its practical value represents a synthesis of the two stages of this research. Moreover, the synthesis of the knowledge obtained as a result of this research provided an answer to the question as to why *the rules and causalities that so unambig-uously exist among the components of the attraction microcosm are of interest to such a small number of people*. The answer lies beyond the dogmatic and non-creative interpretation of the *conversion* property and function of tourism. Namely, the Synthesis procedure yielded the integrated process, mechanism and course of conversion of a tourist resource into a tourist product (Fig. 7.6). To be precise, recent tourism theory and practice have omitted several important links from that chain. Which links are missing? Let us start with conversion.

The conversion property of tourism is one of the postulates upon which tourism, as we know it, is based. It is elaborated and taken over from an earlier publication (Kušen, 2010). The conversion function of tourism makes it possible to include into the economic process many assets which are, otherwise, not considered commodities and do not have an adequate market value. This function of tourism is applicable to many assets that do not have character of commodities or do not have an economic value. The tourism economy is possibly the only factor that can convert them into commodities, explore them economically or transform them into rev-enue. First and foremost, these are potential and real tourism attractions, but some other resources as well, for example, the population with their awareness of tourism value and tourism culture. One of the characteristics of tourism conversions is the fact that, in principle, these assets are not altered during the conversion process, on a condition that the tourism industry treats its tourism assets as a good master, i.e. uses them rationally.

A typical characteristic of the conversion function of tourism is that its effect is economic valorization of those assets that cannot be converted into commodities in any other way or only rarely. With the help of tour-ism, cultural, historic and other social assets become economic resources. Without tourism, they would not even exist as a tangible asset let alone have a market value. Rational exploitation of most of these resources, nat-ural, for example, will not result in their depletion, whereas the exploita-tion of cultural and historical monuments wear and tear is spread over their long lifespan, which is regularly extended through conservation work, funded most commonly from proceeds of tourism as a result of their tourist valorization. Their economic exploitation does not reduce their original value but, rather, increases it, though that is also subject to mar-ket developments. Most of these resources are firmly linked to a location,

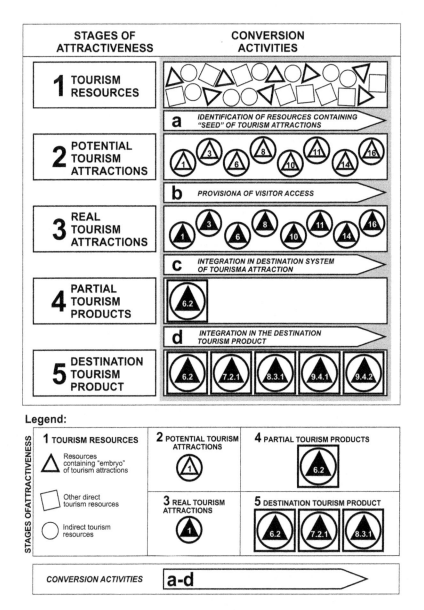

Fig. 7.6   Process of conversion of a tourism resource into a tourism product

i.e. they cannot be moved or copied. Therefore, their aforementioned tourism conversion into sellable commodities coincides with the conversion of those resources into monopolies. Such tourism assets generate tourism rent, which are not expressed by their individual market price, but as part of a total value of tourism products, tourism services and products of other participants in the tourism supply into which that original price has been incorporated.

The multidimensional Tourism Attraction System makes it easy to understand the process of conversion of a tourism resource into a tourism product, the very essence of the conversion phenomenon in tourism. Its mechanism and processes are influenced by natural and social conditions. Within that process, tourism resources pass through different but unavoidable attraction phases, (1) as tourism resources, (2) as potential tourism attractions, (3) as real tourism attractions, (4) as partial tourism products and (5) as parts of a destination tourism product. Such conversion is contingent on very specific activities. A change in a particular attraction phase will occur only under the impact of the following activities: (a) identification and registration of resources that contain 'the seed' of tourism attractiveness, (b) ensuring accessibility of a potential tourism attraction, (c) integration of a real tourism attraction into the attraction framework of a tourism destination and (d) integration of a partial tourism product into a destination tourism product, as illustrated by Fig. 7.6.

There is no awareness on how important it is to identify and register such tourist resources that contain the seed of tourist attractiveness (a); therefore, there can be no data on potential tourism attractions (2) as a separate attraction phase or, if there is data, it is exceptionally rare and typically incomplete. The absence of these two links within the process of converting tourism resources into tourism products is the main reason for the lack of understanding and non-acceptance of the concept of the new Tourism Attraction System and Registry of Tourism Attractions. Moreover, the underdeveloped integration of real tourism attractions into the attraction framework of a tourism destination (c) and partial tourist products into a destination tourist product (d) makes tourism destination management more difficult.

In short, the System of Tourism Attractions has realized most of the previously set partial goals; for example, it offers a new, innovative approach to the tourist-destination development within a general tourism system by putting emphasis on tourism attractions. It also offers functionality within its internal attraction structure, but also from all other aspects of a wider tourism system. Moreover, it has become applicable in most procedures in tourism theory and practice. Furthermore, it contains a functional classification of tourism attractions and a method for determining their properties. Finally, it also offers a three-dimensional model, which shows the internal connectedness of its components. All of these important properties of the System are surpassed by its ability to serve as a base for a Registry of Tourism Attractions.

REFERENCES

Dawkins, C. J. (2003). Regional development theory: Conceptual foundations, classic works, and recent developments. *Journal of Planning Literature, 18*(2), 131–172.

Gunn, C. A. (1972). *Vacationscapes: Designing tourist regions.* Washington, DC: Taylor & Francis.

ICM Guide. (2000). *World tourism attractions.* London: Columbus Publishing Limited.

Kušen, E. (1999). *Metodologija prostorne valorizacije turističkih privlačnosti [Methodology of tourism attractions space valorization].* Zagreb: Arhitektonski fakultet Sveučilišta u Zagrebu.

Kušen, E. (2002a). *Turistička atrakcijska osnova [Tourism attraction Base].* Zagreb: Institut za turizam.

Kušen, E. (2002b). Classification and categorization of basic tourism destinations as a prerequisite for their protection. In *International tourism research conference Reinventing a Tourism Destination, Dubrovnik, 18th – 21st October 2002* (pp.146–148). Zagreb: Institute for Tourism and Croatian Tourist Board.

Kušen, E. (2010). A system of tourism attractions. *Tourism, 58*(4), 409–424.

Kušen, E. (2011). *Tablični prikaz turističkih atrakcija, industrijski dizajn [Tabular presentation of tourism attractions, industrial design].* Zagreb: Državni zavod za intelektualno vlasništvo Republike Hrvatske.

Kušen, E., & Tadej, P. (2003). Functional classification of tourism attractions. *Tourism, 51*(4), 427–442.

Leiper, N. (1990). Tourism attraction systems. *Annals of Tourism Research, 17*(3), 367–384.

Lew, A. A. (1987). A Framework of tourism attraction research. *Annals of Tourism Research, 14*(4), 553–575.

Lew, A. A. (2000). Attraction. In J. Jafari (Ed.), *Encyclopedia of tourism* (pp. 35–37). New York: Routledge.

Mill, R. C., & Morrison, A. M. (1985). *Tourism system*. New York: Prentice Hall.
OECD. (1992). *Tourism policy and international tourism in OECD member countries*. Paris: OECD Publications.
WTO. (1993). *Sustainable tourism development: Guide for local planners*. Madrid: World Tourism Organization.

CHAPTER 8

Implementation of Tourism Satellite Account: Assessing the Contribution of Tourism to the Croatian Economy

Neven Ivandić and Zrinka Marušić

INTRODUCTION

The System of National Accounts (SNA) is a comprehensive accounting framework for compiling and presenting data on complex economic activities within a national economy and its links with the rest of the world. In the 1993's version (Commission of the European Communities, International Monetary Fund, Organization for Economic Cooperation and Development, United Nations, & World Bank, 1993; below SNA 1993), the SNA enables flexible extensions of national accounting through so-called satellite accounts. The satellite accounts are designed to recognize and emphasize important economic activities hidden within the main framework of the SNA. Tourism is one of the activities for which the compilation of satellite account is recommended as 'delineating tourism activities raises a lot of difficulties' (SNA 1993, 21.16). The necessity for a special treatment of tourism resulted in an impulse for the development of a methodological framework for compiling a Tourism Satellite Account (TSA). As a link between tourism statistics and standard national accounts tables, TSA is based on reliable and

N. Ivandić (✉) • Z. Marušić
Institute for Tourism, Zagreb, Croatia

© The Author(s) 2017
L. Dwyer et al. (eds.), *Evolution of Destination Planning and Strategy*, DOI 10.1007/978-3-319-42246-6_8

149

internationally comparable statistical observations organized and reconciled in the form of accounts. It measures the direct economic impact of visitors to a country's economy (Frechtling, 2010). Measurement of the total economic impact, on the other hand, implies the use of different types of economic models. Among them, the most common are input-output models (I-O) and computable general equilibrium (CGE) models (Frechtling, 2013; Los & Steenge, 2010; Song, Dwyer, Li, & Cao, 2012).

Basic TSA concepts have been developed since the late 1970s, and several attempts at the measurement of the contribution of tourism had been made (Alriquet & Herbecq, 1979; Lapierre, 1991; Organisation for Economic Cooperation and Development, 1991; World Tourism Organization, 1983) even before the first international conference with the main topic of TSA was organized in Ottawa in 1991. The framework for internationally harmonized measurements of the macroeconomic contribution of tourism and the calculation of the main tourism macro-aggregates was initially set by 2001 Tourism Satellite Account: Recommended Methodological Framework (Commission of the European Communities, Organisation of Economic Co-operation and Development, United Nations, & World Tourism Organization, 2001; below TSA:RMF 2001). The updated version, 2008 Tourism Satellite Account: Recommended Methodological Framework (United Nations, World Tourism Organization, Eurostat—Commission of the European Communities, & Organisation for Economic Co-operation and Development, 2010a; below TSA:RMF 2008), was aligned with a new version of the International Recommendation of Tourism Statistics (United Nations & World Tourism Organization, 2010b). The inauguration of these documents initialized the compilation of TSAs in many countries. By 2004, 70 countries or regions were in the process of TSA development (Libreros, Massieu, & Meis, 2006), while by 2009, 20 EU countries were regularly compiling TSA or were in the process of its experimental or pilot phase (Eurostat, 2009). In spite of the inaugurated methodological framework, various approaches have been taken to constructing TSA tables, from methods of estimation of internal tourism consumption to the definition and scope of tourism industries and products. The myriad of different solutions is primarily a reflection of an imperfect system of tourism statistics, both from the perspective of its given structure and its development on national levels. Recognizing the underlying issues, the European Commission stresses the 'need to improve the availability, completeness and comprehensiveness of the basic tourism statistics as an input for compiling TSA' (European Union, 2011, p. 17).

Attempts to assess the contribution of tourism have also been made in Croatia. Prior to the international adoption of TSA:RMF 2001, these attempts, due to inadequate tourism statistics and/or nonaligned methods, only partially measured tourism consumption and its contribution (Car, Cicvarić, Radnić, & Sekulić, 1975; Ivandić & Radnić, 1997; Radnić, 1990; Radnić & Ivandić, 1999). Significant improvements of the Croatian system of tourism statistics (STS) occurred in the early 2000s (Horak, Marušić, & Radnić, 1999; Institute for Tourism, 2003), followed by efforts to enrich knowledge of different aspects of tourism impacts (Blažević, 2007; Kesar, 2006) and to evaluate the feasibility of TSA compilation (Institute for Tourism, 2007). An experimental TSA for Croatia was compiled for 2005 (Institute for Tourism, 2008) and 2007 (Institute for Tourism, 2010), followed by the first TSA developed for 2011 (Ivandić, Marušić, Šutalo, & Vuglar, 2014). During that time, parallel efforts were made in the application of tourism impact models based on both the CGE and the I-O approach (Gatti, 2013; Šutalo, Ivandić, & Marušić, 2011).

Since the assessment of the role of tourism in a national economy is a very complex task (Ahlert, 2007) characterized by different solutions in applying the TSA methodological framework on the national level (Eurostat, 2009), this paper aims to discuss the application of theoretical concepts provided by the TSA methodological framework to measure tourism flows in conditions limited by lack of relevant and reliable data. The case of Croatia was used for this exercise, reviewing different issues and possible solutions that arise in the process of TSA development.

The paper has six parts. Following the introduction, the second section deals with the relevance of TSA and its main concepts. The third part reveals an approach to measurement of internal tourism consumption, while, in the fourth part, internal tourism consumption is combined with total output, stressing the issue of unregistered flows. The fifth section is focused on Croatian tourism macro-aggregates and their international comparison, while the last part gives a number of TSA policy implications and recommendations for the future work on TSA development.

TSA—Concepts, Tables and Benefits

Why doesn't the SNA methodology thoroughly assess the contribution of tourism activity? The answer lies in the fact that tourism is not defined by the nature of its output, inputs used or techniques of production employed (SNA 1993) but rather by the position of the customer—the visitor.

Tourism has to be considered as a set of production activities led by demand created by visitors. TSA is 'a step forward in quantifying the direct effects of tourism on the basis of a clearly understandable, uniform and internationally binding accounting system' (Ahlert, 2007, p. 285). Such an assessment of tourism implies, from the perspective of the country of residence of visitors and the country of reference (distinguishing domestic, inbound and outbound tourism), a more specific understanding of a number of issues of which the most important are the visitor, a usual environment, tourism expenditure and tourism consumption (TSA:RMF 2008).

Building on the framework and methodology of the standard SNA tables from a functional perspective (TSA:RMF 2001), a TSA is comprised of ten tables. The core tables (TSA Tables 1, 2, 3, 4, 5, 6, 10) are related to monetary and non-monetary indicators of tourism expenditure and consumption and the output of tourism industries. In particular, TSA Tables 1, 2 and 3 present a division of tourism expenditures by inbound, domestic and outbound visitors, respectively, according to products and services aligned with Central Product Classification and organized into tourism-specific products, tourism characteristic products, non-tourism-related consumption products and non-consumption products. TSA Table 4 presents estimates of total internal tourism consumption, summing inbound (TSA Table 1) and domestic (TSA Table 2) tourism expenditures as well as additional components of tourism consumption. TSA Table 5, based on Supply and Use Table (SUT), connects products (rows) and output of tourism and other industries (columns). Tourism industries, those that produce tourism characteristic products, are in accordance with International Standard Industrial Classification of all Economic Activities. Integrating internal tourism consumption (TSA Table 4) with domestic supply (TSA Table 5), TSA Table 6 is the 'heart' of TSA tables enabling the calculation of the direct contribution of tourism to the economy. Other tables examine employment in tourism industries (TSA Table 7), tourism gross fixed capital formation (TSA Table 8) and tourism collective consumption (TSA Table 9).

In addition to the ten mentioned tables, a TSA includes five macro-aggregates as indicators of the size of tourism in a national economy. Two of them are related to consumption and three to production: (i) internal tourism expenditures, (ii) internal tourism consumption, (iii) gross value added of tourism industries (GVATI), (iv) tourism direct gross value added (TDGVA) and (v) tourism direct gross domestic product (TDGDP). GVATI is a sum of the total gross value added of all establishments belonging to tourism industries, regardless of whether all their output is used by visitors and of the degree of specialization of their production process. TDGVA is a sum of the parts of gross value added generated by tourism industries and other industries of the economy that directly serve visitors, responding to internal tourism consumption. TDGDP is a sum of part of gross value added (at basic prices) generated by all industries in response to internal tourism consumption plus the amount of net taxes on products and imports included within the value of this expenditure at purchaser's prices.

TDGVA and TDGDP are measures of the direct economic contribution of tourism to the economy, but it should be taken into account that they only measure internal tourism consumption and do not consider other components of total tourism demand, namely, tourism gross fixed capital formation and tourism collective consumption. This is of particular relevance when comparing TDGDP with the gross domestic product of other industries.

Despite its limitations (Jones & Munday, 2008; Smeral, 2006), the TSA today represents state-of-the-art methodology for collecting, presenting and comparing national tourism statistics (Kenneally & Jakee, 2012), and it provides a significant advance for those wishing to undertake tourism economic analysis (Jones & Munday, 2008). Numerous potential benefits of TSA are recognized (Frangialli, 2006), among which it is worth mentioning the improvement of the information base for conducting a national tourism policy and marketing strategy and adjustments and fine-tuning of STS and the increase of the use of tourism research results in the private sector (Ivandić & Marušić, 2009).

ASSESSMENT OF INTERNAL TOURISM CONSUMPTION: THE CASE OF CROATIA

A large number of scientific and professional papers deal with the estimation of tourism expenditures as an important economic driver (Sainaghi, 2012). Frechtling (2006) compares seven most frequently used methods for estimation of tourism expenditures and concludes that visitor surveys and cost-factor models, if correctly applied, produce the most valid estimates. Stynes and White (2006) emphasize the importance of measurement units, spending categories and the segmentation of visitors. Wilton and Nickerson (2006) stress the importance of applying the appropriate survey methods in order to reduce non-sampling errors such as recall bias that usually results in spending underestimation.

The assessment of STS in Croatia found it as mostly satisfactory for the estimation of internal tourism consumption within the TSA framework (Ivandić & Marušić, 2009) as it is based on relevant and accurate, although not fully appropriate, surveys. The surveys upon which the data is derived from are (i) Survey on expenditures of foreign visitors in Croatia in 2011, Croatian National Bank (below border survey), (ii) Tourism—monthly survey on tourism arrivals and overnights in commercial accommodation facilities in 2011 (Croatian Bureau of Statistics, 2012; below accommodation occupancy survey), (iii) Survey on attitudes and expenditures of tourists in Croatia in 2010 (Institute for Tourism, 2011; below visitor survey), (iv) Survey on attitudes and expenditures of nautical tourists in Croatia in 2012 (Institute for Tourism, 2013; below nautical visitor survey) and (v) Survey on travel pattern of domestic population in 2011 (Institute for Tourism, 2012; below travel household survey). However, the level of development of STS does not yet allow the compilation of a complete TSA. The limitations of these data sources are that they currently do not cover all segments of tourism demand (e.g., inbound tourists entering Croatia by water and railway border crossings and tourists on Croatian cruise ships), while the level of disaggregation of tourism expenditures does not fully meet TSA criteria (e.g., expenditures for culture, sport and recreation are aggregated as well as expenditures for transport services). Compilation of TSA Tables 1 to 4 therefore assumes partial assessment of expenditures from the supply side based on ad hoc surveys of specific service providers, as well as aggregation of some tourism characteristic products. Regarding the disaggregation of tourism expenditures by segments of demand, the chosen approach and sources presented in Table 8.1 comply with the proposed framework.

Total internal tourism consumption in Croatia in 2011 is estimated at 8.6 billion Euro (Ivandić et al., 2014). Inbound tourism expenditures make up 76.5 per cent, and domestic tourism expenditures 19.5 per cent of internal tourism consumption, while four per cent are related to imputed accommodation services of vacation homes. The accommodation services for visitors generate the largest part of internal tourism consumption (27 per cent) within tourism characteristic products, followed by food and beverage services (22 per cent), transport services (five per cent) and cultural, sports and recreational services (four per cent). Expenditures for other products and services make up 40 per cent of internal tourism consumption. The high percentage of expenditures being attributed to other products and services, idiosyncratic to the Croatian TSA, can be explained by the inclusion of the category Transport equipment rental services in other products and services but also, in a larger extent, a sole reflection of Croatian tourism demand characteristics. Most of Croatian tourists arrive by means of car transport where the dominant types of accommodation facilities are camps and households as well as second homes and friends and relatives accommodation. Finally, this results to a large part of tourist expenditures generated in retail (for food and beverages as well as fuel) and highway tolls.

The applied methodological approach revealed two crucial areas of particular importance due to their significant contribution to the total tourism consumption and due to the reliability of the available data sources used for the obtained estimations: (i) the expenditures of tourists in household accommodation and (ii) the expenditures of nautical visitors (yachting, cruising).

The estimation of total volume of physical demand has shown to be a major issue in calculating the expenditures of tourism in household accommodation. Household accommodation is the most important part (49 per cent in 2011) of Croatian total tourism accommodation capacity measured by the number of beds (Croatian Bureau of Statistics, 2012) which makes 35 per cent of total overnights. Since the official data are based on the supply side approach, they face problems of accuracy of reporting and quality of registers, particularly in the case of household accommodation. Therefore, a specific approach has been developed combining supply and demand side data, as described in Table 8.1, which resulted in doubled estimation of the number of tourists in household accommodation compared to the official data. This has at least two implications for tourism policy in general: (i) recognition of unregistered tourism flows and (ii) distortion of productivity indicators based on TSA. The latter is a consequence of the fact that employment in household accommodation is not taken into account within employment in tourism industries (TSA Table 7). The issue of unregistered tourism flows should also be taken into account in the production side of TSA.

As illustrated by the case of the importance of household accommodation, the process of TSA compilation should be based on linkage and thorough verification of coherence and consistency of data sources. On the other hand, the TSA framework does not allow deeper insight into the importance and characteristics of specific tourism products, such as cultural, business, sun and beach, sport tourism and so on. One example of such products is yachting and cruising tourism, both on the sea and rivers,

Table 8.1 Methodological approach for assessment of internal tourism expenditures in Croatia in 2011

Inbound tourism expenditures	
Number of visitors (NI)	Due to the overestimation of number of inbound visitors obtained by border survey (Ivandić & Marušić, 2009), the estimates are based on: Distribution of inbound visitors by length of stay and type of accommodation: border survey Number of tourist arrivals in hotels and similar accommodation: accommodation occupancy survey The obtained estimates are modified for: Multiple arrivals to hotel and similar establishments during one trip: visitor survey Number of visitors in nautical tourism: nautical visitors survey
Average tourism expenditures (AEI)	Border survey with exemption of expenditures for durable goods
Total tourism expenditures (TEI)	$TEI = \sum_{1}^{n} NI_i AEI_i$, where i represents segments of tourism demand by length of stay and type of accommodation
Domestic tourism expenditures	
Number of visitors	Number of visitors on domestic trips, both within country (NDC) and abroad (NDA): travel household survey
Average tourism expenditures	Trips within country (AEDC): travel household survey Outbound trips (AEDA): travel household survey with expert estimates of share of goods and services used on domestic part of outbound trip
Total tourism expenditures (TED)	$TED = \sum_{1}^{n} NDC_i AEDC_i + \sum_{1}^{n} NDA_i AEDA_i$, where i represents segments of tourism demand by length of stay and type of accommodation
Tourism expenditures per product and service	
Accommodation and food and beverage services	Inbound tourists: border survey with correction for expenditures on package trips Domestic tourists: travel household survey with correction for the expenditures on package trips Package trip expenditures were disaggregated into the components using information on cost structure and margins obtained from tour operators and travel agencies (ad hoc survey)
Passenger transport services	Expenditures of inbound, domestic and outbound visitors on particular transport services are estimated from the supply side based on expert assessments by the main Croatian transport service providers, collected through in-depth interviews; the interviews covered data on passengers and revenues in domestic and international transport and expert assessments of inbound and domestic tourism expenditures; in water passenger transport services, only maritime passenger transport services were included due to lack of data on river and lake transport

(continued)

Table 8.1 (continued)

Inbound tourism expenditures	
Travel agencies and other reservation services	Border and travel household survey for expenditures on package trips and ad hoc survey of tour operators and travel agencies for package cost structure and margins
Cultural, sports and recreational services	Border and travel household survey (this product category also includes expenditures for boat charter and berths in marinas)
Other products and services (retail trade, toll, other)	Border and travel household survey (residual between the total expenditures and expenditures on abovementioned products)
Other issues regarding expenditures	
Expenditures on renting of transport vehicles	Car and other transport vehicles (other than boat charter) rental services are not treated as tourism characteristic products but as expenditures on other products and services
Country-specific tourism goods and services	Not estimated
Other components of tourism consumption	
Housing services provided by vacation homes on own account	Includes imputed accommodation services of vacation homes estimated by share of vacation homes in total housing (11.1 per cent of total housing services in Croatia in 2011); it should be noted that Eurostat (2012) recommends application of a cascade system to trips to vacation homes meaning that those second homes within a municipality would by default be part of the usual environment
Tourism social transfers in kind and other imputed consumption	Not estimated

referred to as nautical tourism (Lück, 2007; Lukovic, 2013). Given the fact that Croatia is internationally recognized for its long rugged coastlines and numerous islands, nautical tourism is of outmost importance for the country, significantly contributing to the total tourism consumption. Nautical tourism is characterized by a specific structure of tourism consumption product expenditures that is significantly different from the majority of other tourism products. Namely, the dominant parts of nautical tourist expenditures are expenditures for sport (berths in marinas), renting and leasing (renting of yachts and recreational boats) and transport (renting yachts with crew, berths in public ports) services. There is almost no expenditure for accommodation services within nautical tourism. Its relevance for total tourism flows in Croatia might cause misunderstanding of the importance of some of tourism-specific products and activities. This requires special attention of tourism policy makers and even compilation of a specific satellite account (Diakomihalis & Lagos, 2008; Dwyer, Deery, Jago, Spurr, & Fredline, 2007) for nautical tourism, having in mind the limited availability of the production side data on such a highly disaggregated level. Alternatively, there is a possibility to extract nautical tourism into the country-specific tourism consumption product. Nevertheless, that extraction is not only having the problem of data availability but is also burdened by the fact that nautical tourism comprises several different tourism products (Marušić, Ivandić, & Horak, 2014).

ASSESSMENT OF THE TOTAL DOMESTIC SUPPLY AND TOURISM RATIOS: THE CASE OF CROATIA

In TSA Table 5, the production of tourism and other industries in the economy is analyzed. For each industry (column), the output (at basic prices) is broken down by product, intermediate input at purchaser's prices and gross value added at basic prices.

The main data sources for compilation of TSA Table 5 for Croatia are those used for the calculation of gross domestic product (GDP) for 2011 (Croatian Bureau of Statistics, 2013a) which is based on the accounting framework given by The European System of National and Regional Accounts (ESA 2010), including estimates of non-observed production. Business entities are grouped within activities as institutional units and not solely as homogenous kind-of-activity units.

According to the TSA framework, tourism activities in TSA Table 5 are in line with the national classification of economic activities for 2007. As Croatian GDP is compiled on a two-digit (division) NACE level only, corrections based on specific surveys were needed in order to obtain reliable estimates at appropriate three- (group) or four-digit (class) NACE levels. As a result of this aggregation of some tourism products in TSA Tables 1 to 4, classification of tourism industries in TSA Table 5 does not fully meet the recommendations. Output of transport equipment rental is allocated to output of other industries, while output of cultural, sports and recreational industries is aggregated together. Finally, no country-specific tourism characteristic industries were specified. The adopted approach is presented in Table 8.2.

TSA Table 6 combines internal tourism consumption and total domestic supply. The rows are identical to those in TSA Table 5, while columns are organized in three blocks: (i) output and tourism share per industry,

Table 8.2 Methodological approach for assessment of output, intermediate inputs and gross value added of tourism industries in Croatia in 2011

Accommodation for visitors	Data for accommodation activities (division 55 of national classification of economic activities 2007) from national accounts are decomposed per specific products based on survey on hotel and restaurant activity (Croatian Bureau of Statistics, 2011) for 2010 Similar to the demand side, housing services provided by vacation homes are imputed accommodation services of vacation homes estimated by share of vacation homes in total housing; issue of housing services (imputed value) provided by vacation homes is of particular importance for Croatia, as for other Mediterranean countries (Frent, 2008)
Food and beverage serving industry	Data for food and beverage service activities (division 56) from national accounts are decomposed per specific products based on survey on hotel and restaurant activity (Croatian Bureau of Statistics, 2011) for 2010
Passenger transport industries	Data from national accounts are decomposed per specific passenger transport industries based on structural business statistics (annual financial statements for legal persons and income tax return for crafts and trades): Railway passenger transport: data on passenger transport from national railway company (exclusive service provider) Road passenger transport: share of other passenger land transport (49.39) and taxi operation (49.32) was applied Water passenger transport: share of sea and coastal passenger transport (50.10) was applied Air passenger transport: data on passenger transport from the biggest national airline company
Travel agencies and other reservation services industry	Data for travel agency, tour operator and other reservation service and related activities (division 79) from national accounts
Cultural, sports and recreational industry	Data for section R—Arts, Entertainment and Recreation from national accounts

(ii) adjustments for calculation of domestic supply at purchaser's prices and (iii) internal tourism consumption and tourism ratio. A detailed approach for compilation of key elements of TSA Table 6 is outlined in Table 8.3.

The presented application of theoretical concepts of the TSA framework in the case of Croatia in 2011 resulted in 5.2 billion Euro value of output of tourism industries or 6.8 per cent of total output of domestic producers (Table 8.4). Tourism products and services generating the highest output are accommodation for visitors (1.7 billion Euro), food

Table 8.3   Methodological approach for assessment of TSA Table 6 in Croatia in 2011

Output of tourism industries	Output (basic prices), intermediate consumption (purchaser's prices) and total gross value added (basic prices) of domestic producers from TSA Table 5
Internal tourism consumption	TSA Table 4
Tourism share by tourism industries	Accommodation for visitors: expert assumption that production is in total generated by tourism demand Food and beverage serving industry: production generated by tourism demand based on border and travel household survey, production generated by local (non-tourism) demand based on household survey and travel household survey Passenger transport, travel agencies and other reservation services industry, culture, sports and recreational industry: internal expenditure at basic prices
Tourism share in other industries	Residual between the total tourism expenditures at basic prices and sum of: (i) expenditures on tourism products and services at basic prices and (ii) imports of goods and services for tourism consumption
Imports of goods and services for final consumption	Imports of goods and services for final consumption are treated as part of other products and services since: (i) accommodation, food and beverage, culture, recreation and sport services are provided by Croatian economic entities only, and (ii) passenger transport services and travel agencies/tour operator services are estimated for Croatian providers only Tourism's share of imports is estimated based on ratio of internal tourism consumption and total output
Taxes on goods and services and subsidies	Ministry of finance budgetary central government revenue for value added tax (VAT), excise duty, other types of taxes on goods and services and subsidies Allocation of VAT by products and services, as well as custom duty on imports of goods and services for final consumption based on SUT for 2005 (Croatian Bureau of Statistics, 2013b) Allocation of excise duty and subsidies by products and services based on expert assessment
Tourism ratio	Internal tourism consumption (at purchaser's prices) as a proportion of domestic supply in per cent. Estimates of internal tourism consumption for accommodation and food and beverage services exceed the total estimated output indicating higher level of unregistered tourism flows than those applied in GDP for 2011

and beverage services (1.5 billion Euro) and cultural, sports and recreational services including mooring services in nautical ports, like marinas (0.7 billion Euro). In total, these three categories account for three quarters of total output of tourism industries.

Table 8.4 Total domestic supply and internal tourism consumption (elements of TSA Table 6) for Croatia in 2011

	Total tourism industries		Other industries		Output of domestic producers (at basic prices)		Imports (of final goods and services) euro mil	Net taxes on products euro mil	Domestic supply (at purchaser's prices) euro mil	Internal tourism consumption euro mil	Tourism ratios in %
	Output euro mil	Tourism share in %	Output euro mil	Tourism share in %	Output euro mil	Tourism share in %					
A. Consumption products	5,214.4	79.5	71,810.7	3.7	77,025.1	8.8	8,008.6	6,318.9	91,352.6	8,581.6	9.4
A.1 Tourism characteristic products	5,006.4	79.4	0.0	0.0	5,006.4	79.4	0.0	509.4	5,515.8	5,145.4	93.3
1. Accommodation services for visitors	2,057.6	99.9	0.0	0.0	2,057.6	99.9	0.0	167.6	2,225.2	2,340.9	105.2
1.a. Accommodation services for visitors other than 1.b	1,704.7	99.9	0.0	0.0	1,704.7	99.9	0.0	167.6	1,872.2	1,987.9	106.2
1.b. Accommodation services associated with all types of vacation home ownership	353.0	100.0	0.0	0.0	353.0	100.0	0.0	0.0	353.0	353.0	100.0
2. Food and beverage serving services	1,529.0	75.0	0.0	0.0	1,529.0	75.0	0.0	220.4	1,749.5	1,856.8	106.1
3. Railway passenger transport services	123.8	25.5	0.0	0.0	123.8	25.5	0.0	-39.9	83.9	38.9	46.3

(continued)

Table 8.4 (continued)

	Total tourism industries		Other industries		Output of domestic producers (at basic prices)		Imports (of final goods and services) euro mil	Net taxes on products euro mil	Domestic supply (at purchaser's prices) euro mil	Internal tourism consumption euro mil	Tourism ratios in %
	Output euro mil	Tourism share in %	Output euro mil	Tourism share in %	Output euro mil	Tourism share in %					
4. Road passenger transport services	79.8	85.0	0.0	0.0	79.8	85.0	0.0	13.6	93.4	83.4	89.3
5. Water passenger transport services	140.6	39.0	0.0	0.0	140.6	39.0	0.0	-22.3	118.3	67.4	57.0
6. Air passenger transport services	295.6	67.7	0.0	0.0	295.6	67.7	0.0	0.4	296.0	246.3	83.2
7. Travel agencies and other reservation services	123.0	92.6	0.0	0.0	123.0	92.6	0.0	18.4	141.4	140.0	99.0
8. Cultural, sports and recreational services	657.0	46.0	0.0	0.0	657.0	46.0	0.0	151.1	808.1	371.7	46.0
A.2 Other consumption products	208.0	81.9	71,810.7	3.7	72,018.7	3.9	8,008.6	5,809.5	85,836.7	3,436.3	4.0
Total output (at basic prices)	5,214.4	79.5	71,810.7	3.7	77,025.1	8.8	8,008.6	6,318.9	91,352.6	8,581.6	9.4
Total intermediate consumption (at purchaser's price)	1,967.0	73.0	37,157.5	3.7	39,124.5	7.1					
Total gross value added (at basic prices)	3,247.4	83.4	34,653.2	3.7	37,900.6	10.5					

Source: Ivandić et al. (2014)

The tourism industry generated 3.2 billion Euro of gross value added or 8.6 per cent of Croatian total value added, making it the industry with the highest gross value added per unit of output.

Tourism generates 79.5 per cent of output and 83.4 per cent of the gross value added of tourism industries. Besides accommodation services for visitors and travel agencies and other reservation services, which are, by default, predominantly generated by tourism (99.9 per cent and 92.6 per cent, respectively), highly tourism-dependent products and services are also passenger transport services and food and beverage serving services. Tourism share of other consumption products is 3.9 per cent.

Domestic supply at purchaser's prices, calculated as domestic output at basic prices increased by imports and net taxes, is 91.4 billion Euro of which tourism characteristic products generate six per cent. A lower share of tourism characteristic products in the domestic supply at purchaser's prices than in domestic output at basic prices is a result of imports of final goods and services, while the share of net taxes in domestic supply at purchaser's prices of tourism characteristic products is higher than that share in other consumption products.

Internal tourism consumption makes up 9.4 per cent of total domestic supply at purchaser's prices. A numerical difference between the tourism share and tourism ratio, the difference being their calculation either from the supply or demand perspective, respectively, indicates a potential problem of unregistered flows. The internal tourism consumption of food and beverage serving services is 6.1 per cent higher than the recorded level of domestic supply at purchaser's prices. Since these services include local consumption as well, the level of unregistered flows is obviously much higher than estimated within the national accounts. The recent process of fiscalization carried out in Croatia during the 2013 has confirmed such findings (Vizek, 2014). Furthermore, a tourism ratio over 100 per cent is also recorded for accommodation services for visitors. Similar discrepancies are also found in some other countries like the Czech Republic, Hungary, Slovenia and the United Kingdom (Eurostat, 2009). The observed issues clearly indicate a need for better understanding and dealing with the flows that are, at least partly, generated within household accommodation. However, it should be noted that the observed differences did not affect the calculation of gross domestic value of tourism since the calculation is derived from the production share of tourism with the purpose of conforming to national accounts.

Finally, tourism directly contributes 10.4 per cent to Croatian GDP (4.61 billion Euro) based on balancing the internal tourism consumption to the level of total output at purchaser's prices in accommodation and food and beverage services.

CROATIA TSA MACRO-AGGREGATES AND INTERNATIONAL COMPARISONS

Among 17 EU member states (Table 8.5), Germany, the United Kingdom and France have the highest internal tourism consumption. Tourism gross value added (at basic prices) is reported by 13 countries, with the highest reported in Germany, Italy and the United Kingdom, among which data for France and Spain were not collected (Eurostat, 2013).

Although Croatia is among countries with a lower level of, both, internal tourism consumption and tourism gross value added, its tourism ratio indicates that Croatia has the highest dependence on tourism demand.

Table 8.5   Tourism gross value added and internal tourism consumption for EU countries (million euro)

Country	Reporting year	Tourism gross value added (at basic prices)	Internal tourism consumption	Tourism ratio in %
Croatia	2011	3,974	8,582	9.4
Austria	2011	16,463	30,437	3.9
Czech Republic	2011	3,609	8,488	1.6
Estonia	2008	539	1,452	3.1
France	2005	–	137,577	–
Germany	2010	97,049	278,317	4.7
Italy	2010	82,833	114,016	3.2
Latvia	2005	416	642	2.2
Lithuania	2010	689	1,397	2.0
Netherlands	2009	13,670	35,145	2.2
Poland	2008	–	13,198	–
Portugal	2007	6,209	15,467	3.8
Romania	2009	1,909	4,527	1.6
Slovakia	2010	1,595	3,560	1.7
Slovenia	2009	1,102	3,348	3.6
Spain	2008	–	120,889	5.7
Sweden	2010	–	25,992	3.1
United Kingdom	2009	81,586	141,507	3.7

Source: Eurostat, 2013, and Ivandić et al., 2014, for Croatia

Particularly, Croatian internal tourism consumption equals 9.4 per cent of domestic supply, while Spain with 5.7 per cent has the second and Germany with 4.7 per cent the third highest tourism ratio. However, regardless the Croatian above average tourism contribution among EU member states, there is a significant growth potential of tourism in Croatia recognized by *Croatian Tourism Development Strategy to 2020* (Ministry of Tourism, 2013).

CONCLUSIONS AND RECOMMENDATIONS

Estimating the size and the importance of tourism for the Croatian economy, the compilation of TSA provides relevant support for the tourism policy formulation. Revealing the high significance of tourism for Croatia and recognizing the set of heterogeneous industries dependent on tourism demand, TSA results presented in this paper give a set of baseline criteria for resource allocation within tourism policy and the further evaluation of its effectiveness, as well as indicators for targets in tourism strategy formulation.

The contribution extends not only to pointing out the macroeconomic policy implications and the related allocation of government expenditure for tourism, but can be crucial to forming a number of policy implications within specific areas of economic policy such as industrial and fiscal policy, investment, marketing, cooperation and improvement of system of tourism statistics. An illustration of some of those implications is given below:

Industrial policy	As prior discussed, Croatian tourism is characterized by dominant share of tourists arriving by means of car transport and those staying in household accommodation, low share of hotel accommodation and low level of expenditures for culture, sport and recreation services. Therefore tourism policy should focus on measures towards the improvement of household accommodation quality, increase of diversity and quantity of hotel accommodation facilities and the development of cultural and sport tourism products. Tourism policy should also incentivize improvement of road service facilities taking into account specific needs of both tourists and same day visitors. Finally, due to the revealed significance of different products and services composing nautical tourism, policy should try to recognize and remove obstacles for growth of this product planned by numerous strategic documents
Fiscal policy	The estimated size of unregistered flows in accommodation and food and beverage services points out the problem of tax evasion and obvious need for a government response

(*continued*)

Investment	As TSA recognizes the key areas of tourism expenditures as well as linkages between tourism and non-tourism products and services, it offers a platform for investment decisions on macro (national), mezzo (destination) and micro (firm) level. For example, the size of expenditure for other consumption products in Croatia emphasizes the relevance of tourism demand in the process of investment justification
Marketing	Statistics on the number of visitors and the structure of expenditures directly points to the segments of tourism demand that should be targeted by marketing activities. For example, TSA results stress a need for attention on currently neglected segments, such as same day visitors and tourist staying in non-commercial accommodation facilities. Keeping in mind that inbound tourists are the most important segment of demand, maximizing the potential results of promotional and communicational activities would require the use of more detailed data such as data by countries and segments, which are not visible in TSA tables
Inter-institutional cooperation	The disclosure of a palette of different industries that generate national tourism product results in the decentralization of the responsibility of governance of the tourism sector under numerous government bodies. This imposes a need for deeper understanding of the specific governance areas of tourism activity of those bodies and their better cooperation in the formulation of tourism policy

This paper also provides a detailed methodological approach for the transfer of TSA theoretical concepts of estimation of the contribution of tourism on the case of Croatia. It contributes to a better understanding of the TSA compilation, which is still characterized by a surprisingly wide range of 'styles' used by different countries (Eurostat, 2009). Giving the evidence that the current STS in Croatia enables estimation of tourism-generated consumption and production based on the widely accepted methodological framework outlined in TSA:RMF 2008, the paper has also facilitated international comparisons with that of other EU member states.

As the TSA becomes an integral and an important element of STS, there is a need to eliminate the limitations associated with data sources in Croatia, not only for the purpose of TSA compilation but also for the improvement of the SNA and STS as a basis for conducting a success-ful tourism policy. Several activities are therefore recognized as priorities. The first group of activities is aimed at improving the information base related to tourism spending. The border survey and travel household sur-vey, as two main sources used for measurement of internal expenditures, need to be further adapted to the needs of TSA compilation, especially in terms of product structure and coverage. Furthermore, the border survey needs to be adjusted for the entry of Croatia into the Schengen area. The second group of activities is related to the accuracy and level of details of SUT table and adjustment of their structure in accordance with the TSA methodological framework. For that purpose it is also necessary to increase the scope and coverage of structural statistics, primarily by updating the register of economic entities and including the monetary indicators. Furthermore, there is a need for deeper investigation of size and characteristics of unregistered flows in Croatia by all stakeholders (Šutalo, Vuglar, & Ivandić, 2012). The third group of activities is focused on further extension of TSA implementation, advocating the measurement of gross investment and collective government spending, as well as introducing country-specific tourism characteristic products and industries, such as retail trade and some forms/parts of nautical tourism. It is also worth considering compiling special TSAs for some relevant tourism products for Croatia (e.g., nautical tourism, sun and beach and so on). Successful implementation of the mentioned activities requires strong inter-institutional cooperation among the main stakeholders.

Finally, in order to most thoroughly capture the potential benefits from TSA and the information base it provides, regional TSAs and TSA approach to measurement of environmental effects of tourism (Frechtling, 2009; Munday, Turner, & Jones, 2013) are seen as an important next step in designing future smart, sustainable and inclusive tourism growth in Croatia.

Acknowledgments This paper is based on the results of project *Tourism Satellite Account for Croatia for 2011 and Estimation of Indirect and Total Contribution of Tourism in Croatia* conducted by the Institute for Tourism and entirely supported by Ministry of Tourism of the Republic of Croatia in 2013 and 2014.

References

Ahlert, G. (2007). Methodological aspects of preparing the German TSA, empirical findings and initial reactions. *Tourism Economics, 13*(2), 275–287.

Alriquet, G. & Herbecq, J.M. (1979). The tourism satellite account: Presentation of accounting tables and the first estimation of domestic tourism expenditure. In: World tourism organization (2001). *The tourism satellite account as an ongoing process: Past, present and future developments*, Madrid, Spain: World Tourism Organization.

Blažević, B. (2007). *Turizam u gospodarskom sustavu*, 2. izmijenjeno i dopunjeno izdanje [Tourism in the Economic System, 2nd ed.]. Opatija, Croatia: Faculty of Tourism and Hospitality Management, University of Rijeka.

Car, K., Cicvarić, A., Radnić, A., & Sekulić, M. (1975). Neki ekonomski efekti inozemnog turizma u Jugoslaviji [Some economic effects of inbound tourism in Yugoslavia]. *Economic Review, 26*(9–10), 509–548.

Commission of the European Communities, International Monetary Fund, Organization for Economic Cooperation and Development, United Nations & World Bank. (1993). *System of national accounts 1993*. Brussels/Luxembourg: Commission on the European Communities.

Commission of the European Communities, Organisation of Economic Co-operation and Development, United Nations & World Tourism Organization. (2001). *Tourism satellite account: Recommended methodological framework*. Brussels/Luxembourg, Paris, New York, Madrid: Authors.

Croatian Bureau of Statistics. (2011). Hotels and restaurants. *Statistical reports* .www.dzs.hr. Date assessed 4 October 2013.

Croatian Bureau of Statistics. (2012). Tourism in 2011. *First release*, from 4.4.2/11. www.dzs.hr. Date assessed 4 October 2013.

Croatian Bureau of Statistics. (2013a). Annual gross domestic product for 2011. *First release*, 12.1.6. www.dzs.hr. Date assessed 24 March 2014.

Croatian Bureau of Statistics. (2013b). Input-output table for 2004 and supply and use tables for 2004 and 2005. *First release*, 12.1.4. www.dzs.hr. Date assessed 24 March 2014.

Diakomihalis, M. N., & Lagos, D. G. (2008). Estimation of the economic impacts of yachting in Greece via the tourism satellite account. *Tourism Economics, 14*(4), 871–887.

Dwyer, L., Deery, M., Jago, L., Spurr, R., & Fredline, L. (2007). Adapting the tourism satellite account conceptual framework to measure the economic importance of the meetings industry. *Tourism Analysis, 12*(4), 247–255.

European Union. (2011) Regulation (EU) No 692/2011 of the European Parliament and of the Council of 6 July 2011. *Official Journal of the European Union*, L 192/2011. http://eur-lex.europa.eu/LexUriServ/LexUriServ.do?u ri=OJ:L:2011:192:0017:0032:EN:PDF. Date accessed 10 May 2014.

Eurostat. (2009). Tourism satellite accounts in the European Union. *Methodologies and working papers*, Luxembourg: Publications Office of the European Union.

Eurostat. (2012). Methodological manual for tourism statistics, Version 1.2. *Methodologies and working papers*, Luxembourg: Publications Office of the European Union.

Eurostat. (2013). *Tourism satellite accounts (TSAs) in Europe*. Statistical working papers, Luxembourg: Publications Office of the European Union.

Frangialli, F. (2006). *The TSA's relevance for policy-makers*. In: Tourism Satellite Account (TSA) – Implementation Project Enzo Paci Papers on Measuring the

Economic Significance of Tourism Vol. 5, Madrid, Spain: World Tourism Organization.

Frechtling, D.C. (2006). An assessment of visitor expenditure methods and models. *Journal of Travel Research*, 45(1), 26–35.

Frechtling, D. C. (2009). Measurement and analysis of tourism economic contributions for sub-national regions through the tourism satellite account. *Enzo Paci Papers*, Volume 6, UNWTO, 189–206.

Frechtling, D.C. (2010). The tourism satellite account: A primer. *Annals of Tourism Research*, 37(1), 136–153.

Frechtling, D.C. (2013). *The Economic impact of tourism: Overview and examples of macroeconomic analysis*, UNWTO Statistics and TSA Issue Paper Series STSA/IP/2013/03 (Online). http://statistics.unwto.org/en/content/papers. Date assessed 7 November 2014.

Frent, F. (2008). The economic importance of vacation homes from the Tourism Satellite Account (TSA) perspective. *Tourism Review*, 64(2), 19–27.

Gatti, P. (2013). Tourism, welfare and income distribution: The case of Croatia. *Tourism*, 61(1), 53–71.

Horak, S., Marušić, Z. & Radnić, A. (1999). *Potrošnja inozemnih putnika u Hrvatskoj i domaćih putnika u inozemstvu u 1998.* godini [Expenditures of inbound and outbound tourists in Croatia in 1998]. Zagreb, Croatia: Croatian National Bank.

Institute for Tourism. (2003). *Turistička aktivnost domaćeg stanovništva u 2002* [Tourist Activity of Population of Republic of Croatia in 2002]. Zagreb, Croatia: Institute for Tourism.

Institute for Tourism. (2007). *Satelitski račun turizma Republike Hrvatske – Studija izvedivosti* [Tourism Satellite Account of Republic of Croatia – Feasibility Study]. Zagreb, Croatia: Institute for Tourism.

Institute for Tourism. (2008). *Eksperimentalni satelitski račun turizma Republike Hrvatske u 2005. godini* [Experimental Tourism Satellite Account of Republic of Croatia for 2005]. Zagreb, Croatia: Institute for Tourism.

Institute for Tourism. (2010). *Eksperimentalna TSA 2007 prema metodologiji Svjetske turističke organizacije: Izravni i neizravni učinci turizma u RH* [Experimental TSA 2007 according to UNWTO methodological framework: Direct and Indirect Impacts of Tourism in the Republic of Croatia]. Zagreb, Croatia: Institute for Tourism.

Institute for Tourism. (2011). *Stavovi i potrošnja turista u Hrvatskoj – TOMAS Ljeto 2010* [Attitudes and Expenditures of Tourist in Croatia – Tomas Summer 2010]. Zagreb, Croatia: Institute for Tourism.

Institute for Tourism. (2012). *Turistička aktivnost domaćeg stanovništva u 2011* [Tourist Activity of Population of Republic of Croatia in 2011]. Zagreb, Croatia: Institute for Tourism.

Institute for Tourism. (2013). *Stavovi i potrošnja nautičara u Hrvatskoj – TOMAS Nautika jahting 2012* [Attitudes and Expenditures of Yachtsmen in Croatia – Tomas Nautica Yahting 2012]. Zagreb, Croatia: Institute for Tourism.

Ivandić, N., & Marušić, Z. (2009). Je li sustav statistike turizma u Hrvatskoj spreman za izradu satelitskog računa turizma? [Is the system of tourism statistics in Croatia ready to create a tourism satellite account?]. *Tourism, 57*(2), 185–205.

Ivandić N., Marušić Z., Šutalo I. & Vuglar, J. (2014). *Satelitski račun turizma RH za 2011. godinu i izračun neizravnih i ukupnih učinaka turizma u RH* [Tourism Satellite Account of the Republic of Croatia for 2011 and Estimation of Indirect and Total Impacts of Tourism]. Zagreb, Croatia: Institute for Tourism.

Ivandić, N., & Radnić, A. (1997). Neslužbeno gospodarstvo u turizmu i ugostiteljstvu [The grey economy in tourism and catering]. *Financial Theory and Practice, 21*(1-2), 231–240.

Jones, C., & Munday, M. (2008). Tourism satellite accounts and impact assessments: Some considerations. *Tourism Analysis, 13*(1), 53–69.

Kenneally, M., & Jakee, K. (2012). Satellite accounts for the tourism industry: structure, representation and estimates for Ireland. *Tourism Economics, 10*(5), 971–997.

Kesar, O. (2006). *Ekonomski učinci turističke potrošnje,* doktorska disertacija [The Economic Effects of Tourism Consumption, dissertation], Zagreb, Croatia: Faculty of Economics and Business, University of Zagreb.

Lapierre, J. (1991). A proposal for a Satellite Account and Information System for Tourism. In: World Tourism Organization (2001). *The tourism satellite account as an ongoing process: Past, present and future developments.* Madrid, Spain: World Tourism Organization.

Libreros, M., Massieu, A., & Meis, S. (2006). Progress in tourism satellite account implementation and development. *Journal of Travel Research, 45*(1), 83–91.

Los, B., & Steenge, A. E. (2010). Tourism studies and input–output analysis: Introduction to a special issue. *Economic Systems Research, 22*(4), 305–311.

Lück, M. (2007). *Nautical tourism: Concepts and issues.* New York: Cognizant Communication Corporation`

Lukovic, T. (Ed.). (2013). *Nautical tourism.* Wallingford, UK: CABI.

Marušić, Z., Ivandić, N. & Horak, S. (2014). Nautical tourism within TSA framework: Case of Croatia, 13th Global Forum on Tourism Statistics, 17–18 November 2014, Nara, Japan. http://naratourismstatisticsweek.visitors.jp/global/ pdf/full_paper/4-4.pdf. Date assessed 22 February 2015.

Ministry of Tourism. (2013). *Croatian tourism development strategy to 2020.* Official Gazette of the Republic of Croatia 55/2013. http://narodne-novine. nn.hr/clanci/sluzbeni/2013_05_55_1119.html. Date accessed 20 November 2014.

Munday, M., Turner, K., & Jones, C. (2013). Accounting for the carbon associated with regional tourism consumption. *Tourism Management, 36*, 35–44.

Organisation for Economic Cooperation and Development. (1991). *Manual on tourism economic accounts*. Paris: Organisation for Economic Cooperation and Development.

Radnić, A. (1990). *Strukturna analiza turističke potrošnje u Jugoslaviji*, doktorska disertacija [Structural Analysis of Tourism Consumption in Yugoslavia, dissertation], Zagreb, Croatia: Faculty of Economics and Business, University of Zagreb.

Radnić, A., & Ivandić, N. (1999). War and tourism in Croatia – Consequences and the road to recovery. *Tourism, 47*(1), 43–54.

Sainaghi, R. (2012). Tourist expenditures: The state of the art. *Anatolia, 23*(2), 217–233.

Smeral, E. (2006). Tourism satellite accounts: A critical assessment. *Journal of Travel Research, 45*(1), 92–98.

Song, H., Dwyer, L., Li, G., & Cao, Z. (2012). Tourism economics research: A review and assessment. *Annals of Tourism Research, 39*(3), 1653–1682.

Stynes, D. J., & White, E. M. (2006). Reflections on measuring recreation and travel spending. *Journal of Travel Research, 45*(1), 8–16.

Šutalo, I., Ivandić, N., & Marušić, Z. (2011). Ukupan doprinos turizma gospodarstvu Hrvatske: input-output model i satelitski račun turizma [Total contribution of tourism to Croatian economy: Input-output model and tourism satellite account]. *Economic Review, 62*(5-6), 267–285.

Šutalo, I., Vuglar, J., & Ivandić, N. (2012). Importance of theoretical value added tax for Croatia's fiscal capacity in the context of the European Union. *Financial Theory and Practice, 36*(3), 297–320.

United Nations, World Tourism Organization, Eurostat – Commission of the European Communities & Organisation for Economic Co-operation and Development. (2010a). Tourism satellite account: Recommended methodological framework 2008. *Studies in methods*, Series F, No. 80/Rev.1, Luxemburg, Madrid, New York, Paris: Authors.

United Nations & World Tourism Organization. (2010b). International recommendations for tourism statistics 2008. *Studies in methods*, Series M, No. 83/Rev.1, New York: Authors.

Vizek, M. (2014). Cijena neuređene države [The Cost of Inefficient State], Jutarnji list. http://www.jutarnji.hr/cijena-neuredene-drzave/1200673/. Date assessed 30 December 2014.

Wilton, J. J., & Nickerson, N. P. (2006). Collecting and using visitor spending data. *Journal of Travel Research, 45*(1), 17–25.

World Tourism Organization. (1983). Determination of the importance of tourism as an economic activity within the framework of the national accounting system. In: World Tourism Organization (2001). *The tourism satellite account as an ongoing process: Past, present and future developments*. Madrid, Spain: World Tourism Organization.

CHAPTER 9

Abandoned Tourism Resorts in Croatia: The Consequences of Discordant Spatial Planning and Tourism Development Policies

Jasenka Kranjčević

INTRODUCTION[1]

The relationship between tourism development and spatial planning is especially complex (Chettiparamb & Thomas, 2012). This is due to the corollary of economic, social, cultural, ecological and political relationships between innumerable stakeholders. Against this complexity, it is open for discussion as to what extent are policy planners, especially at the national level, engaged in critical analysis and assessment of the synergy that exists between spatial planning policies and that of tourism development and their influence on the existing and planned tourism zones.

On the Adriatic's east coast, there are some twenty abandoned tourism zones or resorts, most with hotel complexes within them. These zones are located in some of the most picturesque locations, they are well planned and have all the necessary infrastructure, and some had enjoyed century-old tourism activities. It is important to note at the outset that the land of most of these zones remains in state ownership, while the buildings, such

J. Kranjčević (✉)
Institute for Tourism, Zagreb, Croatia

L. Dwyer et al. (eds.), *Evolution of Destination Planning and Strategy*, DOI 10.1007/978-3-319-42246-6_9

173

as hotels, might be in private ownership or it might be owned by the local municipalities.

The reason for the abandonment of these tourism zones can be viewed from a number of perspectives. However, in this study the focus was on the government's policies on spatial planning and tourism development. These tourism zones were abandoned some 25 years ago, during the Homeland war (1991–1995), and as a result of the subsequent socio-political changes. The new social and political organisation of the country required new legislation which brought about changes in policies in all sectors of governance, including urban and regional spatial planning and tourism development. Thus, the analysis about these abandoned tourism resorts offers an opportunity to investigate the congruence between tourism development and spatial planning policies and its impact on tourism development.

This close relationship between tourism and spatial planning policies was evaluated by analysing two very famous but abandoned tourism resorts: the Haludovo, on the island of Krk in the northern part of Adriatic, an area which was not directly affected by the war, and Kupari resort near Dubrovnik in the south part of the Adriatic, which was damaged by war during 1991–1995 period.

The research was based on the inductive and deductive methods used to analyse tourism and spatial planning policies, the time-slice analysis of tourism development. Although the term policy can be used for all levels of government such as local, regional and national, in this study the term "policy" refers to the policy of the government at the national level. Finally, comparative analysis was used in the case of the two tourism resorts analysed in this study. Of course, this study seeks to contribute to better understanding how important it is to create common tourism and spatial planning policies.

In order to provide a better understanding of the processes behind the development of these tourist zones, and their ensuing abandonment, it is prudent to highlight first the spatial planning as it was under the former Yugoslav socialist government (1945–1990, and the government of the former Socialist Republic of Croatia), when tourist areas all along the Adriatic coast from Savudrija up north to Prevlaka in the south experienced a rapid development and growth in the years between 1960 and 1980. And, second, it is equally important to analyse the demise of these tourist resorts after 1990 and their final abandonment.

The centrally planned tourism development has a long tradition. After the Second World War, most economies of the former socialist bloc countries adopted the practice of centrally planned tourism development, including Yugoslavia, in line with its centrally planned economy model. Coincidently, this type of planning approach to tourism was also evident in countries with a capitalist social system (Beyer, Hagemann & Zinganel, 2013; Breheny, 1991; Buckley & Witt, 1990; Julien, 1989). The importance of tourism planning at the national level was seen as a necessary part of the central policy planning apparatus per se, or the five-year plan, but also to meet the needs of future tourism growth and, therefore, to ensure its development and to develop the most poorest regions of Dalmatia. The benefits of tourism development planning at national level did pay dividends especially for facilitating polycentric development, rational spatial distribution for tourism development and, more broadly, a balanced and centrally controlled use of land and economic development of the poorer regions.

While such plans serve to ensure a controlled and coordinated spatial and tourism development in a desired direction, their implementation depends on a variety of mechanisms, which is often fraught with challenges. Among these is the issue of legislative framework and its implementation, together with the institutional coordination, which are particularly challenging (Pastras & Bramwell, 2013), because spatial planning, the use of building land, infrastructure and tourism development have to be simultaneously assessed, coordinated and implemented.

SPATIAL PLANNING AND TOURISM DEVELOPMENT IN CROATIA DURING 1945–1990

Favourable spatial and geographic and natural conditions on the Adriatic coast sparked the development of tourism resorts before and after the Second World War. It is well known that by the 1930s, tourism and tourism infrastructure on the eastern seaboard and on some of the Adriatic islands, like Lošinj, Brijuni and Hvar, was well established, featuring world-class accommodation and touristic facilities. In the years immediately following the WWII, the new communist state of Yugoslavia appropriated all of the tourism resorts, and tourism was quickly revitalised by the early 1950s as part of the state-run programme for the "vacationing proletariat"; if you were a steel, or mining, or office worker, or any state-employed worker, then you were entitled for an annual holiday at one of these resorts at nominal cost. This kind of tourism soon began to take on unexpected proportions, as reflected in the spontaneous but sharp increase in commercial accommodation facilities, strong growth in the number of domestic and regional tourist arrivals from other eastern bloc countries and growth in domestic tourism investments. Tourism was spreading not only in parts of the Adriatic coastal areas that were planned for tourism development, but it started to develop organically, spreading to the coastal hinterland. Consequently, many places that witnessed an increase in tourism demand lacked operational know-how and quality of marketing, organisational and administrative skills to manage this growth.

It is not surprising, therefore, that due to the hasty and poorly planned tourism development, the tourism industry at the time has shown first signs of disorganisation and a lack of coordination with other sectors of economy with which it was both directly and indirectly connected. As a result, water shortages, poor roads, mismatched passenger-transport scheduling, inadequate communications, traffic congestions in towns and villages and interruptions in supply of electricity were daily realities during the high summer season. In addition, the early hotel construction lacked spatial, functional and technical qualities due to the prevailing building practices that had no spatial plans or the preparation of sites where the building was situated.

Faced with the consequence of such uncontrolled and uncoordinated tourism development, the awareness of the need to plan tourism develop-ment on the national, regional and local level emerged, especially after the national *Economic Development Plans 1957–1961* (the national five-yearly economic plan) further stimulated tourism development as the major eco-nomic goal. In spite of this, the Plan failed to address the complex and multi-layered issues of tourism-related infrastructure, and it had not pro-vided details about the quality and locations of accommodation resorts; the goal was just to build, leaving the rest of the issues "as we go along" (Kobašić, 1981, 1987).

After the official endorsement of tourism as an important economic activity in the national five-yearly economic plan, two types of actions were evident. One set of activities were directed towards regional spatial and tourism planning, while the other set towards collecting relevant data as being the key input to national spatial and tourism development plan-ning. In terms of the latter, it was realised that the entire Adriatic area needed a spatial plan which focused on tourism development. The former Agency for Tourism Economics (today the Institute for Tourism) in 1963 collected key tourism data from coastal areas and tourism development and had drafted several key documents about tourism market demand and the spatial distribution of tourism activities. These documents served as a pretext to national policy for the regionalisation of the Adriatic. In terms of regional planning, it was the spatial planners in Croatia who pioneered spatial for tourism (Marinović-Uzelac, 1986). The first one to be completed was for the Makarska Riviera, a 57 km stretch of pebble beaches in mid-south Dalmatia in 1960 (Kranjčević, 2012a), followed a year later by the tourism spatial plan for the Šibenik region, which is blessed with one of the most beautiful archipelagos in the Adriatic and which was subsequently zoned as a protected national park.

By 1963 the stage was set for the collective drafting of a long-term spatial plan for the Adriatic. This could have only been achieved as a result of the background analyses on tourism growth; natural, geographic, demographic and economic conditions; an understating of tourism and its influence on and dependency on other sectors; activities of the economy; and the experience gained in the process of regional tourism development plans. Although it might have been an overambitious goal, it enabled, for the first time, the collection of documentation on the coastal area, including tourism, based on an analysis of natural, geographic, demographic, economic and infrastructure conditions which served as the basis for policy development for tourism and its spatial distribution. What is important to note here is that the formulation of the policy for spatial planning and tourism development was linked with other sectors of the economy, for example, other socio-economic policies.

Funded by the United Nations Development Programme, the 1963 spatial plan was followed by the spatial plan for the Southern Adriatic in 1964–1968 covering the coastal and hinterland area of Croatia, Bosnia and Herzegovina and Montenegro. It was planned that the number of tourists would increase from 116,000 in 1964 to 900,000 by 1990, of which 820,000 would be holidaying at the coast. It was calculated at the time that to accommodate that number of visitors, there existed a need to have 600,000 beds by 1990.

Two years later a similar plan was launched for the remaining north part of the Adriatic, under the official title—the *Coordinated Spatial Plan of the Upper Adriatic Region*—covering the coastal territory of Slovenia and the upper or northern part of Croatia. It was developed using the same methodology as that for the Southern Adriatic and it was completed in 1972. For that part of the Adriatic, an increase in bed capacity was planned, from 313,7 thousand in 1961 to 1,3 million beds by 2000 (Kranjčević, 2012a, 2012b; Marinović-Uzelac, 1986).

The goal of regional plans for the maritime area of the eastern Adriatic coast, from the late 1960s and early 1970s, was to synchronise tourism, industry, agriculture, culture and environmental protection sectors' policies with the aim to put a stop to the expansionistic, aggressive and destructive forms of tourism such as the occupation of the most attractive areas and construction of an ever-increasing number of hotels and B&Bs, camps and similar. In addition, they aimed at fostering a polycentric development or, in other terms, a rational use and management of land. In addition to spatial distribution of tourism, these regional plans also served as the foundation for the planned urbanisation of the Adriatic coast (Institute for Urbanism, 1967, 1968, 1972).

The planned urbanisation of the coast was directed by the then central government, and as alluded to earlier, this was due to the fact that tourism-designated land was entirely in the state ownership. Hence, there existed a politically expedient mechanism for the plans' unquestioned implementation, and as a result, a large number of hotels and hotel complexes were built according to these regional spatial plans, resulting in a concentration of state-run tourism resorts in Istria, that included Plava Laguna (250 ha; 12,500 beds) and Zelena Laguna in Poreč (130 ha; 13,500 beds); in the northern Adriatic with two smaller zones—Haludovo in Malinska (25 ha; 1,800 beds) and Uvala Scott and Uvala Scott II near Kraljevica (18 ha; 1,200 beds); two in the central Adriatic, Solaris in Šibenik (43 ha; 5,108 beds) and Borik in Zadar (30 ha; 1,700 beds); and in south Adriatic, near Dubrovnik is Babin Kuk (79 ha; 4,400 beds) (Ministry of Tourism, 2012). In addition to these, the state had also built hotels and resorts that were exclusively used by the military personal with restricted public access, such as Duilovo near Split, Kupari near Dubrovnik and Baška Voda near Makarska. In addition to those that have been built, there were ready plans for the additional development of many more tourism resorts. Ironically, many of these state-planned resorts and potential areas for tourism development from the 1970s and 1980s have found their way in the current zoning plans, despite several changes in spatial planning and tourism development legislation (Ministry of Construction and Physical Planning, 2012). Clearly, it can be inferred that the then state had planned for mass tourism on a grand scale.

The development of the tourism zones was governed by the socio-political ideology and socio-political-economic circumstances of the time. Ideologically, it was important to show to the outside world the achievements of the country while caring for its people, the "vacationing proletariat", while the nationalisation of the land and public ownership, meant that the cost-effectiveness or these touristic projects, was not of the uppermost concern to the bureaucrats and policy makers. Critically, however, in the total absence of public and political scrutiny for transparency and cost-effectiveness, the bureaucrats, policy planners and regulatory architects had a complete *carte blanche* for realising their grand ideas (Sallnow, 1985a, 1985b).

Hotels and resorts of the time were predominantly planned and constructed in modern architectural style with a two-fold purpose, one, for showing the world the bright side of socialism and, two, to show the "utopic" conditions that were created for the workers (Kulić, 2009). Hotel designs were based on principles of modern architecture, especially in terms of proportions between built surfaces and surrounding areas, where sport, entertainment and cultural facilities were built and blended into the landscape. These resorts were planned with an idea that they had to be accessible to all society members, regardless of their social position or class. Against this background it comes as no surprise when this slogan first appeared in 1956, "*Yugoslavia is a country of socialism, natural beauty and tourism*" (FNRJ, 1966). Although this "utopian" idea lingered on for a while, but even in a socialist system just like in Orwel's "*Animal Farm*", not all resorts were readily available to all the "proletariat", and in any case, as the time rolled on, the state became more interested in earning foreign exchange from non-domestic visitors, while the idea of the "vacationing proletariat" was quietly consigned to history.

On the downside, these enormous tourism resorts with their equally capacious hotels and other touristic facilities created undesirable impacts too. The most notable, which the bureaucrats, policy planners and spatial planners had failed to "plan" for, was that many of these tourist resorts were giant in size, often dwarfing neighbouring towns or villages, where the number of tourists by far outstripped the number of local residents. The capacity and land area of these large tourism resorts was in vast disproportion to the small Mediterranean settlements, causing dislocated relationships between locals and visitors, to say the least: "*Build them big*" was also another socialist penchant, among many. For example, the Haludovo tourism resort (to be discussed later) is about 2.5 times larger in land area from the adjoining municipality of Malinska (the municipality of Malinska-Dubašnica has 3081 inhabitants and the settlement itself has 971, according to 2013 census). While Grandtis and Taylor (2010) erroneously point out that tourism has brought jobs and slowed down

Table 9.1   Number of beds in the hospitality industry in the period 1955–1984

Year	Number of beds		
	Yugoslavia	Croatia	% Croatia
1955	90,182	39,444	43.7
1960	254,095	151,561	59.6
1965	444,459	286,908	64.5
1970	697,301	453,071	64.9
1975	937,053	614,640	65.5
1980	1.060,803	692,000	65.2
1984	1.235,014	800,121	64.7

Source: SNL (1987), p. 220

the depopulation of coastal areas and islands, if only temporarily, on the other hand, however, large-scale planned urbanisation of the maritime land, such as the Haludovo tourism resort, had irreversibly transformed the existing spatial, aesthetic, cultural, socio-economic and ecological conditions forever, and not necessarily for the better: So much for the "*socialism*" and "*natural beauty*" in the "*Yugoslavia is a country of socialism, natural beauty and tourism*"!

This transformation and large-scale planned urbanisation of the maritime land could have been much more impacting had all the early tourism plans been fully realised. According to the early tourism development plans, by year 2000 it was estimated to have 1.9 million beds in the coastal area of the former Yugoslavia. A glimpse at the aggregate data on bed capacities and overnights in Table 9.1 shows that these early estimates were way overambitious because in 1984 in the entire Yugoslavia there were 1,2 million beds of which 800,000 were in Croatia: "*Big numbers*" was also another socialist penchant.

Nevertheless, the national and regional "build them big" culture by the bureaucrats, planners and other public sector minions at municipal and local levels was well and truly alive right up to the 1990s, where a number of plans were drafted to further increase tourism activities, in particular accommodation capacities in public or state-run ownership. Thus, for example, the Tourism Development Study conducted in 1984, proposed another "*build them big*" project, a 100 per cent increase in accommodation facilities over the next 16 years (Table 9.2). Albeit without a scintilla of information about the spatial needs and distribution for these facilities (Kobašić, 1987).

Table 9.2 Planned accommodation facilities in Yugoslavia for 2000 according to a study from 1984

Accommodation type	Number of beds	Share in %
Hotels total	631,000	23.8
Pensions	34,000	0.4
Motels	35,000	1.3
Holiday resorts	280,000	10.6
Total primary accommodation facilities	**980,000**	**37.0**
Resorts for workers	335,000	12.6
Health resorts	95,000	3.6
Camp sites	555,000	21.0
Private accommodation	632,000	23.8
Other	53,000	2.0
Total complementary accommodation facilities	**1.670,000**	**63.0**
Grand total	**2.650,000**	**100.0**

Source: Kobašić (1987), p. 125

To conclude, in a country with a relatively normal and stable social and political system, spatial planning and tourism development poses considerable challenges. One can hazard to think what a perilous task this must be in societies undergoing fundamental socio-political changes, and a transition from a centrally planned economy to the free market economy, as witnessed in the former socialist-government countries such as Yugoslavia, Hungary, Czechoslovakia, Bulgaria, Rumania and Albania. These transitions have aimed to radically reform the known system, or old order, of making legislation and the administration of legislation. No doubt, the transition from socialism and centrally planned economy required massive and long-term changes in legislation, which, incidentally, are still ongoing today, in particular, for land ownership, agriculture, taxation and spatial reforms.

However, the greatest challenge to date is in the administration and the inconsistent, and unequal implementation of the new policies. The administration of the new legislation at national, regional and local levels is painfully mired by the inertia of the administrative and bureaucratic culture, the people in the office, bureaucrat-led public sector mentality struggling to come to terms and understand the "new order". It must also be said that part of the problem lies in that since the fall of centrally planned economy, spatial and tourism development policies, like many other policies, have been authorised and promulgated often in complete isolation to other socio-economic policies that might have an impact on tourism, which cause dislocation or policy-clash at some later stage of tourism development. To date, internal bureaucratic and administrative policy hurdles still prevail.

ATTITUDES TOWARDS PRIVATE OR NON-STATE TOURISM ENTERPRISES AND INITIATIVES

Immediately after the WWII, the small private sector-operated tourism industry in the former Yugoslavia was almost entirely eliminated mainly due to the war, loss of infrastructure and the nationalisation (confiscation) of land and property. The privately run tourism industry started to develop slowly at first, during the mid-1960s and early 1970s (Kobašić, 1987). While foreign and domestic experts focused on the rapid development of mass tourism in the socialist Yugoslavia, no one was very concerned about the lack of private sector initiative or, later on, about the quality of tourism products offered by the private sector (Allcock, 1986; Sallnow, 1985a, 1985b; Weber, 1989).

The official position and attitude to private sector initiatives were until the mid-1970s restrictive and dogmatic. This position changed fairly quickly with policy changes after the adoption of the 1974 Constitution. Critically, the new constitution allowed for a much needed political power-shift which basically allowed for the decentralised planning of the economy, thus shifting socio-economic planning, including spatial planning and tourism development among others, from the central level to republic level. Significantly in terms of tourism development among other things, the introduction of new constitution granted considerable sovereignties to private ownership and entrepreneurship, a model which the PRC adopted for the transformation of its planned economy in the 1980s, with some success!

Consequently, the official position and attitudes to private sector tourism investment changed with equally corresponding official position, that both public and private investments were important for developing diverse quality and quantity of tourism products and services. In particular, as the tourism market started to change and the large-scale hotel and resort state-run companies began to face serious financial difficulties in not being able to swiftly adapt to rapid market changes in the late 1970s and early

1980s, the advantages of small-scale private investment which was easier to finance, organise and manage made a lot of sense, and it became only too obvious even for the die-hard bureaucrats, that this was the new future of tourism development.

Nonetheless, the tensions between the public and private sectors remained, mostly due to the ideological obstacles manifest in draconian administrative and regulatory barriers for private investors. Faced with unclear regulations and unstable, unpredictable and ambiguous taxation policies, the private sector had not made the necessary investments in tourism development. Not surprisingly, taking commercial risks in such uncertain circumstances forced private investors to think short term and maximise immediate gains, often resorting to fraudulent business practices such as concealment of income, failure to register all tourists staying at an establishment, non-compliance with regulatory requirements, offering low quality of service and similar practices. Given the daft notion that the private sector could not possibly pose a threat to large state-owned hotels, the bureaucrats toyed with a policy idea that would limit the number of beds held by any one privateer to forty (Montana, 1986); although these ideas never materialised, they did stall crucial private investment in tourism development.

Towards the end of the twentieth century, or in the late period of Yugoslav socialism, another policy shift allowed privateers to build small, holiday homes but, once again, in absence of spatial planning and architectural guidelines. Needless to say, as a consequence, in some places complete ad hoc holiday home complexes emerged that were used mostly by their owners and their family and friends. As the demand for beds in the mid-1980s outstripped supply, many of these houses or rooms were rented to tourists. Even so, this spare bed capacity fell short to effectively make a contribution to the development of competitive tourism. As time went on towards the late 1980s, the grinding transition to a market economy aggravated by the lack of clear vision for the private sector initiatives in the tourism industry caused the emergence of unregulated or, as was then referred to, "wild" tourism which, as a matter of reference, was evident in other eastern socialist countries (Bachvarov, 1997; Hall, 1992, 1998).

Both public and private tourism development, and tourism per se, come to an abrupt halt in 1990 with the escalation of hostilities and finally war. Inconceivably, the notion that nobody in former Yugoslavia could have predicted that the public sector development of tourism would be seriously dislocated by the change in the socio-political system, and the war, is plainly a fallacy. Quite a few leading tourism authorities in the EU and elsewhere made an obviously correct prediction that as in any area where there is war on the Croatian territory had seriously scuttled any future plans for tourism development and investment. And, it had put an end to the existing tourism industry (Hall, 1992, 1998); what fool would travel to a war zone for holidays!

SPATIAL PLANNING AND TOURISM DEVELOPMENT IN CROATIA FROM 1990 TO TODAY

In the very first years of Croatian independence, with the fall of socialist order and planned economy system, the end Homeland war, introduction of new legislation in all socio-economic sectors, the commencement of transition to a market economy and the impact of globalisation caused terrific challenges in the functioning of the new state's administrative apparatus at all levels, and rapid legislative changes led to a number of mutually inconsistent rights and obligations. The existing administrative apparatus, mired by inertia and old bureaucratic culture, was unable to adapt quickly to new conditions, and predictably, it used its bureaucratic power to "deal" with the new situation (Simon, 1976), which was to do nothing, a bureaucratic legacy from the early days of Communist Yugoslavia.

The key land-reform legislative changes brought a profound difference in land ownership. After nearly 50 years of state ownership, the new constitution and the subsequent legislation decreed private ownership of land to be the citizens' absolute right. While, on the other hand, the country, as a whole, faced hefty issues such as land reparations for the formerly confiscated land, rebuilding, economic growth and recognition within the international community. As a consequence, both private and public property ownership was now seen as a valuable investment rather than a cheap area or site for appropriation or for collective use (Bramwel & Meyer, 2007).

By 1991 the planning for the new economy commenced in earnest which included a new *Tourism Development Strategy*. Put very simply, it was imperative for the new government to kick-start tourism-sourced foreign income to be able to finance the running of the government. Importantly, the new tourism development strategy clearly instituted spatial resources as being the backbone of long-term tourism planning and development. Importantly, the new strategy directed now the new policy should define spatial within the tourism industry. Likewise, the *National Strategy for Spatial Planning* (Ministry of Physical Planning, Construction and Housing 1997) also singled out valuable land space as a key strategic resource for the nation's tourism development. Incredibly, these strategic recommendations for spatial planning and tourism zoning were mostly ignored by the bureaucrats and the political party in power at the time. Absurdly, the promulgation of the directive about the importance of spatial for tourism was carried over (cut-and-pasted) in all strategic documents including the current *Croatian Tourism Development Strategy to 2020* (Ministry of Tourism, 2013), although the current Strategy is not specific about the spatial distribution of tourism, which, yet again, has a whiff that the Strategy is being less than embraced.

In the first years of independence, the majority of the ex-state-owned hotel and tourist resort companies were sold-off and privatised where the private company often owned all of the accommodation operations such as hotels and touristic services at a destination. These privatisation transactions were often done in a non-transparent way, and sadly, without resolving the now thorny issue of land ownership (new legislation about land ownership). Arising from the old bureaucratic need to "control" in spite of the new legislation, new owners were able to purchase buildings but without the surrounding land area, which hampered the renovation processes. But, it has to be said, this situation did not worry some new owners because they were in it just to make a quick profit in re-selling the buildings to someone else. As new legislation became more effective mainly brought about by public pressure for transparency and to put an end to corruption in the privatisation process, not all ex-state-run tourism enterprises were to be privatised, and by 2013, fourteen tourism companies, that are in the state ownership, are still waiting to be privatised (Ministry of Tourism, 2013).

Relatively free from the regulatory constraints imposed by the government, private investment in tourism started to flourish in the early 2000. The share of privately owned commercial accommodation facilities, popularly called *"zimmer frei"* (owning to the large number of tourists from Germany), increased by more than 50 per cent over the last 20 years. However, this expansion was not regulated by the appropriate spatial plans where development did not follow the pace of investment. In the absence of spatial plans that would ensure proper land use zoning and quality of municipal infrastructure, the rapid construction of accommodation facilities by private investors was ad hoc and disorganised. Thus, in many cases, once such accommodation facilities had been constructed, there would inevitably be shortages of drinking water, or problems with electricity and sewage discharge, sporadic collection of rubbish and traffic issues such as narrow roads, lack of sidewalks and lack of parking spaces. These problems combined had a direct adverse impact on real estate prices.

The reasons for such a rapid construction of private accommodation facilities should be sought not only in the owners' interpretation of what private property is, where many considered that the owner has the absolute right (to do anything) without any obligations, but also within the overall economic restructuring process where many ex-state-run companies found it impossible to adapt to the market economy, as a consequence of which a large number of people lost their source of income and, in the coastal areas, they turned to provision of tourist accommodation as an alternative. In addition, tourism, with the related demand for new building construction, was also seen as a lucrative business by the local and regional governments along the coast, for which the building licence fees and taxes are a major source of income.

Thus, due largely in part to tourism development, quite a few areas on the coast had become huge building sites with all manner of ad hoc construction for accommodation, restaurants, sporting halls, residential buildings, as well as public infrastructure. In short, tourism development has transformed many coastal places beyond recognition. While precise data on spatial areas dedicated to tourism development is not available, the increase of the built-up areas along the coast can serve as firm proxy indicator of the changes in land use. Since there is no accurate data on the built-up area along the coast, that is, from the time of more intensive development of tourism after WWII, it is useful to compare data from the mid-1960s to the present day.

According to the National Report of Situation (State) of Spatial Development (Ministry of Construction and Physical Planning, 2012), there were 2446 settlements in the coastal areas of the Adriatic with 1.4 million inhabitants or 33 per cent of the total population of Croatia. In comparison, in 1961, there were 1.3 million inhabitants or 31 per cent the total population. In which case, there does not appear to be a significant change in the number of people that lived along the coast. However, state-sanitised statistics have conveniently failed to take into account that in the period from 1953 to 1966, some 300,000 to 5000,000 inhabitants either escaped or left the coast and islands for overseas, which would put the 1961 inhabitant figure somewhere in the region of 700,000 to 900,000. Nonetheless, in terms of actual land use, the change was astonishing. Presently, coastal cities, villages and other urbanised areas occupy approximately 1033 km or about 16.5 per cent of the total coastline length (6278 km).

In comparison, in 1960, just before the intensive tourism development, built-up areas occupied 120–150 km of coastline. After the Homeland war, there were significant changes in the structure of commercial accommodation. For example, the proportion of beds in hotels decreased due to the number of hotel resorts that have not been rebuilt or refurbished after 1995. These were mostly state owned. The other reason for the decrease in beds is that the decrease was positively correlated to the *status quo* in quality of the existing state-run hotels, despite trends that showed otherwise. This means that from 1995 to 2011, there was a steady decrease in the number of beds of lower category with a corresponding increase of higher-category hotels, a small increase in the beginning, but quite substantive after 2005. At the same time, there was an increase in the proportion of beds in the private accommodation sector from 32 per cent in 1989 to almost 50 per cent by 2011 (Table 9.3). To deal with this apparent imbalance in accommodation availability, the *Croatian Tourism Development Strategy to 2020* (2013) recommended an

Table 9.3 Accommodation facilities in Croatia (permanent beds) by type of accommodation and hotel category, structure in per cent and rate of change

Year	Total number of permanent beds	Hotels and categories (star rating)					Camp sites	Other collective capacities	Households (private accommodation)
		Total	5	4	3	2 i 1			
		Structure in %							
1989	861.216	15	3	19	74	5	35	19	32
2001	682.721	14	3	2	45	49	28	17	42
2005	784.600	13	5	9	54	32	26	13	48
2011	852.433	13	9	32	44	15	25	13	49
2015[a]	914.058	13	–	–	–	–	25	14	48
		Rate of change in %							
2015/2011 in %	7	7	–	–	–	–	6	13	6
2015/2005 in %	16	18	–	–	–	–	12	19	18
2015/2001 in %	34	28	–	–	–	–	20	9	55
2015/1989 in %	6	-7	–	–	–	–	-23	-24	62

Source: Ministry of Tourism (2013) and Croatian Bureau of Statistics (2015a)
[a]Data for 2015 not available

increase in the share of hotel beds from 13 per cent to 18 per cent by 2020 that include measures to upgrade the quality rankings of private accommodation and to allow developing small family-owned hotels, or boutique hotels, and to re-focus on rebuilding the currently dilapidated ex-state-run resorts in order to ensure, among else, a rational use of land and space. Apart from improving the quality of the overall tourism product, the justification for recommending the upgrading of private accommodation might lay in the fact that hotels have a much better occupancy rate than privateers; however, it is more likely that Croatia is hard up attracting large investment for tourism development and/or redevelopment of large hotel projects given (a) the unresolved issue of land ownership and (b) the seasonality factor which severely detracts large investment, notably in more remote areas.

This recommendation seems rational enough only when the aggregated performance of various types of accommodation facilities is compared with private accommodation which only appears to be underperforming (Table 9.4), compared with the occupancy rates of 39 per cent in hotels. However, it is interesting to note the growth rate in 2005–2011 for the private sector accommodation. Also, the occupancy figures on many islands are the reverse of what is shown in Table 9.4. That is, most of the occupancy is in private accommodation.

To conclude however, given that mechanisms which would enable the implementation of strategic recommendations have not been put in place, it is most reasonable to assume that the implementation of this strategic plan is yet another pipe-dream. Which means that with a sluggish economic activity for the foreseeable future, and where the tourism's contribution to GDP is

Table 9.4 Occupancy rates (permanent beds) according to main types of accommodation and hotel categories in per cent

Year	Hotels					Camp sites	Other collective capacities	Households (private accommodation)
	Total	5ᵃ	4ᵃ	3ᵃ	2ᵃ			
1989	45.8	46.4	52.1	44.8	35.7	13.5	24.7	11.1
2001	37.0	37.8	50.7	42.1	31.5	16.7	21.1	9.2
2005	39.8	41.0	44.3	43.3	32.1	17.4	21.8	10.4
2011	39.0	39.9	43.8	38.5	29.5	18.8	21.2	13.9
2015ᵃ	39.9	–	–	–	–	20.0	22.6	16.9

Source: Ministry of Tourism (2013) and Croatian Bureau of Statistics (2015a)
ᵃData for 2015 not available

continuously increasing (8.3 billion Euro in 2015), the demand for land for tourism development will continue unabated, while developers and investors will resort to taking ad hoc steps when spatial challenges arise.

ABANDONED TOURISM RESORTS: THE CASE OF HALUDOVO AND KUPARI

In this section, assessment and analysis is made about the two well-known, and abandoned, tourist resorts. This section will:

- briefly highlight the approach to tourism development—past and present; and
- discuss the consequences of officious constraints imposed by the government and municipalities who have failed to legally determine the rights and obligations of owners and other communities within these tourism areas.

Two different tourism resorts are presented in Fig. 9.1. Both tourism resorts are located in extremely attractive locations, are well planned and have complete infrastructure. Their current status of the abandoned tourism zones serves to call into question the rationality and cost-effectiveness of spatial in these areas. Importantly, it should be a red flag for the government for allowing so many former tourism resorts to waste in abandonment and for not realising the capital potential of such sites for years, as if the land was worthless. The two tourism zones are Haludovo on the island of Krk in the north Adriatic and Kupari near Dubrovnik in the south Adriatic.

Haludovo Tourism Zone, Malinska, Island of Krk

Haludovo was developed in 1971 as the most modern and up-market hotel resort on Adriatic. It occupied 25 hectares of land, and the resort was planned as an urban-architectural unit that would provide its guests with great comfort, all of the services they need and a direct contact with nature. The entire hotel complex had 1792 beds, the beach area was able to accommodate 2500 users simultaneously and there were 450 parking spaces. The resort consisted of three parts—hotel Palace, hotel Tamaris and Fishermen's Village. Hotel Palace had 485 beds and its restaurant was able to accommodate up to 600 guests. The hotel also had a sports centre

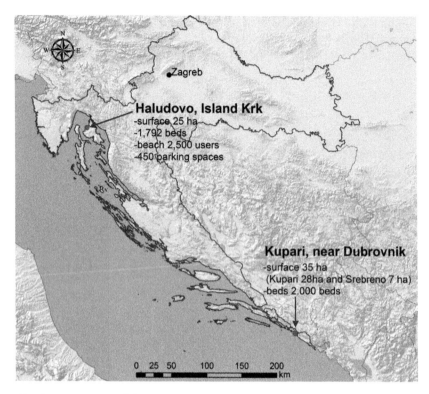

Fig. 9.1 Location of the two abandoned tourism zones in Croatia

and a clinic. Hotel Tamaris had 289 rooms with 526 beds and 119 spare beds. Before renovation, the restaurant seated 447 and after renovation 600. The Fishermen's Village was designed as a fishing village with a small harbour for yachts. In the style of dense Mediterranean architecture, the "village" had 14 luxury suites and 12 rooms with a total of 102 beds. Next to the Village, there were 33 villas with 4 beds each and 18 villas with 6 beds each. The capacity was increased in 1984 with the completion of 20 buildings with family suites, called Lavender. Each building consisted of 4 apartments, and in total they had 320 beds. The population of the Malinska municipality between 1961 and 2011 is shown in Table 9.5.

The investment amounted to 25 million US dollars, and at the time it was, arguably, one of the biggest hotel resorts in the world. Although the investment in infrastructure, facilities and the landscaping did not prove

Table 9.5 Population of Malinska municipality 1961–2011

	1961	1971	1981	1991	2001	2011
Malinska	326	292	700	999	607	965

Source: Croatian Bureau of Statistics (2015b)

Table 9.6 Number of tourist arrivals and overnights in Malinska municipality 1960–2008

Year	Arrivals			Overnights			Average length of stay (nights)
	Total	Foreign	% Foreign	Total	Foreign	% Foreign	
1960	8,556	3,121	36.4	108,731	32,205	29.6	12.7
1971	21,211	13,362	62.9	185,911	134,907	72.6	8.8
1981	58,138	33,177	57.0	438,540	288,001	65.7	7.5
1987	83,396	69,711	83.5	588,551	502,947	85.5	7.1
1991	12,773	8,335	65.2	637,65	39,169	61.4	5.0

Source: Radić (2009), p. 110

cost-effective in the beginning, Haludovo was the genesis of development and modernisation of the local community. The complex provided 270 permanent jobs, and about 250 people found seasonal employment annually (Radić, 2009). The area was also demographically rejuvenated. The population of municipality of Malinska in 1971 was about 300 only to increase to 700 in the following decade (Radić, 2009). The impact of Haludovo resort on tourist arrivals and overnights was significant, as shown in Table 9.6, from 1971, the year of resort completion, the number of arrivals and overnights more than doubled by 1981 (Radić, 2009).

During the Homeland war, Haludovo was used to accommodate refugees and displaced people. The prolonged and less than ideal use of hotels for residential purposes leads to costly damage and their demise, and subsequently, hotel Tamaris was demolished in 2004, and the entire resort was prepared for privatisation.

However, it also needs to be said here that most of these resorts were already on the road towards dilapidation before the Homeland war, and it was only a matter of time until they would have succumbed to commercial redundancy. The reason for this is that during their very active life, the operating budget seldom allowed for proper maintenance, upgrading, landscaping and the 10-year or 12-year overhaul, or the budget was siphoned off for "other" needs. Despite the rhetoric of the time, these monolithic resorts were constructed very poorly. This did not only apply to Haludovo and Kupari resorts but to just about every state-owned tourism infrastructure along the coast and on the coastal islands. Hence, by the 1990s one can reasonably say that the majority of state-run tourism resorts and hotels were already in various stages of decay and obsoleteness, and the Homeland war simply accelerated the decay.

In the privatisation process, a number of unlawful steps were made on purpose to meet a particular investor's interest. For example, the assessment of the resort's true market value was not made transparent, and the final transaction involved the purchase of the resort buildings only and not the complex land. Thus, the buildings were now in private ownership, and the land under them and around them was either owned by the municipality or the Croatian government or both, either way an absurd situation. Obviously, the unresolved issue of land ownership hampered renovation, extension or redevelopment of the accommodation facilities, and by 2001 the decaying buildings and infrastructure were unable to meet the visitor expectations, and the resort was shut down in 2002. Given that this is a very beautiful area already equipped with all the necessary infrastructure and one ready for re-construction, it is more than justifiable to call on the government and local municipality to question their rationality for such an incompetent and almost criminal utilisation of the resort's land. Of course, no one has even bothered to ask what happened to the now unemployed and displaced people of the Malinska community.

Kupari Tourism Zone Near Dubrovnik

The Kupari tourism resort, named after a close-by village of Kupari near Dubrovnik, was developed in the same way as the Haludovo and was one of the prettiest resorts on Adriatic. However, the first construction of this tourism resort began in the early 1920s, when private capital from the Czech Republic was invested in a two-storey hotel "*Kupari*" with pavilions and a Grand Hotel. After the Second World War, the Yugoslav People's Army further developed the resort by building new accommodations for the vacationing military personnel and their families. Due to different ownership and management structure, and a gradual development over time, the Kupari resort did not have a significant impact on the local community. The population of Kupari rose only slightly from 1948 to 1971, from 242 to 354 residents as shown in Table 9.7 (Croatian Bureau of Statistics, 2015b). The entire resort occupied over 35 hectares of land divided in two sub-zones—Kupari with an area of 28 ha and smaller Srebreno resort occupying 7.6 ha. There were 2000 beds in total in four hotels—Mladost, Goričina, Pelegrin and Galeb. As the resort developed, so has the number of tourist arrivals and overnights, and by the 1980, the resort recorded about 57,000 tourist arrivals or about 205,000 overnights (Tables 9.8 and 9.9) (Žabica, 1965).

Table 9.7 Population of Kupari in 1948–2001

Year	1948	1961	1971	1981[a]	1991[a]	2001	2011
Kupari	242	273	354	0	0	553	808

Source: Croatian Bureau of Statistics (2015c)
[a]Year 1981 and 1991 population of Kupari is in Dubrovnik

Table 9.8 Number of tourist arrivals and overnights in Kupari, 1936–1938

Year	Tourist		Overnight	
	Domestic	Foreign	Domestic	Foreign
1936	168	2442	2582	37,258
1937	154	2302	2241	27,932
1938	227	1801	2827	21,734

Source: Žabica (1965), p. 14

Table 9.9 Number of tourist arrivals and overnights in Kupari, 1962–1965 and 1980

	Year	Arrival domestic	Arrival foreign	Domestic overnight	Foreign overnight
Kupari	1962	6,535	–	106,729	–
	1963	9,923	–	126,642	–
	1964	10,801	–	179,229	–
	1965	14,085	–	205,314	–
	1980	57,100	23,000	514,400	80,600

Source: Žabica (1965), p. 15; Stanković (1990), p. 338

Since the Kupari tourism resort is located in the area that was part of the war zone during the Homeland war between 1991 and 1995, all the hotels were destroyed. During the war, the government assumed ownership of the entire resort, and since then, the government has been unsuccessful in selling the property. Owing to the attractiveness of the coast and picturesque Kupari village and its proximity to the UNESCO's World Heritage Site, Dubrovnik, touristic activities take place in the Kupari village vis-à-vis private accommodation. Needless to say, by 2001 the number of tourist arrivals and overnights was about 4100 arrivals and 14,000 overnights, a fraction of what was realised at the resort in 1980 (Ministry of Tourism, 2013).

Despite its extremely attractive location, the government-owned Kupari tourism resort had laid dormant and derelict for over 20 years, and as with the Haludovo resort, one can only beg the question as to why was this resort not rationalised, or crucially, what were the barriers that prevented its sale and redevelopment? The good news is that after all these years, the government has announced in April 2015 that it will call for an international tender to lease, and redevelop, Kupari for 99 years, and that six firms (Karisma Hotels Adriatic; Valamar Business Development; Rixos Group; Home Defence Cooperative Mir; Avenue Osteuropa GmbH, together with the hotel management firm, the Marriott International Inc.; and Titan Real Estate) have expressed an interest in investing up to 100 million Euros in the redevelopment project. At the time of writing this article, it was announced in the media in November 2015 that the Austrian company, Avenue Osteuropa GmbH, together with the hotel management firm, the Marriott International Inc., was awarded the competitive lease.

Discussion and Conclusion[2]

By examining the conditions of tourism development in Croatia between 1945 and 1991, and during the transition period thereafter, it is possible to follow the trajectory of the policy interplay between tourism planning and spatial planning (Fig. 9.2). In doing so, two opposing approaches were contrasted: (1) tourism development of the centrally planned economy in the former Yugoslavia and (2) tourism development in Croatia's free market economy, together with their advantages, disadvantages and long-term consequences.

Relationships between tourism and spatial planning on all levels are closely connected with law, economy and ecology. Any change in their interrelationships could have an impact on tourism and space.

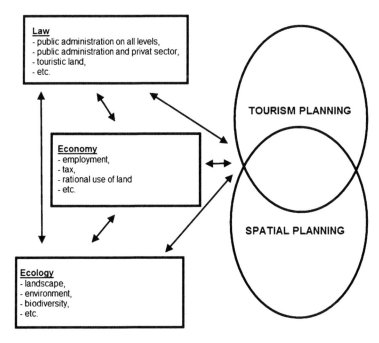

Fig. 9.2 Policy networks between tourism and physical planning

It was strongly argued that the complexity of tourism development, especially in relation to land demand, requires a learned consideration about a multitude of factors and a delicate synchronisation or balancing act of legislation, regulatory policies and implementation. It was also highlighted that such a legislative and regulatory balancing act was something that Croatia did not have due to the rapid socio-political transition and changes to which neither legislation nor bureaucratic culture within its public service could cope efficiently. The consequences of that policy and regulatory dislocation at spatial planning and tourism development level were discussed and highlighted by analysing the two failed and abandoned tourism resorts. This helped to highlight an irrational use of very valuable land as a consequence of failed legislation and regulations, for example, the non-transparent processes of privatisation, and lack of reforms and/or the application of reforms in land ownership.

These arguments were built on a premise that every activity, in terms of spatial that involves tourism, must firstly satisfy legal, economic and ecological requirements. No doubt these factors are important, equally though, to implement and carry on with tourism activities in a legally designated area; it is necessary first to effectively and transparently apply the spatial and tourism development legislation and its regulatory mechanisms. This would go a long way in clearly identifying from the outset, the rights and obligations of all stakeholders, and importantly, it would resolve many of the current conflicts between potential investors and the government (at national, regional and local level). However, the reform process of spatial for touristic purposes at present remains stalled.

The two abandoned tourism resorts presented highlight the consequence of weak and poorly defined policies not only in tourism and spatial planning but also in the management of these resources. Twenty other tourism resorts met with similar consequences. Absurdly, while these resorts lay ruined and deserted, new tourism resorts are being planned in absence of proper access and infrastructure (Ministry of Construction and Physical Planning, 2012:52). The analysis of the two most representative tourism resorts clearly shows how a lack of coordinated policies and legal framework between different governments, coupled with a profound mismanagement of the resorts, has impeded their rejuvenation. No doubt, this will have negative long-term socio-economic impact on the local and regional communities, such as devaluation of land, sectoral unemployment and environmental devastation.

The abandoned resorts are most certainly pointed to an irresponsible use of land from both the economic and socio-environmental perspectives. The destruction of land and poor management of existing natural and human resources demonstrate not only the incompatibility between different policies but also the incompetence of the bureaucrats who manage these policies. The cause for the non-use of these tourism resorts also points the finger at the collusion between the government and private lobby groups whose emergence was the result of the new social and economic conditions and the then government in power right after 1990.

As already tried and tested in other countries with rich tourism history, tourism can significantly contribute to the country's socio-economic development and its regional rejuvenation, but to successfully implement spatial planning for tourism development, a robust mechanism must be in place for a coordinated policy approach to such planning and subsequent development. To implement these mechanisms in Croatia, there is a pressing need for an effective and decentralised legislation at regional and local level (micro level) with a specific role for the planning of regional and local tourist needs, for example, to advise on and regulate spatial planning, to coordinate and synchronise spatial planning with tourism planning, to assess and regulate tourism development and its cost-benefits to the local and regional communities and to affect robust environmental husbandry policies and regulations in all tourism-zoned areas, resort areas including local waterways. In addition, there is a need to have an effective umbrella tourism spatial legislation at national level (macro level), which would address broader tourism spatial issues and provide the necessary legislative framework for tourism development and its spatial planning as a matter of national economic and development policy. Therefore, it is contested here that the future of Croatia's tourism development/redevelopment and spatial planning for tourism is going to be best served by the local and regional communities who are involved with tourism face-to-face, and not necessarily by the tourism policy bureaucrats at the national level. This has proven to be the case with Kupari where spatial planning and tourism development policies, or redevelopment in this case, had been thought about and worked through at local, regional and national level. The very difficult issues of land rights, land ownerships, changes to the land registry, spatial planning, decontamination and sanitation of the resort site, environmental protection, the future scope of redevelopment and even building permits for this former public and military tourism resort were mostly solved at local and regional level, while tourism policy makers at the national level had to make sure that the issues being contested and settled were within the legal framework, hence, assuring a "green light" for the redevelopment of the resort. This clearly shows that when disparate and/or discordant spatial planning and tourism development/redevelopment policies are brought together in accord and harmony, there is little likelihood for any discordant outcomes of such policies. Perhaps, the Kupari's road to redevelopment should serve Croatia well as a model for the redevelopment of its abandoned tourist zones or resorts.

NOTES

1. Notice about term "spatial planning" which is *"terminus technicus" (lat.)*. In European Union and its official documents, the term used is "spatial planning". In the USA, term used is "physical planning" and in Australia the term is "land use".

2. This research is a part of the scientific project Heritage Urbanism (HERU)—
   Urban and Spatial Models for Revival and Enhancement of Cultural
   Heritage (HERU-2032)—financed by Croatian Science Foundation, which
   is being carried out at the Faculty of Architecture University of Zagreb.

References

Allcock, J. B. (1986). Yugoslavia's tourist trade pot of gold or pig in a poke? *Annals of Tourism Research, 13*(4), 565–588.

Bachvarov, M. (1997). End of the model? Tourism in post-communist Bulgaria. *Tourism Management, 18*(1), 43–50.

Beyer, E., Hagemann, A., & Zinganel, M. (2013). *Holidays after the fall. Seaside architecture and urbanism in Bulgaria and Croatia*. Berlin, Germany: Jovis Verlag.

Bramwell, B., & Meyer, D. (2007). Power and tourism policy relations in transition. *Annals of Tourism Research, 34*(3), 766–788.

Breheny, M. J. (1991). The renaissance of strategic planning? *Environment and Planning B: Planning and Design, 18*(2), 233–249.

Buckley, P. J., & Witt, S. F. (1990). Tourism in the centrally-planned economies of Europe. *Annals of Tourism Research, 17*(1), 7–18.

CBS. (2015a). *Croatian Bureau of Statistics*. http://www.dzs.hr. Date accessed 10 May 2015.

CBS. (2015b). *Croatian Bureau of Statistics*. http://www.dzs.hr/App/PXWeb/PXWebHrv/Selection.aspx?px_tableid=Tabela4_08.px&px_path=Naselja%20i%20stanovni%C5%A1tvo%20Republike%20Hrvatske__Stanovni%C5%A1tvo__Naselja&px_language=hr&px_db=Naselja%20i%20stanovni%C5%A1tvo%20Republike%20Hrvatske&rxid=fc9d580f-2229-4982-a72c-cdd3e96307d3. Date accessed 10 May 2015.

CBS. (2015c). *Croatian Bureau of Statistics*. http://www.dzs.hr/App/PXWeb/PXWebHrv/Table.aspx?layout=tableViewLayout1&px_tableid=Tabela4_19.px&px_path=Naselja%20i%20stanovni%C5%A1tvo%20Republike%20Hrvatske__Stanovni%C5%A1tvo__Naselja&px_language=hr&px_db=Naselja%20i%20stanovni%C5%A1tvo%20Republike%20Hrvatske&rxid=fc9d580f-2229-4982-a72c-cdd3e96307d3. Date accessed 10 May 2015.

Chettiparamb, A., & Thomas, H. (2012). Tourism and spatial planning. *Journal of Policy Research in Tourism, Leisure and Events, 4*(3), 215–220.

FNRJ. (1966). *Ilustrirani turistički privredni i hotelski vodič* [An illustrated tourist commercial and hotel guide]. Zagreb, Croatia: FNRJ.

Grandits, H., & Taylor, K. (2010). *Yugoslavia's sunny side: A history of tourism in socialism (1950s-1980s)*. Budapest, Hungary/New York: Central European University Press.

Hall, D. R. (1992). The challenge of international tourism in Eastern Europe. *Tourism Management, 13*(1), 41–44.

Hall, D. R. (1998). Tourism development and sustainability issues in Central and South-Eastern Europe. *Tourism Management, 19*(5), 423–431.

Institute for Urbanism. (1967). *Program dugoročnog razvoja i plan prostornog uređenja Jadranskog područja, Urbanistički institut SR Hrvatske* [Long-term development plan and zoning the Adriatic area]. Zagreb, Croatia: Institute for Urbanism SR Croatian, book 15–43.

Institute for Urbanism. (1968). *Regionalni prostorni plan južnog Jadrana* [The regional spatial plan for the southern Adriatic], Ujedinjene nacije – program za razvoj, Vlada SFR Jugoslavije, Urbanistički institut SR Hrvatske, Republički zavod za urbanizam SR Crne Gore, Urbanistički zavod SR Bosne i Hercegovine, Institut za ekonomiku turizma, međunarodni konzultativni konzorcij Tekne Milano i Cekop Warszawa.

Institute for Urbanism. (1972). *Koordinacioni regionalni prostorni plan Gornji Jadran* [Coordination regional plan for Upper Adriatic]. Zagreb, Croatia: Urbanistički institut SR Hrvatske.

Julien, G. (1989). Stratégie de développement touristique en Languedoc-Roussillon [Tourism development strategy in Languedoc-Roussillon]. *Bulletin de la Société Languedocienne de Géographie, 32*(1-2), 215–221.

Kobašić, A. (1987). *Turizam u Jugoslaviji – razvoj, stanje i perspektive* [Tourism in Yugoslavia – Development, situation and perspectives]. Zagreb, Croatia: Informator.

Kobašić, A. (1981). Lessons from planning in Yugoslavia's tourist industry. *International Journal of Tourism Management, 2*(4), 233–239.

Kranjčević, J. (2012a). Turizam u prostornim planovima Makarskog primorja od 1945–1990. [Tourism spatial plans for Makarska Riviera from 1945–1990]. In M. Mustapić & I. Hrstić (Eds.), Proceedings of scientific meeting *Makarsko primorje danas* (pp. 211–230). Zagreb, Croatia: Institute Ivo Pilar and municipality of Makarska.

Kranjčević, J. (2012b). Spatial planning of tourism – The situation and the consequences. In. Z. Karač (Ed.), *Proceedings of scientific conference rethinking urbanism. Faculty of Architecture* (pp. 127–130). Zagreb, Croatia: University of Zagreb.

Kulić, V. (2009). East? West? Or both? Foreign perceptions of architecture in socialist Yugoslavia. *Journal of Architecture (RIBA), 14*(1), 87–105.

Marinović-Uzelac, A. (1986). *Naselja, gradovi, prostori* [Settlements, cities, places]. Zagreb, Croatia: Tehnička knjiga.

Ministry of Construction and Physical Planning. (2012). Izvješće o stanju u prostoru Republike Hrvatske 2008-2012 [National report on the state of spatial development of the Republic of Croatia 2008-2012]. http://www.mgipu.hr/doc/Prostorno/Izvjesce_SPRH_08_12.pdf. Date accessed 20 November 2014.

Ministry of Physical Planning, Construction and Housing. (1997). *Strategija pro-stornog uređenja Republike Hrvatske* [National strategy for physical planning of the Republic Croatia], http://www.mgipu.hr/default.aspx?id=3662. Date accessed 28 August 2013.

Ministry of Tourism. (2012). *The catalogue of investment projects, Republic of Croatia*. http://www.mint.hr/UserDocsImages/130124--catalogue-FIN. pdf. Date accessed 28 August 2013.

Ministry of Tourism. (2013). *Croatian Tourism Development Strategy to 2020*. Official Gazette of the Republic of Croatia 55/2013. http://narodne-novine. nn.hr/clanci/sluzbeni/2013_05_55_1119.html. Date accessed 20 November 2014.

Montana, M. (1986). Sadržaj i organizacija povezivanja društvenog i privatnog sektora u turističkoj ponudi [The content and organization of connecting the public and private sectors in the tourist offer]. *Tourism, 34*(10), 14–20.

Pastras, P., & Bramwell, B. (2013). A strategic-relational approach to tourism policy. *Annals of Tourism Research, 43*, 390–414.

Radić, M. (2009). *Voljenoj vali – Razvoj turizma u Malinskoj* [Beloved bay – The development of tourism in Malinska]. Malinska, Croatia: Malinka

Sallnow, J. (1985a). Yugoslavia: Tourism in a socialist federal state. *Tourism Management, 6*(2), 113–124.

Sallnow, J. (1985b). Yugoslavia: Booming tourism on the Adriatic coast. *Tourism Management, 6*(4), 295–297.

Simon, H. A. (1976). *Administrative behavior*. New York: Fredd Press-Macmillan.

SNL. (1987). *Veliki geografski atlas Jugoslavije* [Large geographic Atlas of Yugoslavia]. Zagreb, Croatia: SNL.

Stanković, S. M. (1990). *Turizam u Jugoslaviji* (treće izdanje) [Tourism in Yugoslavia – (3rd ed)]. Beograd, Serbia: Turistička štampa.

Weber, S. (1989). Yugoslav international tourism. *Tourism Management, 10*(2), 156–164.

Žabica, T. (1965). Turizam Župe dubrovačke [Tourism in Župa Dubrovačka]. *Tourism, 13*(11), 14–15.

CHAPTER 10

Sustainability Issues in Management of Tourism in Protected Areas: Case Study of Plitvice Lakes National Park

Izidora Marković Vukadin

INTRODUCTION

Protected natural areas, as popular tourism attractions, are burdened by many negative influences largely due to human activities. Their sustainability, in terms of conservation of the underlying phenomenon, is dependent on the quality of management (Alexander, 2008). The protected natural areas are extremely important for the success of Croatian tourism. Croatia belongs to European countries with high percentage of land and sea under various forms of protection and with large number of various protected natural areas. According to the Nature Protection Act in 2012, there were 433 protected areas, covering land area of 682,451 hectares or 12.1 per cent of total land area and sea area of 60.339 hectares or 1.9 per cent of the Croatian territorial sea area (Government of Republic of Croatia, 2013). It is thus no surprise that the natural scenery is the main tourism attraction with over 20 per cent of all tourist arrivals in Croatia motivated primarily by exploring nature protected areas (NPAs), especially national and nature parks (Institute for Tourism, 2006). The constant

I. Marković Vukadin (✉)
Institute for Tourism, Zagreb, Croatia

© The Author(s) 2017   201
L. Dwyer et al. (eds.), *Evolution of Destination Planning and Strategy*, DOI 10.1007/978-3-319-42246-6_10

increase of number of visitors to NPA represents, therefore, a threat to sensitive resources of these protected areas.

With the already large number of visitors that are expected to increase in the coming years, it is extremely important to balance all activities in these areas—protection, education, research, recreation and tourism through mechanism such as spatial planning and management plans. One such area under significant pressure from visitor and facing manifold of management challenge is the Plitvice Lakes National Park. It is the oldest Croatian National Park, under UNESCO protection since 1979, located in the middle of Croatia, on a main route to the Croatian Adriatic. Its main attractions are cascading lakes set amid thick forest, attracting thousands of visitors each year. The Park is the main economic generator of the region, creating jobs and supplementary incomes for local residents in otherwise sparsely populated and economically depressed area of Croatia. The sensitive natural environment, visitor pressure, region's economic dependency on the Park and inadequate infrastructure present management challenge and make it thus an excellent case study for the national park management. The aim of this chapter is, therefore, to illustrate the key challenges faced by the extremely sensitive and equally popular nature protected area based on a research carried out from 2013 to 2015 into environmental, social and economic/tourism sustainability. The chapter starts by a brief overview of the current discourse of the protected areas management and their sustainability issues. Then it moves on to a case study of Plitvice Lakes National Park to identify and discuss the main management challenges arising from tension between the need for environmental protection and much needed revival of an economically and socially deprived rural region.

MANAGEMENT OF PROTECTED NATURAL AREAS

The global network of parks is currently crucial for maintaining and improving conservation of biodiversity and environment in general. Therefore, the need to manage protected natural areas emerged immediately after proclamation of national parks (Marinović-Uzelac, 2001). Initially, only certain aspects were managed, such as forest systems and more prominent ecosystem components (Martinić, 2010; Orlić, 1983), with the management and control system differing from country to country and depending on the particular management objective. Common to all was the significant central government involvement through legislation. As it became clear that the nature protection cannot be achieved by the official designation and regulation acts alone (Dudley et al., 1999), the system of nature protection evolved into an active integrated sustainable management. Such management is regulated with emphasis on sustainable types of tourism (Hockings, Stolton, Leverington, Dudley, & Courrau, 2006), accompanied by monitoring of sustainability indicators to provide measurable units of information on economic, environmental and social condition (Böhringer & Jochem, 2007).

Such integrated sustainable management of NPAs requires a tailor-made approach to each NPA characteristics and particularities (RodríguezRodríguez, 2012). These models of sustainable management are based on cooperation and partnership (Borrini-Feyerabend, Kothary, & Oviedo, 2004), as this makes them more flexible than centralized systems, especially in situations that require quick reaction, such as natural disasters, serious violations of the environment integrity and sudden changes in visitor demand. Furthermore, such models accommodate interest of regional and local communities, the key stakeholders in the process of nature protection and NPAs management. Although the management of the NPAs is becoming more sophisticated and better regulated, there is a growing concern that this dominant discourse in NPAs management is not able to devise a suitable visitor management system when faced with continuous growth of visitors that represent a growing threat to both environment and society (Borrini-Feyerabend et al., 2013).

There are a number of factors that can have significant adverse impacts on biodiversity, especially when corrective actions are not put in place (Martinić, 2010). A study into relationship between management and 26 environmental impacts conducted internationally by the World Wide Fund (Carey, Dudley, & Stolton, 2000) reveals significant correlations between lack of appropriate management and threats to NPAs environment. Since each NPA is unique, there is a great diversity of risks potentially leading to a wide range of negative impacts. Taking into account these risks, the adaptive management is often recommended as an optimal management model. At the core philosophy of adaptive management is its ability to identify critical uncertainties regarding natural resource dynamics and the design of diagnostic management experiments to reduce these uncertainties (Holling, 1978; Walters, 1986). Thus, appropriate strategies are designed to minimize or ameliorate likely risks of each NPA and ensure its sustainability (Growcock & Pickering, 2011; Steven, Pickering, & Castley, 2011).

204 I. MARKOVIĆ VUKADIN

Regardless of a particular management model, the sustainable management of the protected area is, in principle, characterized by the presence of different influences broadly grouped into political, economic and environmental (RodríguezRodríguez, 2012). While sustainable management that takes into account all those influences and devices practices and processes adapted to the specific conditions of each NPAs is a complex and demanding process, it is usually efficient. It is understood as a cyclical process with a set of predefined activities implemented in order to meet the set objectives. Also, it is based on the assessment or evaluation of the NPA's current state, identification of key issues and challenges and definition of clear objectives, so that management actions can be planned and implemented and their impact measured.

The issues of the NPA management and optimal management models discussed so far are not comprehensive but deliberate selected to frame the case study of the Plitvice Lakes National Park. In line with the aim of this chapter, the following section fleshes out the most relevant aspects of the NPA sustainability issues in order to provide a solid foundation of the consequent discussion on sustainable management of the Plitvice Lakes National Park.

SUSTAINABILITY ISSUES IN PROTECTED NATURAL AREA

The issue of sustainability of protected areas was, up to twenty years ago, on the margin of scientific research because of the common perception that the protected natural areas are, by their very existence, sustainable. While their sustainability is threatened in many ways due to transport, foresting, agriculture and global climate changes, a significant threat, as already alluded to in preceding section, are visitors and their projected growth. Thus, when NPAs become popular tourist attractions, they face the similar threats identified in a broad tourism literature on socio-economic impacts of tourism (Cole, 2004; Growcock & Pickering, 2011; Hobbs et al., 2010; Newsome, Moore, & Dowling, 2013; Steven et al., 2011; Wills, 2015). While the visitors bring economic benefits to the community, they often undermine the traditional way of life and cultural identity of local communities with new economic activities substituting traditional ones. While this might not be a significant threat to destination communities in general, in the case of NPA, traditional way of life and local culture that have shaped the cultural and natural landscape are often the key reason for setting up the NPA, and failing to maintain traditional cultural practices can undermine the key values for which the NPAs were created at the outset. This tension between the goals of nature protection and the growth of visitor economy in or around NPAs is likely to increase in the immediate future (Newsome et al., 2013). Namely, given the scope of nature destructions that we are experiencing today, the nature protection is an urgency today. Human manipulation, exploitation and destruction of the natural environment are so great that the entire physical and biological systems of the planet are subordinated to the need for intensive use of our planet's resources. The lack of ethics in dealing with the natural environment (Taylor, 1989) is largely a result of the dominance of profit-oriented values (Pejnović & Lukić, 2014), which has an impact on many aspects of the natural environment.

At the same time, many rural and peripheral regions, faced with economic and population decline, need to devise regeneration strategies, and designation of NPAs is seen as an ideal mechanism for regional economic revival through tourism. Although the prefix eco is often added to this type of tourism, the state of environment is inevitably disturbed by the presence of visitors or, even more so, by their concentration in, usually, the most attractive spots in the NPA. The most adverse impacts relate to waste, wastewater and traffic (Monza, D'Antoniob, Lawsonc, Barberd, & Newmane, 2016; Rodriguez-Jorqueraa, Krollb, Toorc, & Denslowb, 2015), although all infrastructure required for tourism irreversibly alters the natural and social environment (Opačić, Lukić, & Fürts Bjeliš, 2005). Even when the negative impacts are minimal, they are likely to cause severe damage through accumulation (Newsome et al., 2013). Equally important is the visitor pressure in relation to the size of NPA where, as a rule, the larger the area, the easier it will absorb different influences (Growcock & Pickering, 2011). As an illustration, Kruger National Park in South Africa spread over 1.9 million hectares and receives around 800,000 of visitors annually. In contrast, Plitvice Lakes National Park with a surface area of 29,000 hectares receives up to 1.3 million visitors. In addition some recreational activities can cause environmental damage occurring after a short period of use (Cole, 2004), while in other activities, such as camping, negative effects occur gradually. Finally, negative impacts of tourism can occur as a result of construction of tourism facilities, depending on the location sensitivity, building materials, equipment and infrastructure (Martinić, Kosović, & Grginčić, 2008).

Apart from environmental and economic sustainability, there is also social sustainability to consider in NPAs management. While local communities, with their traditions, cultures and lifestyles, are integral to NPAs, they are often marginalized in the management process and their core cultural values and identity undermined by urbanization (Penga, Liua, & Sunb, 2016), class differentiation (Gurneya et al., 2014) and acculturation (Gu & Ryan, 2008; Macloed, 2006; Marinović-Uzelac, 2001; Rekom & Go, 2006; Robinson, 1999).

However, all these potentially adverse impacts that can arise due to tourism in NPAs can be ameliorated or minimized with appropriate management actions. Thus, the management ability to devise and implement appropriate strategies is of crucial importance (Newsome & Lacroix, 2011). For ensuring environmental protection while fostering tourism economy and preserving social fabric, it is important to identify and explain the processes and interrelationships in the ecosystem and the social environment (Hobbs et al., 2010).

With the preceding discussion focused on the importance of management on NPAs, the optimal management models for achieving their ecological preservation and economic and social sustainability, each NPA is a unique case, albeit sharing certain similarities. This case study is focused on relatively small National Park, protecting the extremely sensitive complex of hydrological, geological and biological features, located in otherwise economically depressed region and experiencing a huge pressure from visitors. Management is caught in between the need to preserve its sensitive eco- and geo-system and to act as the chief generator of economic and social revitalization of the region.

CASE STUDY OF NP PLITVICE LAKES

Plitvice Lakes National Park is the oldest national park in Croatia, established in 1949, and the first area in Croatia included on UNESCO world heritage list in 1979. There is tradition of tourism dating back to the nineteenth century (Ivanuš, 2010) with a sharp increase in visitor numbers from the 1970s, corresponding to the tourism boom on the Adriatic coast. Since the very beginning of tourism, it was the engine of regional economic development. The economic importance of the Park is best described by the fact that the Public Institution Plitvice Lakes National Park (PLNP), in charge of Park's management under supervision of the Ministry of Environmental and Nature Protection, employs around 800 people, making it the largest economic entity in the region.

Plitvice is a complex of 16 lakes, connected by travertine waterfalls and surrounded with virgin forests and meadows that spread over 29.7 thousand hectares. The natural phenomenon of Plitvice Lakes is a result of complex interactions between geological, geomorphological, physical-chemical and biological components of the complex ecosystem of the wider area. As a unique water-sediment system closely linked with the environment, the lakes are very sensitive to environmental changes and under constant threats from the surrounding area (Pavletić, 1957).

Located on the main transit route from central Europe to Adriatic Coast and relatively close to the Croatian capital Zagreb (130 km) and Adriatic coast (about 100 km to the closest seaside resorts Crikvenica Riviera) (Fig. 10.1), they are easily accessible to residents and tourists. There are two main entrances to the Park, with parking facilities, info centers and souvenir shops.

The most attractive area around the lakes covers only one per cent of the Park's surface, and it is accessed by 24 km of trails and bridges and

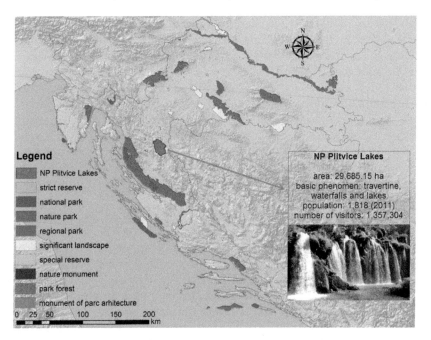

Fig. 10.1 Location and main characteristics of Plitvice Lakes National Park

two 50-m docks on the lake Kozjak (Public Institution NPPL, 2014a). The visitor trails are primarily constructed as wooden bridges on the travertine barriers allowing visitors to see the most attractive parts of the Park. There are two types of trails leading to major attractions, of three, six and eight hours' duration. In addition, there is a dense network of walking and cycling trails throughout the entire Park for those wishing to stay longer and explore all features of the Park.

Although new building construction within the Park's boundary is now forbidden, there are three hotels with 698 beds, built from the 1950s to 1980s and currently owned and managed by the Public Institution NPPL. The Park's infrastructure and the entire region have suffered extensive damage during the Homeland War. Consequently, with the free-market economy after 1995, houses of local residents in surrounding villages have been rebuilt to a modern standard, often with extra accommodation for short-term rental. Micro and small entrepreneurs have set up restaurants and family hotels, and two large camping grounds and hotels were restored and now also managed by the Public Institution NPPL.

The beginning of management and general care for the lakes can be traced back to the Society for Landscape and Beautification of Lakes and Environment founded in 1883 (Vidaković, 1977). In 1949, it was protected as National Park managed by the National Park Directorate set up the same year and in charge of the Park up to 1990. The first period of control was extremely successful against the initial objectives, although some, such as the construction of tourism infrastructure, were not in line with today's management objectives of protected areas (Petrić, 2012). This was achieved despite the lack of management plans that are, nowadays, considered to be the most important for NPAs management. After the Homeland War, management of the area was re-established and focused primarily on the reconstruction of visitor facilities, infrastructure and promotion (Petrić, 2012).

Thus, from its foundation in 1949, the Plitvice Lakes National Park is managed by the federal government through the Directorate before and then the Public Institution after 1995. The local community is considered as an unimportant stakeholder with its role reduced to that of an observer or adviser, without any real influence in decision making process. Initially, this centralized model worked well with the federal government ensuring ample funding for much needed public and tourism infrastructure, management and marketing. However, centralized management proved to be inadequate over time. It has focused primarily on the economic performance of the Park, paying scarce attention to the management of location-specific impact zones. Hotels and restaurants close to the lakes, without proper waste and sewage collection, concentration of visitor facilities in the small and most sensitive area of the Park and pathways erected damaging the travertine barriers are some of the inherited problems.

In contrast to the earlier period, today every Public Institution in charge of managing NPA is required to have management plan, including the Plitvice Lakes National Park. The main objective of the PLNP Management Plan (Šikić, 2007) is protecting the environment and integrating stakeholders, with management aims focused on the preservation and use of natural resources, education and promotion of protected area in the context of its national importance. In practice, however, management does not pay significant attention to stakeholders, while its activities, as outlined in the Public Institution PLNP Annual Plan (2014a), are concentrated on development of recreation facilities and Park's promotion domestically and abroad. This 'practical' management orientation is a result of the situation in which the Public Institution PLNP, formally in charge of nature protection, is, at the same time, the institution that manages the hotel facilities and tourism superstructure, which are in potential conflict with the postulates of protection. While the nature protection calls for control of visitor numbers, the economic viability of tourism and hospitality facilities depends heavily on visitor expenditure. Paradoxically, income generated from visitor entrance ticket sales is often diverted from nature protection into subsidizing low-performing accommodation and restaurant facilities.

TOURISM IN THE NP PLITVICE LAKES

The Park was visited in 2015 by about 1.3 million people (Public Institution PLNP, 2016), mostly day visitors (Table 10.1). Coinciding with the growth of tourist arrivals to the Adriatic since the 1970s, the Park has witnessed a steep increase in visitor numbers from 1970, to reach three quarter of a million by 1985, with a slight decline in 1990, just before the outbreak of War. However, visitor numbers picked up quickly, to exceed the pre-War level by 1995, to about 1.4 million currently. Such growth can be partly attributed to the attractiveness of the Park, overall increase in country's tourism popularity, but also better accessibility brought by significant improvement in road access via an extensive network of highways completed by 2010. With the introduction of new accommodation facilities up to the 1980s, the number of overnight stays has increased similar to the number of arrivals. However, in the post-War period, the

Table 10.1   Number of visitors and overnight stays in Plitvice Lakes National Park, 1970–2011

Year	Number of day visitors	Change rate of day visitors (%)	Number of overnight stays	Change rate of overnight stays (%)
1960	96,708	–	49,210	–
1965	156,570	61.9	103,954	52.7
1970	247,202	57.9	125,876	17.4
1975	400,009	61.8	250,191	49.7
1980	532,253	33.1	318,041	21.3
1985	763,390	43.4	549,784	42.2
1990	667,844	−12.5	431,367	−27.5
1995[a]	0	−100.0	0	−100.0
2000	597,884	100.0	88,763	100.0
2005	855,866	43.1	157,007	43.5
2010	962,322	12.4	173,227	9.4
2015	1,357,304	41.0	201,160	13.9

Source: Public Institution NPPL (2016)
[a]Homeland War period

number of overnights in relation to the number of day visitors is much lower than before. One of the reasons can be better accessibility removing the need for an overnight stay. The other reason is that the visitors are now preferring small hotels and private accommodation in villages near the Park to the large and uniformed hotels within the Park. Whatever the reason, the hotel facilities within the Park, experiencing low occupancy rates, need to be subsidized in contrast to the earlier time when they were the source of the Park's income.

Apart from the prevalence of day visitors, the visitation pattern is highly seasonal. The absolute number of visitors, if evenly spread throughout the year, would not pose a significant threat. However, as Fig. 10.2 clearly illustrates, visitation is concentrated in summer months. In 2013, for example, on 18 days the number of visitors exceeded 10,000, and there were about two months (62 days) with more than 8,000 visitors per day. In addition, visitors have tended to shorten their length of visit over the years. In 2013, 80 per cent of visitors stayed for about three hours, in comparison to 69 per cent in 2007 (Marković, 2015). Such short stay burdens the infrastructure and environment while bringing minimal economic benefits to the Park and regional community. At the same time, carrying capacity for the Park as a whole, but also of its most sensitive locations, is still not determined.

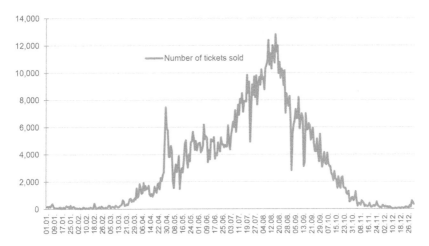

Fig. 10.2 Distribution of visitors in NP Plitvice Lakes in 2013 (*Source*: Public Institution NPPL (2014b))

The growth in visitor number exacerbated by the seasonal concentration in a small area of the Park affects not only the sensitive natural system but also the quality of visitor experience. Visitor surveys conducted in 2013 (Marković, 2015) show a decline in satisfaction in comparison to that conducted in 2006 (Institute for Tourism, 2006). While the overall satisfaction is still high, in particular in relation to information provision and signage, there is a decline of satisfaction with the quality of services—hospitality of employees, provision of parking, interpretation boards, availability and the quality of service facilities (cafes, restaurants, washrooms), souvenirs and provision of additional activities within the Park. The visitor satisfaction varies, though, with the length of stay, with those staying for up to three hours being most, and those staying overnight and using a range of facilities or services within the Park, least satisfied.

SUSTAINABILITY ISSUES

The Plitvice Lakes National Park management is, in essence, faced with three major challenges—to protect the sensitive environmental system, ensure economic sustainability of the region and deal with visitor pressure. Each is a source of unique problems and challenges.

In terms of environmental protection, the Plitvice is facing serious environmental degradation. Current studies of Park's lakes are concentrated on hydrological and microbiological changes in lakes over recent decades coinciding with intensive tourist development. Flow measurements that are conducted since 1954 on lake Kozjak indicate the gradual reduction of flow over the past 60 years (Barešić, 2009; Bonnaci, 2013). This means that the retention time of the water in the lakes has increased; the lakes are becoming more closed from the hydrological point of view, indicating that the area is over-burdened by anthropogenic activities.

Humans by their intensive activities in the environment often cause the so-called cultural eutrophication, which can cause the death of lakes in a very short period. The system of Lower Lakes and river Korana canyon is already under marshification due to eutrophication caused by the increase of the intake of organic matter and bacteriological water pollution. The pollution comes from the household sewage pits (as the entire region does not have sewerage system) from where the wastewater spills easily due to water permeable terrain and underground connectivity of the entire system. This problem is likely to increase as there is already intensive building reconstruction and expansion in surrounding villages for tourism and second-home markets. Research reveals that an increased amount of dissolved organic matter (pollution) has stopped the process of travertine creation in some parts of the lakes (Pribičević, Medak, & Đapo, 2011). While it is a natural process that takes hundreds of years, through human activities (tourism, agriculture, transport, etc.), this process is significantly accelerated. The available biochemical data indicate that the lakes are experiencing intense anthropogenic eutrophication.

These hydrological changes affect the entire lake system. Changes in vegetation and water level are most intensive and noticeable on the smaller lakes. At the same time, there is a trend of increase of water level in the lakes as a result of the growth of travertine barriers and wetlands vegetation (Riđanović, 1989; Rubinić & Zwicker, 2011). However, the most alarming is the fact that the water flow measurement profiles of the lakes are experiencing the greatest declining trend in the whole area of the Croatian karst (Rubinić & Zwicker, 2011).

In addition to hydrological change, another anthropological pollution is the concentration of synthetic surface active agents that are ingredient of detergents which is increasing in the two largest lakes—Kozjak and Prošćansko. This is most likely a consequence of the wastewater from the hotels entering the lake occasionally due, most likely, to malfunctioning of the hotels' sewage systems.

Finally, the wooden trails are anchored in highly fragile travertine barriers. Although these types of structures are highly attractive, they exert stress on the delicate mechanics of travertine barriers. The vibration produced by the excessive number of visitors threatens with the collapse of some travertine barriers. An additional threat to the travertine barriers is the formation of new illegal paths and the vantage points.

While those hydrological changes are very important for the protection of the Plitvice Lakes basic phenomenon, they are not so obvious to a casual observer. In comparison, landscape changes are readily perceived. Landscapes are an essential element of the natural environment in all natural areas and crucial to their appeal and identity. However, it is the fast pace of change that presents the key threat to landscape and ecosystem values. An analysis of the changes in land cover of the Plitvice Lakes from 1991 to 2012 by five main types—water, forests, built surface, fallow and meadows and fields and grasslands—revealed shrinkage of the farming land (grassland and meadows), expansion of forest as well as succession of fallows back to the forest. There was only a small increase in the built area (Fig. 10.3). It seems, thus, that the economic development spurred by tourism has transformed the rural economy and the identity of space through the abandonment of land, rather than through the construction of new surfaces (Marković, 2015). Also, this process is reducing biodiversity of the area, since the grasslands and meadows are richer in total number of species than forests.

Further, similar changes can be observed in the villages in and around the Park. The villages have experienced spatial expansion, introduction of new building forms and materials and changes in landscaping. This transformation from rural to urban forms is more intense in the villages in closer proximity to the lakes, while peripheral villages are abandoned and their rural structures are disappearing.

Since its inception, the Plitvice Lakes National Park was given a role of regional economic rejuvenation via tourism development. However, its central management and poor cooperation with local stakeholders seem to be failing on this promise. Up to 1995, the communities in the vicinity of the Park increased at the expense of peripheral villages that experienced population decline, as people moved close to the Park due to better infrastructure, social services and job opportunities. Since the 1990s, villages

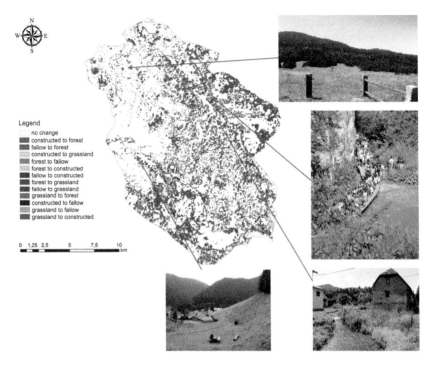

Fig. 10.3   Changes of land cover in area of NP Plitvice Lakes from 1991 to 2012 with illustrations

close to the Park also experienced depopulation, although the rate of emigration is lower than in other parts of rural Croatia (Marković, Pejnović, & Boranić Živoder, 2013). The large proportion of visitors in relation to local residents (annual ratio of resident and visitors is 1:744) and the weak demographic potential is insufficient to independently maintain and expand tourism products and services. The lack of labor and entrepreneurship is substituted by daily migration of workers from distant areas. Tourism demand, as well as the natural beauty of the area and provision of basic infrastructure, has also attracted real-estate investors and, thus, created a certain kind of class differences between the newcomers who have the capital and the local community that benefits minimally from the Park. While local residents consider it important to maintain local identity currently under threat from uncontrolled urbanization and acculturation, for which they blame mostly tourism, a resident survey revealed that over

75 per cent was not able to state one prominent feature of its traditional identity, while only third of them is actively involved in activities aimed at identity preservation, ranging from membership in associations preserving local traditions right through revitalization of traditional production (Marković, 2015).

CONCLUSION

This case study illustrates that the relationship between formal nature protection, nature protection management and its outcome in terms of sustainability is complex and burdened by diverse expectations of many stakeholders. The Plitvice Lakes National Park is an example of many of the tensions inherent in its management—being very attractive natural attractions—it is a magnet for thousands of visitors, yet located in deprived rural area, and it is also an important regional generator of income and jobs. At present, it appears that the centralized management model, although well-functioning in the past, is not able to meet the standards of environmental protection nor bring economic benefits to the region. The protected area is suffering environmental degradation, while the economic benefits are not sufficient to result in demographic rejuvenation.

The intensive tourism development and forecast growth in tourism numbers creates and/or exacerbates a number of diverse issues, ranging from environmental threats (primarily hydrogeological), natural and cultural landscape changes, local community loss of identity and decline in visitor satisfaction. The uncontrolled development of tourism is currently creating a strong imbalance for all sustainability dimensions. With the management caught in between fulfilment of its basic objectives of nature protection and financial performance, it seems that there are no winners. Economic benefits of the Park for local population are not sufficient to reverse the negative economic and population trends and bring the much needed communal infrastructure improvement, while the nature protection is insufficiently implemented and controlled to prevent serious environmental degradation.

The future development of Plitvice Lakes National Park requires continuous research of economic, social and environmental processes, so that the future development can, to a greater extent, be aligned with the principles of sustainable development. Most of the modern management models are based on cooperation with stakeholders and consideration of all three pillars of sustainability, while the management model focused mostly on environmental protection is gradually abandoned. Thus the solution for specific issues in protected areas may be an integral management model that will summarize the best international practices and the specific needs of the NPA and its region. There is no doubt that the further development of Plitvice Lakes area must be based on the concept of mixed economy, in which tourism should be a generator of sustainable development, managed jointly by the State and community, towards sustainability of the environment and the society.

REFERENCES

Alexander, M. (2008). *Management planning for nature Conservation: A theoretical basis and practical guide*. Berlin, Germany: Springer Science.

Barešić, J. (2009). *Primjena izotopnih i geokemijskih metoda u praćenju globalnih i lokalnih promjena u ekološkom sustavu Plitvičkih jezera* [Application of isotopic and biochemical methods in monitoring global and local changes in the ecosystem of Plitvice Lakes]. Zagreb, Croatia: Zagreb: Doctoral thesis at University of Zagreb.

Böhringer, C., & Jochem, P. (2007). Measuring the immeasurable: A survey of sustainability indices. *Ecological Economics, 63*, 1–8.

Bonnaci, O. (2013). Zabrinjavajući hidrološki trendovi na slivu Plitvičkih jezera [Worrying trends in the hydrological basin of the Plitvice Lakes]. *Hrvatske vode, 21(84)*, 137–146.

Borrini-Feyerabend, G., Dudley, N., Jaeger, T., Lassen, B., Pathak Broome, N., Phillips, A., ... Sandwith, T. (2013). *Governance of Protected Areas: From understanding to action*. Gland, Switzerland: IUCN.

Borrini-Feyerabend, G., Kothary, A., & Oviedo, G. (2004). *Indigenous and local communities and protected areas: Towards equity and enhanced conservation*. Gland, Switzerland/Cambridge, UK: IUCN.

Carey, C., Dudley, N., & Stolton, S. (2000). *Squandering paradise? The importance and vulnerability of the world's protected areas*. Gland, Switzerland: WWF International.

Cole, S. N. (2004). Impacts of hiking and camping on soils and vegetation. In R. Buckley (Ed.), *Environmental impacts of ecotourism* (pp. 41–60). Oxford, UK: CABI Publishing.

Dudley, N., Gujja, B., Jackson, B., Jeanrenaud, J.P., Oviedo, G., Phillips, A., ... Wells, S. (1999). Challenges for protected areas in the 21st century. In S. Stolton & N. Dudley (Eds.), *Partnerships for protection: New strategies for planning* (pp. 3–12). Oxon, UK: Earthscan.

Government of Republic of Croatia. (2013). *Zakon o zaštiti prirode* [Nature Protection Act]. *Narodne novine, 08/13*. http://narodne-novine.nn.hr/clanci/sluzbeni/2013_06_80_1658.html. Date accessed 15 May 2016.

Growcock, A. J., & Pickering, C. M. (2011). Impacts of small group short term experimental camping on alpine and subalpine vegetation in the Australian Alps. *Journal of Ecotourism, 120*, 86–100.

Gu, H., & Ryan, C. (2008). Place attachment, identity and community impacts of tourism the case of a Beijing hutong. *Tourism Management, 29*, 637–647.

Gurneya, G., Cinnera, J., Bana, J.C., Presseya, L. R., Pollnacc, R., Campbelld, S. J., ... Setiawand, F. (2014). Poverty and protected areas: An evaluation of a marine integrated conservation and development project in Indonesia. *Global Environmental Change, 26*, 98–107.

Hobbs, R. J., Cole, D. N., Yung, L., Zavaleta, E. S., Aplet, G. H., Chapin, F. S., ... Woodley, S. (2010). Guiding concepts for parks and wilderness stewardship in the era of global environmental change. *Frontiers in Ecology and Environment, 8*(9), 483–490.

Hockings, M., Stolton, S., Leverington, F., Dudley, N., & Courrau, J. (2006). *Evaluating Effectiveness – A framework for assessing management effectiveness of protected areas* (2nd ed.). Amsterdam: World Commission on Protected Areas.

Holling, C. S. (1978). *Adaptive environmental assessment and management.* Chichester, UK: Wiley.

Institute for Tourism. (2006). *TOMAS – Nacionalni parkovi i parkovi prirode 2006* [TOMAS – National and Nature Parks 2006]. Zagreb, Croatia: Institute for Tourism.

Ivanuš, M. (2010). Vrednovanje turističke izgradnje na području Plitvičkih jezera [Evaluation of tourism construction the Plitvice Lakes area]. *Prostor, 18*(1), 123–135.

Macloed, D. V. L. (2006). Power, resources and identity: The influence of tourism on indigenous communities. In P. M. Burnes & M. Novelli (Eds.), *Tourism and social identities* (pp. 111–125). Oxford: Elsevier.

Marinović-Uzelac, A. (2001). *Prostorno planiranje [Spatial Planning].* Zagreb, Croatia: Dom i svijet.

Marković, I. (2015). *Problemi i mogućnosti održivoga upravljanja zaštićenim prirodnim područjima: primjer Nacionalnoga parka Plitvička jezera* [Problems and opportunities for sustainable management of protected natural areas: example of the National Park Plitvice Lakes.]. Doctoral thesis at University of Zagreb, Zagreb, Croatia.

Marković, I., Pejnović, D., & Boranić Živoder, S. (2013). Influence of tourism development on sustainability of local communities in natural protected areas, case study of Plitvice Lakes National Park. In L. Minnaert & S. Čaušević (Eds.), *International critical tourism studies conference V: Tourism Critical Practice: Activating Dreams into Action.* http://cts.som.surrey.ac.uk/publication/ influence-of-tourism-development-on-sustainability-of-local-communities-in-natural-protected-areas-case-study-of-plitvice-lakes-national-park/. Date accessed 25 September 2015.

Martinić, I. (2010). *Upravljanje zaštićenim područjima prirode – planiranje, razvoj i održivost* [Management of protected areas – planning, development and sustainability]. Zagreb: Šumarski fakultet, Sveučilište u Zagreb.

Martinić, I., Kosović, M., & Grginčić, I. (2008). Upravljanje rizicima pri posjećivanju o rekreacijskim aktivnostima u zaštićenim područjima prirode [Visitor Risk Management of recreational activities in protected areas]. *Šumarski list, 132(1–2)*, 33–42.

Monza, C., D'Antoniob, A., Lawsonc, S., Barberd, J., & Newmane, P. (2016). The ecological implications of visitor transportation in parks and protected areas: Examples from research in US National Parks. *Journal of Transport Geography, 51*, 27–35.

Newsome, D., Moore, S. A., & Dowling, R. K. (2013). *Natural area tourism, ecology, impacts and management.* Ontario, Canada: Channel View Publications.

Newsome, D., & Lacroix, C. (2011). Changing recreational emphasis and the loss of the "natural experiences" in protected areas: An issue that deserves consideration, dialogue and investigation. *Journal of Tourism and Leisure Studies, 17(2)*, 315–333.

Opačić, V. T., Lukić, A., & Fürts Bjeliš, B. (2005). Sustainable development of recreation and tourism in the protected areas of Croatia: Issues and indicators. *Problemi na geografijata, 3–4*, 209–223.

Orlić, S. (Ed.). (1983). *Prirodni šumski rezervat "Čorkova uvala – Čudinka"* [Natural forest reserve Čorkova Cove – Čudinka]. Zagreb, Croatia: Opće udruženje šumarstva, prerade drveta i prometa Hrvatske.

Pavletić, Z. (1957). Ekološki odnosi briofitske vegetacije na slapovima Plitvičkih jezera. *Acta Botanica Croatica, 16*, 63–88.

Pejnović, D., & Lukić, A. (2014). Uloga geografije u obrazovanju prostornih planera: primjer Hrvatske [The role of geography in education spatial planners: Croatian example]. In N. Drešković (Ed.), *Zbornik radova 3. kongres geografa Bosne i Hercegovine* (pp. 98–117). Društvo geografa BiH: Sarajevo.

Penga, L., Liua, S., & Sunb, L. (2016). Spatial–temporal changes of rurality driven by urbanization and industrialization: A case study of the Three Gorges Reservoir Area in Chongqing, China. *Habitat International, 51*, 124–132.

Petrić, K. (2012). *Pejsažna i prostorno-organizacijska obilježja tradicijskih naselja na području Nacionalnog parka Plitvička jezera* [Landscape and spatial organizational characteristics of traditional settlements in the Plitvice Lakes National Park]. Zagreb, Croatia: Master Thesis at University of Zagreb.

Pribičević, B., Medak, D., & Đapo, A. (2011). Geodetic and hydrographic research in the area of Plitvice Lakes National Park. In B. Šutić & A. Dujmović (Eds.), *Zbornik radova znanstveno-stručnog skupa Nacionalnog parka Plitvička jezera* (pp. 68–92). Plitvička jezera: Javna ustanova Nacionalni park Plitvička jezera.

Public Institution NPPL. (2014a). *Godišnji program zaštite, održavanja, očuvanja, promicanja i korištenja Nacionalnog parka Plitvička jezera za 2014. godinu* [Annual program for protection, maintenance, preservation, promotion and use of Plitvice Lakes National Park for 2014]. http://www.np-plitvicka-jezera.hr/ files/file/dokumenti/Godisnji-plan-rada-za-2014--godinu.pdfž. Date accessed 10 October 2015.

Public institution NPPL. (2014b). *Business information Plitvice Lakes National Park.*

Public institution NPPL. (2016). *Business information Plitvice Lakes National Park.*

Rekom, R. V., & Go, F. (2006). Cultural identities in globalizing world: Conditions for sustainability of intercultural tourism. In P. M. Burnes & M. Novell. (Eds.), *Tourism and social identities: Global frameworks and local realities* (pp. 79–91). Amsterdam: Elsevier.

Riđanović, J. (1989). Prvi rezultati suvremenih hidroloških mjerenja na Plitvičkim jezerima [The first results of the contemporary hydrological measurements at Plitvice Lakes]. *Geografski glasnik, 51,* 129–135.

Robinson, M. (1999). Is cultural tourism on the right track? *UNESCO Courier, 52(7/8),* 22.

Rodriguez-Jorqueraa, I. A., Krollb, K. J., Toorc, G. S., & Denslowb, N. D. (2015). Transcriptional and physiological response of fathead minnows (Pimephales promelas) exposed to urban waters entering into wildlife protected areas. *Environmental Pollution, 199,* 155–165.

RodríguezRodríguez, D. (2012). New issues on protected area management. In B. Sladonja (Ed.), *Protected area management* (pp. 19–42). http://cdn.intechopen.com/pdfs-wm/38181.pdf. Date accessed 11 February 2016.

Rubinić, J., & Zwicker, G. (2011). Hidrologija sustava Plitvičkih jezera i gornjeg toka Korane – praćenja, spoznaje i izazovi [Hydrology system of the Plitvice Lakes and the upper flow of Korana – monitoring, findings and challenges.]. In B. Šutić & A. Dujmović (Eds.), *Zbornik radova znanstveno-stručnog skupa Nacionalnog parka Plitvička jezera* (pp. 46–59). Plitvička jezera, Croatia: Javna ustanova "Nacionalni park Plitvička jezera".

Šikić, Z. (Ed.). (2007). *Plan Upravljanja NP Plitvička jezera* [Management Plan of Plitvice Lakes National Park]. Zagreb, Croatia: JU NP Plitvička jezera.

Steven, R., Pickering, C., & Castley, G. (2011). A review of impacts of nature based recreation on birds. *Journal of Environment Management, 92,* 2287–2294.

Taylor, C. (1989). *Sources of the self: The making of modern identity.* Cambridge, MA: Harvard University Pres.

Vidaković, P. (1977). *Plitvička jezera, zaštita i turistička valorizacija* [Plitvice Lakes, protection and tourism valorization]. Plitvička jezera, Croatia: Nacionalni park Plitvička jezera.

Walters, C. J. (1986). *Adaptive management of renewable resources.* New York: Macmillan.

Wills, C. (2015). The contribution of cultural ecosystem services to understanding the tourism–nature–wellbeing nexus. *Journal of Outdoor Recreation and Tourism, 10,* 38–43.

CHAPTER 11

Identifying Trends in Tourism Demand Using Longitudinal Survey

Zrinka Marušić, Ivan Sever, and Sanda Čorak

INTRODUCTION

Tourism demand is affected by various economic, social, cultural, political, technological and environmental trends (Dwyer et al., 2008; Kasriel-Alexander, 2016). The underlying trends, impacting both, the size and the characteristics of tourism demand, heavily influence tourism destination management and, specifically, tourism product development that have to meet tourists' needs and expectations. The key challenge for a successful tourism industry is in its' ability to recognize and adapt to underlying trends in a highly complex and dynamic environment, particularly evident at the destination or regional level. Tourism destinations should, therefore, monitor profile and expectations of their tourists and adjust their strategies to market trends in order to maintain their competitiveness and deliver tourism products and services that stimulate tourists' satisfaction and, thus, create loyal guests in the constantly evolving tourism market.

Determinants of tourism demand are commonly assessed through cross-sectional surveys (Dwyer & Forsyth, 2006; Xiao & Smith, 2006).

Z. Marušić (✉) • I. Sever • S. Čorak
Institute for Tourism, Zagreb, Croatia

© The Author(s) 2017   221
L. Dwyer et al. (eds.), *Evolution of Destination Planning and Strategy*, DOI 10.1007/978-3-319-42246-6_11

Conducting a single cross-sectional survey reveals the valuable characteristics of tourism demand in a destination at a given point in time and could be very useful for gaining insight into current tourism activity. But, such survey could also lead to misleading inferences because it does not support analysis of change over time. Since dynamics of tourism environment make the monitoring of change a primary interest when assessing destination development (Dwyer et al., 2008), single cross-sectional survey is inappropriate for gaining a comprehensive knowledge on the main determinants of tourism demand. To appropriately capture underlying dynamics in tourism system, to detect, examine and monitor patterns of change over time, a longitudinal research, sometimes referred to as a 'trend analysis', is required (Moscardo & Benckendorff, 2010; Ritchie, 2005).

Although the number of longitudinal surveys overall has multiplied in recent years (Lynn, 2009), there is almost no published trend studies with a significant time-span tracking both quantitative and qualitative characteristics of tourism demand on a region or a destination level. The purpose of this chapter is, therefore, to fill this gap by presenting empirical research on a case of a longitudinal survey of Croatian tourism demand characteristics and behavior. Croatia, a Mediterranean country that has shown a strong and steady increase in tourism demand over the past decades, is an emerging economy heavily dependent on tourism demand. Croatia has the third highest tourism receipts per capita in the Mediterranean (1,750 Euro; World Tourism Organization, 2015), following Malta and Cyprus, while tourism directly contributes 10.4 per cent to Croatian GDP (Ivandić, Marušić, Šutalo, & Vuglar, 2014). Croatia is the sixth most preferred main holiday destination for the Europeans traveling outside their country of residence (European Union, 2016). In accordance with geographical position and climate characteristics, the majority of tourist activity in Croatia is taking place along the coast, over the four summer months (88 per cent of total number of overnights in commercial accommodation facilities in 2015) (Croatian Bureau of Statistics, 2016).

Recognizing the importance of monitoring the tourist experience and assessing the long-term effects of tourism policies and managerial pitfalls responsive to the changing environment in which tourism operates, the Institute for Tourism launched a longitudinal survey of tourists' attitudes and expenditures in Croatia in 1987, under the name TOMAS Summer survey. Since then, the survey has been conducted nine times (Institute for Tourism, 1987, 1989, 1994, 1997, 2002a, 2005a, 2008a, 2011, 2015), giving tourism policy an appropriate information base for timely response to changes to the tourism market. Underlining the usefulness and advocating the use of longitudinal studies in tourism research, the aim of this chapter is twofold. It gives guidelines how to approach some methodological issues in application of longitudinal research design in a study of tourism demand but also reveals some mega trends observed in Croatian summer tourism demand over almost thirty years of the country's tourism development.

The chapter has four main parts. Following the introduction, the second part gives an overview of longitudinal surveys in tourism demand research, emphasizing the main issues and challenges of longitudinal research design. The third part presents the case study—the longitudinal TOMAS Summer survey on attitudes and expenditures of tourists in Croatia. It provides an overview of all aspects of the survey process and the resulting trends in Croatian tourism demand in the 1987–2014 period. The conclusion discusses some limitations of the current research and suggests areas for possible improvements of the future longitudinal research of tourism demand.

LONGITUDINAL SURVEYS IN TOURISM DEMAND RESEARCH

According to Ritchie (2005, p. 131), a rationale for a longitudinal research is 'to monitor and understand how and why various aspects of the tourism market are changing over time'. Longitudinal research could be defined as 'research in which (a) data are collected for each item or variable for two or more distinct time periods; (b) the subjects or cases analyzed are the same or at least comparable from one period to the next; and (c) the analysis involves some comparison of data between and among periods' (Menard, 1991, p. 4). The longitudinal data could be collected using different approaches, both quantitative and qualitative, which include personal interviews, focus groups, observation and documentation method (Pettigrew, 1990). In the past decade, online interviews have become increasingly popular, although various issues, such as sample representativeness, undermine the value of online data collection method. Some researchers recommended to combine the above techniques to utilize advantages of different methods in the process of longitudinal data collection (Cooke, Watkins, & Moy, 2007).

Without any doubt, longitudinal research is a highly demanding research method, confronting researchers with different challenges and requiring broad methodological knowledge, long-term commitment as well as adequate resources (Ritchie, 2005). A number of methodological challenges are involved in conducting longitudinal research. They are primarily related to the appropriate survey design, statistical methods and measures applied and accurate interpretation of the results (Chen & Miller, 2005; Diggle, Liang, & Zeger, 2002; Watkins, 2010). Survey design is an essence of any research, defining *what* and *how* it will be measured. Longitudinal research is subjected to different design issues. One of these issues is related to a number of data points (time periods) and a time interval between the consecutive data points which are appropriate for the analysis and answering of research question at hand, while keeping in mind the available research budget (Watkins, 2010; Chen & Miller, 2005). Furthermore, both sampling method and sample size should be adequate. Sampling method should accurately reflect the population from which the sample was drawn so that the sample is a representative of a population and proper inferences could be drawn. Different probability sampling methods could be used, such as simple random sampling, systematic, stratified or cluster sampling. Following the sample design, a proper sample size should be specified to enable accurate inferences about population of interest, while taking into account variability in data, targeted precision of estimates and budget constraints. Even random samples of large size are not necessarily representative, and usually the weighting process has to be applied to reflect accurately the structure of the entire population of interest (Lynn, 2009). The Horvitz–Thompson estimator is frequently applied data weighting procedure in survey analysis to account for sampling bias (Rendtel & Harms, 2009).

Longitudinal studies deal with two main types of data: panel data and repeated cross-sectional data (Andreß, Golsch, & Schmidt, 2013; Dwyer, Gill, & Seetaram, 2012; Ritchie, 2005). Both panel and repeated cross-sectional studies could be used to address changes in behavior and attitudes over time but differ in information gained. Panel studies that repeatedly collect data from the same individuals are better suited to answering the 'why' question—why people behave in certain manner and what affects their behavior and attitudes (Bissell, MacKay, & Vogt, 2008). However, as tourism destinations are not closed systems, fixing the sample population could lead to inaccurate inference about the tourist population as it does not account for potentially significant changes in population structure over time. Furthermore, a greater gap or time intervals between measurements raise concerns for selection bias and attrition. In examining social change through time, such as change in characteristics and behavior of tourists in a destination, obtaining a large and representative sample of tourist population is essential (Dwyer et al., 2012). For these purposes, repeated cross-sectional surveys are more suitable as they are administered to a new random sample of respondents at each successive point in time. Repeated cross-sectional surveys provide better answer to 'how many' type of questions. By selecting completely new sample of respondents at each point in time, repeated cross-sectional surveys are only suitable for monitoring aggregate changes in a variable of interest over time, that is, patterns in overall population of interest or in different sub-population groups. When assessing changes, it is critical to identify subgroups or trajectories that follow different patterns on variable(s) of interest. Identification of these subgroups forms a basis for market segmentation analysis, which is widely used in tourism research to better understand various groups within a population of tourists and to identify critical market segments. By identifying these segments or groups with different needs and expectations, the tourism product could be adjusted to provide more satisfactory tourist experience.

General patterns in population as well as patterns in identified homogeneous subgroups that do not conform to the general pattern can often be revealed even by the means of simple descriptive analyses. Data exploration through descriptive data analysis is an important step in longitudinal data analysis and should not be overlooked (Chen & Miller, 2005). This refers to the numeric or graphical reporting of summarized data. Plotting different groups over time to illustrate both cross-sectional and longitudinal relationships could be particularly useful and informative. This step addresses the characteristics of change—is it linear or not, positive or negative and so on—or stability in the variable(s) of interest over time. Different indicators of change could be reported with longitudinal data, such as a scale score or percentage above cut (PAC) score (Almond & Sinharay, 2012). Using a single scale score, such as a mean, is usually admirable due to the appealing interpretation. However, the mean change is biased in the case of non-normality or variance heterogeneity. Although other measures of central tendency could be used, such as medians and geometric means, all such measures are point estimates and provide limited conclusions. Finally, assessing multiple points in a distribution better reflects situation across the whole population of interest. Longitudinal research also enables modeling the effects of different sociodemographic and other factors and their interactions on a variable of interest, which could provide even deeper insight into determinants of tourist behavior (Spini & d'Epinay, 2003).

Therefore, a plethora of reporting methods is available for presenting the results of longitudinal research, and researcher should use the ones that are the most appropriate and informative in specific situation.

Despite the importance of longitudinal studies in tourism research, existing literature is relatively restricted (Moscardo & Benckendorff, 2010; Ritchie, 2005; Moscardo, 2004). In the review of the most relevant tourism journals, Xiao & Smith (2006) found out that most of the case studies adopted one-time cross-sectional approach and only a smaller number of studies could be classified as longitudinal. However, interest in longitudinal research methods has been increasing (Bissell et al., 2008; Song, Dwyer, Li, & Cao, 2012). Tourism research adopting longitudinal research methods has mainly been focused on changes in tourism demand over time rather than on the changes in behavior and characteristics of tourists in a destination itself (Moscardo, 2004). Most researchers focused on forecasting tourism flows (arrivals and nights) by developing econometric models based on time-series analysis (Marrocu & Paci, 2013; Dwyer & Forsyth, 2006; Dwyer et al., 2012; Song et al., 2012). With the lack of longitudinal studies focused on tourist behavior in a destination, this paper presents methodological guidelines and empirical trend study to stimulate much needed research in this area.

CASE STUDY: TOMAS SUMMER SURVEY 1987–2014

TOMAS Summer survey derives its name 'TOMAS' from the research originally conducted in Switzerland under the name 'TOuristisches MArktforschungssystem Schweiz' (Tourist market research system Switzerland) in winter season in 1982–1983. The newly established survey of tourism demand in Croatia that was launched in 1987 was based on the Swiss TOMAS study experiences. Although the survey methods in Croatia have been updated and adapted over time to the characteristics of Croatian tourism demand and the needs of Croatian tourism industry, 'TOMAS' name has been retained as a research brand.

Methodological Challenges

TOMAS Summer survey is a repeated cross-sectional survey aimed to obtain relevant, reliable and representative data on characteristics, behavior, satisfaction and consumption of domestic and international tourists in Croatia and to identify the relevant trends and/or changes in tourism demand over the time. An additional requirement has been to obtain the representative and reliable data on a regional (county) level by type of accommodation and country of tourist's origin. To meet the aims, TOMAS research methodology follows modern statistical practice of both practitioners and scholars engaged in tourism research (Frechtling, 2006; Gunn, 1994; Henning, Levy, & Ritchie, 2005; Oh, Kim, & Shin, 2004; Pizam, 1994; Ritchie, 2000, 2005; Ritchie & Sheridan, 1988; Smith, 1989; Weber, 1991; Zins, 2007) and complies with a number of recommendations on tourism statistics and research methods and techniques given by the United Nations and World Tourism Organization (2010), Eurostat, the statistical office of the European Union (2014), and the professional association of market researchers (European Society for Opinion and Marketing Research).

TOMAS Summer survey has been conducted in 1987, 1989, 1994, 1997, 2001, 2004, 2007, 2010 and 2014, recording two- to five-year time-span between the two consecutive surveys and covering four significant periods of Croatian recent history: (i) Croatia as one of the former Yugoslav republics (1987 and 1989), (ii) Croatian Homeland War (1994), (iii) Croatia as an independent country (1997, 2001, 2004, 2007 and 2010) and (iv) Croatia as an independent country and member of the EU (2014). Over the years, the survey methodology has adjusted to significant changes in the structure of tourism demand regarding the type of accommodation and generating markets. Furthermore, the survey methodology accounts for global trends in technology development and changes in European lifestyle preferences and also reflects the improvement in the Croatian summer tourism product, as well as expansion of stakeholders' interests in the industry. At the same time, a focus has constantly been kept on the need to retain comparability of the survey results over time. This has been achieved by either keeping the core characteristics of tourism demand unchanged or enabling aggregation and, thus, comparability of the results.

TOMAS Summer survey population is defined as 'tourists (foreign and domestic) in commercial accommodation facilities (hotels and similar, campsites and households) along seven Croatian coastal counties during four summer months', covering the most of the officially registered tourism flows in Croatia. The exemption was survey population in 1987 and 1989 when the survey coverage was limited to foreign tourists only. One of the peculiarities of any visitor survey is the absence of a sample frame needed for a probability sample design. In the case of TOMAS Summer survey, the official data on tourists' overnights in the commercial accommodation facilities recorded the previous year has been used as a proxy for the sample frame. Data on tourists' overnights, rather than those on tourists' arrivals, has been used in order to avoid multiple counting caused by possible changing of an accommodation facility. In order to obtain a sample representative for tourists' population (within the circumstances where there is no available sample frame in advance), a stratified quota sample has been used, with strata defined as a month (June to September), a county (seven coastal counties), an accommodation facility (hotels, campsites and households) and a country of tourist's origin (domestic and 12–15 main foreign generating markets accounting for at least 85 per cent of total tourists overnights realized along the area during the summer season). Many authors argue that such a mixed sampling method, accompanied with a sufficient knowledge on population frame and its attributes, is a good approximate of stratified random sample (Groves et al., 2009; Teddlie & Yu, 2007).

A sample size has been determined based on previous survey estimates of variations in an average daily consumption and desired precision of the estimates at the county level, and the availability of the research funds. Sample size of TOMAS Summer survey has usually been between 4,000 and 5,000 respondents, with the biggest samples obtained in the first two survey years (8,000 respondents). The size of strata at the county level has been proportional to the number of realized tourist overnights recorded previous year, while accounting for a minimal number of respondents acceptable per strata. The sample has been allocated to several hundreds of randomly chosen accommodation facilities within sample strata. Once the official data on tourist overnights in the survey year became available, results have been weighted by actual data to be representative of tourists' population in the survey year. Weights are defined as:

$$w_{z,s,n} = \frac{N_{z,s,n}}{n_{z,s,n}},$$

where $N_{z,s,n}$ is the officially recorded number of tourist overnights in county z, realized by country of origin n in the accommodation facility s. On the other hand, $n_{z,s,n}$ is the number of survey respondents from country of origin n, in accommodation facility s in county z. Reliability of the sample estimates is assessed by calculating standard errors and 95 per cent confidence intervals of estimates.

Data collection method used in TOMAS Summer surveys is a personal interview conducted by professional market research agency. Both sample allocation and fieldwork are under the supervision of the Institute for Tourism in order to minimize the occurrence and the impact of non-sampling errors. The Survey instrument is a structured questionnaire printed in Croatian and in a number of foreign languages corresponding to the main tourists' generating markets. The questionnaire is divided into four main parts:

- Basic trip characteristics covering travel motivation using a set of both push and pull travel motives, information sources, main mean of transport, travel party, loyalty to Croatia and tourism destination tourist is staying in and type of accommodation booking,
- Characteristics of travel behavior in destination including length of stay, activities engaged in during the stay and consumption pattern,
- Satisfaction with various elements of the Croatian tourism product, overall and in relation to competing Mediterranean destinations visited before and
- Basic sociodemographic characteristics covering gender, age, education level and income status.

Except for consumption and age, all questions are close-ended, some of them with multiple responses. Satisfaction is measured on a 5-point Likert scale anchored by 1-very poor and 5-excellent marks. Some illustrations of survey content improvements over time are introduction of the Internet option into the question on information sources in 1997, introduction of low-cost carrier option into the question on means of transport in 2004, constant expansion of the list of the activities offered in accordance with the tourism product development, introduction of crowdedness evaluation, as well as evaluation of destination suitability for disabled tourists in 2014, upgrading the 5-point Likert scale to the 7-point Likert scale due to better discrimination between the tourists' satisfaction (Sever, Marušić, & Čorak, 2016) and so on.

Descriptive analysis applied to TOMAS Summer survey data revealed some general patterns, trends and long-term changes in behavior of Croatian summer tourist population over the time. Some of these will be illustrated in the next section, while the complete survey results are published in the corresponding books (Institute for Tourism, 1987, 1989, 1994, 1997, 2002a, 2005a, 2008a, 2011, 2015).

TOMAS Mega Trends in Summer Tourism Demand

Trends of Croatian summer tourism demand characteristics should be analyzed in the light of changes that occurred between 1987 and 2014, primarily the Homeland War (1991–1995) and the transition to market economy, each having had a significant impact on tourism activity. For illustration (Čorak, Marušić, & Ivandić, 2009; Croatian Bureau of Statistics, 2015), Croatia exceeds in 2014 the total number of tourist arrivals in the commercial accommodation facilities registered in 1987 (by 25 per cent) but has still not reached (97.5 per cent) the number of tourist overnights realized in the prewar years. At the same time, total commercial accommodation capacity measured by number of available permanent beds has increased by 8 per cent, lowering the gross occupancy rate from 22.6 per cent in 1987 to 20.3 per cent in 2014. Furthermore, although hotel accommodation increased, both in capacity and quality, the share of hotel overnights in the total overnights in 2014 (31.6 per cent) is still lower compared to 1987 (32.3 per cent). Rooms and apartments in households have become the primary type of commercial accommodation which increased in share of the total number of overnights from 19 per cent in 1987 to 36 per cent in 2014. Significant changes are also observed in the structure of foreign tourism demand. For example, while the United Kingdom and Germany have lowered their share in total overnights, the Czech Republic, Slovakia, Hungary and Poland have significantly increased their share in total overnights in the 1987–2014 period.

Regarding the TOMAS Summer survey results on tourist's motivation for visiting Croatia, '(passive) rest and relaxation' is the primary motive for visitation during the summer months at the seaside destinations. It has been dominant over the years and motivates at least 60 and up to 90 per cent of tourists per year. Recent surveys recorded a stable level of 75 per cent of those motivated by '(passive) rest and relaxation'. Although not fully comparable, the results are partly in line with the preferences of Europeans towards tourism in 2015 (European Union, 2016) which revealed that sun or beach was chosen by almost four in ten respondents (39 per cent) as one of their main reasons for going on holiday.

One of the major TOMAS trends observed in the reference period refers to secondary tourist motivation (Fig. 11.1), revealing the increased diversification and strengthening of the secondary motives during the study period. Thus, since 1997, the entertainment, new experiences and gastronomy are becoming more and more important. Entertainment motivates 43–44 per cent of tourists; the importance of new experiences

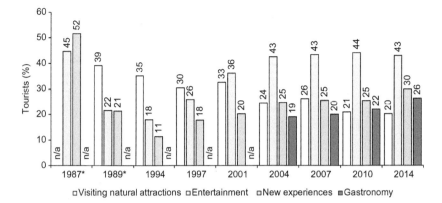

Fig. 11.1 Secondary motives for visiting Croatian coastal destinations (*Foreign tourists only. Note: Multiple response (up to three answers). *Source:* Institute for Tourism (1987, 1989, 1994, 1997, 2002a, 2005a, 2008a, 2011, 2015))

grew from 11 to 30 per cent, while gastronomy, included into the survey in 2004, motivated more than a quarter of all tourists ten years later. At the same time, tourist motivation for visiting natural attractions has decreased steadily—in 2014 it was the fifth most important motive, while in 1989 it ranked second in importance. These changes in motivation are likely to be a result in both push and pull factors. They are reflectors of the changed demographics and lifestyle of the European population (European Travel Commission, 2006), and an increase in diversity of tourist destination offer.

In line with these findings are also the TOMAS Summer survey trends on tourist behavior or activities. Monitoring tourist activities from 1997, when the question was introduced, to 2014, confirms that the trends in motivation are mirrored in tourists' engagement in a variety of activities. The question on participating in an activity was a dichotomous choice (yes/no) in 1997, while from 2001 it has been measured on a 3-point ordinal scale (never/sometimes/often). The options 'sometimes' and 'often' were grouped and marked as 'participation in an activity' in order to enable comparison of the results over the whole time period. Furthermore, over the years, new activities were added to reflect diversification of tourism product portfolio, such as introduction of visits to olive oil/wine roads. Thus, the total number of the activities offered for survey purposes varied from 24 to 31.

Swimming and bathing has remained the most popular activity (with participation rate from 87 per cent in 1997 to 99 per cent in last two survey rounds), in line with the steady and dominant motive of rest and relaxation on the beach. However, the strong increase in the participation rate has been observed for a number of other activities. For example, with the increase of the importance of gastronomy as the motive for visiting Croatia, the share of tourists dining in restaurants has also increased (51 per cent in 1997, 84 per cent in 2007 and 91 per cent in 2014), and thus interest for gastronomy-related products is also evident. In 2014, wine and olive roads were visited by 28 and 21 per cent of tourists, respectively. Similarly, the increased participation in 'health, recreation and wellness programs' (4, 11, 24, 25, 33 and 36 per cent of tourists in 1997, 2001, 2004, 2007, 2010 and 2014, respectively) is also noticeable.

Generally, the increased participation in a number of sports and recreation, entertainment, cultural and educational activities since 1997 reflects the changes in tourists' expectations. Regardless of whether they are motivated with a specific destination offer or not, tourists are keen to expand their knowledge, increase the level of their physical condition and experience the culture and customs of different regions, while focusing on some kind of creative, physical and/or spiritual self-development (European Travel Commission, 2006; Nordin, 2005). Finally, influenced by many social changes, the concept of 'sun and sea' tourism is also changing (Ivandić, Telišman-Košuta, Čorak, & Krešić, 2006), affecting the characteristics of this, still the most important, tourism product for the Europeans.

Results also reflect the broad trends in shortening the length of stay observed in European tourism population due to more pressured leisure time (European Travel Commission, 2006; Nordin, 2005). Both the official statistics and TOMAS Summer trends confirm that length of stay of tourists in Croatia is shortening (Fig. 11.2). Although the stay from 8 to 14 nights remains stable and dominant throughout almost the whole period (44–46 per cent of all holidays since 1997), the share of guests having shorter holidays (one to seven nights) has been increasing steadily, while the share of those staying 15 or more nights is constantly decreasing and, in 2014, fell to one-third of that recorded in 1989.

TOMAS Summer survey is also tracking information sources used for trip planning. The most important source is previous visit (35 per cent in 2014), owing to a large proportion of repeat foreign visitors (between 60 and 73 per cent depending on the year already visited Croatia for three

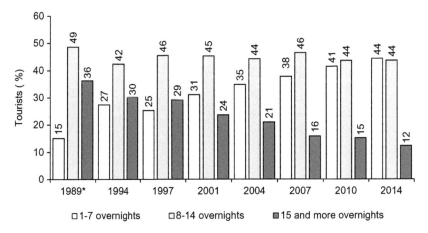

Fig. 11.2   Length of stay in Croatian coastal destinations (*Foreign tourists only. *Source:* Institute for Tourism (1989, 1994, 1997, 2002a, 2005a, 2008a, 2011, 2015))

or more times), although it is gradually decreasing in importance (Fig. 11.3). A question on Internet use was introduced in 1997, when only 2 per cent have used it for trip planning. It increased to about 30 per cent by 2007, without further growth. Similar trends are observed at the European level (European Union, 2016). Nevertheless, there are large differences in Internet use between different segments. For example, 43 per cent of young tourists (up to 29 years of age) and 47 per cent of first-time visitors rely on the Internet. In 2010, the question on Internet use was refined with the introduction of more specific Internet sources—social media, Croatian tourism boards' web pages, accommodation web pages and online travel agencies portals. The accommodation sites were the most often used, while 12 per cent reported the use of social media. It can be concluded that Croatian tourists, gathering information from multiple sources, are well informed about the country's tourism products. This, in turn, puts the additional requirements on promotional materials whose design and content should be coordinated in order to achieve a complete, synergic effect.

TOMAS Summer survey tracks also tourist satisfaction with a battery of about 30 elements (Table 11.1) of destination tourism products and services. There were some changes in the satisfaction measure over time, relating to satisfaction elements/items and measurements. In terms of

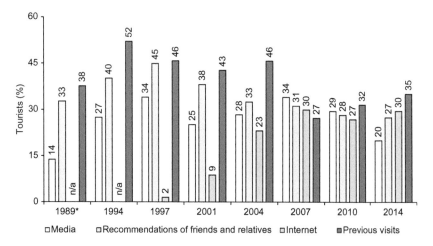

Fig. 11.3 Use of information sources by tourists in Croatia (*Foreign tourists only. Note: Multiple response. *Source:* Institute for Tourism (1989, 1994, 1997, 2002a, 2005a, 2008a, 2011, 2015))

items, few were added/deleted or modified but in a way to always retain a sufficiently large subset for tracking the changes over time. In terms of measurement, a 5-point Likert scale was used up to 2010. Five categories of satisfaction were defined based on the share of grades four and five according to the following: 50 per cent or less indicated very low level of satisfaction, 50 to 59.9 per cent indicated low level of satisfaction, 60 to 69.9 per cent indicated intermediate level of satisfaction, 70 to 79.9 per cent indicated high level of satisfaction and share of grades above 80 per cent indicated very high level of satisfaction with a specific element. However, the 5-point scale proved to be insufficiently precise. Up to 2010 tourist satisfaction increased steadily, and that yet none of the elements were classified into very low or low satisfaction category, calling into question a sensitivity of the 5-point scale. Therefore, a 7-point scale was introduced in 2014, while the five categories of satisfaction were defined based on share of grades six and seven. The change in the length of scale does not allow direct comparison of 2014 survey results with the previous ones. However, comparison is still possible by comparing the average scores, following the adjustment of the scales or elements' ranks.

TOMAS Summer survey results indicate an almost constant increase in tourist satisfaction with each of the elements of destination tourism products and services (Table 11.1). Regarding the rank of elements according

Table 11.1 Tourist satisfaction

Elements of destination tourism products and services	Level of satisfaction rank**								
	1987*	1989*	1994	1997	2001	2004	2007	2010	2014
Climate	1	2	1	-	-	-	-	-	-
Scenic and natural beauty	2	1	2	1	1	1	1	1	1
Friendliness of staff in the accommodation	9	7	7	4	3	4	5	4	2
Suitability for a family holiday	6	5	4	2	2	2	2	2	3
Personal safety	3	3	6	5	4	3	3	6	4
Picturesquesness and tidiness of town/ resort	5	4	3	9	7	8	19	10	5
Friendliness of local people	9	7	7	3	5	6	10	7	6
Service quality in the accommodation	8	8	-	10	11	10	7	12	7
Value for money' for the accommodation	-	-	-	-	-	-	11	18	8
Comfort of accommodation	13	9	-	12	14	13	9	11	9
Food quality in the accommodation	12	11	-	8	12	12	14	8	10
'Value for money' for gastronomic offers	-	-	-	-	-	-	13	17	11
Quality of food outside the accommodation	7	6	5	6	6	5	8	5	12
Clean beach	-	-	-	-	13	14	17	14	13
Suitability for short break holiday	-	-	14	7	10	11	12	9	14
A wealth of gastronomic offers	-	-	10	13	9	15	16	13	15
Environmental preservation	-	-	15	14	15	9	18	15	16
Quality of information provided in destination	10	14	17	17	16	19	22	16	17
Supply of organised sightseeing trips	4	10	9	16	17	16	20	19	18
Accessibility of this place	17	20	12	-	-	18	21	21	19
Shopping opportunities	23	21	25	22	21	25	25	27	20
Equipment on the beach/ beach tidiness	-	-	-	19	19	21	24	26	21
Presentation of cultural heritage	-	-	-	-	-	-	28	22	22
Wealth of sport activities offered	15	17	18	18	20	20	23	20	23
Quality of tourism signage for attractions	-	-	16	20	23	22	26	23	24
Variety of entertainment opportunities	19	19	23	21	22	24	27	24	25
Variety of cultural events	20	18	24	23	24	26	30	25	26
Quality of local transport	21	22	20	24	25	23	29	28	27
Destination suitable for people with special needs	-	-	-	-	-	-	-	-	28
Entire stay	-	-	-	-	-	-	4	3	-
Value for money of entire stay	11	12	21	15	18	17	6	-	-
Quietness	16	15	-	11	8	7	15	-	-
Foreign language knowledge	-	-	8	-	-	-	-	-	-
Opportunities for nature walks / mountaineering	18	16	11	-	-	-	-	-	-
Quality of post services	-	24	13	-	-	-	-	-	-
Suitability for business meetings	22	23	19	-	-	-	-	-	-
Quality of road services	-	25	22	-	-	-	-	-	-
Service in restaurants	14	13	-	-	-	-	-	-	-

* Foreign tourists only.
** Rank according to share of grades four and five in 1987-2010, rank according to share of grades six and seven in 2014.
- n/a.

Legend	
Level of satisfaction:	very low
	low
	intermediate
	high
	very high

Source: Institute for Tourism (1987, 1989, 1994, 1997, 2002a, 2005a, 2008a, 2011, 2015)

to tourist satisfaction, the highest-rated element during the whole study period has been scenic and natural beauty, followed by, not necessarily in the same order, a friendliness of staff in the accommodation establishment, a suitability for a family holiday and a personal safety. On the other hand, a set of cultural, entertainment, sport and shopping opportunities, together with a quality of local transport and beach equipment, have traditionally been among the lowest-rated elements and could be considered as weakness of Croatian tourism.

Finally, TOMAS Summer survey tracks tourist expenditures in destination as one of the most relevant indicators of tourism performance and competitiveness. However, its estimation is, especially when monitoring the change during a long period of time, subjected to a number of methodological issues such as using current and constant prices. The recorded changes in the amount and distribution of tourist expenditures by different products and services reflect not only changes in inflation and exchange rates but also those in tourism demand characteristics and destination tourism products. The average daily expenditures (at current prices) of tourists during the summer season in Croatia in 2014 are estimated at 66 Euros per person (with standard error of one Euro), 14 per cent nominally more in comparison to 2010 and 36 per cent more than ten years before (Fig. 11.4). In 2014, 55 per cent of total daily expenditures was spent on accommodation, 18 per cent on food and beverages in restaurants and bars outside the accommodation facility and 27 per cent for entertainment, sport, culture and other services. The share of non-accommodation services, although oscillating over the time, indicates a slight growth in importance, confirming the improvement in the structure of the destination tourism product in Croatia.

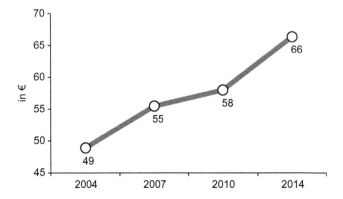

Fig. 11.4 Average daily tourist expenditures in Croatia in Euro (at current prices) (*Source:* Institute for Tourism (2005a, 2008a, 2011, 2015))

CONCLUSION

Longitudinal data on Croatian tourism obtained by the TOMAS Summer surveys in 1987–2014 period has revealed a huge number of scientifically based, relevant and accurate information on changing nature of tourism demand. The primary goal of this chapter was to present experiences in longitudinal research implementation, but also to illustrate type of information that can be extracted and derived from such research. The chapter brought insight into the basic trends of the aggregate tourism demand in Croatia indicating a significant change/shift in both tourism demand and tourism offer in Croatia. Knowledge about tourism demand can further be expanded analyzing different sub-segments of demand, for example, tourists in specific type of accommodation, from specific generating markets, in specific counties, age groups and so on. Furthermore, for the purpose of this chapter, only descriptive analysis was presented, but more complex methods and analysis have been applied by scholars to assess the effects of multiple factors and broaden the knowledge on both methods applied and results interpretation (Dwyer et al., 2012). TOMAS Summer research has prompted a number of scholars to further reveal and explain data obtained by the surveys (Krešić, Mikulić, & Miličević, 2013; Krešić & Prebežac, 2011; Mikulić, Krešić, & Kožić, 2015; Mikulić, Krešić, Prebežac, Miličević, & Šerić, 2016; Miličević, Mihalić, & Sever, 2016; Pejić Bach, Dumičić, & Marušić, 2009; Prebežac & Mikulić, 2008).

The information obtained by TOMAS Summer surveys is used for tourism market segmentation, tourism product development and innovation, assessment of tourism destination competitiveness and tourism impact assessment in Croatia as illustrated in Chap. 7. TOMAS Summer survey data, enabling long-term monitoring of tourism demand, are regularly used for the formulation of tourism policy as well as for the strategic tourism development plans on national and regional levels. Realizing the necessity of such data, TOMAS survey has been further used to track tourism demand in nautical (Institute for Tourism, 2002b, 2005b, 2008b, 2012) and city tourism (Institute for Tourism, 1999, 2004, 2006, 2007, 2009, 2013), under the name TOMAS Nautica survey and TOMAS Zagreb survey, respectively. Furthermore, the methodological framework of TOMAS surveys was transferred and applied to track tourism demand in Bosnia and Herzegovina (Marušić et al., 2010) and Montenegro (National Tourism Organization of Montenegro, 2014). The application of the standardized TOMAS methodological framework allows further comparison among different segments of demand, thereby gaining the additional knowledge on tourism phenomenon.

TOMAS Summer survey has also some limitations. In terms of coverage, it addresses the characteristics, attitudes, behavior and expenditures of tourists staying in commercial accommodation facilities. However, the importance of tourism demand in non-commercial accommodation facilities is unquestionable due to the large segment of second home tourism demand in Croatia and European trends predicting its further growth. The improved mobility increases the segment traveling to visit relatives and friends, while higher purchasing power enables acquisition of own second homes or apartments (European Travel Commission, 2006). There is almost no information on that segment in Croatia. The future TOMAS surveys should therefore be expanded in order to cover tourism demand in non-commercial accommodation. Further, Croatia is striving to extend tourism activity on the continental part of the country and, thus, reduce the growing pressure on the narrow coastal strip. Similarly, one of the main strategic directions of further country's tourism development (Ministry of Tourism, 2013) is to reduce the pronounced seasonality of tourism demand and stretch the demand over the whole year. The survey population should, therefore, be extended, covering the tourism demand throughout the country and all year around, in order to obtain a more comprehensive picture of Croatian tourism.

TOMAS Summer survey also opens a series of new questions about tourism in Croatia and has prompted a need for a more detailed study of specific aspects of tourism demand such as tourist lifestyle or deeper insight into tourist satisfaction. In the future, TOMAS research will be demanding in terms of the coverage and content extension, that will challenge further trend analysis, but that is the challenge facing all longitudinal studies. Finally, an area that should attract a lot of attention of further research on tracking nature of tourism demand worldwide is the ever-present need to harmonize longitudinal research design and methodology in order to facilitate cross-national comparison and benchmarking of tourism destinations.

REFERENCES

Almond, R. G., & Sinharay, S. (2012). What can repeated cross-sectional studies tell us about student growth? *Educational Testing Service Research Report Series, 2*, i–20.

Andreß, H. J., Golsch, K., & Schmidt, A. W. (2013). *Applied panel data analysis for economic and social surveys*. Berlin/Heidelberg, Germany: Springer Science & Business Media.

Bissell, L., MacKay, ,K., & Vogt, C. (2008). Using panel studies in travel research: Issues of participation, participant attitudes and best practices. *Canadian Travel and Tourism Research Association Proceedings*, Victoria, BC.

Chen, X., & Miller, J. G. (2005). Introduction to longitudinal research on human development: Approaches, issues and new directions. *International Society for the Study of Behavioural Development Newsletter*, 2(48), 1–7.

Cooke, M., Watkins, N., & Moy, C. (2007). Market measurement: The next frontier for panel research. *Panel Research* 2007, ESOMAR World Research Conference, Orlando, 28–30 October.

Čorak, S., Marušić, Z., & Ivandić, N. (2009). Trendovi TOMAS Ljeto: od 1987. do 2007. Godine [TOMAS Summer Trends: from 1987 to 2007]. In S. Čorak & Z. Marušić (Eds.), *TOMAS trendovi – Stavovi i potrošnja turista u Hrvatskoj 1987–2008* (pp. 11–43). Zagreb, Croatia: Institute for Tourism.

Croatian Bureau of Statistics. (2015). Tourist arrivals and nights in 2014. *First Release*, 4.3.2., www.dzs.hr. Date accessed 4 April 2016.

Croatian Bureau of Statistics. (2016). Tourist arrivals and nights in 2015. *First Release*, 4.3.2., www.dzs.hr. Date accessed 4 April 2016.

Diggle, P. J., Liang, K. Y., & Zeger, S. L. (2002). *Analysis of longitudinal data* (2nd ed.). New York: Oxford University Press.

Dwyer, L., & Forsyth, P. (2006). *International handbook on the economics of tourism*. Cheltenham, UK: Edward Elgar Publishing Limited.

Dwyer, L., Edwards, D., Mistilis, N., Roman, C., Scott, N., & Cooper, C. (2008). *Megatrends underpinning tourism to 2020: Analysis of key drivers for change*. Queensland, Australia: CRC.

Dwyer, L., Gill, A., & Seetaram, N. (2012). *Handbook of research methods in tourism: Quantitative and qualitative approaches*. Cheltenham, UK and Northampton, MA: Edward Elgar.

European Travel Commission. (2006). *Tourism Trends for Europe*. www.etc-corporate.org. Date accessed 18 February 2015.

European Union. (2014). Methodological manual for tourism statistics. *EUROSTAT Manuals and Guidelines*. Luxembourg: Publications Office of the European Union. ec.europa.eu/eurostat/documents/. Date accessed 4 April 2016.

European Union. (2016). Preferences of Europeans towards tourism. *Flash Eurobarometer*, 432, January 2016. ec.europa.eu/growth/tools-databases/vto/eurobarometer. Date accessed 2 May 2016.

Frechtling, D. C. (2006). An assessment of visitor expenditure methods and models. *Journal of Travel Research*, 45(1), 26–35.

Groves, R. M., Fowler, F. J., Couper, M. P., Lepkowski, J. M., Singer, E., & Tourangeau, R. (2009). *Survey methodology* (2nd ed.). Hoboken, NJ: Wiley.

Gunn, C. A. (1994). A perspective on the purpose and nature of tourism research methods. In J. R. B. Ritchie & C. R. Goeldner (Eds.), *Travel, tourism, and hospitality research: A handbook for managers and researchers* (2nd ed., pp. 3–12). Hoboken, NJ: Wiley.

Henning, G. K., Levy, S., & Ritchie, J. R. B. (2005). An inquiry into the nature and composition of tourism, leisure and hospitality research. *Tourism, 53*(3), 187–203.

Institute for Tourism. (1987). *Stavovi i potrošnja turista u Hrvatskoj – TOMAS '87. I Izvještaj* [Attitudes and Expenditures of Tourists in Croatia – TOMAS '87 Report I]. Zagreb, Croatia: Author.

Institute for Tourism. (1989). *Stavovi i potrošnja turista u Hrvatskoj – TOMAS '89* [Attitudes and Expenditures of Tourists in Croatia – TOMAS '89]. Zagreb, Croatia: Author.

Institute for Tourism. (1994). *Stavovi i potrošnja turista u Hrvatskoj – TOMAS '94* [Attitudes and Expenditures of Tourists in Croatia – TOMAS '94]. Zagreb, Croatia: Author.

Institute for Tourism. (1997). *Stavovi i potrošnja turista u Hrvatskoj – TOMAS '97* [Attitudes and Expenditures of Tourists in Croatia – TOMAS '97]. Zagreb, Croatia: Author.

Institute for Tourism. (1999). *Stavovi i potrošnja turista i posjetitelja Zagreba – TOMAS Zagreb 1998* [Attitudes and Expenditures of Tourists and Visitors in Zagreb – TOMAS Zagreb 1998]. Zagreb, Croatia: Author.

Institute for Tourism. (2002a). *Stavovi i potrošnja turista u Hrvatskoj – TOMAS Ljeto 2001* [Attitudes and Expenditures of Tourists in Croatia – TOMAS Summer 2001]. Zagreb, Croatia: Author.

Institute for Tourism. (2002b). *Stavovi i potrošnja nautičara u Hrvatskoj – TOMAS Nautika 2001* [Attitudes and Expenditures of Nautical Tourists in Croatia – TOMAS Nautica 2001]. Zagreb, Croatia: Author.

Institute for Tourism. (2004). *Stavovi i potrošnja turista i posjetitelja Zagreba – TOMAS Zagreb 2003* [Attitudes and Expenditures of Tourists and Visitors in Zagreb – TOMAS Zagreb 2003]. Zagreb, Croatia: Author.

Institute for Tourism. (2005a). *Stavovi i potrošnja turista u Hrvatskoj – TOMAS Ljeto 2004* [Attitudes and Expenditures of Tourists in Croatia – TOMAS Summer 2004]. Zagreb, Croatia: Author.

Institute for Tourism. (2005b). *Stavovi i potrošnja nautičara u Hrvatskoj – TOMAS Nautika 2004* [Attitudes and Expenditures of Nautical Tourists in Croatia – TOMAS Nautica 2004]. Zagreb, Croatia: Author.

Institute for Tourism. (2006). *Stavovi i potrošnja turista i posjetitelja Zagreba – TOMAS Zagreb 2005* [Attitudes and Expenditures of Tourists and Visitors in Zagreb – TOMAS Zagreb 2005]. Zagreb, Croatia: Author.

Institute for Tourism. (2007). *Stavovi i potrošnja turista i posjetitelja Zagreba – TOMAS Zagreb 2007* [Attitudes and Expenditures of Tourists and Visitors in Zagreb – TOMAS Zagreb 2007]. Zagreb, Croatia: Author.

Institute for Tourism. (2008a). *Stavovi i potrošnja turista u Hrvatskoj – TOMAS Ljeto 2007* [Attitudes and Expenditures of Tourists in Croatia – TOMAS Summer 2007]. Zagreb, Croatia: Author.
Institute for Tourism. (2008b). *Stavovi i potrošnja nautičara u Hrvatskoj – TOMAS Nautika 2007* [Attitudes and Expenditures of Nautical Tourists in Croatia – TOMAS Nautica 2007]. Zagreb, Croatia: Author.
Institute for Tourism. (2009). *Stavovi i potrošnja turista i posjetitelja Zagreba – TOMAS Zagreb 2009* [Attitudes and Expenditures of Tourists and Visitors in Zagreb – TOMAS Zagreb 2009]. Zagreb, Croatia: Author.
Institute for Tourism. (2011). *Stavovi i potrošnja turista u Hrvatskoj – TOMAS Ljeto 2010* [Attitudes and Expenditures of Tourists in Croatia – TOMAS Summer 2010]. Zagreb, Croatia: Author.
Institute for Tourism. (2012). *Stavovi i potrošnja nautičara u Hrvatskoj – TOMAS Nautika Jahting 2012* [Attitudes and Expenditures of Nautical Tourists in Croatia – TOMAS Nautica Yachting 2012]. Zagreb, Croatia: Author.
Institute for Tourism. (2013). *Stavovi i potrošnja turista i posjetitelja Zagreba – TOMAS Zagreb 2012* [Attitudes and Expenditures of Tourists and Visitors in Zagreb – TOMAS Zagreb 2012]. Zagreb, Croatia: Author.
Institute for Tourism. (2015). *Stavovi i potrošnja turista u Hrvatskoj – TOMAS Ljeto 2014* [Attitudes and Expenditures of Tourists in Croatia – TOMAS Summer 2014]. Zagreb, Croatia: Author.
Ivandić, N., Marušić, Z., Šutalo, I., & Vuglar, J. (2014). *Satelitski račun turizma RH za 2011. godinu i izračun neizravnih i ukupnih učinaka turizma u RH* [Tourism Satellite Account of the Republic of Croatia for 2011 and Estimation of Indirect and Total Impacts of Tourism]. Zagreb, Croatia: Institute for Tourism.
Ivandić, N., Telišman-Košuta, N., Čorak, S., & Krešić, D. (2006). Ljetni odmorišni turizam [Sun and sea tourism]. In S. Čorak & V. Mikačić (Eds.), *Hrvatski turizam – plavo, bijelo, zeleno [Croatian tourism: Blue, white and green]* (pp. 1–38). Zagreb, Croatia: Institute for tourism.
Kasriel-Alexander, D. (2016). *Top 10 global consumer trends for 2016.* London: Euromonitor International. http://go.euromonitor.com/consumer-trends-2016.html. Date accessed 2 May 2016.
Krešić, D., & Prebežac, D. (2011). Index of destination attractiveness as a tool for destination attractiveness assessment. *Tourism: An Interdisciplinary Journal, 59*(4), 227–238.
Krešić, D., Mikulić, J., & Miličević, K. (2013). The factor structure of tourist satisfaction at pilgrimage destination: The case of Medjugorje. *International Journal of Tourism Research, 15*(5), 484–494.
Lynn, P. (2009). Methods for longitudinal surveys. In P. Lynn (Ed.), *Methodology of longitudinal surveys* (pp. 1–20). Chichester, UK: Wiley.
Marrocu, E., & Paci, R. (2013). Different tourists to different destinations. Evidence from spatial interaction models. *Tourism Management, 39*, 71–83.

Marušić, Z., Čorak, S., Sever, I., Krešić, D., Miličević, K., & Ivandić, N. (2010). *Stavovi i potrošnja turista u Federaciji Bosne i Hercegovine – TOMAS FBiH pilot 2010 [Attitudes and Expenditures of Tourist in Federation of Bosnia and Herzegovina – TOMAS FBiH pilot 2010].* Zagreb, Croatia: Federal Ministry of Environment and Tourism & Institute for Tourism.

Menard, S. (1991). *Longitudinal research.* Newbury Park, CA: Sage Publications.

Mikulić, J., Krešić, D., & Kožić, I. (2015). Critical factors of the maritime yachting tourism experience: An impact-asymmetry analysis of principal components. *Journal of Travel & Tourism Marketing, 32*(1), 30–41.

Mikulić, J., Krešić, D., Prebežac, D., Miličević, K., & Šerić, M. (2016). Identifying drivers of destination attractiveness in a competitive environment: A comparison of approaches. *Journal of Destination Marketing and Management, 5*(2), 154–163.

Miličević, K., Mihalić, T. & Sever, I. (2016). An investigation of the relationship between destination branding and destination competitiveness. *Journal of Travel & Tourism Marketing* (in press).

Ministry of Tourism. (2013). Croatian Tourism Development Strategy until 2020. *Official Gazette of the Republic of Croatia* 55/2013. http://narodne-novine.nn.hr/clanci/sluzbeni/2013_05_55_1119.html. Date accessed 20 November 2014.

Moscardo, G. (2004). Exploring change in Asia Pacific tourism markets. In K. Chon, C. Hsu, & N. Okamoto (Eds.), *Globalization and tourism research: East meets West* (pp. 369–378). Hong Kong: Asia Pacific Tourist Association.

Moscardo, G., & Benckendorff, P. (2010). Mythbusting: Generation Y and travel. In P. Benckendorff, G. Moscardo, & D. Pendergast (Eds.), *Tourism and Generation Y* (pp. 16–26). Oxfordshire, UK: CAB International.

National Tourism Organization of Montenegro. (2014). *Guest Survey (2014): Stavovi i potrošnja turista u Crnoj Gori* [Guest Survey (2014): Attitudes and Expenditures of Tourist in Montenegro]. Podgorica, Montenegro: Author.

Nordin, S. (2005). *Tourism of tomorrow – Travel trends and forces of change.* Ostersund, Sweden: ETOUR – European Tourism Research Institute. miun.diva-portal.org/smash/record.jsf?pid=diva2%3A1660&dswid=1527. Date accessed 4 April 2015.

Oh, H., Kim, B. Y., & Shin, J. H. (2004). Hospitality and tourism marketing: Recent developments in research and future directions. *Hospitality Management, 23*, 425–447.

Pejić Bach, M., Dumičić, K., & Marušić, Z. (2009). Application of association rules method in tourism product development. In L. Zadnik Stirn, J. Žerovnik, S. Drobne, & A. Lisec (Eds.), *Proceedings of the 10th International Symposium on Operational research* (pp. 565–574). Nova Gorica, Slovenia, September 23–25.

Pettigrew, A. M. (1990). Longitudinal field research on change: theory and practice. *Organizational Science, 1*(3), 267–292.

Pizam, A. (1994). Planning a tourism research investigation. In J. R. B. Ritchie & C. R. Goeldner (Eds.), *Travel, tourism, and hospitality research: A handbook for managers and researchers* (2nd ed., pp. 61–75). Hoboken, NJ: Wiley.

Prebežac, D., & Mikulić, J. (2008). Measuring perceived destination image: A comparative case study of Croatia and Hawaii. In *Proceedings of the 4th International Conference An Enterprise Odyssey: Tourism - Governance and Entrepreneurship* (pp. 1942–1955). Cavtat, Croatia, June 11–14.

Rendtel, U., & Harms, T. (2009). Weighting and calibration for household panels. In P. Lynn (Ed.), *Methodology of longitudinal surveys* (pp. 1–20). Chichester, UK: Wiley.

Ritchie, J. B., & Sheridan, M. (1988). Developing an integrated framework for tourism demand data in Canada. *Journal of Travel Research, 27*(1), 3–9.

Ritchie, J. R. B. (2000). Research and the tourism industry: Building bridges of understanding and insight. *Tourism Recreation Research, 25*(1), 1–8.

Ritchie, J. R. B. (2005). Longitudinal research methods. In B. W. Ritchie, P. Burns, & C. Palmer (Eds.), *Tourism research methods: Integrating theory with practice* (pp. 131–148). Oxfordshire, UK: CAB International.

Sever, I., Marušić, Z., & Čorak, S. (2016). Assessing the reliability of percentage above cut scores in monitoring tourist satisfaction levels. *ISCCRO'16 – The 1st International Statistical Conference in Croatia*, Zagreb, May, 5–6, 2016.

Smith, S. L. J. (1989). *Tourism analysis: A handbook*. Singapore: Longman Publishers Ltd..

Song, H., Dwyer, L., Li, G., & Cao, Z. (2012). Tourism economics research: A review and assessment. *Annals of Tourism Research, 39*, 1653–1682.

Spini, D., & d'Epinay, C. L. (2003). Measuring attitudinal change in repeated cross-sectional surveys: Beliefs about the self, life, and society among Swiss elders (1979–1994). *Swiss Journal of Psychology, 62*(1), 27–35.

Teddlie, C., & Yu, F. (2007). Mixed methods sampling a typology with examples. *Journal of mixed methods research, 1*(1), 77–100.

United Nations & World Tourism Organization. (2010). *International Recommendations for Tourism Statistics 2008*. Studies in Methods, Series M, No. 83/Rev.1. New York: Authors.

Watkins, M. N. (2010). A longitudinal study of changeability in leisure meanings. *Leisure Studies, 29*(4), 361–376.

Weber, S. (1991). Problem areas and sources of errors in tourism demand research. *The Tourist Review, 3*, 2–8.

World Tourism Organization. (2015). Tourism in the Mediterranean, 2015 edition. *UNWTO Tourism Trends Snapshot*. Madrid, Spain: World Tourism Organization. www.e-unwto.org. Date accessed 2 May 2016.

Xiao, H., & Smith, S. L. J. (2006). Case studies in tourism research: A state-of-the-art analysis. *Tourism Management, 27*, 738–749.

Zins, A. H. (2007). Exploring travel information search behavior beyond common frontiers. *Information Technology & Tourism, 9*, 149–164.

CHAPTER 12

Longitudinal Assessment of the Carrying Capacity of a Typical Tourist Island: Twenty Years On

Jakša Kivela and Zoran Klarić

A Brief Historical Account of Vis and a Correction of the Popular View About Vis' Tourism

Vis in ancient Greek is known as *"Ισσα"* and in Latin as *Issa*. This is a small Croatian island in the Adriatic Sea (Fig. 12.1) and is the farthest larger inhabited island of the Croatian mainland. Vis with adjacent smaller islands has an area of 101 square kilometres (39.0 square mile), and in the 2011 census, it had a permanent population of 3,460. The island Vis itself has an area of 90.3 square kilometres (34.9 square mile) and a population of 3,445. The island's two largest settlements are the town of Vis on the eastern side of the island, with a population of 1,672, and Komiža, on its western side, with a population of 1,397. It is often portrayed by the marketing and advertising blurb as "the pearl among the Croatian Adriatic islands," "left untouched by the development of tourism for so many years due to it being a strategic military zone" in its long history and then from

J. Kivela • Z. Klarić (✉)
Institute for Tourism, Zagreb, Croatia

© The Author(s) 2017
L. Dwyer et al. (eds.), *Evolution of Destination Planning and Strategy*, DOI 10.1007/978-3-319-42246-6_12

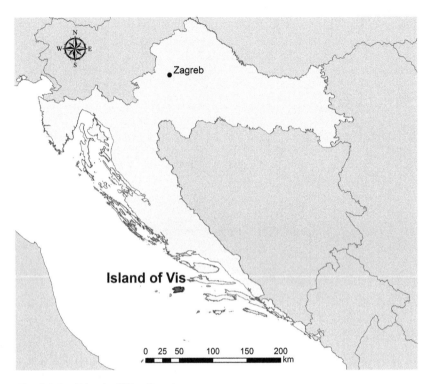

Fig. 12.1   Island of Vis, Croatia

1945 until 1989. While true only in part, the island has most definitely been "touched by tourism," actually going back to the days of the Austro-Hungarian Empire (1867–1918).

In about 3000 B.C., the first people to settle on Vis were from the Mediterranean, most probably Greeks. By 2000 B.C. they were overrun by the Illyrian tribes which formed their own government in the fifth century B.C. The Syracuse warlord, Dimitri, the Elder, in approximately 397 B.C., established a colony on Vis, and its settlers expanded their influence towards the central Dalmatian islands and the coast. By the 219 B.C., Vis or *Issa* was under the authority of Rome. The Croat tribes started to settle on Vis in the seventh century. Centuries later, Vis was occupied by the Venetians, and it stayed under Venetian rule from 1420 until 1797, when Venice handed it over to the Austrian Empire. In 1805 it was briefly under French possession, but by March 1811, the English fleet annihilated Napoleon's fleet just off Vis, and the English occupied and defended Vis (fort St. George) until 1814. The Regulations of the Vienna Congress of 1814 saw Vis being returned to Austria and later the Austro-Hungarian Empire until 1918, when it was occupied by the Italians just after WWI. In 1921, the Rapallo agreement (signed on 12 November 1920 in Rapallo near Genoa in Italy) ceded Vis to the Kingdom of Serbs, Croats and Slovenians. In 1941 it was again occupied by the Italians until the capitulation of Italy in 1943. After this, it became an army and naval base for the People's Army of Yugoslavia. As noted earlier, Vis was then closed to all outside (foreign and select domestic) visitors because of its strategic military position, a regulation that was terminated in 1989, just before the fall of Yugoslavia: Quite a history for such a very small place! However, it must be noted that from the late fifties until 1990, Vis enjoyed considerable tourism numbers and had developed substantial tourism facilities and, importantly, its tourism infrastructure, albeit for the domestic market which was significant as, by the mid-sixties, Yugoslavia had a population of over 20 million. At present, popular tourism literature would let us believe that Vis was bereft of tourism and tourism infrastructure, save for the military. This is quite false and misleading.

For the record, Vis, in the years 1963–90, enjoyed a substantial and successive year-on-year growth in tourism numbers and bed-nights from the then Yugoslav market place. By the end of 1966, hotels, roads, electrification, water and sewerage infrastructure, concert halls and cinemas, museums, fast and modern passenger ships, restaurants, supermarkets and such were all in place for the island's growing tourism: All this for the military tourists only? Not true. It is a matter of fact that Vis was then one of the most exotic and exclusive tourist destinations in Yugoslavia, on par with island Hvar, Dubrovnik, Opatija and the Brijuni islands up north (Hrvatska Enciklopedija, 2013a, 2013b). Since Croatia's independence in 1995, Vis had resumed its tourism know-how but this time allowing foreign nationals as its guests also, offering its uniqueness, history, cultural heritage and natural beauty to all. Just recently one of its beaches (Stiniva) was voted as the best beach in Europe for 2016 (Croatia Week, 2016). Table 12.1 shows tourism and related growth figure for the years 1988 and 2014, including 1981 as a historical reference point.

One can note that in the period 1988–14, the actual number of visitors to Vis has almost doubled including the number of nights. What is of some concern is that if one takes a look the growth of the number of tourists per square kilometre, the figures show almost a threefold growth

Table 12.1 Tourism indicators for Vis, 1981, 1988, 2014

Indicators	2014	1988	1981
Number of permanent residents[a]	3,460	4,361	4,134
Population density	33.7	37.0	41.0
Total number of tourists[b]	36,698	27,499	10,733
Total number of domestic tourists	10,401	27,470	10,721
Total number of foreign tourists	26,297	29	12
Total number of nights[b]	216,115	166,923	50,222
Including private not-registered accommodation	312,000		
Total number of nights—domestic	56,629	166,778	50,128
Total number of nights—foreign	159,486	145	94
Total accommodation capacity[c]	4,758	1,391	449
Percentage of private accommodation capacity	65 %	23 %	21 %
Number of tourists per inhabitant[b]	10.6	7.4	2.6
With day trippers and yacht crews in 2014 (54,198)	15.7		
Number of tourists per square kilometre	406.7	285.7	111.5
Including day trippers and yacht crews in 2014	600.5		
Nautical tourism: number of yachts berthed overnight at Vis and Komiža harbour for the entire season	9,360	420	27

Source: Dragičević, Kušen & Klarić (1991), Kivela (2004–2015) and Statistical Yearbook (2015)
[a]Number of permanent residents in 2014 refers to census data from 2014 and in 1988 to census data from 1991. For the census records from the year 1991 and 1981 registered residents, however, as many as 15 per cent of registered residents live in other parts of Croatia and overseas for part of the year and at times for many years, for example, about 350 residents who live permanently overseas but who are registered as the island's permanent residents
[b]Excludes day trippers and yacht crews which in 2014 was just over 17,500 visitors
[c]Including private accommodation

in the 1988–14 period. And, this does not include occupation and use of the nearby marine environment. Given author's observation and field count, on average during the 2014 season, there were 85 yachts moored in the Vis harbour and 47 yachts in Komiža harbour, respectively, every day (based on six-day week) of the season or 9,360 yacht berths during the entire season. Arguably, Vis is now gaining a reputation for one of the most popular tourist island destinations in the Mediterranean; however, it comes at a cost to its infrastructure, culture, heritage and ecology.

Tourism can be a real benefit to the local island economy and Vis is no exception. However, there is a point where enough might become too much. In the 2014 season, the number of tourists outnumbered the local population by ten to one, noting that the tourist season on Vis is from June to the end of August. And, if day trippers and yacht crews are also taken into account, the ratio of tourists to local population is over 15 to one during the three-month season. Vis with its few thousand residents is practically overrun by tourists in peak season. One can argue that it is akin to an experiment in population growth and decline repeated on an annual basis, and the strain on population and its ageing infrastructure quickly becomes evident.

In 1988 there were 27,499 visitors to the island, and by the outbreak of war in 1990, there were only 14,125 visitors during the season. During the 2014 season, there were 36,698 visitors to Vis excluding about 17,500 day trippers and yacht crews. This is sizeable increase for such a small place and in a short time span of a season and is one that brings to mind the growth trends that populations exhibit as they are near carrying capacity (Dragičević et al., 1991).

Importantly, tourism for Vis has followed the same S-shaped or logistic curve. The initial number of visitors after the end of war of independence in 1995 was at a slow trickle, but once the island was re-discovered, the number of arrivals soared. As a consequence, prices rose sharply, both land and marine ecology began to show signs of distress, summer crowding becomes an issue and the crumbling 50-year-old infrastructure is often on the verge of collapse.

Arguably, the carrying capacity for tourism is similar to ecological carrying capacity where physical resources limit both population and tourist levels. Shortage of rooms, or decline in the quality of environment, weak infrastructure and overcrowding, can quickly put the brakes on tourism growth (Chamberlain 1997). But importantly for Vis however, cultural resources must also be a cause for concern. Observations over a ten-year period have confirmed that Vis' unique culture and heritage that attracted visitors in the first place is fast-becoming spoiled and diluted, which might end in losing the draw Vis once had. Culturally, Vis is a far cry of what it once was.

Equally, it is not always obvious that there might be a relationship between limits on tourist capacity and ecological carrying capacity. Tourists' demands are similar to those of their everyday life, only greatly multiplied. For example, while on holidays, service is expected where it otherwise would not be, and consumption is higher, for example, how many people wash their towels on a daily basis when at home? Or, eat at a restaurant every day? (McCool & Lime, 2001). Convincingly, the holidaymakers on Vis are testing the limits of the island's infrastructure and environment.

TOURISM CARRYING CAPACITY

Tourism Carrying Capacity is generally defined as the maximum number of people that may visit a tourist destination at the same time, without causing destruction of the physical, economic, socio-cultural environment and an unacceptable decrease in the quality of visitors' satisfaction (UNWTO, 1981). Other authors, such as Middleton and Hawkins (1998) and Chamberlain (1997), define carrying capacity in a similar way as the level of human activity that an area can accommodate without the area deteriorating, the resident community being adversely affected or the quality of visitors experience declining. Despite the unfavourable rhetoric about the concept of carrying capacity from the academia, these time-tested definitions have stood the test of time by pin-pointing carrying capacity at the point at which a destination or attraction starts experiencing stress as a result of the number of visitors. For example, in areas which have an objective of maintaining pristine ecological condition, any level of visitor use creates a negative impact, suggesting that the carrying capacity should be zero. In which case, an acceptable level of interference becomes a matter of human judgment, and it is not an inherent quality of a particular tourist site or destination (Coccossis & Mexa, 2004).

As noted above, tourism carrying capacity is arguably an outdated approach to managing visitors in protected areas and national parks. However, it still has credence when assessing the tourist carrying capacity of a small island, for example, 50–400 sq/km, where tourism is the main form of economic activity, such as the islands of Brač, Hvar, Korčula, Mljet, Vis and Šolta. Traditionally, wildlife managers have attempted to determine the largest population of a particular species that could be supported by a habitat over a long period of time. Many authors, such as Buckley (1999), Washburne (1982) and McCool, Stankey and Clark (2007), have critiqued the concept as being flawed in both the conceptual assumptions made and its limited practical application. For example, the notion of a carrying capacity assumes that the social-ecological systems in which protected areas and tourism destinations are situated are stable. However, we know that island tourist destinations are dynamically complex and difficult to predict as to their carrying capacity. We also know that to implement a carrying capacity at a practical level assumes a level of control of entries into a destination which is often not practical. We also know that a carrying capacity requires considerable financial and technical resources to administer; and we know too well that when demand exceeds a limit, the ways in which economic opportunities are allocated are often controversial and come at a cost.

Opponents of Carrying Capacity

Carrying capacity assumes a stable and predictable world, a "J-shaped" curve in the relationship between use level and impact and value judgments. However, on the practical level, it can be difficult to calculate a maximum number of visitors because this is also dependent on other factors such as the way in which the tourists behave, for example, a large number of tourists using the island's water, sewerage and garbage disposal resources every day during the season will have a different impact on the environment compared to the resident population's use throughout non-season. Therefore, in the case of island destinations such as Vis, visitor impacts change with seasons. What is important to know is that these impacts can be cumulative and are often subject to acceptability, an issue that is largely dependent on social and cultural value systems at the destination (Coccossis & Mexa, 2004).

In the context of island Vis tourism, "carrying capacity" is a concept to be thought about when we intend for sustainable versus full utilisation of resource for a purpose. In fragile island systems such as Vis, a full utilisation of infrastructure or resource for tourism should be a restricted long-term mandate. Hence, in addition to "carrying capacity," it is also prudent to have strict guidelines for regulating tourism development and for prohibiting tourism of any kind in select sensitive areas, without altering the cultural, social and biophysical heritage of the island (Anderson, Hardy, Roach, & Witmer, 1976).

Limits of Acceptable Change

Limits of acceptable change is the first of the post carrying capacity visitor management frameworks developed to respond to the shortcomings of carrying capacity by the US forest service in the 1980s. It is based on the notion that rather than there being a threshold of visitor numbers, since any tourist activity has an impact, therefore management should be based on constant monitoring of the site as well as the objectives established for it. It is possible that within the limit of acceptable change framework, a visitor limit can be established, but such limits are only one tool available. The framework is frequently summarised in to a nine-step process:

Identify area of concerns and issues; define and describe opportunities/ challenges; select indicators of resource and social conditions; inventory existing resource and social conditions; specify standards for resource and social indicators for each opportunity; identify alternative opportunity allocations, for example, sacrificial tourist zones and no-go tourist zones; identify management actions for each alternative; evaluate and select preferred alternatives; and implement actions and monitor conditions.

Economic Carrying Capacity

This relates to a level of acceptable change within the island's local economy; it is the extent to which the island is able to accommodate tourist functions without the loss of local activities. Economic carrying capacity can also be used to describe the point at which the increased revenue brought by tourism development is overtaken by inflation caused by tourism.

Physical Carrying Capacity

This is the highest number of tourists that an island is actually able to support, not accommodate, though this can be misleading, for example, when food and daily necessities are shipped in plentiful supply from the mainland.

Social Carrying Capacity

This relates to the negative socio-cultural related to tourism development. The indicators of when the social carrying capacity has been exceeded are a reduced local tolerance for tourism as described by Doxey's Index of irritation (Butler, 1980; Doxey, 1975). Reduced visitor enjoyment and increased friction between locals and visitors are also indicators of when the social carrying capacity has been exceeded.

Biophysical Carrying Capacity

This deals with the extent to which the island's natural environment is able to tolerate interference from tourists. This is made more complicated by the fact that because it deals with ecology which is able to regenerate to some extent so in this case the carrying capacity is when the damage exceeds the habitat's ability to regenerate. Environmental carrying capacity is also used with reference to ecological and physical parameters, capacity of resources, ecosystems and infrastructure.

METHODOLOGY

The approach used in this study relied on systematic observational research methodology, field notes, subject interviews, non-participant interviews and analysis of official tourist data over a period of ten years. Observation of the Vis field setting involved:

- A long engagement with Vis community and Vis tourists, during tourist seasons and off seasons;
- A methodical plan for observation developed for this study;
- Clearly expressed field notations recorded of what and how was observed;
- Cross-checking one's observation notes with participants, relevant tourism data and previous field notes.

Participant Observation

Participant observation allowed for a combined participation in the lives of the Vis population and Vis tourists while at the same time allowing some distance between the researchers and the subjects or, what Fetterman (1998, pp. 34–35) suggested, "a professional distance that allows satisfactory observation and recording of data." This also allowed participants to be as unbiased and/or free of obligations, real or perceived. The range of roles one may play as a participant observer have been described by Atkinson and Hammersley (1994) and others, while Bernard (1988) suggested that participant observation must be learned in the field, which in this case amounted to making fine adjustments in one's approach to different island groups.

In this study, there were a variety of reasons for collecting observational data, for instance:

- because the nature of the study necessitated what and how type questions;
- because the topic was relatively unexplored and little was known to explain how tourism affected Vis and its population over a long period of time;

- when understanding the issues in a detailed way was valuable;
- when it is important to study the impact of tourism on Vis from a distance and in situ;
- when self-report data (asking people what they do) was likely to be different from actual behaviour (what people actually do), for example, difference between self-reported and observed garbage recycling on Vis.

Non-participant Observation

After field notes, the non-participant observation mode of data collection dominated throughout this study. As implied, this allowed for observation with limited interaction with the island's people and tourists observed. For example, observational data was best collected unobtrusively by recording day/time of the affluent outflow in the harbour as indicators of pollution in the Vis harbour or observing when/how garbage was collected and what happened to it at the garbage depot. This data collection approach resulted in detailed recording of the actual events over a time period and provided the researchers with a track record and a cross-check of actions versus what's been said by participants.

Field Notes

In research, field notes have a long tradition in descriptive sciences such as ethnography, biology, geology and archaeology (Canfield, 2011). While participant observation approach in this study used multiple methods to gather data, the primary method in this study, as noted, involved writing field notes. Field notes are qualitative notes recorded by researchers during or after their observation of a specific phenomenon they are studying. These were intended to be read as evidence that gave meaning and understanding of the tourism development and impact of Vis over a long period of time. Field notes have allowed the researchers to access the subjects and record what they have observed in an unobtrusive manner and when gathering sensitive information.

There is, however, a shortcoming of taking field notes, and that is that they are made by an observer and can therefore be prone to the conscious or unconscious bias of the observer (Emerson, Fretz, & Shaw, 1995). Despite this however, field notes in this study were particularly valued. Two types of notations were usually recorded: descriptive information and reflective information. Descriptive information was factual data, such as time and date, the state of the infrastructure, social environment, descriptions of the subjects being studied and their roles in the Vis community and examining official documents. Reflective information were the observers' reflections about how this study is being conducted on Vis and/or the stages of. These reflections included ideas, questions, concerns and other related thoughts, as well as sketches, diagrams and other drawings. Visually capturing a happening or a task, for example, refuse collection, required the observers to pay more attention to every detail as to not overlook anything.

SELECT FINDINGS, DISCUSSION AND RECOMMENDATIONS

Over the course of this longitudinal study, considerable data has been acquired by way of field notes, subject interviews, non-participant interviews and analysis of official tourist data. Careful attention has been paid to systematically examine and categorise the data into the following Vis' tourism-related issues and vulnerabilities that were observed and investigated which are presented in Table 12.2.

While it is beyond the scope of this article to fully address each one of these issues in detail, the following issues, such as nautical tourism, sewage infrastructure, garbage collection and culture and heritage, will be discussed next.

Nautical Tourism

As shown in Table 12.3, the growth in nautical tourism has been exponential for Vis, no doubt causing tremendous pressure on marine ecology around the island and in its two key harbours. Critically however, to date regulations which prevent pumping out of ship's holding tanks into the sea is neither enforced nor robust enough in Croatia, as is in other nautical tourism countries. In any case, even if the conscientious skipper did not pump out to sea, there are no facilities on Vis to pump out the heads holding tank. As a consequence one can safely estimate that 95 per cent of the visiting yachts, or 8892 yachts, had pumped out their heads directly into the sea around Vis, and at an average of 40 litres per tank, that amounts to 355,680 litres of raw sewage per season. This is a conservative field calculation because the researcher did not take into account large yachts and small coastal cruise ships that also frequent the island.

Table 12.2   Vis' tourism-related issues and vulnerabilities

Environmental issues
   Noticeable disregard for the environment at general public and municipal government
   level
   Profound lack of awareness and support for sustainability and sustainable tourism
   growth/development (at municipal and local tourism authority level)
   Waste management—open and unlined garbage dumps/landfills, lack of recycling due
   to lack of awareness and/or lack of government/county support; ageing sewage
   system allowing untreated affluent into local waters and Vis harbour; unregulated and
   uncontrolled pumping of waste from yachts into local waters and Vis harbour; poor
   waste collection outside the main towns and beaches
   Water—water shortages and water over-usage during the season (Vis has its own water
   supply)
   Overfishing, illegal fishing and lack of water ecology strategies at local level
   Energy—little if any renewable energy usage, no support for alternative energy
   investment
   Erosion—for example, trail erosion, removal causing erosion
   Noise pollution
   Crumbling infrastructure
   Crowding—pressure of tourist traffic in main towns
Social/cultural issues
   Vis' unique island culture and heritage is becoming spoiled and diluted
   Marketing—lack of a unified brand to promote the island, marketing cooperation
   issues
   Competition with other islands/island insularity
   Quality standards—not all businesses/attractions have similar levels of service quality
   Branding—lack of promotion of the island as a brand instead focus is fragmented
   Lack of vision for the island's future of sustainable tourism (by the local tourism
   office)
   Unregulated and uncodified construction of houses
Economic issues
   Leakage—almost all of the income from harbour—fees and tourism taxes leaving the
   island—to central and county governments
   Seasonality—relatively short tourist season hence the mentality of "get as much as you
   can in the shortest time possible"
   Inflation—rise in house prices/goods due to holiday home/tourist presence
   Infrastructure upkeep—roads, sewage system, overall building maintenance
   Day tripper and yachting market—lack of seasonal contribution to island and potential
   high environmental impact
   Employment—seasonal and/or part time employment
   Depopulation—younger population moving off the island in search of work, ageing
   population
   Education—lack of awareness of environmental/social issues in the community
   Lack of cooperation between key authority—city offices, tourism authorities, harbour
   authorities, chambers of commerce

Table 12.3   Indicators of nautical tourism growth

Indicators	2014	1988	1981
Number of permanent residents[a]	3,460[a]	3,729[a]	4,134[a]
Population density	33.7	37.0	41.0
Total number of tourists	36,698[b]	27,499[b]	10,733
Total number of domestic tourists	10,401	27,470	10,721
Total number of foreign tourists	26,297	29	12
Total number of nights	216,115[b]	166,923	50,222
Total number of nights including private not-registered accommodation	312,000		
Total number of nights—domestic	56,629	166,778	50,128
Total number of nights—foreign	159,486	145	94
Total accommodation capacity	4,758[c]	1,391[c]	449[c]
Percentage of private accommodation capacity	65%	23%	21%
Number of tourists per inhabitant	10.6[b]	7.4	2.6
With day trippers and yacht crews in 2014 (54,198)	15.7		
Number of tourists per square kilometre (90.26 square kilometres)Including day trippers and yacht crews in 2014	406.7600.5	285.7	111.5
Nautical tourism: number of yachts berthed overnight at Vis and Komiža harbour for the entire season	9,360	420	27

a) Number of permanent residents in 2014 refers to census data from 2011 and in 1988 to census data from 1991. The census records from the year 1991 and 1981 include approximately 15 per cent residents living in other parts of Croatia or overseas, but registered as island's permanent residents
b) Excludes day trippers and yacht crews which in 2014 was just over 17,500 visitors
c) Includes private accomodation
Source: Dragičević et al. (1991) and Kivela (2004–2015)

This state of affairs has been going for quite some time, and without a doubt, this is an ecological disaster in the making, and it is only a matter of time before we see Vis' marine environment, and that of other islands, collapse. Incredibly but not surprisingly, both county and national tourism and environmental safety officials had turned a blind eye to this, concentrating on the income that the growing nautical tourism brings to the country.

What is the solution? One solution is to adopt best practices from countries such as Australia, Canada and New Zealand. First, legislation needs to be robust and practicable. For example, all pleasure and cruise craft in Croatia's Adriatic waters must have its direct-to-sea-holding tank vents sealed by the marine authorities until such time as the seal is opened by the sanitary officer who pumps out the holding tank at port, in an environmentally appropriate manner. These pumping out stations should be in every popular port along the coast. And, in instances of breaching this regulation, for example, the seal is opened before the tank is being officially pumped out, heavy on-the-spot fines including confiscation of the vessel should be imposed on offenders. Despite the latest annual bathing water report for 2014 giving Croatia's 917 beaches an excellent report for sea water quality and clearness, the dumping of yachts' black water is widespread along the coast (Croatia Week, 2016). What would be interesting to know is when these tests were done; in winter or at the peak of the summer season? The people of concern have been rather shy when broached with this question, including when asked about tests, if any, done of seafloor sedimentation.

Sewerage Infrastructure

The island's sewage infrastructure is now 53 years old. Conservatively, in the period between 1981 and 2014, the number of tourists has grown five-fold, and yet no major improvements had been carried out on the Vis town sewage system since 1963. Over the years, rough and ready patch-up work is done when the system collapses, usually in the season. For instance, in the 2014 season, when an ageing pump failed, thousands of litres of raw sewage was dumped in Vis harbour daily. Incredibly, sections of the system are connected to storm water drains, sending raw sewage directly into Vis harbour and nearby beaches on day-to-day basis: One wonders where the bathing water quality scientists were! As is, all of the Vis' sewage is pumped out to sea some distance from the main two townships. According to one insider who works for the island's sewage and water firm, "the whole system needs to be re-built with proper treatment facilities, but I'm not holding my breath because neither the company nor the county are interested. One day, the system will collapse to such an extent that it won't be fixable." Here again is an example of official/political myopia who only seem to be interested in tourism income. What is the solution? It seems that in absence of official and political will to totally upgrade and rebuild the island's sewage system, there is no foreseeable solution.

Garbage Collection

Like its sewage counterpart, the island's garbage collection and treatment system is straining even out of season. Although garbage collection is efficient, it isn't very effective. For example, while there are on-the-street provisions for separation and recycling, all the refuse ends up in the same truck and in the same dump. Figure 12.2 shows Komiža's open garbage dump, just under one of the most scenic and pristine (used to be) areas of the island. This dump is not lined nor is it effectively regulated as to what goes in it. Over the years, old batteries, engine oil, metals, paint and other nasties have been deposited here. The Vis town garbage dump is the same.

The island's average resident's daily garbage production is about 1.5 kg for organics and 560 g for non-organics, or about seven tonnes per day.

Fig. 12.2 Komiža's open garbage dump (Author: Jakša Kivela)

During the tourist season, this figure quadruples to over 28 tonnes of untreated garbage per day. Over the years both Vis and Komiža municipalities have been at loggerheads about the issue, with little if any progress, although, in 2015 there was a veiled announcement by the Vis municipality that "something was going to be done about the town's garbage dump." One councillor even suggested that a mini thermo-electric station was going to be built at the site to convert burned garbage into steam and electricity. What is the solution? Again, in absence of county/state will and financial support, it seems that, as in the case of sewage, there is no foreseeable solution for this ecological problem.

Culture and Heritage

Vis' unique island culture and its unique heritage is also becoming diluted, and nowhere is this more noticeable than in the island's demise of its folkloric *Klapa* songs. A Klapa song is a form of traditional male singing in Croatia's Dalmatia region. Uniquely on Vis, it is sung unaccompanied and exclusively in the Vis and Komiža dialect. The word Klapa means "a group of male friends" in English and traces its roots to coastal and island church singing of long ago (Ćaleta, 1997), (Fortunato, 1997), although there are now female Klapa groups throughout Dalmatia.

These ballads of old and new celebrate traditions, people's livelihood, love, tragedies, the homeland and, of course, the sea and fishermen. The main elements of the music and unaccompanied singing are anchored in harmony and melody, and in 2012 Klapa and Klapa music was inscribed in UNESCO Intangible Cultural Heritage of Humanity. Sadly, during the tourist season on Vis, jazz, rock and modern disco beat have now all but replaced these traditional Klapa groups. Author's recollection throughout the 1960s and 1970s is that there were at least four to five regular Klapa groups in Komiža and Vis towns. One author's father and brothers were all part of a Klapa group. As of 2014 there were only two Klapa groups left on Vis performing on irregular basis. When asked to comment about Klapa's demise, this is what one of the local poets had to say about Vis' tourism: "Tourism is a phenomenon on Vis that was once strongly linked to the attractiveness of our culture and heritage, however, as tourism increased, especially as mass tourism evolved, it now threatens Vis' identity and culture, and our uniqueness will disappear, if it already hasn't already." While another resident from Komiža town said, "we used culture and heritage like souvenirs, which is just appalling. People on Vis are still attached to their culture and traditions, but tourism is disrupting this; the diversity of local culture and heritage is being homogenized. So, we now offer a standardised 'Dalmatian or Mediterranean package' to foreigners, which has nothing to do with Vis."

Lack of money and support have gutted what was once the essence of Vis' cultural heritage. One can safely argue that of all the cultural and heritage travesties on Vis, the demise of Klapa groups has been one of the most destructive because, with it, it also swept away a unique island-dialect language and therefore a rich cultural storytelling tool for the next generations: So much for the UNESCO's Intangible Cultural Heritage of Humanity! There is little doubt that successive waves of tourism growth, notably in international arrivals, have had a very devastating impact on Vis' Klapa heritage which is irreplaceable.

CONCLUSION

This article provides a succinct snapshot of the many challenges facing Vis. Granted, Vis has in the past broached many challenges; no doubt, it has yet to reconcile its destiny with tourism, even though these challenges are not for the faint of heart. Of course, the difficulty with all of these issues is that tourism does have positive qualities too. For instance, as a direct result of tourism, some of the people, but not all, on Vis have become richer, and the economic standard of living has increased overall, and many say that they are satisfied with the way tourism has developed anyway. On the other hand, the very same people lament that Vis' youth is distancing itself from its culture and heritage which is often perceived as too traditional and overbearing. Faced with the fact that tourists on Vis are now testing the limits of the island's infrastructure, environment and cultural heritage, hard decisions at county, state and local levels need to be made to put in place solutions to safeguard the island's uniqueness, which is why tourists come to it in the first place.

Alas, when it comes to tourism, it's not in the beast's (government) nature to make hard long-term decisions except how to squeeze more money from tourism. Of course, this will not help Vis' tourism sustainability in the long term. Even if compliant government and quasi-government organisations and tourism businesses do what is required by the regulations and/or from pressure by key stakeholders, tourists, this does not mean that they will go beyond the compliance to adopt sustainability that can be directly linked to how Vis' environmental and cultural heritage can be protected for generations to come. Such strategic sustainability would be a logical extension of eco-efficiency and cultural husbandry which would mean that such strategy can be used as a competitive strategy and one linked with quality tourism. In the long term however, this approach is not enough. The hard decisions for Croatia's tourism, including Vis, need to be fundamentally different to the previous approaches in that the primary goal is a clear and significant contribution to the well-being of its tourism areas, including Vis, and in the quality of life for people in these areas. Simply put, tourism activities and tourism businesses would need to examine not just the short-term impacts of tourism but redress negative tourism impacts throughout the entire lifecycle of tourism, consider the social value of tourism to the communities, decentralise tourism policy to local level, keep tourism income within local community and actively work at safeguarding and improving sustainability beyond the immediate future. To conclude, this study demonstrates that there needs to be a change the way government, county and Vis community think about tourism and sustainability. Importantly, this study highlights only too well that Vis' and county tourism planners, managers and businesses need to become sustaining rather than just being sustainable, if barely.

REFERENCES

Anderson, J. R, Hardy, E. E., Roach, J. T., & Witmer, R. E. (1976). *A land use and land cover classification for use with remote sensor data.* U.S. Geological Survey Professional Paper 964.

Atkinson, P., & Hammersley, M. (1994). Ethnography and participant observation. In N. K. Denzin & Y. S. Lincoln (Eds.), *Handbook of qualitative research* (pp. 248–261). Thousand Oaks, CA: Sage Publications.

Bernard, H. R. (1988). *Research methods in cultural anthropology.* Newbury Park, CA: Sage Publications.

Buckley, R. (1999). An ecological perspective on carrying capacity. *Annals of Tourism Research, 26*(4), 705–708.

Butler, R. W. (1980). The concept of the tourist area life-cycle of evolution: Implications for management of resources. *Canadian Geographer, 24*(1), 5–12.

Ćaleta, J. (1997). Klapa singing, a traditional folk phenomenon of Dalmatia. *Narodna umjetnost Croatian Journal of Ethnology and Folklore Research* . Zagreb. Institute of Ethnology and Folklore Research,, *34*(1), 127–145.

Canfield, M. R. (2011). *Field notes on science & nature.* Cambridge, MA: Harvard University Press.

Chamberlain, K. (1997). *Carrying capacity, UNEP industry and environment*, 8. Paris: UNEP.

Coccossis, H., & Mexa, A. (2004). Tourism carrying capacity: Future issues and policy considerations. In H. Coccossis & A. Mexa (Eds.), *The challenge of tourism carrying capacity assessment. Theory and practice* (pp. 277–288). Aldershot, UK: Ashgate Publishing Limited.

Croatia Week Online Magazine. (2016). *Croatian Beach Tops Europe's Most Beautiful for 2016.* http://www.croatiaweek.com/croatian-beach-tops-europes-most-beautiful-for-2016/. Data accessed 10th January 2016.

Doxey, G. (1975). A causation theory of visitor-resident irritants: Methodology and research inferences. *Proceedings of the 6th Annual Conference of the Travel and Tourism Research Association* (pp. 195–198).

Dragičević, M., Kušen, E., & Klarić, Z. (1991). *Ocjena kapaciteta podnošljivost turističkog razvoja otoka Visa: Program prioritetnih akcija* [Carrying capacity assessment for tourism activities on the island of Vis: Priority actions]. Zagreb – Split: Centar za regionalne aktivnosti.

Emerson, R. M., Fretz, R. I., & Shaw, L. L. (1995). *Writing ethnographic fieldnotes.* Chicago: University of Chicago Press.

Fetterman, D. M. (1998). *Ethnography step by step* (2nd ed.). Thousand Oaks, CA: Sage Publications.

Fortunato, A. R. (1997). *Libar Viškiga Jazika* [The book of Vis language]. Toronto, Canada: Libar Publishing.

Hrvatska enciklopedija [Croatian encyclopedia]. (2013a). *Vis (otok) [Vis (island)].* Zagreb: Leksikografski zavod Miroslav Krleža.

Hrvatska enciklopedija [Croatian encyclopedia]. (2013b). *Grčka kolonizacija na Jadranu* [Greek colonization on the Adriatic]. Zagreb, Croatia: Leksikografski zavod Miroslav Krleža.

Kivela. J. (2004–2015). Field notes on Splitsko-Dalmatinska County, municipality of Vis and Komiža, tourism data figures.

McCool, S. F., Stankey, G. H., & Clark, R. N. (2007). *An assessment of frameworks useful for public land recreation planning.* General Technical Report GTR-705. Portland, OR: Pacific Northwest Research Station.

McCool, S. F., & Lime, D. W. (2001). Tourism carrying capacity: Tempting fantasy or useful reality? *Journal of Sustainable Tourism, 9*(5), 372–388.

Middleton, V. C., & Hawkins, R. (1998). *Sustainable tourism: A marketing perspective.* Oxford, UK: Butterworth-Heinemann.

Statistical Yearbook of the Republic of Croatia. (2015). 47 Year, December 2015, Croatian Bureau of Statistics, Zagreb

UNWTO. (1981). *Saturation of tourist destinations.* Report of the Secretary General. Madrid, Spain: UNWTO.

Washburne, R. F. (1982). Wilderness recreation carrying capacity: Are numbers necessary? *Journal of Forestry, 80,* 726–728.

CHAPTER 13

Gastronomy Tourism: Croatia, a Land of Wine and Plenty, or Beyond Pizza and Grill!

Jakša Kivela

INTRODUCTION

The relationship between gastronomy and tourism is affirmed in select social sciences literature, but only a few studies are reported in the hospitality literature that specifically addresses gastronomy and tourism relationship. This exploratory study intends to bridge this gap by focusing on gastronomy's influence how tourists experience a destination (Wolf, 2006).

GASTRONOMY AND TOURISM

It was Long (2002) who first coined the term 'Culinary Tourism' in 1998 to express the idea of experiencing other cultures through food. Wolf (2006, p. 20), however, defines culinaria and gastronomy tourism as 'travel in order to search for, and enjoy prepared food and drink....and unique and memorable gastronomic experiences'. This supports earlier research (Finkelstein, 1989) which suggests that feelings and memories make dining out when on holiday, very special and attractive, because

___

J. Kivela (✉)
Institute for Tourism, Zagreb, Croatia

© The Author(s) 2017
L. Dwyer et al. (eds.), *Evolution of Destination Planning and Strategy*, DOI 10.1007/978-3-319-42246-6_13

these become transposed into experiences that are often very personal. Importantly, these experiences also have the power to modify our eating preferences and tastes as well as imbue us with experiences of the culture that we are visiting (Chang, Kivela, & Mak, 2010, 2011; Johns & Clarke, 2001; Johns & Kivela, 2001; Kivela & Crotts, 2009; Kivela & Johns, 2002). In this context, one of the functions of the destination's food service industries is the provision of those experiences and feelings that individuals believe they should be having while on holiday or while travelling. It is normal that we should experience pleasure as an essential part of a holiday experience, and dining out should be a pleasurable and memorable part of that experience. So much in fact, that culinaria and gastronomy play a pivotal role in the marketing of some tourist destinations. For example, some travel organizations (Travel, 2015) regularly offer gourmet or culinary holidays to Asia, Italy and France and holidays with cooking classes in Tuscany and Provence; Melbourne and Sydney in Australia are often marketed as the food and wine and restaurant destinations. (The Australian Tourist Commission—ATC—was one of the first destination marketing organizations to make a commitment to culinary tourism.) For tourists, this means that the destination's restaurants' ambience and cuisine are legitimate sources of pleasure which generates emotions and experiences, hopefully pleasant ones, that they are supposed to be having while on holiday (Kivela & Chu, 2001; Kivela & Crotts, 2009). However, while tourists often dine out in search of new taste and culinary experiences, they also encounter disappointment from time to time: an eatery that is a parody of the destination's image or what Finkelstein (1989) calls the 'manufactured images'. Nevertheless, an increasing number of tourist destinations are very sought-after because of their unique culinaria and gastronomy (Hjalager, 2002). Lifestyle and travel media also vigorously promote gastronomy, for example, magazines such as the *Epicure* and *Gourmet*. In search of new recipes and taste sensations, both food critics and celebrity chefs scour the world for new and different gastronomy, rediscovering old, long-forgotten recipes and discovering new ingredients and new culinary destinations. Therefore, it is appropriate to say that the relationship between gastronomy and a tourist destination is symbiotic because the destination provides the food, recipes, chefs and the cultural backdrop that makes gastronomy an ideal product for tourist consumption (Chang et al., 2010, 2011; Fields, 2002; Richards, 2002; Scarpato, 2002). Simply stated, gastronomy is an inextricable part the holiday experience.

Hjalager (2003) offers phenomenological model of culinary tourism experiences. The model of tourism and gastronomy lifestyles depicts tourist attitudes and preferences for food and eating according to four categorizations—*recreational, existential, diversionary* and *experimental* gastronomy tourists. The *existential* gastronomy tourists seek food combinations and eating experiences that foster (culinary) learning. For these tourists food consumption and drinking do not only satisfy hunger and thirst, importantly for them, such consumption means gaining in-depth knowledge about the local or regional cuisine and of the destination's culture. For these tourists, the holiday's success is measured by that special restaurant 'where only the locals eat'. The *existential* gastronomy tourist will actively seek and visit working farms and participate in cooking classes and harvesting of fruits, vegetables and wines; they will visit cheese and wine makers and go fishing with professional fishermen.

The *experimental* gastronomy tourists symbolize their lifestyle through food—usually trendy and 'in' foods. These tourists will actively seek the destination's smartest designer cafes and restaurants that serve innovative menus and offer equally chic service. The *experimental* gastronomy tourists keep up-to-date about trendy and fashionable foods, ingredients and recipes. They actively pursue trying out new ingredients and new ways of eating and preparing food. Yesterday's food trends are quickly replaced by today's food fashions. For the *experimental* quality and fashionability value of food is a major consideration—being part of their overall lifestyle.

The *recreationalist* gastronomy tourists are the more conservative type, that is, they appreciate and actively seek, while holidays, the familiarity of their home cuisine. The *recreationalist* gastronomy tourists actively engage in self-catering while on holidays. They also prefer to stay in self-contained accommodation such as holiday apartments if available. Often, they bring ingredients with them so that they will not have to do without. Dining ambiance and service style have little impact on *recreationalists*. They also do not like foreign foods, except those foods that have long become part of their everyday life.

The *diversionary* gastronomy tourists are the kinds of tourists that want to escape from the everyday life—mundanity (Finkelstein, 1989)—that includes day-to-day shopping and cooking for the family. For these tourists, while on holiday, food must come easily, without too much effort, and there must be plenty of it, for example, popular and chain restaurant operations. They prefer and actively seek menu items that are familiar. For the *diversionaries* quantity, not quality, of food is essential, for example, large meat joints, jumbo-sized desserts and big plates of pasta are taken into consideration rather than haute cuisine. The *diversionary* gastronomy tourists have a dislike for exotic foods.

METHODOLOGY

A descriptive research design was adopted that utilized quantitative techniques for data collection and analysis involving the use of a survey questionnaire. A survey sample should normally represent the population, particularly when a random sampling method is used. In this instance, however, it was not prudent to apply a random sampling methodology to disparate tourist subjects. The alternative strategy was to employ a systematic approach in selecting the subjects, and the subjects' age and gender were selected by a judgmental method. The sample size was set at 3600 (400 per summer per each island each year). The survey was conducted with the assistance and cooperation of selected restaurants at these main towns on Vis (towns of Vis and Komiža), Hvar (towns of Hvar and Stari Grad) and Korčula (town of Korčula). Based on the researcher's prior experience, the proposed sampling design minimized undue inconvenience to other guests and the participating organizations. The survey was conducted at the participating restaurant properties. The survey was randomly administered once per day from 7:00 pm to 9:00 pm, two times per week on a continual basis over the three-month period. The reliability analysis was calculated to measure the internal consistency of each of the research instrument's main item banks. The coefficients for all item banks exceeded the recommended level of 0.50 (Hair, Anderson, & Black, 1995), ranging from 0.84 to 0.95.

In analysing the data, descriptive statistics were used to examine variables of interest, including Chi-square ($x^{\wedge 2}$). In order to compare samples across perceptual and experience dimensions or demographic grouping, appropriate comparative analyses such as ANOVA were used. Multivariate analysis (factor and regression) was also used. Only the findings of the select regression analysis are presented in this article.

RESULTS AND DISCUSSION

A select example of demographic characteristics of the sample is presented in Table 13.1.

Of particular interest is that almost 30 per cent of the sample indicated that their main reason for travelling to these islands was to taste the local

Table 13.1 The demographic characteristics of the sample

Main purpose for visiting Hvar or Vis or Korčula	Frequency	Per cent
Holiday/pleasure	2050	59
Business/meeting	139	4.0
Visiting friends or relatives	244	7.0
Stop-over	35	1.0
Because of the island's authentic food	1007	29.0
Total	3475	100.0

cuisine. In real terms, one could argue that about 700,000 to 1.5 million tourists might be coming to Croatia to savour its gastronomy as well. These numbers are not inconsequential, and a 'culinary or gastronomy' tourism segment representing 10–12 per cent of the total visitor market is, by any measure, a significant market segment. For Croatia, this represents a substantial gastronomy tourism market segment possibility, and evidence suggests that motivation to travel for gastronomy reasons is a reasonably valid construct to use for tourism market segmentation purposes in Croatia. Croatia's tourism authority promotes Croatia as a great tourist destination vis-à-vis its tourist information offices in Croatia and abroad, and although it mentions Croatia's authentic foods, it does not specifically market Croatia's gastronomy to the international gastronomy tourism market segment, as is done, for example, by the Regional Tourism Authority in Tuscany or by the New Zealand's tourism board.

Factor Analysis

The Principal Components and Orthogonal (varimax) rotation method was used for the analysis. A variable was considered of practical significance and included in a factor when its factor loading was equal to or greater than 0.5 (Norušis, 1994, 2000), with a Bartlett Test of Sphericity value of 5922.133. The Kaiser-Meyer-Olkin overall measure of sampling adequacy (MSA) was 0.872. From the Orthogonal (varimax) rotated factor matrix, seven factors with 21 variables were defined by the original variables that loaded most heavily (loading $\geq$ 0.5) on them. The factor analysis produced a clean factor structure with relatively higher loadings on the appropriate factors with most variables loaded heavily on the first five factors but not on the sixth and seventh. The seven-factor solution resulted in 67.9 per cent of the variance explained. The communality of each variable was relatively high, ranging from 0.39 to 0.81. A six-factor solution resulted in the following factor labels:

- Factor 1: Expectations of gastronomy
- Factor 2: Importance of gastronomy
- Factor 3: Gastronomy experiences at destination
- Factor 4: Gastronomy as reason for travel
- Factor 5: Evaluation of gastronomy experiences at destination
- Factor 6: Culture and gastronomy

Regression Analysis

The regression analysis showed that all predictors except (F#2) 'Importance of gastronomy', (F#4) 'Gastronomy as reason for travel' and (F#6) 'Culture and gastronomy' were included in the model for the prediction. The sample's gastronomy-tourist group 'Expectations of gastronomy' with Beta = 0.871 accounted for a very high 87 per cent of the variance explained, and together with (F#3) 'Gastronomy experiences at destination' with Beta = 0.041, and (F#5) 'Evaluation of gastronomy experiences at destination' with Beta = 0.043, was found to be the most important predictor groups which would consider returning to Croatia's islands to sample their gastronomy sometime in the future.

Both the literature and evidence from this study suggest that when travellers' expectations were met and/or were exceeded, they were likely to return to the destination sometime in the future. Importantly in this study, it appears that this also applies to gastronomy tourists and arguably that the 'existential' and 'experimental' gastronomy tourists, who are knowledgeable in gastronomy, are the most likely groups who would return to the same destination because of its unique gastronomy, providing they had satisfying gastronomy experiences (Evaluation of gastronomy experiences at destination). These results provide evidence suggesting that as a result of favourable experiences, repeat visits to a destination because of its unique gastronomy is a reasonably valid construct to use for destination marketing purposes. The results from this study clearly indicate that Croatia's gastronomy was a significant factor that positively contributed to the respondents' desire to return to Croatia again. Hence, it is argued here that Croatia's gastronomy plays a contributing role in the creation of a high-quality travelling experience and return behaviour. In addition, the analysis of the findings also reveals that Croatia's gastronomy might be increasingly converging as a significant element in a range of touristic experiences. That is, gastronomy is increasingly vital to a whole range of tourism products and services that are offered in Croatia.

CONCLUDING REMARKS

The study described here finds that gastronomy is inextricably linked to the destination and the destination's image, in multi-dimensional forms, some of which are not yet clearly understood. From this study it can also be hypothesized that gastronomy and culinary experiences are powerful tools for marketing Croatia's uniqueness.

While the study confirms that Croatia's gastronomy is an integral part of the visitor's experience, Croatia's tourism marketing has not really focused on integrated strategies to develop, refine and capitalize on interest in gastronomy, and yet there is evidence which shows that various tourism authorities use gastronomy to create niche markets for their destinations, for example, Italy, France, Australia, Spain and New Zealand. Croatia's tourism marketing promotes its gastronomy in a peace-meal and uncoordinated manner as an adjunct to its overall tourism promotions, and yet, gastronomy promotions for the local consumption abound. That is, Croatia's tourism authorities do not have a clearly defined strategy to market, and defend, Croatia's unique and authentic gastronomy. There are several notable destinations that demonstrate such leadership in the gastronomy tourism niche. Noteworthy examples include Sydney and Melbourne, Australia; Western Australia; Singapore; Taiwan; Macau; New Orleans; New Zealand; Spain; and Greece. Space precludes discussing them here (for further reading, see Hjalager, A.M. (2003). What do tourists eat and why? Towards a sociology of gastronomy and tourism, in, J. Collen, and G. Richards, (red.). *Gastronomy and Tourism. ATLAS – expert meeting. Sandrio (Italy) 21–23 November 2002.* Academie Voor de Streekgebonden Gastronomie, Belgium).

SOME PRACTICAL SUGGESTIONS FOR CROATIA'S TOURISM PLANNERS

The literature suggests that destinations with best chances for developing gastronomy tourism products are those destinations that already have the advantageous 'ingredients' to support a gastronomy tourism strategy. Such resources include unique and/or multi-ethnic cuisine, creative chefs, unique marine and agricultural products, unique culinary heritage and so on. No doubt, Croatia is endowed with all of these 'ingredients' and more. Although gastronomy tourism is the primary tourism product in only a handful of destinations, a gastronomy destination like Croatia if serious about refining and niching its gastronomy tourism products, it should first perform an asset inventory. The inventory is then sorted according to type (cuisine type, culinary regions of significance with authentic and unique foods, authentic restaurants, growers and suppliers, markets and such). How many resources exist in each category? Then an informal ranking should be performed, for example, what is the quality of each resource on a scale of 1 to 5. Next, it should list what are Croatia's unique gastronomy assets? Does Croatia produce/prepare a unique food items? What are Croatia's gastronomy strengths/weaknesses? Should Croatia ban pizza from traditional-cuisine areas? Should Croatia trademark its indigenous foods/recipes like Tuscany does? That is, what exists in Croatia's gastronomy market that could be an opportunity of threat? And, what kinds of partnerships could Croatia forge to take gastronomy tourism product development to a marketable level, outside Croatia?

As the regional gastronomy tourism niche market intensifies, and as more professionals begin to understand its role within their tourism industry, we will see more gastronomy tours; more food-oriented travel guidebooks; more focus on travel in epicure magazines; and more itineraries that celebrate food/drink as an integral part of the travel experience. In the Croatian context and assuming that gastronomy tourism growth is to continue, business owners and the destination's marketers will have to consider innovative and synergetic opportunities for strategic partnerships. The matrix shown in Table 13.2 gives an idea of the types of gastronomy tourism alliances or business relationships that are likely to be successful in Croatia. As implied by the matrix, gastronomy tourism is a complexly interesting and potentially a very unique product to add to Croatia's destination product mix, if only because as all other tourists, gastronomy tourists leave their money within the local business economy before they return home. Importantly in the Croatian context, gastronomy tourism if strategically marketed as a unique product niche, it would greatly help in overcoming the Croatia's stereotype identity as the 'sun & sand' paradise. It would also provide additional opportunities for local businesses that are in some way connected to tourism. On a more positive note, regional competition and the synergy of complementary products help to raise the overall quality of the visitor's experience and the products

Table 13.2 Croatia's gastronomy tourism—Alliance/relationship matrix

	Indigenous island cuisines	Indigenous Dalmatian cuisine	Indigenous Zagorje cuisine	Indigenous Slavonian cuisine	Indigenous Istrian cuisine	Indigenous Primorje cuisine	Western-European restaurants	Hotels	Home stay	Country/Efarm/agro-tourism	Local markets	Retail/mar-food and wine shops	Food festivals and events	Indigenous cultural and food festivals	Heritage/cultural/tours	Farms/fishing villages	Indigenous retail food shops	Boutique wine and food shops	Destination's Tourist Authority	Media—lifestyle and epicure	Museums, cultural/historic sites
Indigenous island cuisines											★		★	★	★	★	★		★	★	★
Indigenous Dalmatian cuisine										★	★		★	★	★	★	★		★	★	★
Indigenous Zagorje cuisine										★	★		★	★	★	★	★	★	★	★	
Indigenous Slavonian cuisine										★	★		★	★	★	★	★		★	★	★
Indigenous Istrian cuisine										★	★	★	★	★	★	★		★	★	★	★
Indigenous Primorje cuisine														★			★				
Hotels	★	★★	★★	★★	★★		★★		★	★★	★★	★★	★★		★★	★★		★★	★★	★★	
Home stay	★	★★	★★	★★	★★		★★	★		★★	★★	★★	★★		★★	★★		★★	★★	★★	

(continued)

Table 13.2 (continued)

	Indigenous island cuisines	Indigenous Dalmatian cuisine	Indigenous Zagorje cuisine	Indigenous Slavonian cuisine	Indigenous Istrian cuisine	Indigenous morje cuisine	Western-European cuisine	Western restaurants	Hotels	Homestay	Country/farm/Efarm/agro-tourism	Local markets	Retail food and wine shops	Food festivals and events	Indigenous cultural food festivals	Heritage/cultural tours	Farms/fishing villages	Indigenous retail food shops	Boutique wine and food shops	Destination's Tourist Authority	Media—lifestyle and epicure	Museums, cultural/historic sites
Country/farm/agro-tourism	★	★	★	★	★	★	★	★	★	★	★	★		★	★	★	★	★	★	★	★	
Local markets	★	★	★	★	★	★	★	★			★	★		★	★	★	★	★	★	★	★	
Retail food and wine shops	★	★			★		★	★	★	★	★	★	★	★		★		★	★	★	★	
Food festivals and events	★	★	★	★	★	★	★	★	★	★	★	★	★	★	★	★	★	★	★	★	★	★
Indigenous cultural/food festivals	★	★	★		★	★	★					★		★	★	★	★	★	★	★	★	★
Heritage/cultural tours	★	★	★	★	★	★					★	★		★	★	★		★	★	★	★	★
Farms/fishing villages	★	★	★	★	★	★	★	★			★	★		★	★	★		★	★	★	★	★
Indigenous retail food shops	★	★	★	★	★	★	★					★		★	★	★	★			★	★	★

Boutique wine and food shops		★	★	★	★	★	★	★	★	★	★	★	★	★	★	
Destination's Tourist Authority	★	★	★	★	★	★	★	★	★	★	★	★	★	★	★	★
Media—lifestyle and epicure	★	★	★	★	★	★	★	★	★	★	★	★	★	★	★	
Museums, cultural/historic sites	★	★	★	★	★			★	★	★	★	★	★	★	★	

offered in all destinations. However, in developing gastronomy tourism niche for tourists visiting Croatia, it is not enough to simply offer a gastronomy experience; gastronomy tourism is also about making the tourist feel good as a result of their visit to Croatia. Making tourists feel good about being in Croatia is highly desirable, but it is even more desirable to make the tourists feel good about themselves. This is an important, and appealing, emotional dimension of gastronomy. To achieve this, however, requires an effort on the part of the destination's tourism planners and gastronomy providers to educate tourists about why the local cuisine and its associated culture are ubiquitous to the region they're in. If we are to consider the destination's gastronomy as a pleasurable experience, the pre-and-post elements of that experience gain added significance. This is because tourists appear to evaluate their holiday experiences against often-vague holiday ideas influenced by general motivators in the pre-holiday phase and re-assessed in the post-holiday phase. From the analysis of the results of this study, it can be said with confidence that respondents' satisfaction with gastronomy in Croatia was dependent on the image they had of the destination's gastronomy before visiting, compared with the actual experience of gastronomy that they had experienced. This before-after relationship is important when developing strategies for gastronomy tourism in Croatia because its gastronomy is much more likely to be mentioned by repeat visitors than by first-time visitors. Hence, since tourists' level of knowledge of the local gastronomy prior to consumption is likely to be less than their post-visit knowledge, this knowledge-gap knowledge must also be addressed when marketing gastronomy tourism.

In summary, it can be said that the impression of gastronomy present in the respondents' perceptions of their dining-out experiences offers a rich and an alternative perspective from which to understand the experiences of holiday-makers. The precepts investigated can also provide a rational framework for a future study about tourists' perceptions of various gastronomy products in Croatia and in other destinations. For Croatia's tourism planners, the emotive nature of gastronomy offers considerable potential in terms of the niche marketing. Offering experiences that dovetail with the motivations of individual tourists can ensure that gastronomy tourism in Croatia becomes even more popular in the future. Finally, the analysis of respondents' perceptions about their dining-out experiences in this study has underpinned the structuring of the hypothesis for a more in-depth investigation sometime in the future, that gastronomy plays an increasingly deciding role in the way tourists select a destination.

REFERENCES

Chang, C. Y. R., Kivela, J., & Mak, H. N. A. (2010). Food preferences of Chinese tourists. *Annals of Tourism, 37*(4), 989–1011.

Chang, C. Y. R., Kivela, J., & Mak, H. N. A. (2011). Attributes that influence the evaluation of travel dining experience: When east meets west. *Tourism Management, 32*(2), 307–316.

Fields, K. (2002). Demand for the gastronomy tourism product: Motivational factors. In H. A-M & G. Richards (Eds.), *Tourism gastronomy* (pp. 36–50). London: Routledge.

Finkelstein, J. (1989). *Dining out: A sociology of modern manners.* Cambridge: Polity Press.

Hair, J. F., Anderson, R., & Black, W. C. (1995). *Multivariate data analysis with readings.* New Jersey: Prentice Hall.

Hjalager, A.-M. (2002). A topology of gastronomy tourism. In A.-M. Hjalager & G. Richards (Eds.), *Tourism gastronomy* (pp. 21–35). London: Routledge.

Hjalager, A.M. (2003). What do tourists eat and why? Towards a sociology of gastronomy and tourism. In J. Collen & G. Richards (Eds.), *Gastronomy and tourism. ATLAS – expert meeting* (pp. 54–74). L. Sandrio (Italy) 21–23 Nov 2002. Academie Voor de Streekgebonden Gastronomie, Belgium.

Intrepid Travel. (2015). *Intrepid gourmet traveller* (p. 3). Melbourne: Intrepid Travel. http://www.intrepidtravel.com. Date accessed 18 Jan 2015.

Johns, N., & Clarke, V. (2001). Mythology as a basis for service expectation and experience: A study of Norfolk Broads Boating Holidays. *Annals of Tourism, 28*(2), 334–359.

Johns, N., & Kivela, J. (2001). Perceptions of the first time restaurant customer. *Food Service Technology, 1*(1), 5–11.

Kivela, J., & Chu, Y. M. C. (2001). Diagnosing favourable and unfavourable service encounters in restaurants. *Journal of Hospitality and Tourism Research, 25*(3), 251–271.

Kivela, J., & Crotts, J. (2009). Understanding travellers' experiences of gastronomy through etymology and narration. *Journal of Hospitality and Tourism Research, 33*(2), 161–192.

Kivela, J. & Johns, N. (2002, 18–21 October). A mythological approach in analysing dining out experiences: Implications for remaking of tourist destinations. *Proceedings of An International Tourism Research Conference "Reinventing a Tourism Destination"* (pp. 98–100). Institute for Tourism Zagreb and the Croatian Tourist Board, Dubrovnik.

Long, L.M., (2002). A Folkloristic perspective on eating and otherness. In L.M. Long, (Ed), *Culinary tourism* (pp. 20–50). U.S.A.: University Press of Kentucky.

Norušis, M. J. (1994). *SPSS advanced statistics 6.1.* Chicago: SPSS Inc.

Norušis, M. J. (2000). *SPSS advanced statistics 11.0*. Chicago: SPSS Inc.

Richards, G. (2002). Gastronomy: And essential ingredient in tourism production and consumption? In H. A-M & G. Richards (Eds.), *Tourism gastronomy* (pp. 36–50). London: Routledge.

Scarpato, R. (2002). Gastronomy as a tourist product: The perspectives of gastronomy studies. In H. A-M & G. Richards (Eds.), *Tourism gastronomy* (pp. 51–70). London: Routledge.

Wolf, E. (2006). *Culinary tourism: The hidden harvest*. Kendall/Hunt Publishing.

CHAPTER 14

Tourism Future: Towards Transformational Tourism

Larry Dwyer, Irena Ateljević, and Renata Tomljenović

A Look Back

This book has discussed the challenges and opportunities in tourism planning, strategic development and management of tourism in Croatia. It is a county whose main sun&sea product has reached maturity at the time when tourism emerged as one of the main pillars of national economy.

This book represents an effort to better understand the broad spectrum of Croatian tourism challenges. The content of the various chapters ranged over issues such as the history of tourism in Croatia, trends in tourism demand, crafting a national tourism vision, shaping destination identity, the influence of political factors in fashioning destination image, the relevance of EU accession to tourism development, challenges to DMO, the tourism attraction system, the economic contribution of tourism to Croatia using TSA, the consequences of discordant spatial planning and tourism development policies, management of tourism in protected areas, carrying capacity issues for small islands and gastronomic tourism. These

L. Dwyer (✉)
University of Ljubljana, Slovenia; Griffith Institute for Tourism (GIFT), Griffith University; School of Marketing, University of New South Wales

I. Ateljević • R. Tomljenović
Institute for Tourism, Zagreb, Croatia

© The Author(s) 2017
L. Dwyer et al. (eds.), *Evolution of Destination Planning and Strategy*, DOI 10.1007/978-3-319-42246-6_14

types of issues present both challenges and opportunities to all tourism destinations, particularly emerging destinations. Croatia, as a country still in transition to a free market economy, faces particular challenges that must be addressed if it is to develop in a sustainable way into the future.

The contributions to this book have made use of existing theories and practice. In Chap. 2, Tomljenović and Ateljević build on the value-driven approach to national vision creation and outline an approach to its practical application. It is deliberately positioned within a wide social context where the urgency of the need for societal transformation is recognized in face of the manifold crisis that we as humanity are experiencing today and which are affected and affect tourism and its future, nationally and globally. As such, it steps aside from the positivistic paradigm dominating tourism studies seeking to tease out broader political, economic and social issues as tourism cannot be separated from the broader national or global context.

The tendency to treat tourism in isolation is not only to be found in tourism scholarship but also in national policies where tourism is treated as a 'gift from heaven', with governments paying scant attention to its management and strategic development. Kunst, in Chap. 3, discusses obstacles that tourism management and development face in a fragmented planning process, lack of consensus in political priorities and poor coordination between government bodies, nationally and locally. Many and varied deficiencies in regulatory framework and overall business environment have a detrimental effect on the competitiveness of Croatian tourism. Croatia has recently joined the Europe Union. Comparing the experience of EU accession's implication for tourism, with reference to most recent member states and those seeking to join, Kunst argues that tourism can benefit through better media exposure, the Commission's pressure for structural reform in order to improve investment climate and overall economic performance and easier access to funding.

While destination promotion and branding is crucial for tourism industry and its competitiveness, it also plays an important role in forging an overall national image, domestically and abroad. Telišman-Košuta in Chap. 4 focuses on the role of branding in reshaping Croatia's tourism image away from that of a 'sea, sun and summer destination'. A fragmented approach to branding, with a lack of leadership and coordination, is detected as the most important barrier to delivering the brand articulated in strategic documents. Similar to overall tourism development discussed in the preceding chapter, collaboration and leadership theories are suggested as a new context for destination branding. In a broader context, Skoko, Miličević and Krešić in Chap. 5 explore the role of tourism promotion in the national image formation, especially important for a newly formed state seeking to distance itself from its past association with Yugoslavia. They convincingly argue that, while Croatia has successfully repositioned its image from a little-known Yugoslav republic to an attractive tourism destination, its current national image in Europe and globally is predominantly related to tourism, with its beaches and pristine nature perceived as a holiday playground. While it is advantageous for tourism, it shows the lack of other agencies' efforts in forging an overall country image for achieving political, economic, social and cultural interest.

Tourism policy and its implementation, destination governance and marketing depend heavily on destination management capabilities. How to achieve efficient and effective destination management is a topic hotly debated in professional and scholarly circles in Croatia, which set up hierarchically organized destination management organizations some 20 years ago. While the competition and market trends, as well as variety of development pressure on destination, are changing rapidly, the system of DMOs has remained intact. In Chap. 6, Čorak and Boranić-Živoder identified barriers to efficient destination management, relating mostly to the lack of funding and human resources and inadequate stakeholder involvement and coordination as the key barriers to successful destination management.

While the early focus on some of the key aspects of tourism planning and implementation, with Chap. 7 the focus shifts from the essentially marketing to destination development issues. Kušen's starting premise is that the prevailing economic considerations in tourism planning and development have pushed aside the question of destination resources, their inherent attractiveness and their development potential. The attractions of a destination, a relatively neglected area of scholarly interest, are fundamental not only for long-term tourism resource planning but also for their appropriate protection from degradation, destruction or inappropriate use. The System of Tourism Attractions, presented in this chapter, is a theoretically founded and empirically tested system for identification, classification and evaluation of real and potential tourism attractions, of value to practitioners in daily operations as well as in strategic planning, academic research and consulting.

As a complex, yet often perceived as a hedonistic diversion, many problems with appropriate planning, implementation and coordination of tourism management and development arise from tourism not treated as a serious economic activity. This perception can be countered demonstrating tourism's economic importance. As tourism is not defined by the nature of its output-inputs used, or techniques of production employed, but rather as a set of production activities led by demand created by visitors, measuring its economic contribution is challenging. The common approach is Tourism Satellite Account (TSA) that links tourism statistics and standard national accounts tables. In Chap. 8, Ivandić and Marušić provide a detailed methodological approach for the transfer of theoretical concepts given by the TSA methodological framework to the estimation of the direct contribution of tourism to the Croatian economy. The 10.4 per cent estimation for Croatia reveals the highest dependency on tourism demand among EU countries—Croatian internal tourism consumption equals 9.4 per cent of domestic supply, while Spain with 5.7 and Germany with 4.7 per cent are second and third, respectively.

The complexities of tourism planning are exposed again by Kranjčević (Chap. 9), this time in the context of relationship between tourism and spatial planning. Kranjčević highlights the tension that has existed between developers' pressure for opening up new tourism zones against existing 20 tourism zones devastated during the Homeland War but retaining obsolete building construction and infrastructure. Two different approaches to spatial planning and tourism development are juxtaposed—that of centralized planning in former Yugoslavia against the planning practice in market-led economy of Croatia today. Fragmentation of government departments and their complex and often conflicting laws and regulation are identified yet again for the lack of the rejuvenation of this existing zones and, overall, chaotic approach to tourism land zoning.

While in spatial planning there was a transition to market-led forces, the management of the most attractive nature protected areas is still centralized. While central government in this way exercises a high level of control over the most financially lucrative nature protected areas, such a system creates threats to environmental and social security, often with questionable economic benefits to local communities. Marković in Chap. 10, in a case study of Plitvice Lakes, Croatia's most popular national park, identifies a number of adverse impacts created by visitor pressure coupled with inefficient centralized management model. In effect, these problems again relate to the lack of cooperation and participatory decision making at the regional level.

While Marković has investigated the long-term change in natural environment, Marušić, Sever and Čorak, in Chap. 11, focus on tracking the changes in tourism demand through longitudinal research in order to identify patterns of change, monitor tourist experiences and satisfaction and, indirectly, assess the long-term effects of tourism policies as well and managerial pitfalls. Similarly, the longitudinal study on a small tourism island of Vis by Kivela and Klarić (Chap. 12) highlights the carrying capacity challenges associated with tourism. Faced with the fact that tourists on Vis are now testing the limits of the island's infrastructure, environment and cultural heritage, they advocate a change the way government, county and Vis community think about tourism and sustainability. Obviously, one of the possibilities is to de-season islands' tourism demand by fostering visits in shoulder season through introduction of new products. One such niche market is gastronomy, and in Chap. 13, Kivela provides evidence of the strong demand for gastronomy tourism on the southern Croatian islands, traditionally the hot spots for lovers of the sun and sea. While the ubiquitous offerings of pizza and grilled meats might seem like standard tourist fare, this study strongly suggests that about 30 per cent of tourists return to these holiday islands for their authentic gastronomy. Put in another way, about 1.5 million tourists are returning to Croatia to savor its gastronomy.

Fashioning Croatia's Tourism Future

While Croatia's travel and tourism competiveness is low at present—ranking 33 out of 141 countries (WEF, 2015)—various issues have been identified that, if addressed, could improve this ranking. These include addressing impediments within the business environment, human resource skills and greater cooperation between private and public sector stakeholders. A major impediment to Croatia's tourism development, as noted in various papers in this volume, is the persistence of a fragmented and uncoordinated approach to tourism development.

While it is obviously in the interests of Croatia to address barriers to tourism development and to capitalize on opportunities to develop tourism in a sustainable way, it is important that its stakeholders avoid the 'business as usual' approaches that predominate in both developed and developing destinations worldwide. An implicit assumption of much of the tourism planning literature is that the market requires increasing economic growth. The appropriateness of the 'growth ethic' largely remains an unexamined issue in the tourism research literature. On the standard view, economic growth is paramount—more is better—despite the fact that tourism's obsessive drive for expansion is destroying the very environments that attract visitation. Tourism planning typically consists of a SWOT analysis followed by strategies to build on strengths to promote growth, address weaknesses to growth, counter threats to growth and capitalize on opportunities for growth (Dwyer & Edwards, 2010). In the WTTC *Blueprint for New Tourism* purporting to address sustainability issues, tourism growth is lauded as an important goal for all destinations (WTTC, 2003). An explicit growth ethic also underpins UNWTO (2016) publications which promote tourism as a driver of economic growth, inclusive development and environmental sustainability, as well as the bulk of the destination competitiveness literature wherein better attractions and better management imply greater demand for tourist industry products and services.

The reality is that a substantial array of negative impacts are associated with tourism developments worldwide despite the espousal of sustainability principles and practices in planning processes. The negative effects of tourism growth, which the chapter authors have identified for Croatia, suggest that the established ways of thinking which underpin tourism development are 'not working'. Given the forces that underpin continued tourism growth, the 'business as usual' approach to tourism development can be expected to lead to more adverse environmental and social impacts. Despite the adoption of sustainability practices worldwide, such as Corporate Social Responsibility (CSR) (Nicolau, 2008), and Triple Bottom Line Reporting (Dwyer, 2005), there is no indication that tourism's problems globally are being solved. There is also little evidence that such issues are being seriously addressed in Croatia. Even if a growing proportion of tourism operators were each to reduce the size of their negative social and environmental impacts, the expansion of tourism nationally (and globally) means that, under current practice, the absolute volume of negative impacts will continue to increase.

The foundations for the 'business as usual' approach comprise elements of the established model, otherwise known as the 'Industrial Model' (Pollock, 2012, 2015) or 'Production Model' (TII, 2012). This way of thinking reflects the dominant economic model that is undergoing substantial criticism of late (Fullerton, 2015; Hurst, 2014). It also reflects the influence of traditional management theory which is under sustained fire from many quarters (Birkinshaw, 2010; Mackay & Sisodia, 2014).

An alternative ('responsible', 'conscious') perspective involves a more serious effort on the part of all tourism stakeholders to adopt 'sustainability' practices. This perspective recognizes that the standard approach provides no real insight into how to control behavioral effects to realize true sustainability in tourism development. The alternative perspective begins with an exhortation for all tourism stakeholders to expose the unexamined assumptions that have guided their behavior and to take more responsibility for all the stakeholders affected by their actions. Whereas the established mindset sees human needs, financial returns, economic growth, jobs, rising incomes, production, facilities investment and expanded tourism numbers as indicators of a successful industry, the alternative mindset sees economic and financial health as inseparable from human, societal and environmental health, responsibilities to others, environmental and socio-cultural stewardship, inspiring experiences and developing a sense of place with a broader conception of the ideal tourist (Pollock, 2012, 2015; TII, 2012). The relevance of this alternative mindset as a potential driver of Croatian tourism deserves serious attention from analysts.

Two major trends are taking place that have the potential to drive the alternative mindset. These two trends have particular relevance for an emerging destination such as Croatia. On the demand side, *new consumer values* are emerging. New and growing demographics of individuals are 'values aspirational', placing a higher value on healthy living, environmental and social justice and ecological sustainability in the products and services they purchase, the companies in which they invest, the politicians and policies they support, the companies for which they work and, ultimately, the lifestyles they lead (Szmigin, Carrigan & McEachern, 2009). Aspirational consumers make purchase decisions based on total value not lowest price, seeking meaningful experiences rather than more 'things', actively co-creating content, products and experiences rather than acting as a passive recipient of brand communications, and are prepared to pay extra for products and services from companies that demonstrate similar values. These changing consumer values are not passing trends or superficial changes in operator values or consumer preferences, but reflect a much deeper more radical shift in demographic changes and worldview (Mackay & Sisodia, 2014). They are now starting to underpin new management concepts such as '*Consumer* Social Responsibility' (CnSR), the demand-side counterpart to '*Corporate* Social Responsibility' (Devinney, Auger & Eckhardt, 2012).

This shift has been particularly accelerated by the latest recession that seems to be serving as a key tipping point. Not only social science but also many popular writings and market research agencies confirm the trend. For example, Richard Florida in his book *The Great Reset* (2010) speaks about how new, more responsible ways of living and working drive post-crash prosperity. A white paper *A Darwinian Gale* (2010) from the Futures Company has announced the current shift towards the 'new era of consequences' with the value found in responsibility as opposed to the twentieth century 'era of indulgence' when the values were based in trading and consuming, while the eighteenth and nineteenth centuries were characterized as the 'era of readiness' when value was found in new frontiers. Similarly, Euro RSCG Worldwide (2010), a major global study that included an in-depth survey of 5,700 adults in seven countries including Brazil, China, France, Japan, the Netherlands, the United Kingdom and the United States, has shown that people in mature markets have grown tired of the constant push to accumulate more. They claim that even well before the recession, we were seeing signs of discontent being played out in positive ways. Once-fringe movements such as organic foods and recycling are becoming mainstream in mature markets, part of a growing consciousness about the impact our personal consumption choices are having on our bodies, other people and the planet we share. Then along came the global downturn—a.k.a. the 'Great Recession'—giving people an opportunity or necessity to stop and think, to consider and reassess their lives and lifestyle choices. Across the markets surveyed, people are fed up with a culture built on trips to the mall and hours spent parked in front of televisions and computer screens. Seven in ten global respondents (69 per cent) worry that society has become too shallow and focused on things that don't really matter. In the United States, France and the United Kingdom, that figure rises to 79, 77 and 75 per cent, respectively. Six in ten (60 per cent) believe society has grown intellectually lazy, while nearly seven in ten (67 per cent) believe we have grown physically lazy. In both cases, the percentages are the highest in the United States and United Kingdom. Saturated by meaningless hyper consumerism, 'new consumers' still want more, but they are defining that differently. Not more mountains of consumer goods but, rather, more meaning, more deeply felt connections, more substance and a greater sense of purpose. Similarly, an Ogilvy and Mather (2010) market study speaks about the emerging post-recession consumer consciousness in which 75 per cent of those surveyed said that they would rather get out of the 'rat race' than climb the corporate ladder—and instead, 76 per cent said they would rather spend more time with family than make more money. In its report *Eyes Wide Open, Wallet Half Shut*, the agency identifies 'awake, alert and aware' conscious consumers across all ages and genders. Advertisers have already captured them as the market labelled LOHAS—conscious consumers with lifestyle of health and sustainability (LOHAS, 2015).

The rise of the socially responsible consumer is also generating new patterns of tourist behavior (European Travel Commission, 2010). Organizations need to become more proactive with respect to *Consumer* Social Responsibility if they want their *Corporate* Social Responsibility initiatives to have a greater impact. To do so, Croatian tourism managers in both the private and public sectors need to recognize the complexity of the consumer decision-making process with respect to social purchasing and take appropriate actions to guide and educate consumers.

It is in this context that we see the increasing trend of the growing need for *transformative* holidays in which travel appears to provide the means to change both one's own life(style) and the impact one makes on places of visit. Academic and industry-based research increasingly confirms this trend, albeit using different terms to communicate the shift towards the new travelling mindset. Some frame it as the transmodern tourism of the future (Ateljevic, 2009, 2011), while others call it transformative tourism (Reisinger, 2013, 2015), hopeful tourism (Pritchard, Morgan & Ateljevic, 2011), transformational travel (Lean, 2009) or conscious travel (Pollock, 2015). Yet, regardless of the terminology employed, all research points in the same direction that also goes beyond the recognition of responsible tourism that has been widely promoted by the industry and UNWTO. For example, through the 2012 campaign *One Billion Tourists: One Billion Opportunities*, tourists are called upon to make their actions count in terms of caring for places and communities they visit (e.g., saving energy, respecting local culture, buying locally).

However, transformative/conscious travelers are recognized to be going *further* by using travel to re-invent themselves and the world. They travel in order to volunteer and make a difference; they value what's slow, small and simple and aim for self-reliance; they are connected and communicative; they seek meaningful experiences that help them to develop personally and collectively. In sum, they use travel to reflect upon their lives and get the courage to make crucial life changes upon their return back home, not only in terms of their lifestyle but also the type of work they do. As Deville and Wearing (2013, p. 151) neatly point out:

> Tourism must not only operate in a more sustainable manner... To be trans-
> formational, tourism must result in changes that go beyond generating local
> economic contributions or stimulate donations ... Tourism must stimulate
> change by provoking a deep questioning of the purpose and meaning of
> people's life through empathic, engaged, authentic and invited, rather than
> imposed, encounters with the lives of others.

Many various types of tourism have been identified that allow for developing new experiences and transforming one's personality and worldview,
such as educational, volunteer, survival, community-based, eco-, farm,
extreme sports, backpacking, cultural, wellness, religious, spiritual and
yoga tourism (Reisinger, 2013).

Yet, limited studies on transformative tourism show that it is not sufficient to provide 'alternative and special interest tourism' experiences only.
The seismic changes in consumers' lifestyles, values and consumption patterns described above must be met by an equally seismic shift in the firms
producing goods, services and experiences for the 'silent revolution' to
come to fruition. The free-market capitalism that has driven business activity for centuries is now itself under question. Some would say it is broken,
and different norms and drivers of business activity are needed. In Naomi
Klein's (2014) book *This Changes Everything: Capitalism vs. the Climate*,
she addresses the urgency of transforming the broken economic system
while also addressing climate change. She eloquently points to the need to
drop our addiction to free-market ideologies, put an end to greed and corporate power, restructure local economies and strengthen our democracies.

A commitment to go beyond profit interests to create societal value, and
that the social and environmental impacts of firm operations should be built
into firms' business models, rather than being addressed as 'optional extras',
firms 'under new management' attempt to attract stakeholders who are in
alignment with company values and purpose. These so-called conscious
firms (Mackay & Sisodia, 2014) are characterized by their commitment to
drive positive social/environmental change as an organizational objective;
creating mutually beneficial, 'flourishing' relationships with stakeholders;
long-time horizons for slower growth; and build community and support personal growth and positive leadership (Fullerton, 2015; Haigh &
Hoffman, 2012). Continuously generating more value for stakeholders is
not just the goal for the CEO or the marketing department: it becomes
the operational goal of everyone in the organization. Conscious firms have
also changed the investment world on individual and institutional levels
through socially responsible investing, favoring promotion of human and

consumer rights, environmental management and social justice. There is evidence that a collective values shift is occurring—a shift in focus from 'I' to We, a shift from self-interest to the common good and shift from being the best *in* the world to the best *for* the world (Denning, 2010). Two types of justification support this wider view of firms' responsibilities:

- *Ethical perspective:* 'It's the right thing to do'. Privately owned businesses have a moral and ethical responsibility to address the impact of their operations on all stakeholders, just as government bodies must (Haigh & Hoffman, 2012).
- *Pragmatic perspective:* 'Its good for profits'. Evidence is mounting that conscious such businesses significantly outperform traditional businesses in financial terms while also creating many other forms of well-being (Mackay & Sisodia, 2014). The enterprises that differentiate themselves by 'making a difference' and 'delighting stakeholders' tend to enjoy higher brand equity and profitability than those focused primarily on profit (Denning, 2010; Sheth, Sisodia & Wolfe, 2003).

This requires tourism firms to re-examine how they fit into the emerging society described above and to reflect on a new raison d'être—one which addresses the needs of the planet and the fundamental changes affecting tourists' consumption patterns and lifestyles. The common wisdom is that the pure profit maximization goal must now stand side by side with goals for societal well-being. Otto Scharmer describes this shift as moving from ego-centric behavior (maximizing self-interest) to eco-centric behavior (contributing to the social, cultural and environmental eco-systems within which the firm operates). Many business gurus (Porter & Kramer, 2011, Senge, Scharmer, Jaworski & Flowers, 2004; Scharmer & Kaufer, 2013) endorse this shared value approach to corporate activity and call for firms to wake up to their impact on the eco-systems in which they operate. This is more urgent now than it ever has been. Without such a shift, we will not '... cross through the gate to an economy that operates more consciously, inclusively, and collectively ...' (Scharmer & Kaufer, 2013:18). Greed, corporate power and corruption have no place in the new economy. Instead collaboration, sharing and common values characterize economic behavior. All avenues of business activity are undergoing this disruption, and the travel industry is not being spared. In fact, because it is so huge, so global and—in its traditional form—so consumptive of resources, it must be one of the leading sectors ushering in the new economy. Whether tourism will step up to this moral challenge is yet to be seen; hence, the rationale behind this chapter is to provide an insight into the motivations and behaviors of the new, conscious traveler as well as the emerging best practices of transformative travel businesses and destinations.

While various Corporate Social Responsibility (CSR) programs are increasingly recognized to be rather token in nature, more forward-looking, responsible firms are strategically integrating social responsibility into their missions and their core activities. Michael Porter recommends that firms first examine the societal needs in the communities/destinations where they operate and respond by designing products and services to meet those needs. He terms this 'creating shared value'. Researchers purport that the sincere adoption of this approach creates more successful companies in all aspects (Pfizter, Bockstette & Stamp, 2013; Porter & Kramer, 2011), although the tourism industry rarely features in the reporting of this phenomenon.

Even as this welcome shift is happening in corporate activity, the urgent desire by conscious citizens to address the world's problems is giving rise to a deeper and more fundamental disruption of the economic status quo. To respond to the gaps in societal well-being left by governments, corporations and NGOs, new economic and social agents are emerging. The initiators and supporters of these are often new consumers themselves. They see needs in society—in health, education, agriculture, poverty alleviation—and address them with innovative business models outside the status quo economy. New forms of NGOs, not-for-profit organizations, for-benefit enterprises and social entrepreneurs are a few examples.

Perhaps the most impactful of these is the rapidly growing social entrepreneurship sector fired by creative individuals who are resourceful, opportunity oriented and innovative. They intentionally pursue the public good to create value in society while making a reasonable profit. They seek meaning and a sense of contribution in their work lives and act as change agents of social and economic progress. Some seek to address local social needs, some to build alternative structures addressing social needs that government or business cannot, and others seek to create newer, more effective social systems that replace old ones (Volkmann, Tokarski & Ernst, 2012).

David Bornstein's (2007) book *How to Change the World: Social Entrepreneurs and the Power of New Ideas* and Elkington and Hartigan's (2008) book *The Power of Unreasonable People* both highlight the significant global impacts of social entrepreneurs and their contributions to the UN Millennium Development goals and other pressing world problems. Every year the Skoll World Forum (2016) honors the most successful social entrepreneurs in all parts of the world and all sectors such as health, education and agriculture. Rarely is a travel or tourism enterprise one of the award winners, pointing again to the need of the tourism sector to step up to the plate and make its impact. However, the Ashoka Foundation (2016), one of the first international agencies that supports social entrepreneurs and matches them with funding sources, currently has 184 projects underway that relate to tourism.

A similar, yet equally powerful, change agent is the social intrapreneur—an individual who seeks to affect change within a company as an employee. (S)he disrupts old ways of doing things from the inside and stimulates corporate policies and actions for social good. Visionary tourism companies can actively seek these individuals to bring sparks of innovation and social contribution into traditional structures and methods of doing business.

Another sign that the traditional economic system is crumbling is the emergence of the shared economy. The shared economy is fueled by individuals who exchange resources among each other to acquire the goods or experiences they desire. This is akin to bartering where smaller amounts of money or none at all are exchanged. The tourism sector has already been shaken by examples such as the ride-sharing services Uber and Lyft and AirBnB which matches travelers seeking accommodation with residents with extra rooms. These initiatives are strong competition for traditional travel products and also can save environmental resources. As development pressures compromise more and more destinations, such sharing systems can unlock underutilized resources and should be encouraged.

Another economic disruption is the investment behavior of awakened, conscious citizens and consumers. Wanting their investments to have positive social impact, they invest only in companies with a social conscience. In the United States, for example, sustainable, responsible and impact (SRI) investing grew from $3.74 trillion in 2012 to $6.57 trillion in 2014, an increase of 76 per cent. These assets account for one out of every six investment dollars under professional management and add additional pressure on firms to be socially responsible (The Forum for Sustainable and Responsible Investment, 2014). Klein (2014) stresses the need for conscious investors to pull out of extractive industry investments such as oil and coal to help mitigate climate change. The tourism sector, as both a contributor to and victim of climate change, will be affected by this.

The economic growth paradigm has been the gold standard of success for centuries. But our planet cannot survive more growth and remain healthy. Given the state of its strained resources, non-growth models are gaining more traction with governments, destinations and communities. Tourism also is seeking more holistic measures of success than simply growth in arrivals and expenditures. Since much tourism is driven by the (over)consumption of natural environmental and cultural resources, a re-think is urgently required. The holiday experiences that conscious travelers seek are rarely found in crowded and congested mass tourism destinations. Travelers with consciousness want their travel experiences to contribute to their own physical, mental, emotional and spiritual well-being and to also help rectify the various market failures created by the free market economy in the destination. They too want to move from ego-centric to eco-centric behavior. This requires new systemic design of tourism experiences to provide transformative and meaningful experiences that meet the needs of new consumers. Experiences, which harness the energy and vision of conscious travelers to create social and environmental good, will also nourish the destinations.

Many believe that the world's ills, and tourism's ills, will only be healed through collaboration of governments, private sector and civil society (Lowitt, 2013). The collaborative approach can transform destinations into ones that nourish their precious resources and cultures and survive into the future. Tourism companies and stakeholders have a responsibility not only to respond to this societal paradigm shift but to step forward and lead it. Firms can still make a fair profit and join hands with government and civil society to disrupt tourism and turn it around for the better. Embracing the ideas of creating shared value, the collaborative economy, the search for meaning and social good can replenish our spirits and create the transformation that destinations—and the planet—need to survive. We envision the Croatian tourism industry to take on this inspiring opportunity to potentially become a global leader of transformational tourism for Croatian and planetary sustainable futures.

References

Ashoka Foundation. (2016). *Ashoka innovators for the public.* http://publications.unwto.org/. Date accessed 15 May 2016.
Ateljević, I. (2009). Transmodernity – Remaking our (tourism) world? In J. Tribe (Ed.), *Philosophical issues of tourism* (pp. 278–300). Bristol: Channel View Publications.
Ateljevic, I. (2011). Transmodern critical tourism studies: A call for hope and transformation. *Revista Turismo em Análise, Special Issue: Critical Issues in Tourism, 22*(3), 497–515.
Birkinshaw, J. (2010). *Reinventing management: Smarter choices for getting work done.* London: Wiley.

Bornstein, D. (2007). *How to change the world: Social entrepreneurs and the power of new ideas*. Oxford: Oxford University Press.

Elkington, J. and Hartigan, P. (2008). *The power of unreasonable people*. Boston: Harvard Business Press.

Euro RSCG Worldwide. (2010). *The new consumer: In the era of mindful spending* (Vol. 8). Prosumer Report. New York.

Denning, S. (2010). *The leaders Guide to Radical Management: Reinventing the workplace for the 21st century*. London: Wiley.

Devinney, T. M., Auger, P., & Eckhardt, G. (2012). Can the socially responsible consumer be mainstream? *Journal for Business Economics and Ethics, 13*(3), 227–235.

Deville, A., & Wearing, S. (2013). WWOOFing tourism: Beaten tracks and transformational paths. In Y. Reisinger (Ed.), *Transformational tourism: Tourist perspectives* (pp. 151–168). Oxfordshire: CABI.

Dwyer, L. (2005). Relevance of triple bottom line reporting to achievement of sustainable tourism. *Tourism Review International, 9*(1), 79–94.

Dwyer, L., & Edwards, D. (2010). Sustainable tourism planning. In J. Liburd & D. Edwards (Eds.), *Understanding the sustainable development of tourism*. Oxford: Goodfellows Publications.

European Travel Commission. (2010). *Demographic change and tourism*. Madrid, Spain: United Nations World Tourism Organization/European Travel Commission.

Florida, R. (2010). *The great reset: How new ways of living and working drive post-crash prosperity*. Ontario: Random House Canada.

Forum for Sustainable and Responsible Investment. (2014). *Report on US sustainable, responsible and impact investment trends 2014*. http://www.ussif.org/trends. Date accessed 15 May 2016.

Fullerton, J. (2015). *Regenerative capitalism*, Capitalism Institute, Working Draft.

Futures Company. (2010). *A Darwinian Gale and the era of consequences*. A White paper published by the Futures Company.

Klein, N. (2014). *This changes everything: Capitalism vs. the climate*. London: Penguin Books.

Haigh, N., & Hoffman, A. (2012). Hybrid Organisations: The next chapter of sustainable business. *Organisazional Dynamics, 41*(2), 126–134.

Hurst, A. (2014). *Purpose economy*. Boise, ID: Elevate Publising.

Lean, G. L. (2009). Transformative travel: Inspiring sustainability. In R. Bushel & P. Sheldon (Eds.), *Wellness and tourism: Mind, body, spirit, place* (pp. 191–205). New York: Cognizant.

Lohas. (2015). *Lifestyle of health and sustainability – LOHAS online*. http://www.lohas.com. Date accessed 16 June 2015.

Lowitt, E. (2013). *The collaboration economy: How to meet business, social and environmental needs and gain competitive advantage*. San Francisco: Jossey Bass (A Wiley Brand).

Mackay, J., & Sisodia, R. (2014). *Conscious capitalism: Liberating the heroic spirit of business*. Cambridge, MA: Harvard Business Review Press.

Nicolau, J. L. (2008). Corporate social responsibility: Worth creating activites. *Annals of Tourism Research, 35*(4), 990–1006.

Ogilvy & Mather. (2010). *Eyes wide open, Wallet Half Shut*. New York: Ogilvy and Mather.

Pfitzer, M, Bockstette, V. & Stamp, M. (2013). Innovating for shared value. *Harvard Business Review*. http://www.philoma.org/docs/2013_2014_Valeur_actionnariale_a_partagee/Pfitzer_and_co_-_HBR_-_Innovating_for_shared_value.pdf. Date accessed 15 May 2016.

Pollock, A (2012). *Conscious Travel: Signposts towards a New Model for Tourism*, contribution to the Second UNWTO Ethics and Tourism Congress, Conscious Tourism for a New Era, September 12, Quito.

Pollock, A. (2015). *Social entrepreneurship in tourism: The conscious travel approach*. Tourism Innovation Partnership for Social Entrepreneurship (TIPSE), UK.

Porter, M., & Kramer, M. (2011). Creating shared value. *Harvard Business Review, 89*(1/2), 62–77.

Pritchard, A., Morgan, N., & Ateljevic, I. (2011). Hopeful tourism: A new transformative perspective. *Annals of Tourism Research, 38*(3), 941–963.

Reisinger, Y. (Ed.). (2013). *Transformational tourism: Tourist perspective*. Wallingford: CABI.

Reisinger, Y. (Ed.). (2015). *Transformational tourism: Host perspectives*. Oxfordshire: CABI.

Senge, P., Scharmer, O., Jaworski, J., & Flowers, B. (2004). *Presence: Human purpose and the field of the future*. Cambridge: SoL.

Scharmer, O., & Kaufer, K. (2013). *Leading from the emerging future: From ego-system to eco-system economies*. Sydney: ReadHowYouWant.com.

Sheth, J. N., Sisodia, R., & Wolfe, D. (2003). *Firms of endearment: How world class companies profit from passion and purpose*. Prentice Hall, NY: Pearson.

Skoll World Forum. (2016). *About Skoll*. http://skoll.org/skoll-world-forum/. Date accessed 15 May 2016.

Szmigin, I., Carrigan, M., & McEachern, M. (2009). The conscious consumer: Taking a flexible approach to ethical behavior. *International Journal of Consumer Studies, 33*(2), 224–231.

Tourism Intelligence International. (2012). *The paradigm Shift in Travel and Tourism: Win or die new rules for competitive success, Mini market Intelligence Brief*. www.tourism-intelligence.com

Volkmann, C., Tokarski, K., & Ernst, K. (Eds.). (2012). *Social entrepreneurship and social business*. Wiesbaden: Springer Gabler.

UNWTO. (2016). *UNWTO e-library*. http://www2.unwto.org/. Date accessed 20 May 2016.

INDEX

A

abandoned tourism resorts/zones, 10, 11, 173–98
Haludovo, Krk, 174, 178–80, 189–92, 194
Kupari, near Dubrovnik, 174, 178, 189, 192–4, 197
acceptable change, 12
limits of, 215–2
Act on Tourism boards and the Promotion of Croatian Tourism, 105, 106, 111
alternative development perspective, 33, 276, 285
alternative mindset, 285
architecture of hotels, 179, 190
attitudes to private initatives (former Yugoslavia), 182, 194
attitude to tourism
local goverment, 43, 47–9, 51, 52, 61, 74, 106–11, 113
public sector leaders/DMO, 26
tourism boards/DMOs, 47–52, 100–3, 106–12, 114, 115, 233

B

basic functional classification of tourism attractions, 120, 126–31
basic functional classification of tourist motives/activities, 127
brand management, 8, 75, 88
brand positioning, 70
business as usual, 283, 284

C

carrying capacity, 12, 132–4, 210, 245–62, 279, 283
biophysical, 252–3
debate, 107, 281
economic, 252
island, 245–62, 279, 283
physical, 252
social, 252
centralized management model, 215, 282
centrally planned economy, 175, 181, 194
collaborative advantage, 75

Note: Page numbers followed by "n" denote footnotes.

© The Author(s) 2017
L. Dwyer et al. (eds.), *Evolution of Destination Planning and Strategy*, DOI 10.1007/978-3-319-42246-6

collaborative approach, 292
commercial accommodation capacity, 230
  Croatia, 230
competitive identity, 70
conscious citizens, 290, 291
conscious consumers, 17, 25, 287
conscious firms, 288
conscious travel, 7, 16, 17, 287
conscious travelers, 287, 290, 292
Consumer Social Responsibility (CnSR), 285, 287
consumer values, 285
contribution of tourism, 10, 279, 282
  Croatia, 149–67
Corporate Social Responsibility (CSR), 284, 285, 287, 290
crisis
  economic, 15, 16
  environmental, 7, 15, 17, 207, 212, 215, 282
  social, 15, 280, 282
Croatia
  attractions, 38, 46, 62, 72, 88, 135, 136, 140, 143, 178, 188, 201, 202, 231, 279
  challenges, 4, 8, 10, 67–75, 81–6, 100, 107, 114, 181, 184, 189, 279, 280
  commercial accommodation, 46, 53, 154, 166, 176, 185, 187, 222, 227, 228, 230, 238
  cultural heritage, 41, 68, 80, 90, 105, 247
  destination branding, 8, 69–74, 75n1
  destination image, 69, 88, 279
  destination management, 4, 7, 9, 23, 39–41, 43, 59, 60, 62, 71, 75, 100, 103, 106, 107–14
  destination management organization (DMO), 7, 26,
    39, 40, 43, 56, 71, 75, 100, 103–15, 279, 281
  facts and figures, 8, 26, 38, 39, 41, 46, 47, 56, 59, 62, 68, 70–3, 80–2, 85, 90–5, 95n2, 151, 157, 158, 178, 188, 206, 212, 247, 283
  funding destination management organizations (DMOs), 99, 100, 105, 106, 109, 110, 115
  history of tourism, 21–5, 279
  national image, 8, 81, 84, 95, 280, 281
  national image formation, 281
  national tourism planning, 21–5
  nature protected areas (NPAs), 201–6, 208, 282
  tourism demand and supply, 10, 39, 55, 68, 89, 155, 165, 226, 227, 237, 238, 279, 282
  tourism development, 6, 7, 9, 37–63, 68, 103, 105, 107, 108, 112, 114, 173–98, 283–5
  tourism development challenges, 279
  tourism position in Europe, 2, 9, 80, 104
  tourism promotion, 8, 73, 79, 80, 85, 88–90, 92, 95, 271
Croatian gastronomy
  marketing, 13, 226, 269–72, 276, 280–3, 286–8, 292
  strengths and weaknesses, 272
Croatian national image, 8, 84, 89, 95, 280, 281
Croatian summer tourism, 223, 227, 230
Croatian summer tourists
  activities, 6, 104, 229, 231, 232
  expenditures, 6, 104, 223, 236
  length of stay, 132–4, 156, 191, 211, 229, 232, 233

motivation, 6, 104, 229–31
satisfaction, 6, 104, 229, 233–5,
    238
trip planning, 232, 233
Croatian tourism, 1, 2, 4–7, 12, 17,
    21–5, 32, 38–40, 43, 46–57, 59,
    62, 72, 80, 86–90, 92, 114, 135,
    151, 155, 165, 201, 222, 223,
    226, 229, 233, 236–8, 279, 280,
    285, 287, 292
comparative advantage, 80, 86–8
Croatian tourism competitiveness, 40,
    50–61
improvement, 41, 44, 56–8, 60, 61
Croatian tourism development
effectivness, 46–50
obstacles, 40, 50–6
*Croatian Tourism Development
    Strategy to 2010,* 22
*Croatian Tourism Development
    Strategy to 2020,* 43, 68, 90, 107,
    165, 185, 187
Croatian Tourist Board (CTB), 8, 22,
    68, 71, 80, 87, 89, 90, 95, 105,
    106, 113
culinaria, 265, 266
culinary experiences, 266, 271
culinary tourism experiences, 267
phenomenological model, 267

D
descriptive research design, 267
destination
attraction evaluation, 132, 134,
    135–9
types of, 136
destination branding, 8, 69–74, 75n1,
    281
Croatia, 71–4
limitations, Croatia, 70, 72, 74
destination brending

Croatia,
destination developers, 102
destination identity, 8, 9, 67–75
destination image, 7, 8, 69, 79–95,
    123, 279
Croatia, 8, 69, 90–4
destination leadership, 8, 75
destination management, 4, 7, 9, 12,
    23, 39–41, 43, 59, 60, 62, 71,
    75, 99–103, 106, 107, 110, 114,
    135, 146, 221, 281
challenges, Croatia, 9, 12, 71, 75,
    99–101, 103, 114, 221
Croatia, 4, 7, 9, 23, 39–41, 43, 59,
    60, 62, 71, 75, 100, 114, 135,
    281
efficiency, Croatia, 4, 71, 101, 281
destination management organizations
    (DMOs)
Croatia, 7, 9, 26, 39, 40, 43, 56,
    71, 75, 99, 100, 103–15, 279,
    281
funding, Croatia, 99, 100, 105,
    106, 109, 110, 115
restructuring,Croatia, 5, 55, 186
destination transformation, 99–115
DMO model, 103
domestic supply, 152, 158–65, 282
domestic tourism expenditures, 154,
    156

E
eco-centric behavior, 289, 292
economic contribution of tourism, 10,
    150, 153, 279
economic growth, 22–6, 33, 40, 184,
    283–5
economic growth paradigm, 292
ego-centric behavior, 289
environmental impacts, 203, 284, 288
environmental sustainability, 284

EU accession, 7, 21, 37–63, 279, 280
Europe 2020, 24
EU structural funds, 56–61
    national priorities, 57

F
free market economy, 181, 194, 208, 280, 292
functional classification of tourism attraction, 120, 126, 129–32, 147
    destination perspective, 138

G
gastronomy, 13, 68, 230–2, 283
gastronomy tourism, 13, 265–76, 283
    implications for Croatia, 13, 272
gastronomy tourism alliances, 272, 273
gastronomy-tourism market segment, 269
gastronomy tourism products, 271, 272
    Croatia, 271, 272
gastronomy tourism products development, 272
gastronomy tourists
    Croatian island, 283
    typology, 245,
global downturn, 286
globalization, 16, 40
Great Recession, 286
gross value added of tourism industries, 152, 159, 163
growth ethic, 283, 284

H
Haludovo tourism resort, 179, 180
history of tourism planning, Croatia, 21–5, 279
household accommodation, Croatia, 155, 163, 165

I
Inbound tourism expenditure, 154, 156, 157
inclusive development, 284
Industrial Model, 284
Institute for Tourism, 3–6, 22, 23, 32, 67, 68, 75n1, 92, 93, 107, 114, 119, 135, 151, 154, 176, 201, 211, 222, 229, 231, 233–7
    journal *Tourism*, 6
integrated sustainable management, 203
internal tourism consumption, 150–4, 159–65, 282
island tourism development, 37, 46, 175, 245–62
island Vis
    garbage collection, 255, 258–60
    nautical tourism, 248, 255–8
    sewerage infrastructure, 247, 258
    threats to culture and heritage, 249, 255, 256, 260–1
    tourism development, 251, 252, 254
    tourism development issues, 252, 254–6, 261

J
Josip Broz Tito, 83
journal *Tourism*, 6

K
Klapa song, 260
Kupari tourism resort, 192, 194

L
Legislations
    Act on Tourism Boards and the Promotion of Croatian Tourism, 105, 106, 111
    Nature Protection Act, 201

longitudinal research implementation, 237
longitudinal surveys, 12, 221–38

M
mindset, 285, 287

N
national image, 8, 81, 84, 95, 280, 281
repositioning of Croatia, 71
national image formation, 281
National Park Plitvice Lakes
anthropogenic eutrophication, 212
management, 201–16
regional economic rejuvenation, 213
sustainabilitiy issues, 201–16
tourism, 201–16
visitor satisfaction, 211, 215
National strategies and plans
Coordinated Spatial Plan of the Upper Adriatic Region, 177
Croatian Tourism Development Strategy to 2020, 43, 68, 90, 107, 165, 185, 187
Economic Development Plans 1957 - 1961, 176
National Strategic Reference Framework 2012-2013, 21, 57
Strategic Marketing Plan of Croatian Tourism, 68, 90
national tourism marketing policy, 84
national tourism vision, 15, 20, 26, 28, 30, 279
acceptance of value driven vision, 7, 15–33
approach to vision building, 18, 25, 28
basic value propositions, 28–30
vision statement, 30–2

nautical tourism, island Vis, 255–8
new consumers, 39, 285, 286, 290, 292
Non-Aligned Movement, 83

P
paradigm
of economic growth, 23
materialistic *vs.* spiritual, 19
neoliberal, 23, 27
perspective, 33, 68, 71, 73, 74, 102, 122, 123, 138, 150, 152, 163, 174, 196, 276, 285, 289
planned urbanisation, 178, 180
policy networks between tourism and physical planning, 195
Production Model, 284
protected natural areas
environmental impacts, 203, 284, 288
management, 11, 201–16, 250, 279, 282
sustainability issues, 201–16

R
region, definition, 135
Registry and Atlas of Tourism Attractions, 120, 130, 132–3, 140, 143
Registry of Tourism Attractions, 132, 134, 135, 137, 143, 146, 147
research
destination image survey, Croatia, 7, 8, 69, 79–95, 123, 279
national park visitor survey, 104, 153, 154, 156, 211, 227
restaurant visitor survey, 186, 189, 190, 208, 209, 211, 232, 235, 236, 247, 249, 266–8, 272–4

research (*cont.*)
  stakeholder survey, 26, 43, 45, 50,
    51, 61, 74, 75, 105, 107, 111,
    114, 215, 283
  TOMAS Summer survey, 222, 223,
    226–34, 236–8
  tourism demand, 223
  vision workshop, 26–9
research methods
  field notes, 253–5
  image survey, 95n2
  longitudinal surveys, 12, 222–6
  non-participant observation, 254
  participant observaton, 253–4
  qualitative, 5, 223, 254
  TOMAS Summer survey, 222, 223,
    226–34, 236–8
  workshop, 7, 17, 26–9, 32, 33
responsible tourism, 287

S
shared economy, 291
SNA. *See* System of National Accounts
  (SNA)
social entrepreneurship sector, 290
social intrapreneur, 291
socially responsible consumer, 287
spatial planning
  Croatia, 4, 9–11, 173–98, 279, 282
  tourism development, 173–98
spatial planning, Adriatic, 173–8, 186,
  189, 192, 194
spatial planning policies, 173, 174
stakeholders, 4, 7, 10, 11, 17–20, 23,
  26, 27, 39, 41–3, 45, 50, 61, 70,
  71, 73–5, 99, 100, 102, 105–7,
  111–15, 167, 173, 196, 203,
  209, 213, 215, 227, 261, 283,
  285, 288, 289, 292
  attitudes to tourism, 26
strategic management, 38, 41, 42, 63

*Strategic Marketing Plan of Croatian
  Tourism 2010-14,* 90
structural reforms, Croatia, 57, 60, 62
sustainable management, 203, 204
  models, 203, 204, 206, 215, 216,
    282
sustainable, responsible and impact
  investing (SRI), 291
System of National Accounts (SNA),
  149, 151, 152, 166
system of tourism attractions, 10,
  119–25, 129, 131–43, 146, 281
system of tourism statistics (STS), 150,
  153, 154, 165, 166
  Croatia, 151, 154, 166

T
TOMAS research methodology, 227
TOMAS Summer survey
  data collection, 229
  mega trends, 230–6
  population, 227
  sample size, 228
  survey instrument, 229
tourism attractions
  basic functional classification, 120,
    126–31
  Croatian gastronomy, 281
  definition, 122–4
  destination, 120–6, 128, 130, 131,
    133–40, 143, 146
  evaluation, 10, 126, 130–3
  potential, 123–6, 129, 136, 137,
    146, 281
  Registry/Atlas, 120, 130, 132, 133,
    140, 143
  system, Kušen, 9, 119–47, 279
  theoretical framework, 120, 121
tourism attraction system, 9, 119–47,
  279
Tourism Attraction Typology

Mill and Morrison, 121, 128
UN World Tourism Organization
    (UNWTO), 6, 101, 102, 250,
    284, 287
tourism branding, 84
tourism characteristic products, 152,
    154, 157, 161, 163, 167
tourism competitiveness, 7, 23, 38,
    40, 44, 50–60, 62
tourism development
    building expansion, 32
    complexity, 18, 100–2, 130, 173,
        195, 287
    constraints, Croatia, 7, 39, 40, 44,
        50, 52, 62, 100, 110, 111,
        185, 189, 224
    human resources, Croatia, 8, 49, 52,
        55, 57, 109, 111, 112, 114,
        115, 125, 196, 281
    management, 44, 58
    planning/implementation, 7, 9,
        175, 176, 281
    post-1990, 40, 53, 54, 69, 104,
        124, 151, 184–9, 192, 196,
        208–10, 213
    spatial planning, 4, 9–11, 58,
        173–98, 279, 282
    Vis, 245–62, 283
tourism direct gross domestic product
    (TDGDP), 152, 153
tourism direct gross value added
    (TDGVA), 152, 153
tourism expenditure
    domestic, 154, 156
    inbound, 154, 156, 157
tourism in Croatia, 1–4, 13, 61, 67,
    165, 238, 276, 279
tourism planning, 5, 9–11, 13, 18, 20,
    21–5, 43, 48, 104, 134, 139,
    175, 176, 184, 194, 197, 279,
    281–4
    ideology, 178

tourism policy, 4, 41, 140, 153, 155,
    158, 165, 166, 197, 222, 237,
    262, 281
tourism product, 5, 10, 12, 23, 31,
    32, 41, 43, 60, 62, 88, 104–6,
    115, 124, 136, 140, 143–7, 155,
    157, 158, 160, 165–7, 182, 188,
    214, 221, 225, 227, 229, 231–7,
    271, 272
tourism promotion, 8, 73, 79, 80, 85,
    88–90, 92, 95, 111, 271, 281
tourism Ratio, Croatia, 159–65
tourism resorts
    impacts, 174, 179, 180, 182, 184,
        186, 191, 192, 196
    privatisation, 185, 191, 192, 195
Tourism Satellite Account
    concepts, 151–3, 159, 166, 282
    core tables, 152
    macro-aggregates, 10, 150–2,
        164–5
    methodological approach, Croatia,
        17, 28, 155, 156, 159, 160,
        166, 282
    methodological framework, 149–51,
        166, 167, 237, 282
Tourist Attraction Typology, Lew,
    127, 128
tourist motives/activities, 126, 127
transformative holidays, 16, 287
transformative tourism, 16, 287, 288
transmodern tourism, 16, 287

U
UNESCO Intangible Cultural
    Heritage of Humanity, 260
United Nations Development
    Programme, 177
unregistered tourism flows, 155,
    160
use of land, 175, 188, 196

V

value driven tourism vision, 7, 15–33
values shift, 289
vision
   effectivness, 18, 21, 23, 183
   national tourism vision, 15, 20, 26,
      28, 30, 279
   qualities of, 20
   typology, 20
visioning
   methodological approach, Croatia,
      17, 28, 155, 156, 159, 160,
      166, 282
   strategic, 18, 19
   in transformational studies, 19

   in visionary/spiritual/
      transformation leadership, 19
visitor management frameworks, 251
visitor pressure, 202, 205, 211, 282

Y

Yugoslavia, 2–4, 24, 79, 81–6, 91, 93,
   94, 105, 175, 179–84, 194, 247,
   281, 282
Yugoslav socialist government, 174

Z

zimmer frei, 185

Lightning Source UK Ltd.
Milton Keynes UK
UKOW07n1400100717
305040UK00001B/1/P